WHERE ARE WE HEADING?

WHERE ARE WE HEADING?

BY SUMNER WELLES

AUTHOR OF "THE TIME FOR DECISION"

HARPER & BROTHERS PUBLISHERS

NEW YORK AND LONDON

For my grandson,
ALEXANDER WELLES,
with the hope that his generation may enjoy
the Four Freedoms
which we of today so painfully seek.

CONTENTS

CHAPTER 1   Progress Toward World Order   1

CHAPTER 2   Peacemaking   60

CHAPTER 3   Reconstruction of Europe   114

CHAPTER 4   The Inter-American System Is in Jeopardy   182

CHAPTER 5   Shadows Over the Near East   242

CHAPTER 6   The Nationalist Surge in Asia   284

CHAPTER 7   Our Foreign Policy: Its Achievements and
              Its Failures   334

ON the following right-hand pages are reproduced two pages of the second draft of the Atlantic Charter, which Sumner Welles prepared, with President Roosevelt's corrections, and a handwritten letter from Franklin D. Roosevelt to the author regarding the principles contained in Article 4 of the final text of the Charter.

Opposite the facsimile reproductions of these documents are printed, for the convenience of the reader, the pages of the second draft of the Charter, as corrected by Mr. Roosevelt, and the text of his letter.

Second, they desire to see no territorial changes that do not accord with the freely expressed wishes of the peoples concerned;

Third, they respect the right of all peoples to choose the form of government under which they will live; and they hope that self-government may be restored to those from whom it has been forcibly removed.

Fourth, they will endeavor to further the enjoyment by all peoples of access without discrimination and on equal terms to the markets and to the raw materials of the world which are needed for their economic prosperity.

Fifth, they hope to see established a peace, after the final destruction of the Nazi tyranny, which will afford to all states and peoples the means of dwelling in security within

Second, they desire to see no territorial changes

that do not accord with the freely expressed wishes of the

peoples concerned;

Third, they respect the right of all peoples to choose

the form of government under which they will live; *and they hope*

that self government may be restored to those from whom

Fourth, they ~~will strive to promote mutually ad-~~ *it has*

been forcibly

~~vantageous economic relations between them through the~~ *removed.*

~~elimination of any discriminations in either the United~~

~~States of America or in the United Kingdom against the~~

~~imports of any product originating in the other country;~~

~~and~~ they will endeavor to further the enjoyment by all

without discrimination and

peoples of access on equal terms to the markets and to

of the world

the raw materials which are needed for their economic

prosperity.

Fifth, they hope to see established a peace, after

the final destruction of the Nazi tyranny, ~~which by~~

which

~~effective international organization~~, will afford to all

states and peoples the means of dwelling in security within

their own boundaries and the means of assurance that human beings may live out their lives in freedom from fear. They likewise hope to see established by such a peace safety for all peoples on the high seas and oceans, and the adoption of such measures as will prevent the continuation of expenditures for armaments other than those which are purely defensive.

Sixth, because the future of peace is impossible if armament by land, sea and air continues in the hands of any nation which threatens or may threaten to use force outside its frontiers we believe that disarmament of such nations is essential. We say this in the hope that the whole world may be guided in spirit to the goal of abandonment of force.

their own ~~bounds~~ boundaries, and the means of assurance that

human beings may live out their lives in freedom from

fear.   They likewise hope to see established by such

a peace safety for all peoples on the high seas and oceans,

and the adoption of such measures as will ~~reduce unnecessary~~ prevent
the continuation of expenditures for armaments
~~a continued burden of all armaments~~ other than those which

are purely defensive.

Fifth : Because the future of peace is impossible
if armament by land sea and air can-
tinues in the hands of any nation
which threatens or may threaten to
use force outside its frontiers we
believe that disarmament of
such nations is essential. We say
this in the hope that the whole
world may be guided in spirit to
the goal of abandonment of force.

U.S.S. Augusta
Mon. 2:30 p.m.
August 11

Dear Sumner:

Time being of the essence I think I can stand on my *own* former formulas—to wit: access to raw materials. This omits entirely the *other* subject which is the only one in conflict: discrimination in trade.

The fourth paragraph would then read "of access to the raw materials of the world etc."

For *me* that is consistent.

Yrs
FDR

U.S.S. Augusta Mm
2 30 pm
May 11

Dear Sumner —

Time being of the essence I think
I can stand on my own former
formulas — Twist : access to
raw materials . This omits entirely
the other subject which is the only
one in conflict : discrimination in
Trade .

The 4 — A would then read
" of access to the raw materials of the
world etc "

to me that is consistent
Yrs F.R.

WHERE ARE WE HEADING?

Chapter I

Progress Toward World Order

WE STAND confused and uncertain at the threshold of a new era. At the close of the greatest revolution which the world has known we have as yet no sure sign of what the future holds.

Man now has within his hands the means of destroying all life upon this planet. He also holds the means whereby humanity can be assured that the new day which is dawning will be a day of peace, of security, of human progress and of liberty.

At this moment of writing the prospect is obscured. There is no freedom from that fear which afflicted all peoples during the uneasy truce between the great wars. Greed and the lust for power are still omnipresent. The insane delusion that democracy and Communism cannot simultaneously exist in the world is rampant. Stupidity, reaction and timidity dominate the councils of the nations.

Opportunity after opportunity for understanding between all peoples has been lost.

Yet those who like myself believe that the ultimate end of man is good rather than evil must see those lost opportunities not as a cause for futile regret, but rather as an impelling reason for redoubled effort. We cannot recall them. But we can, through our understanding of past mistakes, better avail ourselves of the new opportunities to come.

The peoples of the world without exception passionately desire peace and security. In their majority they need no longer resign themselves to accept the consequences of the incapacity or the criminal ambitions of their leaders. For democracy has made it possible for men and women to control events. It will be owing only to their lethargy if they permit themselves now to be controlled by events. They possess the power to shape to their own welfare, and to that of generations to come, the cataclysmic revolution through which humanity is passing.

After ten years during which I had been given some opportunity to take part in the conduct of this government's foreign policy, and consequently to know at first hand the inner working of international affairs, I have found myself during the past three years in the role of a detached observer of the scene.

Since the illness and death of Franklin Roosevelt the scene has darkened. Ancient antagonisms and new rivalries have made themselves felt, the knowledge of the discovery of atomic fission has spread like a poisonous miasma over the relations between governments. Popular confidence in the abilities of the leaders of the people has been gravely undermined. And hope that the end of the war would at once bring security and freedom has now vanished.

The record of these times is profoundly discouraging. Yet there are many reasons for realistic optimism. The greatest is that there functions today a new international organization forged in the fires of conflict. Fifty-one nations of the earth are joined together "to save succeeding generations from the scourge of war."

So long as the United Nations continues, so long as the chance exists for it to draw all peoples into closer union and for it to enhance its authority as the agency of the countless men and women who demand that peace must be maintained, we have in it the surest promise of a new and better world to come.

In *The Time for Decision* I touched briefly upon the negotiation by President Roosevelt and Prime Minister Churchill of the Atlantic Charter. That declaration became the foundation upon which this new structure of international organization has been built. It is timely to throw more light upon the motives which led the chiefs of the two major English-speaking peoples to bind their countries to the principles set forth in the charter as well as upon their views about what those principles should be.

The only instrument which welded the wartime alliance between the Soviet Union and these English-speaking powers, as well as with the other countries joined with them in the struggle against the Axis—the United Nations Declaration—was based upon the Atlantic Charter. Every member of the United Nations thereby subscribed to its provisions. The Atlantic Charter was the beacon which the English-speaking democracies held aloft to the peoples struggling for liberty, to light them forward to peace, to human progress and to a free world.

As I have earlier written, President Roosevelt since the autumn of 1936 had become ever more deeply engrossed with foreign policy. No matter how urgent the problems of domestic reform and recovery might be, he had long since recognized that neither recovery nor reform could be enduring in a world so rapidly rushing toward war. He was already obsessed with the dangers by which the United States was confronted. By the summer of 1941 the dangers had become imminent.

From what he said to me I do not believe that the President had ever felt, since the rejection by the United States of the Treaty of Versailles, that the League of Nations, as an international organization, could succeed in achieving the objectives for which it was created. Circumstances had permitted it to become more and more the tool of Great Britain or of France, to be employed in the furtherance of their occasionally joint, but frequently divergent, interests.

Franklin Roosevelt passionately believed that civilization could not survive unless an international organization was established. But he did not believe that a workable international organization could be built up upon the inadequate and weakened foundations of the League of Nations.

By the summer of 1941 the overwhelming issue was his need to obtain the support of the people of the United States, and of their Congress, for those measures which were indispensable if the United States was to be prepared to defend herself should she be drawn into war and if, in the meantime, she was to be able to render such assistance as was available to the British people then fighting alone against the Axis. Isolationist sentiment was still widespread. The Congress was so far from recognizing the threatening dangers that at the very time when President Roosevelt and Mr. Churchill were meeting at Argentia the House of Representatives extended the operation of the Selective Service Act by a majority of only one vote.

President Roosevelt often said, "first things must come first." In the summer of 1941, the "first thing" was for the United States to prepare and for the Axis to be defeated. After that there would be time, he felt, to decide upon the precise nature of the international organization to be created, and upon the part which the United States should play in it. It should be added that the President had a further conviction which was typical of his temperament. This was that before any international organization could be effective, some policemen armed with the necessary force must undertake an extended cleaning-up job.

He frequently spoke of the waste resulting from the military establishments of the smaller European powers. In time of war, as he put it, these armies proved to be valueless against the modern military equipment of the major powers. In time of peace, the cost of these military establishments was a crushing burden upon the men and women who had to pay for them. I remember that he once showed me an estimate which he had had prepared which demonstrated that the budgetary deficits that the majority of these smaller countries had been incurring over a period of many years were almost exactly equivalent to the cost of maintaining their armies. Worst of all in his opinion the maintenance of these standing armies was the chief reason so many of the smaller countries were constantly embroiled in wars, as in the Balkans, which ultimately affected the interests of the major powers, and involved them also in the conflict.

In 1941 his general thesis was that before any durable and effective international organization could be set up, some policing powers must first undertake the task of disarming the smaller countries, thereby ridding the world of an unnecessary burden upon humanity as well as of a danger to international peace. Only the major powers, Great Britain, the Soviet Union, and the United States could undertake such a responsibility.

The way the mind of the President was running at that time is shown in some notes which I made on August 11, during the time of the Atlantic Charter meeting, of a conversation which I had with the President on the afternoon of that day:

I said I had been surprised and somewhat discouraged by a remark that the President had casually made in our morning's conference, which was that nothing could be more futile than the reconstitution of a body such as the Assembly of the League of Nations. I said to the President that, if he conceived of the need for a transition period upon the termination of the war, during which period Great Britain and the United States would undertake the policing of the world, it seemed to me that it would be enormously desirable for the smaller powers to have available to them an Assembly in which they would all be represented, in which they could make their complaints known, and in which they could join in recommendations as to the policy to be pursued by the major powers who were doing the police work. I said it seemed to me, that an organization of that kind would be the most effective safety valve that could be devised.

The President said that he agreed fully with what I said and that all that he had intended by the remark which he had made in the morning was to make clear his belief that a transition period was necessary, and that during that transition period no organization such as the Council or the Assembly of the League could undertake the powers and prerogatives with which they had been entrusted during the existence of the League of Nations.

I further said that, while from the practical standpoint I was in agreement that the United States and Great Britain were the only powers which could or would exercise the police work, it seemed to me that it would be impossible to exclude from the responsibilities involved the other American Republics or, for that matter, such occupied countries as Norway, the Netherlands, and even Belgium.

The President replied that he felt that a solution for this difficulty could probably be found through the ostensible joining of those powers to Great Britain and the United States but that it would have to be recognized that this must be only ostensible, since none of the nations mentioned would have the practical means of taking any effective or at least considerable part in the task involved.

It will, of course, be noted that the President made no reference to the Soviet Union. But it must be remembered that in the early days of August, 1941, the Soviet Union had only just been invaded by the Nazi armies. The highest military authorities of the United States were continually advising the President not only that the Soviet Union could resist the German onslaught for but a brief period, but also that the occupation of the whole of Russia west of the Urals was inevitable. It must also be remembered that relations between the United States and the Soviet Union, particularly during the period of the German-Soviet agreement, had been practically nonexistent. Our knowledge of the views of the Kremlin about the future establishment of world order or, for that matter, about any other aspect of Russian foreign policy was very slight.

President Roosevelt, before he had left Washington for the Atlantic meeting, had told me in some detail how he thought the approaching meeting with the British Prime Minister should be utilized to hold out hope to the enslaved peoples of the world. The English-speaking democracies both stood for principles of freedom and of justice. They should jointly bind themselves now to establish at the conclusion of the war a new world order based upon these principles.

He was firm in the conviction that equal opportunity to enjoy the world's natural resources must be available to all peoples. He was particularly impressed with the need to find co-operative methods through which standards of living would be steadily raised. He frequently discussed the most effective method of persuading the nations of the so-called "have" countries that an increase in the standard of living of the nationals of the "have-not" countries would redound to their own benefit by enlarging the purchasing power in foreign markets for the goods produced by the more prosperous and advanced nations.

Finally, the President had uppermost in his mind the fact that an agreement on principles between the British and American governments would remove the danger that the British government might enter into such secret arrangements as those concluded during the course of the First World War, which had rendered the subsequent task of writing a just peace so difficult.

There had been no prior exchange of views between the President and Mr. Churchill about issuing a declaration such as the Atlantic Charter. The initiative was taken by Mr. Churchill after his arrival at Argentia on the evening of August 9. On the following morning Sir Alexander Cadogan, the British Permanent Under Secretary, handed me a draft which Mr. Churchill had prepared. The text was as follows:

The President of the United States of America and the Prime Minister, Mr. Churchill, representing His Majesty's Government in the United Kingdom, being met together to resolve and concert the means of providing for the safety of their respective countries in face of Nazi and German aggression and of the dangers to all peoples arising therefrom, deem it right to make known certain principles which they both accept for guidance in the framing of their policy and on which they base their hopes for a better future for the world.

First, their countries seek no aggrandizement, territorial or other;

Second, they desire to see no territorial changes that do not accord with the freely expressed wishes of the peoples concerned;

Third, they respect the right of all peoples to choose the form of government under which they will live; they are only concerned to defend the rights of freedom of speech and thought without which such choice must be illusory;

Fourth, they will strive to bring about a fair and equitable distribution of essential produce not only within their territorial boundaries but between the nations of the world;

Fifth, they seek a peace which will not only cast down forever the Nazi tyranny but by effective international organization will afford to all States and peoples the means of dwelling in security within their own bounds and of traversing the seas and oceans without fear of lawless assault or the need of maintaining burdensome armaments.

The first three articles in Mr. Churchill's draft seemed to me both essential in their import and admirable in their clarity. It was, however, more than doubtful that the American Congress would at that moment have approved a pledge by the government of the United States to "defend the rights of freedom of speech and thought" when those rights were abrogated in every Axis country.

The fourth and fifth points offered by Mr. Churchill seemed to me either questionable in meaning, or far too limited in their scope.

The assurances proposed by Article 4, for example, meant precisely nothing. They were reminiscent of the pious hopes expressed in a thousand and one economic conferences that "a fair and equitable international distribution of commodities" would come into being, during the very years when tariffs were being built up in the United States, and when every variety of discriminatory trade barrier was being erected in an increasingly autarchic world.

Through its Trade Agreement program the American government had been the one major power to attempt to arrest the tide. The British government had made no such effort before the war. Since 1939 it had been of course in no position to do so.

But in 1932, by the Ottawa Agreements, the United Kingdom had placed the final stone upon the grave of those liberal trade policies—first advocated by Cobden and the Manchester School—which had done so much to increase the power and wealth of the British people, and, by freely opening the British Empire to the commerce of all nations, had contributed so notably to the maintenance of world peace during the two generations prior to the First World War. The Ottawa Agreements were designed to force every component part of the British Empire, covering a quarter of the globe, to trade solely within that area. Theoretically other countries would still be able to purchase what they wished within the Empire. But, unless they were willing to come within the sterling area, because of the hindrances otherwise placed upon their ability to sell their own goods to the Empire, they could not long continue so to buy for lack of sterling exchange. Tariffs, quotas, blocked currencies had become almost as much a part of the British trade policy after 1932 as they had become a part of Germany's trade policy under Schacht.

Unless the declaration now to be issued contained the firm commitment that the British government would join the United States after the war in trade policies which would eliminate all such fatal impediments to international trade as American high protectionist tariffs, and British Ottawa Agreements, there would patently exist no assurance of any new and better world economic order to come.

Moreover, in the Churchill draft there was no reference to the imperative need of giving peoples everywhere some clear hope that the two English-speaking powers intended to guide the world, as soon as conditions made it possible, down the road which would lead eventually to a true reduction and limitation of armaments.

It was with these purposes that the alternative draft which I submitted to the President early on the morning of August 11 had been written. It read as follows:

The President of the United States of America and the Prime
Minister, Mr. Churchill, representing His Majesty's Government in
the United Kingdom, being met together, to consider and to resolve
the steps which their Governments should take in order to provide for
the safety of the respective countries in face of the policies of world
wide domination and of military conquest upon which the Hitlerite
Government of Germany and the other dictatorships associated there-
with have embarked, and in face of the dangers to all peoples arising
therefrom, deem it right and proper to make known certain principles
which they both accept for guidance in the framing of their respective
policies and on which they base their hopes for a better future for
the world.

First, their countries seek no aggrandizement, territorial or other;

Second, they desire to see no territorial changes that do not accord
with the freely expressed wishes of the peoples concerned;

Third, they respect the right of all peoples to choose the form of
government under which they will live;

Fourth, they will strive to promote mutually advantageous economic
relations between them through the elimination of any discrimination
in either the United States of America or in the United Kingdom
against the importation of any product originating in the other country; and they will endeavor to further the enjoyment by all peoples of
access on equal terms to the markets and to the raw materials which
are needed for their economic prosperity;

Fifth, they hope to see established a peace, after the final destruction of Nazi tyranny, which by effective international organization,
will afford to all states and peoples the means of dwelling in security
within their own boundaries, and the means of assurance that human
beings may live out their lives in freedom from fear. They likewise
hope to see established by such a peace safety for all peoples on the
high seas and oceans, and the adoption of such measures as will prevent the continuation of expenditures for armaments other than those
which are purely defensive.

The President considered and discussed every word. He eliminated the greater part of the suggested preamble because of his
belief that American public opinion was not as yet prepared for so
drastic a statement of policy, and that it was preferable to limit the
scope of the entire declaration to principles, rather than include
therein references to immediate issues. It was for that reason as
well that he struck out the first half of the suggested fourth article.

He wrote in in his own handwriting, however, in the remaining portion, the words "without discrimination," which had been of course the essential point in the first part of the article, now eliminated.

He wrote in the second half of the third article the clause: "and they hope that self-government may be restored to those from whom it has been forcibly removed."

In the fifth article the President omitted all reference to "international organization" for reasons which he later made clear in his subsequent conference with Mr. Churchill.

He then wrote upon the draft a further, and sixth, article, in these words:

Sixth, because the future of peace is impossible if armament by land, sea and air continues in the hands of any nation which threatens or may threaten to use force outside its frontiers, we believe that disarmament of such nations is essential. We say this in the hope that the whole world may be guided in spirit to the goal of abandonment of force.

The President then suggested that I return to the *Tuscaloosa*, where I was quartered, and prepare a further draft containing the changes and amendments he had indicated, as well as any further provisions, along the general lines we had been discussing, which might seem desirable to me.

I prepared the third draft in this form:

The President of the United States of America and the Prime Minister, Mr. Churchill, representing His Majesty's Government in the United Kingdom, being met together, deem it right to make known certain common principles in the national policies of their respective countries on which they base their hopes for a better future for the world.

First, their countries seek no aggrandizement, territorial or other;

Second, they desire to see no territorial changes that do not accord with the freely expressed wishes of the peoples concerned;

Third, they respect the right of all peoples to choose the form of government under which they will live; and they wish to see self-government restored to those from whom it has been forcibly removed;

Fourth, they will endeavor to further the enjoyment by all peoples of access, without discrimination and on equal terms, to the markets and to the raw materials of the world which are needed for their economic prosperity;

Fifth, they hope to see established a peace, after the final destruction of the Nazi tyranny, which will afford to all nations the means of dwelling in security within their own boundaries, and which will afford assurance to all peoples that they may live out their lives in freedom from fear and want;

Sixth, they desire such a peace to establish for all safety on the high seas and oceans;

Seventh, they believe that all of the nations of the world, for realistic as well as spiritual reasons, must come to the abandonment of the use of force. Because no future peace can be maintained if land, sea or air armaments continue to be employed by nations which threaten, or may threaten, aggression outside of their frontiers, they believe that the disarmament of such nations is essential. They will likewise further all other practicable measures which will lighten for peace-loving peoples the crushing burden of armaments.

This third draft came up for discussion at a meeting held on the President's flagship, the *Augusta*, at 11 A.M. on August 11. At this meeting the President, Mr. Churchill, Sir Alexander Cadogan, Harry Hopkins and myself were present.

We sat around informally in the admiral's quarters, which the President used as his study as well as his messroom. The President was dressed in a gray suit with his shirt open at the collar. The Prime Minister was dressed, as he was throughout the meetings, in uniform. The bright sunlight streamed in through the open portholes.

The hasty notes of this meeting which I made at the time follow:

Mr. Churchill then said that he desired to bring up for discussion the proposed joint declaration by the President and himself.

The President said that he believed the best solution of this problem was for an identic statement to be made in London and in the United States, probably on Thursday, August 14, to the effect that the Prime Minister and the President had met at sea, accompanied by the various members of their respective staffs; that these members of the two governments had discussed the question of aid under the terms of the Lease-Lend Act to nations resisting aggression, and that these military and naval conversations had in no way involved any future commitments between the two governments, except as authorized under the terms of the Lease-Lend Act; that the Prime Minister and the President had between them discussed certain principles relating to a better future for the world and had agreed upon a joint declaration which would then be quoted verbatim.

Mr. Churchill dissented very strongly from the form in which the President had desired to make it clear that no future commitments had been entered into. The President stated that that portion of the proposed statement was of extreme importance from his standpoint inasmuch as a statement of that character would make it impossible for extreme isolationist leaders in the United States to allege that every kind of secret agreement had been entered into during the course of these conversations.

Mr. Churchill said that he understood that side of the question, but that he believed that any categorical statement of that character would prove deeply discouraging to the populations of the occupied countries and would have a very serious effect upon their morale. He likewise made it clear that a similar effect would be created by British public opinion. He asked if the statement could not be worded in such a way as to make it positive rather than negative, namely, that the members of the staffs of the Prime Minister and of the President had solely discussed questions relative to the furnishing of aid to the countries resisting aggression under the terms of the Lease-Lend Act. The President replied that he believed that the statement could be drawn up in that way and that if he then were queried in the United States he need merely reply that nothing had been discussed or agreed upon other than that which had already been indicated in his public statement.

I then gave the President, Mr. Churchill and Sir Alexander Cadogan copies of a redraft which I had made this morning of the proposed joint declaration before Mr. Churchill had arrived and had had an opportunity of going over it with the President, and the latter had approved it. Mr. Churchill then commenced to read it. He suggested that there be inserted in the text of the third point before the word "self-government" the words "sovereign rights and." This was agreed upon.

Mr. Churchill then read the fourth point which read as follows: "Fourth, they will endeavor to further the enjoyment by all peoples of access, without discrimination and on equal terms, to the markets and to the raw materials of the world which are needed for their economic prosperity."

He immediately inquired whether this was meant to apply to the terms of the Ottawa Agreements. I replied that of course it did, since the policy which the United States Government had been pursuing for the better part of nine years had been addressed primarily toward the removal of all of those artificial restrictions and controls upon international trade which had created such tragic havoc to world economy during the past generation. I said I understood fully the immediate difficulties which this occasioned him, but I pointed out that the phraseology was "they will endeavor to further" and that this naturally did not imply a formal and immediate contractual obligation on the part of his government. The President stated that he believed the point was of very great importance as a measure of assurance to the German and Italian peoples that the British and the United States governments desired to offer them, after the war, fair and equal opportunity of an economic character.

The Prime Minister said that of course he was without any power himself to agree upon this point. He set forth in considerable detail the position of the United Kingdom vis-a-vis the Dominions and emphasized his inability, without the agreement of the Dominions, to enter into the proposed declaration insofar as this point was concerned. He said that insofar as he himself was concerned the issue was one with which his own personal life history was connected. He referred to the days at the outset of the century when Joseph Chamberlain first brought up the proposal for Empire preferences and the predominant part which this issue had played in the political history of Great Britain during the past forty years. He said that he felt that the proposal as now phrased would have the enthusiastic support of all the liberals everywhere. He said that he himself was heartily in accord with the proposal and that he himself had always been, as was well known, emphatically opposed to the Ottawa Agreements. He said, however, that it would be at least a week before he could hope to obtain by telegraph the opinion of the Dominions with regard to this question.

Harry Hopkins then suggested that Sir Alexander Cadogan and I be requested to draft new phraseology which would take care of these difficulties and prevent the delay of which Mr. Churchill spoke. He said it was inconceivable that the issuance of the joint declaration should be held up by a matter of this kind.

I said that in my own judgment further modification of that article would destroy completely any value in that portion of the proposed declaration. I said that it was not a question of phraseology, but that it was a question of a vital principle which was involved. I said that if the British and the United States governments could not agree to do everything within their power to further, after the termination of the present war, a restoration of free and liberal trade policies, they might as well throw in the sponge and realize that one of the greatest factors in creating the present tragic situation in the world was going to be permitted to continue unchecked in the postwar world. I said that the trade policies of the British Empire during the latter portion of the nineteenth century had, I felt, contributed enormously to the sane and prosperous condition of the world at that time, and that, of course, I realized that the tariff policies pursued by the United States and many other countries during that period had played an important part in the creation of the evils which had sprung up after the last war. I said, however, that it seemed to be imperative that we try to agree now upon the policy of constructive sanity in world economics as a fundamental factor in the creation of a new and better world and that except through an agreement upon such a policy by our two governments there would be no hindrance whatever to a continuation later of the present German practices of utilizing their trade and financial policies in order to achieve political ends.

Mr. Churchill agreed very emphatically to this policy. He and Sir Alexander Cadogan both agreed that it was not a question of phraseology, but that they were up against a material obstacle which Mr. Churchill had already indicated. The Dominions would have to be consulted. It might well be that an agreement could not be had from the Dominions and that consequently the proposed joint declaration could only be issued some time after news of the meeting between the President and the Prime Minister had been given out. Mr. Churchill suggested that the inclusion before the phrase "they will endeavor to further" of the phrase which would read "with due regard for our present obligations" might ease the situation.

The President suggested, and Mr. Churchill agreed, that the latter would try and draft some phraseology which would make that situation easier, and it was arranged that I would call later in the afternoon upon the Prime Minister and Sir Alexander Cadogan to go over with them such redraft as they might have in mind.

Mr. Churchill was in entire accord with points five and six.

He then read point seven and after discussion at the meeting of this point it was agreed that the phrase "to use force" be replaced by the word "aggression" in the second sentence of the seventh point.

Mr. Churchill said that, of course, he was heartily and enthusiastically in favor of this point seven, which had been initiated by the President. He inquired, however, whether the President would not agree to support some kind of "effective international organization" as suggested by the Prime Minister in his original draft of the proposed joint declaration.

The President replied that he did not feel that he could agree to this because of the suspicions and opposition that such a statement on his part would create in the United States. He said that he himself would not be in favor of the creation of a new Assembly of the League of Nations, at least until after a period of time had passed and during which an international police force composed of the United States and Great Britain had had an opportunity of functioning. Mr. Churchill said that he did not feel that he would be candid if he did not express to the President his feeling that point seven would create a great deal of opposition from the extreme internationalists. The President replied that he realized that, but that he felt that the time had come to be realistic and that in his judgment the main factor in the seventh point was complete realism. Mr. Churchill then remarked that of course he was wholeheartedly in favor of it and shared the President's view.

The meeting then broke up and I arranged with the President that I would drop by to see him after my conference later in the afternoon with the Prime Minister. The latter stated that he would not be able to leave until at least 5:00 P.M., tomorrow, August 12, and that he felt it of importance to reach a complete meeting of minds with the President upon all of the issues involved, that he would be willing to spend an additional twenty-four hours should that be necessary.

Before leaving the President's flagship for the *Tuscaloosa*, I urged him to see whether Mr. Churchill might not be induced to cut corners and expedite his communications with the Dominion governments so that a favorable decision might be obtained on the article which dealt with economic policy. The article would be of far less value in its bearing upon the future if the phrase "without discrimination" were left out. If Mr. Churchill's suggestion that this phrase be eliminated, and that the phrase "with due respect for their existing obligations" be inserted, were to be adopted, the article would have no application to the Ottawa Agreements, and its force would be gravely weakened. The President appeared to be strongly of the same opinion. I can only surmise that afterwards Harry Hopkins persuaded him that the questions at issue would not be of sufficient importance to warrant any delay in reaching an agreement upon the final text of a declaration.

I was due to meet with Sir Alexander Cadogan at 3:00 P.M. that afternoon. Five minutes before that hour a messenger brought me the following memorandum from the President:

The White House
Washington

U.S.S. Augusta
Mon. 2:30 P.M.
August 11

Dear Sumner:

Time being of the essence I think I can stand on my *own* former formulas—to wit: access to raw materials. This omits entirely the *other* subject which is the only one in conflict: discrimination in trade.

The fourth ¶ would then read "of access to the raw materials of the world" etc.

For *me* that is consistent.

Yrs
FDR

In view of this decision of the President there could be no further reason for delaying an understanding with Sir Alexander on the text of a redraft of the declaration with a view to its approval at the final meeting between the President and Mr. Churchill scheduled to take place at 11 A.M. on the following day. A new article was now suggested by Mr. Churchill which read:

They desire to bring about the fullest collaboration between all nations in the economic field with the object of securing for all peoples improved labor standards, economic advancement and social security.

This was incorporated in the fourth draft of the declaration prepared the afternoon of August 11 by Sir Alexander Cadogan and myself. This in turn was slightly modified, in phraseology rather than in substance, at the final meeting between President Roosevelt and Mr. Churchill on August 12.

I believe that this detailed account of the genesis and negotiation of the Atlantic Charter, showing how every word employed in it represented the considered, and the joint, decision of the heads of the American and British governments, may help to eradicate that extraordinary suspicion which later grew up, that because the Atlantic Charter was neither a treaty nor a written agreement with signatures and seals affixed thereon, it therefore lacked validity as the official pronouncement of the policies of the two governments concerned.

The Atlantic Charter was issued as a joint declaration to the press only because of the circumstances under which it was agreed upon. It was precisely as valid in its binding effect as if it had been signed and sealed. It was exactly what it purported to be: notice to the world by the President of the United States and the Prime Minister of the United Kingdom, that in accordance with their constitutional authority to speak for their countries and their governments, the two nations which they represented would adhere to the great principles set forth in the declaration.

As an indication of the President's feeling this message, dated Tuesday, August 12, sent to me by Admiral Stark as I was leaving the harbor, is of interest:

> U.S.S. Augusta
> Ship Harbor, Newfoundland
> August 12, 1941

. . . .
The President said he would like no release of the names of those who accompanied the President until Saturday on which day you may release it.

His reasons are that he wants the press release to stand out (to use his expression) "like a sore thumb," (I'd say a "beacon") with nothing to detract from it or to cause any other discussion; then when it has had time to be thoroughly digested, just of itself, to go ahead and give out the names of the rest of the party—on Saturday.

> H. R. Stark.

The final text of the Atlantic Charter did not, of course, contain all that either the President or Mr. Churchill would have liked to see incorporated in it. But however material the omissions and the defects of the Atlantic Charter may now seem to be, it must be read in the light of the moment when it was written.

Except within the Western Hemisphere, world order had long since collapsed. The very semblance of international law had vanished. Except by the American Republics, any attempt at international co-operation had been abandoned. The United States herself had refrained from all efforts to co-operate with nations outside of her own region for over twenty years.

The Atlantic Charter represented the first major reversal of the isolationist policy which the American people had been pursuing since the close of the First World War. It represented the first effort at joint leadership on the part of the two leading English-speaking democracies. It was the first assurance for a quarter of a century to the free peoples outside the New World that the United States had undertaken a positive, rather than a negative, foreign policy. Far more than that, it represented, as soon as the United States had been drawn into the war, the one policy of enlightened international co-operation upon which the peoples struggling against Axis domination could base their hopes for a better world of the future.

I have related these details of the manner in which the Atlantic Charter was drafted, and certain of the conversations which I held with President Roosevelt at that time, because some of the confidential records which I dictated during the days of the Atlantic meeting were published during the course of the Pearl Harbor investigation. A few of the statements made to me by the President at that time have been lifted out of their context and have appeared in the press as isolated statements. They have been used to charge that the President was at heart an isolationist.

There must be few among his fellow citizens who can take such a charge as being other than unfounded. The President's magnificent record of constructive achievement in the field of foreign policy proves how ludicrous that charge must be. But it may be well to emphasize this salient consideration. At the time of the Atlantic meeting, President Roosevelt was primarily concerned with the dangers which he saw rapidly approaching the country that he loved. He was concentrating to the best of his great ability upon the need for defense.

I remember that a good many months later, at a time when I was urging him, as others were, to speak to the people of the United States of their need to prepare for the peacemaking task, and to consider the means by which this country could best play its full part in preventing new world wars, he said to me that he believed his primary obligation was to concentrate the attention of public opinion upon the winning of the war. He was convinced that if he spoke to the American people, under the conditions which then existed, of postwar problems, they might be distracted from the cardinal objective of victory, and controversies might develop which would jeopardize national unity. He also, he said, believed that it was imperative that he should do nothing and say nothing which would make the people feel that he was not dedicated exclusively to his responsibility as Commander-in-Chief.

Franklin Roosevelt had by no means that "one track mind," which Woodrow Wilson once insisted he himself possessed. But he was always inclined to segregate the urgent from the not-so-urgent. He always preferred to devote himself to the task which was immediate rather than to the task which could be undertaken later on. It was, I think, only in that sense that during the Atlantic meeting he refused to consider urgent the need to reach a decision as to the precise kind of international organization to be created after the defeat of the Axis powers. After this country had become involved in the war, he never faltered in his conviction, as I will later show, that every effort should be made to obtain an agreement between the major powers upon the main lines of an international organization, and to have such an organization functioning, in at least provisional form, before the conclusion of the war. In August, 1941, his attention was fixed upon the defense of the United States. But clearly he was already convinced that the new American foreign policy, set forth in the Atlantic Charter, would later on be of great help in laying the foundations for a free and a secure world, and that the Atlantic Charter in itself would, in the meantime, hold out to the enslaved peoples of the earth the assurance that such a world would be achieved.

The Department of State had been carrying on its studies of postwar policy, and of the task of peacemaking for some time before the public learned of it.

I had long believed that, had the United States been able before the end of the First World War to reach firm agreements with its allies as to the nature of the peace settlements, and as to the exact charter of the international organization to be established, the Treaty of Versailles might well have produced far different results. Before the conclusion of the war the United States had a far greater measure of authority and, from the practical standpoint, a far more potent leverage in achieving its own objectives than it could possibly possess after the victory was won. One of the chief reasons President Wilson had not followed that course was that, owing to lack of proper preparation, the policies of the United States with regard to the approaching peace settlements had not been clarified. The work of Colonel House's "Enquiry" was carried on to the exclusion of the Department of State. It had only been partially concluded when the Armistice was signed.

It seemed to me after the United States entered the Second World War that this government should have learned two lessons from those pages of history. The first was that the executive branch of the government charged with the conduct of American foreign relations, namely, the President and the Department of State, should from the outset call in representative leaders of the legislative branch in formulating peace plans. The second lesson was that such preparations should be commenced at the earliest possible date in order that the end of the war might not once more find this government inadequately prepared for the peace task and consequently unable to determine its postwar policy.

There was at first some opposition within the Department of State to such preparatory work. It was considered necessary to avoid making public any knowledge that such work was going on. During the early weeks of 1942 I was primarily engrossed with the Second Consultative Meeting of the American Foreign Ministers, held at Rio de Janeiro in January, to which the President had appointed me the representative of the United States. The conversations which I had during that conference with the representatives of the other American Republics gave me assurance that the entire hemisphere was looking to the United States for leadership in the tasks which would have to be confronted when the war was over.

Upon my return from Brazil, I was for some months Acting Secretary of State. The urgent problems which were then daily arising made it difficult to find the time necessary to decide how best the Department might commence its preparatory peace studies. In April, however, I discussed with the President the desirability of creating a small confidential body within the Department to take charge of the general preparatory work, and of associating with the officials selected for this purpose a few members of the Congress and a few individuals outside of official life who possessed special qualifications. The President was wholly in favor of the suggestion. He warmly endorsed the need for starting such preparations without delay.

The plans were about to be carried out when a jurisdictional dispute arose as a result of an executive order which the President had signed and which delegated to the newly created Board of Economic Warfare authority over the formulation of postwar economic policy. The conflict which then developed held up for some time all preparatory work by the Department of State.

When it was finally settled, a small group of State Department officials was first appointed. These undertook the preparation of the factual material required. From private life we called in Dr. Isaiah Bowman, the president of Johns Hopkins University, one of the most eminent geographers of the present day, as well as one of the experts who had attended President Wilson at the Paris Conference of 1919; Myron C. Taylor, whose broad grasp of international affairs, and whose experience and knowledge of economic problems, made his co-operation invaluable; Professor James Shotwell and Dr. Clark Eichelberger of the Association for the United Nations, whose devoted service to the cause of international organization was recognized at home and abroad; Anne O'Hare McCormick, whose exceptional knowledge of European affairs, and whose penetrating insight into all aspects of international relations have for so long been demonstrated in her brilliant articles in the New York *Times*; and Hamilton Fish Armstrong, the head of the Council of Foreign Relations, whose experience and great ability were of outstanding value. The late Norman Davis, then chairman of the American Red Cross, gave us his help whenever his arduous duties in the Red Cross made it possible.

To these were added outstanding members of the Foreign Relations Committee and of the Foreign Affairs Committee of the Senate and of the House of Representatives. The first Congressional members who participated were Senator Connally, Senator George, and Senator Thomas of Utah, Democratic members of the Foreign Relations Committee. Senator Austin of Vermont, not yet a member of the Foreign Relations Committee, and Senator White of Maine, one of the ranking Republican members of the committee, as well as the chairman and the ranking Republican member of the Foreign Affairs Committee of the House, Congressman Bloom and Congressman Eaton, completed the Congressional representation.

President Wilson had excluded the Congress from any part in preparing for the peace after the First World War. President Roosevelt desired that both the Senate and the House participate from the outset in determining the objectives which the United States would seek.

For a period of some months this group met once a week in my office at the State Department. I arranged my own work so that each Saturday was devoted to these meetings. The work of the group was from the outset divided into three separate categories of research. The first had to do with future peace settlements, the second with questions of economic and financial policy, and the third with the formulation of international organization and security. A number of subcommittees were delegated to prepare the groundwork during each week for the consideration of the members of the committee at their Saturday meetings. After a short time a large secretariat was appointed, many of its members being loaned to the department by the Council of Foreign Relations. The Saturday meetings were wholly informal. They were, in fact, open discussions. They accomplished within a relatively brief period a surprising, practical result. It became possible after only a few months to formulate tentative recommendations on many aspects of the subjects with which the committee had dealt.

It would be impossible to single out any individual as having contributed more than his fellows to the accomplishments reached at this early stage. But it would be equally impossible to avoid emphasizing the contribution made by Dr. Bowman, because of his exceptional gift for making available to others the unique knowledge of geographic questions which he possesses, or to omit mention of the devotion with which Myron Taylor gave his

services to the committee and of the practical solutions which he
so often found for controversial problems. I must also stress the
invaluable help rendered by the members of the Congress, some
of whom gave up much-needed vacations in order to continue
their work in the Department of State.

Personal supervision of the meetings of the committee was
eventually taken over by the Secretary of State himself. The
original group was ultimately greatly enlarged. Some of the early
members dropped out. I retained, however, the active chairman-
ship of the committee on international organization and security,
and in the early winter of 1943 officers of the War and Navy
departments were added to this committee.

By that time our recommendations upon international organization and security were crystallizing. The recommendations of
the representatives of the General Staff and of Naval Operations
were indispensable.

During the early stages of this preparatory work the President
gave me frequent opportunities to report to him the progress
being made, especially by the committee on international organization and security. In this way he could give us continuously
his own wishes about the shape which our projects should take.

Personally, I had come to believe that in the future international
organization the difficulty arising from the need to reconcile the
sovereign equality of all states with the inevitable demand by the
major military powers to retain such freedom of action as might
be required—at least during an initial period—to assure them of
security, might best be solved by establishing the new world
organization upon a foundation of regional organizations, each
subordinate to the ultimate control of the world organization.
Such regional systems, similar in general nature to the inter-
American system of the Western Hemisphere, would be required
to assume the primary responsibility for maintaining peace in
their respective parts of the world. Only if these regional systems
proved unable to compose disputes or to restrain an aggressor
would the supreme universal authority be required to intervene.
In that manner each state in every region, no matter how weak
it might be, would be required as well as enabled to contribute in

proportion to its resources the assistance needed in maintaining regional, and world, peace.

In the supreme executive agency of the world body, now termed in the United Nations organization the Security Council, the smaller states would be given full representation. But the major powers possessing the armed force required to keep the peace would necessarily have to be given all the authority needed to act when action was indispensable to avert war.

From the practical standpoint, no one of the great powers would be willing to join an international organization where the police power, composed of a pooling of military contingents from all the great powers and presumably the lesser powers as well, would be greater than its own military resources, unless it had some means of controlling the operation of that police force. The Covenant of the League of Nations had, in part, evaded this difficulty and had, in part, attempted to meet it by requirements for unanimity. On this fundamental issue the League of Nations had not been able to function successfully. It is this issue which has now come to be known as the veto issue. It was apparent to the departmental committee that if the new organization was to have any hope of success, this issue must be solved in such a way as to give the greater powers security, while at the same time making it impossible for any one major power to block the efforts of the organization to check aggression from whatever quarter.

In the drafts for international organization made by the departmental committee, it was determined that the supreme executive agency of the organization should be composed of eleven members, seven of these representing regional systems, each of the seven members to be elected periodically by all the states comprising the region which he represented. The remaining four members were allotted to the United States, the Soviet Union, Great Britain and China. Each major power was to have a permanent seat upon the agency. No feature of the discussions received more consideration than the precise authority that should be given to the great powers represented on the supreme executive agency. It finally became the consensus that no decisions that involved the employment of armed force should be made by the

executive agency unless nine members of the body voted affirma-
tively, and unless these nine affirmative votes included at least
three votes from the four permanent members. It was believed
that from the practical standpoint, such a provision would guarantee the legitimate security of every great power and would
vest a fair measure of authority in the lesser powers. At that time
there was no certain prospect that France could soon regain her
status as a great power, and the four great powers for which
permanent representation was envisioned were the United States,
Great Britain, the Soviet Union and China. What the provision
therefore established was that the major powers were granted
only a qualified veto right within the agency. It was our belief
that if three of the major powers, and six of the lesser powers,
voted for military sanctions, no one major power should have the
right to block action. For in such event the presumption must
clearly be that that major power itself must be guilty of a violation of the principles upon which the international organization
was founded. We could not admit the right of any power, great
or small, to veto action against itself if it undertook to pursue
policies of aggression.

Subsequently that position was modified to provide for exactly
that total veto right of the major powers upon all sanctions. It
had become unmistakably clear that the Soviet Union would not
otherwise participate in any international organization. It was
equally plain that the United States Senate would in all probability
refuse to ratify any charter of world organization in which the
United States did not possess such a right. And from a purely
practical point of view, it has become increasingly evident that
no international organization such as the United Nations could
function during the first years of its life should any one of the
major military powers refuse to co-operate with its associates
and embark upon aggression.

It is still my conviction, however, that if the United Nations
survives its early ordeals the present sweeping veto rights granted
to each of the five major powers must be modified. And the first
step toward the eventual creation of a more truly democratic
world order might well be an amendment of the present United

Nations Charter to achieve the modification of the veto right as provided in the earlier projects of the State Department Committee of 1943.

In June, 1943, I gave the President the copy of the final plan drafted by the State Department Committee. The President left open for further consideration certain questions of detail, notably, I remember, the method of electing the representatives of the smaller nations in the executive agency, or Security Council. He was attracted by the idea of regional election because this would diminish the probability that the delegates of the lesser powers would act primarily in the interest of their respective governments. He was, however, doubtful that this would at first prove practical. But of the general structure proposed for a new world organization he heartily approved. It was this general formula which was adopted at the subsequent meeting at Dumbarton Oaks. This, in turn, greatly enlarged and improved, eventually became the United Nations Charter.

During these months of 1942 and 1943 the British government was also accelerating its preparations for postwar decisions. The British Foreign Office was primarily in charge of the preparatory work. It received, however, the assistance of several quasi-unofficial groups, notably those working under the supervision of Chatham House. At a later period a considerable measure of discussion went on between the American and British governments.

Many of the governments of the smaller nations of western Europe approached this government from time to time with respect to postwar problems, and the suggestions of many of them were singularly helpful. The views advanced by the Netherlands and Norwegian governments were in the highest degree useful. It is necessary to say, however, that in most of these cases the views were regional rather than universal. At that time the governments of the occupied countries of western Europe leaned definitely toward that kind of an Atlantic community of nations that Mr. Walter Lippmann has so eloquently urged upon us. The basic concept was that the nations of the Western Hemisphere and of western Europe that are primarily concerned in the Atlantic should join together in a league for the maintenance of peace in the Atlantic, both south as well as north, and that this Atlantic community of nations should become one of a series of communities, all of which would tend to create a new balance of power—a balance between continents.

The thinking of the Government of the United States was, however, never along those lines. The approach made by the Department of State to the problem of international organization was always universal. Most of us, I think, never believed that world peace could be maintained unless some international organization could be created which was universal in its scope. But most of us also believed that this organization should be fashioned in such a way as to leave to the nations in the several geographical regions of the world, namely, the Western Hemisphere, Europe, the Far East, and the Near East, the utmost responsibility for maintaining peace, and for furthering social and economic progress within their respective areas. It appeared to us not only that it would prove impossible to create new and artificial groupings of states, but that any such arrangements would tend to set up military spheres of influence, each dominated by one major military power, and that eventually the creation of such spheres of influence would give rise to conflicts of interest which would promote, rather than check, new wars.

As the tides of victory flowed ever more strongly, the President became more deeply engrossed in postwar problems. He studied ever more attentively every detail of international organization. He became more and more confident that no lasting peace was possible and that no progress would be made in solving the world's economic difficulties, in raising general living standards, and in guaranteeing human freedoms, unless an effective international organization were founded, and founded, if possible, before the conclusion of the war.

I had left the Department of State in August of 1943. The President sent for me to visit him at Hyde Park in the latter part of September. He there went over with me once more in the greatest detail the project for international organization. At that moment he regarded as the key to the whole problem, as of course it was, the question whether the Soviet government would see eye to eye with this government regarding the need for the immediate establishment of such an international organization, or whether the Soviet government believed that its ultimate objectives and its own security might be better advanced by remaining outside such an organization. In the latter event, there could, of course, be no hope of assurance that world peace could be maintained. He regarded it as imperative that our two governments reach an immediate understanding. He had, however, at that time, and he never wavered from it in any subsequent conversation which I had with him, the positive conviction that the Soviet government would in its own interests recognize that its security could best be assured, and its legitimate objectives most readily attained, by co-operating fully with the United States in a universal international organization.

The President sent for me to come to see him at the White House a few days before he left on his long and fateful journey to meet at Teheran with Stalin and Churchill, and at Cairo with Chiang Kai-shek.

The President received me in his bedroom where I had so often been called during the past years when he wished to talk over quietly some of the problems in foreign affairs with which he was engrossed.

It was one of those warm gray November days which are typical of Washington. The mist hung heavy over the vista which framed the distant Potomac. The windows were half open, and the President, who was propped up in bed, had over his shoulders the dark blue cape which he so often wore. The tables by his bedside were crowded with books and littered with papers.

He had not been well. He had suffered increasingly from the constant sinus infection which he found it so hard to shake off, and he said laughingly that he believed the desert air of Africa would prove a good remedy. But he was unusually serious. He felt deeply the import of the conferences which lay ahead, and he spoke far more than was customary with him of the future which lay before the world after the war had been won. At times his face had that luminous aspect and his eyes that remote look which struck so deeply into the hearts of those who loved him, as his life drew to its close.

His days had recently been devoted to staff conversations and to the military planning for the conferences. For it was now that Stalin was to be told of the final plans for the second front.

He discussed with me the general principles which he believed should be established with regard to the Far East, as they were later to be embodied in the Declaration of Cairo. He spoke as well of the emerging problems of the Mediterranean and of the Balkans, fully anticipating the inevitable clash of interests between the Soviet and England.

But during the two hours in which I was with him by far the greatest part of the conversation was devoted to the details of international organization, and of the manner in which he might best achieve at the meeting with Stalin a firm agreement upon the general nature of the organization, and upon the manner in which it should be established.

The President had upon his bed the copy of the draft which I had given him in June. He told me he had been studying it again the night before. On the backs of some of the pages he had jotted down notes and suggestions. Most of these had to do with the powers and constitution of the Security Council.

He spoke with hope of his ability to reach a "meeting of the minds," as he put it, with Stalin. He regretted that no meetings had taken place before, and he complained rather sharply of the difficulties which had been raised in Moscow to making the present conference possible. Stalin insisted that his own military responsibilities prevented his going far from Moscow. He could not understand, he said, that the President of the United States, while Congress is in session, must remain in close touch with Congressional leaders, and must be able to pass upon legislation which is enacted, within the ten-day period fixed by the Constitution.

But he was under no illusions as to the magnitude of the basic problem of finding a co-operative understanding with Russia. He said to me in so many words, "We won't get any strong international organization unless we can find the way by which the Soviet Union and the United States can work together to build it up as the years go by." That to him was the key issue.

By that time, November, 1943, Franklin Roosevelt was as determined to use every bit of his remaining physical and mental capacity to create the only foundations upon which lasting peace and human progress could be constructed as he had already proved determined to sacrifice himself to win the victory of the United Nations. As was always the case, he spared no effort in translating the objectives nearest to his heart into facts. By his inspiration the declaration already issued by the representatives of the Soviet Union, Great Britain, China and the United States at Moscow on October 30, 1943, had contained this provision:

They recognize the necessity of establishing at the earliest practicable date a general international organization, based on the principle of sovereign equality of all peace-loving states, and open to membership by all such states, large and small, for the maintenance of international peace and security.

At Teheran on December 1, he himself secured this pronouncement:

And as to peace—we are sure that our concord will win an enduring peace. We recognize fully the supreme responsibility resting upon us and all the United Nations to make a peace which will command the good will of the overwhelming mass of the peoples of the world and banish the scourge and terror of war for many generations.

With our diplomatic advisers we have surveyed the problems of the future. We shall seek the co-operation and active participation of all nations, large and small, whose peoples in heart and mind are dedicated, as are our own peoples, to the elimination of tyranny and slavery, oppression and intolerance. We will welcome them, as they may choose to come, into a world family of democratic nations.

By the leadership which he exercised in the conferences at Moscow and at Teheran and by the inspiration for which he was essentially responsible, President Roosevelt laid the ground for a firm understanding between the major partners. Without it there could be no durable international organization.

In the meantime this government went forward with the practical plans for social, economic and financial co-operation.

During the preceding year the President had frequently elaborated to me his conception of the shape these plans should take. He believed that the most practical method of insuring success for international co-operation in the economic and social fields lay in holding functional conferences, each dealing with a separate aspect of the general problem. He was strongly in favor of having each of these separate conferences held in different capitals.

I remember that upon one occasion he canvassed the possibility of holding, within the United States, a United Nations conference on the problems of food and agriculture, a conference in London on financial policy, a conference in Moscow upon the most equitable method of making available the oil resources of the world, and a conference in Rio de Janeiro to work out an international agreement upon the distribution of other essential raw materials. It was his thought that each one of these conferences should first of all strive to secure an international agreement upon policies and conclude by deciding upon the best kind of machinery to carry out the policies laid down. Later, in his judgment, the organizations established by each conference should be taken over and become integral parts of the permanent United Nations organization.

This general concept of the President was wholly in line with the idea which he had as to the manner in which the permanent international organization itself should function. He told me that he was strongly opposed to having all the machinery of the new organization located permanently in any one place. He objected strongly to a return to Geneva, except perhaps for some one functional branch of the organization, such as the International Labor Organization, which might make its headquarters there. He saw the need, of course, for some permanent headquarters where the secretariat and the archives would be located. But he felt strongly that the executive agency, or the Security Council, should be continuously in session, and be prepared to meet at short notice in any part of the world where trouble might arise.

He was firmly of the opinion that the meetings of the General Assembly should be held in some place where the delegates would be completely free from any form of undue pressure, whether exercised by organized groups, or by the press or radio. For that reason, he told me several times, he believed that a permanent site for the Assembly meetings should be established in the Azores. Air communication would make headquarters there accessible to all officials at short notice. But undesirable or unnecessary visitors could be readily excluded, and no individual or selfish influences could be exerted.

The President's views on the means of creating implementary machinery were carried out, except that the major part of the preliminary economic, social and financial conferences were held in different cities in the United States rather than in other parts of the world as well. This was due, of course, to war conditions.

The food and agriculture conference met originally at Hot Springs. There, and at its subsequent meetings in other places, general policies as well as organizational structure were agreed upon. The United Nations Relief and Rehabilitation Administration, designed to cope with the relief problems which would arise as soon as the war in Europe had ended, was likewise established at this time.

In July, 1944, the representatives of forty-five nations met at Bretton Woods and there arrived at a series of accords. Through these were established an International Bank for Reconstruction and Development, with a capital of $9,100,000,000, to make loans to governments to help rehabilitate and develop the war-torn countries after the war, and an $8,800,000,000 International Monetary Fund intended to bring about the postwar stabilization of world currencies and thereby to foster a high level of international trade. These agreements had been ratified by twenty-eight governments before the end of 1945. They thereupon became operative, since among the ratifying powers were the United States, Great Britain, France and China. The Soviet Union, however, abstained. Organizational meetings subsequently were held at Savannah, and in May, 1946, the two institutions actually came into being.

The subscription of the United States to the capital of the International Bank was $3,175,000,000, and its fund quota was $2,750,000,000. The contribution is large. But it is a contribution to world peace and world prosperity. No more practical measures in the field of international economic co-operation have been devised, for they offer to the war-devastated peoples the chance to help themselves. They can resume production; they can return to a position where they can once more buy in the world market. The operation of the International Monetary Fund will to a large extent eliminate those former disastrous fluctuations in world currencies, which not only impeded the free flow of commodities, but also resulted in those crippling exchange restrictions which prevented the seller of goods in one country from being paid in another country save in currencies which he could not exchange into the money of his own country.

An international conference upon civil aviation was held in Chicago. It was hoped that a basic agreement could be found which would insure world co-operation in the development of air communications. Unfortunately, no accord was reached upon some of the fundamental principles which must be established if any real approach to non-discriminatory practices is to be achieved. Other meetings, of a more limited nature, subsequently took place. But aviation is one field where no success in international co-operation has yet been encountered.

However, the United Nations have met with success in their effort to strengthen the International Labor Organization, and in their handling of several other social and economic problems.

All of these several agreements represented the keystones fashioned upon the instigation of President Roosevelt for later insertion in the great arch of international organization.

In the early autumn of 1944 there was held at Dumbarton Oaks in Washington, the conference in which the United States, Great Britain, and the Soviet Union, and later China, participated in order to formulate specific proposals for the new international organization. The Dumbarton Oaks proposals—proposals, since they were theoretically the recommendations of the major powers to the smaller members of the United Nations—were based upon the plan drafted in the Department of State the preceding year.

In the preparation for the conference, however, this government was responsible for a serious miscalculation, if the whole-hearted, rather than the nominal, co-operation of the lesser powers was to be secured. For it held no prior consultation with the other twenty American Republics regarding its views on world organization. Yet the spirit of all the recent inter-American agreements required an intimate understanding between the United States and its American neighbors as soon as the United States determined to sponsor a proposal by which the destinies of every one of the other American Republics would be shaped.

More than that, the Inter-American Consultative Meeting of Foreign Ministers held in Panama in 1939 had established a juridical committee, with its headquarters in Rio de Janeiro, which had been charted with the specific responsibility of formulating inter-American proposals for world organization. A United States delegate was a member of this committee.

It is true that eventually the governments of the other American Republics were given the opportunity of presenting their proposals for world organization, and of commenting upon the agreements reached at Dumbarton Oaks. But it was notorious that neither their proposals, nor their suggested amendments were given serious consideration. More than that, a series of seminars upon the subject of world organization, undertaken for the benefit of the Latin-American diplomatic representatives in Washington by a minor official in the Department of State, created a considerable measure of antagonism, because of the belief of the Latin-American governments that the United States had not only studiously ignored their views, but was now attempting to dictate the course which it expected them unquestioningly to follow. Had the Department of State during the twelve months prior to the meeting at Dumbarton Oaks taken the other American Republics into its confidence, and discussed with them its own concept of the most desirable nature of the organization to come, the American Republics would have felt themselves to be true partners in a common enterprise. Moreover, this government would have profited greatly by the exceedingly valuable suggestions which could have been offered by several of the Latin-American governments, all of which had played a prominent part in the League of Nations and had learned much through their participation in that organization.

What was still more serious, from the standpoint of the United States, was that through the procedure adopted the Western Hemisphere lost the chance of uniting behind the project for the new world order. The nations of the Americas have evolved the most decent and enlightened international relationship which civilization has yet known. It would have proved of great value at San Francisco if all of the United Nations had recognized that the Western world spoke with one voice in favor of the advanced form of world organization there proposed.

In the same way neither Great Britain nor the United States attempted to obtain the benefit of the advice of the smaller powers of Europe. These governments, like those of Latin America, had taken a prominent part in the League of Nations. They were among the most worthy citizens in the world community. Their recommendations would have been of great value.

In consequence, the conference at Dumbarton Oaks antagonized the smaller powers. The four major powers ignored them all until after the conclusion of the conference. Since the Soviet government had insisted that the conference be limited to the delegates of the great powers, the exclusion of the small countries from this preparatory meeting was inevitable. But that by no means prevented the United States from reaching a prior, even if informal, understanding with its American neighbors.

The meeting at Dumbarton Oaks was protracted. The delay in reaching a final decision was due to the refusal of the Soviet government to agree with the United States and Great Britain upon the nature of the power to be vested in the major states. The Soviet government insisted upon an absolute veto right for each of the major powers in the Security Council. The governments of the English-speaking powers urged that the veto right be less extensive. In the final result, no agreement upon this point was reached. In the proposals finally drafted specific reference had to be made to the fact that "the question of voting procedure is still under consideration."

Shortly thereafter, Franklin Roosevelt embarked for the Crimea on his last great mission, although his final election campaign had been exhausting and the reserves of his physical strength were running very low. But the differences which had arisen between the Soviet Union and her Western allies during the summer and autumn months of 1944 were becoming constantly more accentuated. The disagreement concerning the powers of the major countries in the coming international organization threatened to become insoluble. President Roosevelt determined that no further time must be lost in reaching a binding accord with the Soviet Union on all questions concerning international organization, as well as in ending such dangerous controversies as that which had recently arisen with regard to the future of eastern Europe.

There is no statesman of recent times who has possessed a more accurate realization of the importance of the time element in the conduct of foreign policy. President Roosevelt knew that if the growing discord between the Soviet Union and the Western powers was permitted to continue unchecked the very creation of an international organization would be jeopardized. He believed that he had found by experience that a personal meeting between himself and the chief of the Soviet government could secure the kind of understanding that was indispensable if co-operative policies, rather than antagonistic policies, were to be pursued by the two greatest powers. To Franklin Roosevelt a firm agreement with the Soviet Union was the indispensable foundation for peace in the future. He never feared differences with Great Britain. Differences between the two English-speaking countries would inevitably arise from time to time, but he realized that these would from now on be only superficial.

The relations between the United States and the Soviet Union he regarded as in a wholly different category. In the narrower sense, neither country depended upon the other. But in the wider sense he saw that each could achieve security only if it had the co-operation of the other. He told me in one of the final talks I had with him that he believed that Stalin saw this fact as clearly as he did himself. Neither the Soviet Union nor the United States could be safe unless each was confident that there was no reason for it to defend itself against the other. Each could prosper only if it could live in a safe and prosperous world. Each could progress only if the community of nations witnessed a universal rise in living standards.

Franklin Roosevelt saw no need to fear Communism if an international organization existed. To him it need be feared as a disruptive force only if the world were divided into two armed camps, one headed by the Soviet Union and the other by the English-speaking powers.

He once said to me that he believed that if the world could remain at peace the following phenomenon would probably take place. He regarded the American form of democracy as being at the opposite pole from the original form of Soviet Communism. In the years which had elapsed since the Soviet revolution of 1917, the Soviet system had advanced materially toward a modified form of state socialism. In the same way, the American polity since that time had progressed toward the ideal of true political and social justice. He believed that American democracy and Soviet Communism could never meet. But he told me that he did believe that if one took the figure 100 as representing the difference between American democracy and Soviet Communism in 1917, with the United States at 100 and the Soviet Union at 0, American democracy might eventually reach the figure of 60 and the Soviet system might reach the figure of 40. The gap between these two final figures it seemed to him would never lessen.

He felt, therefore, that even though the internal systems of the two countries could never conceivably become identical, some progress toward approximation had already been made, and that this approximation made for a better understanding between the peoples of the two nations. He regarded this trend as making it more likely that no fundamental conflict between the two countries need ever become inevitable, provided Soviet Communism had permanently abandoned its doctrine of world revolution. He felt it was indispensable that both governments should realize that in the field of world affairs their respective courses could always be parallel and need never be antagonistic.

At that dangerous time, in the late autumn of 1944, he was willing to make material concessions in order to achieve such an understanding and to make it possible for the United Nations organization to be established. But in return for such concessions he must have complete assurance that the United Nations organization would be supported from the outset by the Union of Soviet Socialist Republics as well as by the United States.

It was in that spirit and with that purpose that Franklin Roosevelt attended the meeting at Yalta. Though rapidly failing, he achieved in the declaration of February 11, 1945, which he signed together with Prime Minister Churchill and Generalissimo Stalin this culminating triumph. The declaration contains these provisions:

We are resolved upon the earliest possible establishment with our allies of a general international organization to maintain peace and security. We believe that this is essential, both to prevent aggression and to remove the political, economic and social causes of war through the close and continuing collaboration of all peace-loving peoples.

The foundations were laid at Dumbarton Oaks. On the important question of voting procedure, however, agreement was not there reached. The present conference has been able to resolve this difficulty.

We have agreed that a conference of United Nations should be called to meet at San Francisco in the United States on April 25, 1945, to prepare the Charter of such an organization, along the lines proposed in the informal conversations at Dumbarton Oaks.

Our meeting here in the Crimea has reaffirmed our common determination to maintain and to strengthen in the peace to come that unity of purpose and of action which has made victory possible and certain for the United Nations in this war. We believe that this is a sacred obligation which our Governments owe to our peoples and to all the peoples of the world.

Only with the continuing and growing co-operation and understanding among our three countries and among all the peace-loving nations can the highest aspiration of humanity be realized—a secure and lasting peace which will, in the words of the Atlantic Charter, "afford assurance that all the men in all the lands may live out their lives in freedom from fear and want."

Franklin Roosevelt's death, only a few weeks after his return to the United States, came as a shattering blow to millions of people in every corner of the globe. To tens of millions in the United States his death represented a personal loss. But at the moment it seemed to me that his death was felt almost more keenly and more emotionally in other countries. Throughout the war years, the suffering people of Europe and of the Far East as well as those of the Western Hemisphere had come to regard him as more than a brilliantly successful war leader. To them he had become also a personification of their hopes for peace and security and a better life. With his death the assurance that these hopes would be realized seemed greatly lessened.

The world felt immediately the loss of a great quality of leadership. For the masses of the people everywhere had had confidence in him. They had gained the conviction that he truly loved his fellow men. And however much antagonized many powerful elements in the United States had been by his pursuit of the objectives in which he believed, and however reluctant they might have been to admit it, there was an almost universal acceptance of his superior wisdom in the conduct of the nation's foreign policy, and recognition of the national asset represented by the experience which he had acquired during his long years as Chief Executive.

There was a very general feeling that no one could take his place. The public recognized that at this critical moment in the history of the world, before the war had even been won, and when the great task of consolidating the gains of victory had not even commenced, the qualities of sincerity and of patriotism, and the good intentions which President Roosevelt's successor undoubtedly possessed, were not enough. It was a moment when proven capacity on the part of the Executive, and confidence on the part of the public in the wisdom of the Executive, were required as they had not been since the days of the American Civil War.

It was not unnatural that at the United Nations Conference in San Francisco, when it convened only a few days after the President's death, the delegates assembled in a spirit of gloom and uncertainty. Their spirits were scarcely revived by the inaugural addresses to which they were obliged to listen. For these, unfortunately, were more suited to a chamber of commerce meeting than to the inauguration of one of the most momentous conferences which the world has yet known.

No assemblage called to frame the constitution of a new world order could have seemed more wholly uninspired.

Among the delegations there were few brilliant or outstanding figures. It would have seemed probable that after the war years new and striking personalities should have come to the fore. Of such there was no evidence. With a few exceptions, by far the ablest delegates to be found at San Francisco came from the smaller countries. The British Dominions were in the forefront with such truly able leaders as Marshal Smuts of South Africa, Prime Minister Mackenzie King of Canada, and Dr. Herbert Evatt, the Foreign Minister of Australia. From the Netherlands and Belgium, Dr. Van Kleffens and Mr. Spaak towered above the average of their colleagues. And the quality of the Latin-American delegations was high. But at San Francisco there were no such great personalities as those who had been present at the signing of the Treaty of Versailles.

The eyes of the world, not unnaturally, were focused upon the delegation from the Soviet Union. The course pursued by Mr. Molotov at San Francisco may be summarized in this way. In drafting the United Nations Charter he sought primarily to insure that the Soviet Union retained its unrestricted and untrammeled sovereignty. The major objective was to secure for the great powers a blanket veto power, not only within the Security Council, but in all other agencies of the United Nations as well, and to keep the Assembly a debating society and nothing more. In general terms, Mr. Molotov attempted, as in his sponsorship of the dependent peoples, to increase popular sympathy for the Soviet Union as well as to weaken the world influence of other major powers. Finally, he tried to have incorporated within the charter provisions which the Kremlin might readily make use of in maneuvering if the United Nations organization later proved an obstacle to the expansion of Russian influence and to the achievement of whatever Russian "security" the Soviet leaders considered necessary.

The reluctance of the smaller states to be relegated to the role of meek subservience intended for them by Mr. Molotov soon became apparent. As the conference progressed, the delegations of the small powers were ably led by Dr. Evatt of Australia and by Prime Minister Frazer of New Zealand, both vigorously supported by an increasingly solid bloc of the Latin-American Republics.

Great Britain attempted to act as middleman. The French delegation, unable to indulge in even the barest platitude without the specific prior approval of General de Gaulle, remained wholly in the background.

The role played by the United States was negative save for the individual achievements represented by the admirable work of Commander Stassen in drafting the provisions covering the International Trusteeship System, and the invaluable support given by Senator Vandenberg in defense of the rights of the smaller nations.

The only occasion upon which the United States delegation as a whole came prominently into the limelight was hardly beneficial. The incident arose through the sponsorship by the United States of Argentina's admission to the United Nations organization, a step vigorously combated for bargaining purposes by the Soviet Union.

At the Inter-American Conference held at Mexico City two months before, the United States had agreed, if Argentina adhered to the inter-American agreements there reached, to secure her entrance into the United Nations organization. At San Francisco the United States delegation attempted to back out of its commitment, but was held to it by the other American Republics. The details of the controversy will be discussed in a subsequent chapter. At this point it is merely necessary to state that the manner in which the United States delegation permitted itself to be placed under a cloud of public obloquy by the Soviet Union was incredibly inept. For Mr. Molotov at the outset had been quite willing to accept Argentina in return for White Russia and the Ukraine. It was only when he raised his stakes to include Poland in the bargain, and the United States objected, that the storm broke. Had the public been informed of these facts the situation would have been clear. As it was the United States, as a result of exceedingly clever footwork on the part of Mr. Molotov, was made to appear the ardent supporter of a Fascist régime. But what was far worse in its ultimate effect was the fact that the unskillful handling of the incident by the American delegation led to the immediate crystallization within the conference of two blocs, one composed of the Soviet Union and its handful of satellites, and the other consisting of the large group of Western states, led by Great Britain and the United States.

The United Nations Charter as finally adopted at San Francisco has grave defects. It has serious weaknesses. But in the last analysis, the United Nations Charter offers to the peoples of the world a far more promising basis for effective international organization than did the League of Nations. It offers a far greater measure of hope that an international organization has come into being which can keep the peace, which can stimulate social progress and understanding between peoples, and which can bring about effective international economic co-operation, than would have seemed even remotely possible a few years before.

To my mind the major improvements over the Dumbarton Oaks proposals which were achieved at San Francisco are the admirable Preamble, the broader powers granted to the Assembly, the elaboration of the functions of the Economic and Social Council and of the Trusteeship Council, the provisions which safeguard the existence of regional systems, and the compromise adopted with respect to the Security Council.

Among the gravest defects in the charter is the provision which unduly restricts the possibility of amendment. Since it is provided that any one great power can veto any amendment, even one approved by all the other member states, it is probable that no amendments will be adopted until after a period of ten years has elapsed, when, under the terms of Article 109 of the charter, a conference to consider amendments may be called even over the objections of a major power. Yet the United Nations cannot become the true embodiment of the hopes of humanity unless it can always be open to those modifications and improvements which a great majority of the peoples of the United Nations believe to be essential.

The United Nations, like the League of Nations, is founded upon the concept that a league of sovereign states pledged to unite their strength "to maintain international peace and security and to insure, by the acceptance of principles and the institution of methods, that armed force shall not be used, save in the common interest," as stipulated in the Charter of the United Nations, can not only prevent war, but can also achieve the other common objectives set forth in the charter. The basis of the two international organizations is, therefore, precisely the same. But the experience of the years between the great wars and the practical demonstration of the inherent defects and weaknesses in the machinery of the League of Nations brought about a material strengthening of the form of the league envisioned in the Charter of the United Nations.

The Paris Conference of 1919 refused to adopt the French contention that the League of Nations should have authority over an armed force to be used to carry out the League's decisions. The Council of the League of Nations was empowered only to "recommend" the military steps to be taken by each of the member states in any common endeavor to repress aggression. The Charter of the United Nations, on the contrary, authorizes the Security Council of the United Nations to "take such action by air, sea, or land forces as may be necessary to maintain or restore international peace." Moreover, under Article 43 of the charter, all the member states "undertake to make available to the Security Council, on its call and in accordance with a special agreement or agreements, armed forces, assistance, and facilities, including rights of passage, necessary for the purpose of maintaining international peace and security"; and by Articles 45 and 47 the member states obligate themselves to "hold immediately available national air force contingents for combined international enforcement action" and to submit to such plans for the application of this armed force as may be made by a special military staff committee created to function under the authority of the Security Council.

From the standpoint of its ability to exercise police power, the United Nations is consequently far more potent than the League of Nations.

And by the authorization granted through Chapter 8 of the charter to states in any given region to enter into regional pacts for the purpose of insuring their security and achieving the pacific settlement of local disputes, the Security Council is strengthened from another practical point of view through the authority which it is enabled to exercise over these regional policing arrangements.

In every other functional aspect as well, the United Nations is a stronger organization than the League of Nations. Moreover, through the creation of one agency which did not exist in the League of Nations, namely, the Economic and Social Council, the United Nations has been enabled, should this agency be used to the fullest possible extent, to contribute greatly to the prevention of war. For the potential usefulness of the Economic and Social Council is almost unlimited. It is empowered to solve through international co-operation the basic social and economic problems which have so gravely afflicted humanity during the past centuries and which have so frequently engendered conditions that have made for international controversy and for wars of aggression.

From the standpoint of organization, the Economic and Social Council possesses one great advantage over the Security Council. There is no veto power exercised within it. It is composed of the delegates of eighteen countries, all of whom have equal rights. Decisions within the Council are taken by a majority of those delegates who are present and who vote.

The chief and the most valid criticism of the United Nations is that in the Security Council the five major powers are granted an absolute veto right, except upon procedural matters and except when they are parties to disputes which the Security Council is attempting, under Chapter 6 of the charter, to settle by pacific means. This veto right means that, in practice, any one of the five major powers can prevent the United Nations from undertaking any kind of punitive action against it and can further block all effective action by the United Nations once pacific settlements have proved to be futile and the nature of the controversy has been publicly ventilated.

Certainly from the standpoint of any sincere perfectionist the veto powers granted to the major states are totally incompatible with the fundamental principles of international democracy, with the reiterated assertion by the United Nations of its respect for the equal sovereignty of all countries, great or small, and with the concept that world order should be subject to law rather than to military power.

But had these special veto rights been eliminated from the charter, there would exist today no United Nations organization. The Soviet Union was adamant in its insistence on this right. It was only owing to the urgent endeavors of President Roosevelt that the Soviet government agreed to waive its insistence upon a blanket veto power and conceded the limitations finally embodied in the charter. More than that, the Senate would not have agreed to ratify the participation by the United States in the United Nations organization without these veto rights. It is in the highest degree doubtful that the majority of American public opinion would have supported the entrance of the United States into the United Nations organization on any other terms.

Under these conditions the only constructive policy for the United States Government to pursue was the negotiation of a charter embodying these veto rights in the Security Council for the major powers with the understanding that, should the United Nations organization succeed, should world order thereby be maintained, and should the nations of the earth consequently enjoy for a protracted period a true reign of peace, this discrimination between the major and the lesser powers might then be abolished.

All that stands today between those hundreds of millions of men and women who desire peace and the assurance of security, and world anarchy and an ultimate war of annihilation is the United Nations organization. The fears and suspicions engendered by the discovery of atomic fission and the deep-rooted rivalries that have so rapidly increased between the major powers since the end of the Second World War have created a widespread feeling of panic. This panic fear, in turn, has brought about an insistence on the part of an increasing number of high-minded and sincere people that the United Nations organization, as it has now been established, cannot possibly succeed and that it should be immediately replaced with some new type of international organization

to which they generally refer as a "federal world government."
To most of these the term "world government" implies an indispensable relinquishment of sovereignty by the present sovereign
nations. The concept is best set forth by Mr. Emery Reves in his
book *The Anatomy of Peace* in these words: "As the twentieth
century crisis is a world wide clash between the social units of
sovereign nation-states, the problem of peace in our time is the
establishment of a legal order to regulate relations among men,
beyond and above the nation-states."

If we were living in a world where the mere announcement of a
desirable objective was sufficient to assure its achievement, every
intelligent man and woman would enthusiastically support such
objectives as those set forth by Mr. Emery Reves and by his associates and followers. But unfortunately the world of today is of a
wholly different character. The basic defect in the appeals for
world government now being made by Mr. Reves, Justice Owen J.
Roberts, Mr. Humber and many others of the same school is the
fact that no form of world government can today be created in
which both the Soviet Union and the United States will take part.
The Soviet government has repeatedly and officially declared not
only that it opposes any form of world government but also that
an international organization such as the United Nations, to prove
successful, must depend, at least during its initial period, upon the
domination of all the rest of the world by the three major powers.
There is no evidence which can lead an objective observer of
American public opinion to believe that any considerable number,
let alone a majority, of the people would support the entrance of
the United States into a federal world government which subjects
the determination of American security and of American foreign
policy to any such form of federal world legislative body as that
envisioned by most of these schemes.

In view of the increasing tension which has arisen between the
Soviet government and the Western powers during the past
twelve months, it would be a true optimist who could affirm that
even so relatively liberal and effective a charter could now be agreed
upon as that signed at San Francisco in June, 1945. Yet notwithstanding the clearly shown sentiment of a majority of the Ameri-

can people and notwithstanding the trenchant assertions of the Soviet government that it will not even consider such a proposal, a number of advocates of world government actually propose that the United States Government take the lead today in summoning a new world conference in order to obtain an international agreement upon an immediate federal world government. This group of world government advocates illustrates again that strange American characteristic: the desire to believe that because some proposal is righteous and desirable, the formulation of it in writing is necessarily equivalent to the actual realization of the objectives sought. For it seems to me that nothing could today be more fantastic than to assume that the peoples of the Soviet Union and of the United States would be willing to entrust the determination of their destinies to any kind of international legislative body elected by popular vote, no matter how weighted, of the masses of the people of the world.

Another school of these proponents of World Government now has, however, an additional motive behind its appeals which should be carefully noted and which must be as carefully analyzed.

This motive can be most clearly seen in some of the addresses on behalf of world government made within recent months by Justice Roberts. Justice Roberts frankly states that he recognizes that if a world government is to be immediately constituted, there are in fact "people who feel that they are not able to join." Justice Roberts makes no effort to conceal who these "people" are. The "people" in question are the Russians. He and his followers, consequently, urge that the world government which he envisions should immediately be organized "to represent us and all the other people in legislating for the common welfare" but, more particularly, for "defense." If such a world government were set up, excluding the Soviet Union, can it for a moment be assumed that the Soviet government and its satellite states would not immediately regard it as an alliance directed against them? Would they not be more firmly convinced than ever that the Western world is engaged in a capitalistic conspiracy against Soviet Communism, and, what is more important, embark without delay upon whatever methods the Kremlin might consider best designed to insure Soviet "security" and its own defense? Could there be any more effective method than that proposed by Justice Roberts to bring about a prompt crystallization of the world into two major spheres of influence, each armed to the teeth and each feverishly preparing for a new and atomic war?

The most deplorable effect created by the advocates of World Government now comes through their ability to undermine the faith of many here in the United States in the capacity of the United Nations to serve the cause of world peace and thereby to weaken popular support for the new international organization. Unquestionably, many like myself believe that the ultimate objective of the United Nations should be the attainment of some form of federal world government wherein peoples, rather than governments, can have a direct and controlling influence. It is our hope that, as the United Nations becomes stronger, as political and social progress gathers momentum, and as the capacity of governments and of peoples to work together toward their common objectives becomes more firmly established, the initial charter of the United Nations may be continuously amended so as to bring about that kind of truly democratic international organization now seen through a glass darkly. But of no one thing am I more firmly convinced than that, if the United Nations Charter were today to be scrapped and the effort to be made to bring about a general international agreement upon a world government, humanity would secure neither world government nor anything other than chaos.

After many months of discussion of procedure and mechanics by its provisional and preparatory committees, the first meeting of the General Assembly of the United Nations took place in London in the early winter of 1946. The accomplishments of this first meeting were necessarily limited to the determination of procedural matters and to the creation of the several agencies for which provision was made in the charter.

As a result of a protracted dispute it was finally determined that the permanent site of the United Nations should be in the neighborhood of New York City, and that pending the construction of the necessary facilities, the provisional headquarters should be set up in New York City itself. No more unwise or illogical

decision could have been reached. The location of the permanent
headquarters of the United Nations within the territory of any
one of the major powers will inevitably give rise sooner or later
at a moment of crisis to the charge that public opinion, and in particular the press and radio, of that major power, is creating an
unwarranted influence upon the delegates and that such an atmosphere is not conducive to an impartial and objective consideration
of their problems. The site was chosen over the strong objections
of the western European nations, partly because of the stubborn
refusal of the Soviet government to agree to the location of the
United Nations at the old headquarters of the League of Nations
in Geneva and because of its desire that the site should be outside
western Europe. The Latin-American Republics favored a site
within the Western Hemisphere, but in their majority they, like
China, favored San Francisco as the permanent headquarters.
When this location proved unacceptable to Great Britain and to
France, a compromise was effected by choosing the eastern sea-
board of the United States. The facility with which the charge of
undue influence can be raised against any site within the territory
of one of the major powers was demonstrated when the Preparatory Commission was studying the relative advantages of several
areas along the eastern coast of the United States. At that time the
Soviet government announced that under no conditions would it
agree to the selection of a site near Boston because of what it
alleged was the anti-Soviet feeling prevalent in that area.

Had the members of the United Nations been guided solely by
the long-range interests of the organization, they would not have
agreed on New York as the permanent headquarters. The ideal
site would have been within the territory of a smaller nation, and
a smaller nation free from the suspicion of ulterior national
motives. The site should have been centrally located, easily accessible by air to all governments, and geographically situated so
as to be as free as possible from the presence of pressure groups
and of organized lobbies.

The correctness of President Roosevelt's belief that the best
site would be the Azores is becoming more and more evident.
The islands are readily accessible by air. Entrance to the islands

could easily be regulated by the authorities of the United Nations, and the deliberations of all of the official members of the United Nations and the work of its agencies could be carried on in an atmosphere wholly free from the suspicion of undue influence.

At the preparatory meeting of the Assembly, Mr. Trygve Lie, who had served throughout the war as the Foreign Minister of the Exiled Government of Norway, was elected the first Secretary General of the United Nations. Mr. Lie had won the respect of the governments of the major powers and of the governments-in-exile located in London for the qualities of courage, determination and indefatigable energy which he possessed to so eminent a degree. Nor could there be any question of his truly democratic and liberal spirit. His ability was unquestioned. His election was the result of a compromise between the Soviet Union and the Western powers, although it has been generally assumed that he was, in reality, the first candidate upon the list favored by the Soviet government.

In a very real sense the initial success of the United Nations may depend upon the vision and qualities of statesmanship possessed by the Secretary General. He is the chief administrative officer of the organization. He acts in that capacity in all meetings of the General Assembly, of the Security Council, of the Economic and Social Council, and of the Trusteeship Council.

By Article 99 of the charter he is specifically empowered to bring to the attention of the Security Council any matter that in his opinion may threaten the maintenance of international peace and security. President Roosevelt had urged that these powers be even more ample. He had specifically favored the proposal that the Secretary General be empowered to participate, although without a vote, in all the discussions of the Security Council; and his general concept of the proper functions to be vested in the chief administrative officer of the United Nations may best be grasped from the fact that he preferred the title of "Moderator" for this official rather than the title of "Secretary General."

But the authority now granted the Secretary General by the charter and by the procedural regulations adopted by the Security Council is so broad that it makes it possible for him to stimulate or retard the functioning of the organization, and to facilitate or impede the solution of the problems which come before the several agencies of the United Nations. It rests, therefore, with Mr. Lie as the first incumbent to establish the precedents which will determine whether the position of Secretary General will come to be considered as having the full significance which it potentially possesses. The demonstration which he has so far given of his realization of the importance of these precedents has necessarily been limited. The staff which he has appointed under the powers granted him by Article 101 of the charter has unfortunately been exceptionally mediocre. Logically, the individuals appointed to key positions have been selected with due regard to geographical distribution, but at a moment when demonstrated capacity should have been the primary consideration, official influence seems unfortunately to have been the predominant cause for selection.

At the preparatory meeting no Trusteeship Council was elected owing primarily to the reluctance of Great Britain and of the other colonial powers to expedite the negotiation of the special agreements required by the terms of the charter before a Trusteeship Council could be officially installed. What was even more regrettable was the long delay in the establishment of the Economic and Social Council notwithstanding the fact that the activities of the Council, once constituted, could have proved invaluable in furthering European peace settlements. The International Court of Justice was finally elected and, like the World Court, was established with its permanent headquarters at The Hague. The judges elected to the Court, except in the case of a few eminent jurists who were nationals of smaller powers, hardly reached the level of mediocrity. It was in the highest degree regrettable in the case of the United States that the American government permitted the replacement of Judge Manley O. Hudson, who had served for long years with outstanding distinction as a member of the old World Court.

The most important step taken at the London meeting was the election of the members of the Security Council and the supplementary decision that the Council should at once convene in New York City.

By the terms of the charter, the Security Council is composed of eleven members, of which five, the United States, Great Britain, the Soviet Union, China, and France, have permanent seats, and of which the remaining six are elected by the General Assembly for terms of two years. The Security Council is entrusted with "primary responsibility for the maintenance of international peace and security." It is organized so as to function continuously, and by the rules of procedure adopted, the Council is obligated to meet at brief intervals whether or not it is called upon to consider urgent questions. Its authority under Chapters 6 and 7 of the charter with respect to the pacific settlement of disputes and its powers to take action to prevent or to repress breaches of the peace is exceedingly wide. While it was alleged upon one occasion by the Australian representative upon the Security Council that the Council is not "the executive committee of the United Nations," for all practical purposes that is precisely what the Council actually is, especially during the formative period of the United Nations before the organization as a whole has had the opportunity to commence to function and the component parts of the mechanism to settle into place.

During the first period of the United Nations organization, before any peace settlements had been reached and while the entire world was in a stage of rapidly increasing chaos, it was in the highest degree important that the Security Council, while remaining within the limits of the powers conferred upon it by the charter, should nevertheless exercise the fullest measure of its authority and assert that authority in every rightful way. That was clearly the intent of the authors of the charter.

The election of the first non-permanent members of the Security Council by the General Assembly resulted in the selection for the six seats accorded to the lesser powers of Brazil, Mexico, Australia, Egypt, the Netherlands and Poland. It was clearly the obligation of every one of the governments entrusted with the responsibility of appointing representatives to the first sessions of the Security Council to choose the ablest men available for the tremendous responsibilities devolving upon them.

To any impartial observer the contrast between the hopes and anticipations, and the reality, was shocking. No mechanism such as the Security Council can be successful in solving the problems with which humanity is afflicted unless the human material of which it is composed is of a caliber sufficiently broad to avail itself of the opportunities entrusted to it. With but a few exceptions, the members of the Security Council failed lamentably to meet those standards.

The delegate selected by the Soviet government, Mr. Andrei Gromyko, had served first as Counsellor and then as Ambassador in Washington. A competent functionary of the younger generation of Soviet diplomats, Mr. Gromyko had represented his government both at San Francisco and during the preparatory meetings of the United Nations in London. It was well known that he was not authorized to assume any responsibility or to take any action save in accordance with the specific instructions issued to him from Moscow. He was consequently unable to make any such notable contribution to the work of the Security Council as that made in former years to the Council of the League of Nations by Maxim Litvinoff, even had his personal experience or his personal capacities made such contributions conceivable.

The representative of Great Britain was Sir Alexander Cadogan, who had served for many years as Permanent Under Secretary of State for Foreign Affairs in London and who had previously had a long record as a competent British diplomatic officer. But not by the widest stretch of the imagination could Sir Alexander Cadogan be regarded as possessing vision or a capacity for initiative, or as capable of reaching political decisions in a moment of crisis. The best type of high-minded and honorable Civil Service official, he was at the same time bound by the traditional limitations of the service to which he belonged.

The American delegate, Mr. Edward Stettinius, had scarcely demonstrated during his brief career as Secretary of State any of the qualifications required in the position to which he had now been appointed. Of his good intentions there could be no question. Of his wholehearted desire to bend his every effort toward making the Security Council a success there could likewise be no doubt. But, devoid of any knowledge of international relations or even of modern history and lacking the personal qualifications desirable in so high an office, Mr. Stettinius, it was painfully evident from the outset, could play only a meager part.

The appointment in June, 1946, of Senator Austin as successor to Mr. Stettinius strengthened immeasurably the representation of the major powers upon the Security Council. Senator Austin possessed much knowledge of foreign affairs. He had played a large part in the creation of the United Nations. A man of character and of ability, he could make an individual contribution to the work of the Council of which his predecessor had been incapable. His courage and his vision were unquestioned.

The original French representative, France's Ambassador in Washington, M. Henri Bonnet, was distinguished for his liberal point of view, but more particularly for his early devotion to the cause of General de Gaulle. He was soon succeeded by M. Alexandre Parodi, who had been one of the outstanding leaders of French resistance during the German occupation.

The representative of China, Dr. Quo Tai Chi, who had served previously as Chinese Foreign Minister and earlier as Chinese Ambassador in London, was distinguished more for his conciliatory spirit than for his capacity to play any determining part in the work of the Council.

Of the representatives of the smaller powers, Dr. Pedro Velloso, Brazilian Minister for Foreign Affairs during the last period of the government of President Vargas, and for many years prior thereto a Brazilian diplomatic representative in the Far East, assumed a large negative role. It was a strange anomaly that a nation like Brazil, which has for so long been outstanding in her exceptionally brilliant representatives abroad, should not have selected for this position a statesman of more marked vigor and initiative.

The Polish representative, Dr. Oscar Lange, whose brief experience as an American citizen had been ended by his acceptance of the position as Ambassador in Washington of the new Polish government, was noted chiefly for his subservience to the line laid down by Moscow.

The original representative of Egypt, Mahmoud Hassan, Egypt's Minister in Washington, like his successor, Dr. Afifi, demonstrated both personal force and a laudable desire to contribute toward the strengthening of the authority of the Council.

But it was the representatives of the three remaining powers, Australia, the Netherlands and Mexico, who alone showed any real ability to rise to the requirements of their positions. The Dutch delegate, Dr. Eelco Van Kleffens, Foreign Minister of the Netherlands during the years of the war, revealed a remarkable lucidity of intellect, and time and again during the debates of the Council, he would lay before his colleagues the true issues and indicate methods of solution. This was made particularly evident during the Council's debate on the Iranian problem.

In this he was consistently supported by the Mexican Foreign Minister, Dr. Castillo Najera, whose many years of service in the League of Nations and whose profound understanding of international relations contributed greatly to the effective assistance which he was able to give.

But of all the eleven members of the Council, it was the representative of Australia, Colonel Hodgson, who was the most valuable during the first weeks of its sessions. Undaunted by opposition, entirely realistic in his approach to the problems before the Council, he insisted undeviatingly that it meet the requirements for which it was created and adhere to the principles upon which it was founded. No greater service has been rendered the United Nations than that given by the government of Australia from the time of the drafting of the charter, and Colonel Hodgson's share in it during the relatively short period when he was on the Council was considerable.

Upon two occasions it was Colonel Hodgson's proposals for practical solutions which were adopted by the Council, and which ended dangerous stalemates. And while Colonel Hodgson's reiterated demand that the Council deal with "facts," rather than rumors or opinions, occasioned some cause for mirth to the press, his insistence in that regard lessened the probability that the Council would at the outset become a sounding board for purely political propaganda.

It has, therefore, been by no means surprising, since most of the eleven governments concerned failed to appoint outstanding statesmen to the Security Council and selected in their stead men of secondary abilities, that the Council has so frequently fallen far short of the expectations legitimately held by the adherents of the United Nations.

During the first months of its existence, the Security Council was called upon to deal with three matters. The first, the adoption of rules of procedure, the lack of which materially handicapped its early sessions, occasioned no insurmountable obstacles.

The second problem which arose from the demand, technically presented by Poland but in reality emanating from Moscow, that the United Nations break all relations with the Franco regime in Spain in order to bring about a change of government, gave rise to a sharp cleavage of opinion. Both the United States and Great Britain, supported by Brazil, China, the Netherlands, Egypt and Australia were reluctant to have the question ventilated in the Security Council on the ground that the Franco government, under present conditions, constituted no real menace to world peace, however objectionable intrinsically it might be. The Soviet Union and Poland, supported by France and Mexico, persisted, however, in the demand for positive action. The problem was temporarily solved through the adoption of a proposal offered by Australia that the Security Council appoint a special committee to take evidence on the real situation in Spain and on the existence of any plans or preparations for aggression by the Spanish government. The Security Council could then reach a decision upon the basis of facts authoritatively gathered.

When this subcommittee rendered its report, recommending that final action be deferred until a decision could be reached by all of the United Nations at the meeting of the General Assembly in September, 1946, and that the Security Council merely recommend that the United Nations sever diplomatic relations with the Spanish government, should Franco still be in power when the Assembly met, a further, and even more violent, controversy arose.

The Soviet delegate insisted that the Security Council itself, and not the General Assembly, must take action. When it proved impossible for him to obtain approval for his demand, he officially interposed the veto of the Soviet Union to the adoption of the report of the subcommittee. All further action on the Spanish problem was consequently blocked, at least for the time being.

It was the third problem, however, the problem of Iran, which became by far the most dangerous as well as the most pressing. For the problem of Iran possessed fundamental significance. The specific questions which it raised were basic.

As a consequence of the conference at Teheran in 1943, the United States, Great Britain and the Soviet Union had agreed to withdraw all their forces of occupation from Iran not later than March 2, 1946. During the months immediately prior to that date the government of Iran had already protested to the major powers of the West against the interference by Soviet authorities in the northern provinces of Iran occupied by Russian troops. These protests had given rise to various interchanges between the three major powers, but no satisfactory understanding had been reached. What actually transpired, however, was that on March 2 both American and British troops had been withdrawn while Soviet troops remained on Iranian territory, counter to the specific pledges given by the Soviet Union. The question was then brought before the Security Council upon two issues: that the Soviet government had failed to abide by the commitment made to withdraw its troops from Iran upon the date set, and that Soviet forces were directly interfering in the internal affairs of Iran, and were preventing the central government at Teheran from dealing effectively with the dissident elements centered in the northern province of Azerbaijan.

After long discussions and acrimonious debates, one fundamental principle was established by the Council. This was that the appeal of a small state to the Council cannot be discarded because of the objection of a major power, and that a small nation will, consequently, not be deprived of the right to make its grievances known to public opinion through the Security Council.

The Soviet Union made every effort to prevent the Security Council from hearing the Iranian complaints, and before entering into a new agreement with the Iranian government by which it pledged itself to withdraw all its armed forces from Iran not later than May 6, went so far as to instruct Mr. Gromyko, its delegate upon the Council, to boycott all sessions of the Council at which the Iranian question came up for discussion. The test of the the Security Council lay in its ability to prove that its power exceeded the authority of any one of its members. While the Soviet delegate walked out of the sessions of the Council whenever Iranian matters were being considered, his government nevertheless at the crucial moment recognized the superior authority of the Council by replying to the inquiry addressed to it by the Secretary General on its intentions in Iran.

It was likewise true that, before the evacuation of Iran's northern provinces had commenced, the Soviet had obtained from Iran an agreement granting Russia entire control over oil concessions in northern Iran for a long period of years. She had also compelled the government of Teheran officially to recognize the notorious Soviet interference in the province of Azerbaijan as "a purely internal affair." It is further true that long after May 6 no conclusive evidence had been presented to the Security Council that the Red Army had completed its evacuation of Iran. The Iranian government on May 22 officially notified the Council that "according to trustworthy local people" the Soviet armies had evacuated Azerbaijan on May 6. The official radio in Moscow broadcast a statement that Soviet armies had been withdrawn. It was patent, however, that the Iranian government was undergoing a constantly intensified pressure from the Soviet Union, and the Security Council by a large majority voted on May 22 to keep the Iranian question upon its agenda for an indefinite period. The suspicion was expressed that the Soviet government was continuing to interfere in the internal affairs of Iran, and had both established and armed a dissident faction in Azerbaijan which was intent upon placing the province under the real control of the Soviet Union.

An important school of thought in the United States has insisted that the decision of the Security Council to continue to deal with the Soviet-Iranian controversy over the objections of the Soviet Union, and notwithstanding the technical statement by the government of Teheran that the Soviet evacuation of Iranian territory had been completed, was unwise and uncalled for, particularly in view of the present inability of the Security Council to take any effective action in the matter. There can, of course, be no question that the refusal of the major powers of the West to accede to the Russian contentions has added to the deterioration in relations between the Soviet Union and the West. In my judgment, however, the harm so done even at this critical moment in world history weighs far less in the balance than the harm which would have resulted had a majority of the Security Council taken a different course. Had the Security Council given in to the Russian threat and refused to continue to consider the Iranian controversy, its action would have been tantamount to the immediate admission that no smaller power had any right of appeal to the Security Council in the face of aggression by a major power; that the Council would accept at its face value a denial of aggression or threat of aggression made by a small power under pressure from a major power. Under such conditions what shadow of confidence could any smaller nation have in the ability of the Security Council or of the United Nations to safeguard its rights and its independence?

Apart from this achievement, and it is by no means small, the Security Council has established one precedent which is of outstanding value. That is its decision to make public all its proceedings. Every debate involving the Iranian controversy has been open to the public. The people have thereby been enabled to understand fully every development which has taken place and the reasons for such development. Had the sessions of the Security Council been held in secret, public opinion would have been hopelessly confused. Propaganda would have made it possible for the public in all the democracies to misinterpret the facts and to fail to recognize the gravity of Soviet machinations in Iran. These activities involved the very fundamentals of international order. It is only because the people of the democracies have been able to grasp this fact readily as a result of their knowledge of the details of each debate that public opinion has rallied overwhelmingly in support of the position taken by the Security Council on this point.

CHAPTER II

Peacemaking

THE First World War ended with the surrender of the imperial German armies on November 11, 1918. The Peace Conference of Paris commenced on January 18, 1919. The Peace Treaty of Versailles was signed on June 28, 1919. The peace settlements imposed upon Germany's allies were concluded soon thereafter.

The Second World War came to an end in Europe when German resistance collapsed on May 8, 1945. At this moment, fourteen months later, not only has no peace treaty been imposed upon the German people, but there is no semblance of an agreement between the victorious nations as to what the terms of the treaty should be. There is as yet no agreement upon a final peace treaty with Italy. There is no understanding upon the peace settlements to be concluded with the Axis satellites of eastern Europe and of the Balkans.

Before the end of the war in Europe the United Nations had proclaimed that it was their purpose to make of their victory a new epoch in human affairs. They declared that they intended to bring about an era in which the peoples of Europe would obtain peace, liberty and economic as well as physical security.

Any lasting reconstruction of Europe can be based only upon peace settlements designed to attain these ends. The longer the peace settlements are delayed, the more difficult it will be to attain them. No advance can be made toward reconstruction until a state of peace actually exists. Political stability will prove impossible until the peoples of each European country know what their boundaries are to be. Economic and financial recovery cannot be started until political stability is a fact. Increasing social unrest is inevitable until the peoples of Europe can be confident that the days of hunger and of panic terror are past, and that both political and economic security are in sight. Prolonged uncertainty can

only arouse the fierce passions of exaggerated nationalism, and
lessen the opportunity for liberal democracy to make headway.
It can only drive desperate men and women to seek the remedies
that will be held out to them by the demagogues of the extreme
right or of the extreme left.

In 1919 the people in every one of the Allied countries were
clamoring because of the prolonged delay—as it then seemed to
be—in finishing up the task of peacemaking.

Winston Churchill said to me a few months ago, "Do you remember the outcry against the delegates at the Peace Conference
of Paris because of the time they took to conclude the Treaty of
Versailles? Yet that treaty and the Covenant of the League of
Nations were agreed upon within four months. At the end of that
time the terms of peace had been decided and we all knew where
we were. Today, almost a year has gone by since Germany surrendered, and no start has yet been made to find an agreement upon
the terms of peace. It is enough to make one despair of the future."

There were two desirable alternatives open to the future peacemakers as the Second World War was drawing to its close.
Either would have made for a rapid and an enduring peace.

The first alternative lay in the creation of the United Nations
organization before the end of the war in Europe so that it
not only might have been competent to function as soon as the
victory was won, but also might have been prepared to take over
immediately the work of peacemaking.

None of the major powers, however, favored this alternative.
Official opinion in Washington quite as much as in Moscow
strongly deprecated the possibility that the smaller powers should
have anything to say about the terms of a peace to be concluded
as the result of a victory for which the three major powers had
been chiefly responsible. Had the task of peacemaking been entrusted to the United Nations organization, the smaller powers
would necessarily have had a voice in the determination of the
peace terms. Yet it can hardly be denied that such participation
by the smaller powers, and particularly those smaller powers of
Europe, which—in proportion to their population and to their
resources—had suffered far more at the hands of the German

people than some of the major powers, might well have resulted in far more practical and far more equitable peace settlements than those we are now likely to obtain.

The second alternative lay in the ability of the United States, the Soviet Union, and Great Britain to agree before the close of the war on the broad outlines of all the European settlements. It would have involved the establishment of some political council similar to the military allied agency known as the Combined Chiefs of Staff. Had such a political agency existed, all the future peace terms could have been settled in advance. Then a peace conference of all the United Nations could readily have been held not later than three months after Germany's surrender. In that case, peace treaties could have been concluded with Italy, and with all the Balkan and eastern European countries as soon as they had established democratic governments. The conference could likewise have defined the final frontiers of Germany, as well as the long-range policy to be adopted toward the German people, leaving the conclusion of an actual peace treaty with Germany until such time as the United Nations considered the German people fitted to elect their own representative government.

The adoption of either of these two alternatives would have prevented the present interminable delay. It would have lessened the chances of acute friction between the victorious governments, and in particular between the Soviet Union and the major democracies of the West. No major power could have used the uncertainties resulting from the lack of peace settlements to extend its political, military, and economic control over its weaker but sovereign and independent neighbors. The whole of Europe would have been spared much needless suffering, loss of life and much dangerous suspicion, jealousy and recrimination.

Both alternatives were ignored. Those who fixed upon the procedure adopted appeared deliberately to spurn the lessons which should have been drawn from the experience of the Allies after the First World War, and deliberately to risk every one of the dangers which the peacemakers of 1919 had been wise enough to avoid.

At the Crimean conference Roosevelt, Churchill and Stalin had

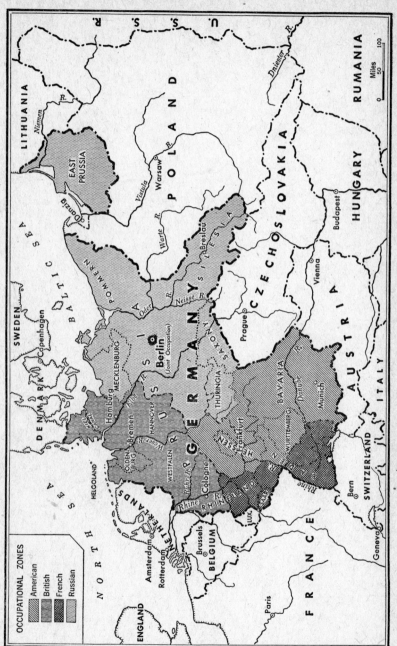

GERMANY, showing border countries and occupation zones

decided to meet again immediately after the victory in order to proceed with the preparation of the peace settlements, and in order to strengthen the United Nations, which they agreed should be organized within two months after their conference.

This meeting was held as scheduled in the latter part of July of 1945. It was attended on behalf of the United States by both President Truman and his newly appointed Secretary of State, James F. Byrnes. Neither of these two new directors of American foreign policy possessed the slightest knowledge of international relations. It is no disparagement of President Truman to state that he had neither the familiarity with modern history, the grasp of international affairs, nor the innate flair for foreign relations possessed by his predecessor. Nor did Secretary Byrnes display any of these qualities. No two representatives of the United States could have gone to this critical meeting with a greater realization of the responsibilities involved, nor have shown a more determined disposition courageously to assume their obligations than did the new President and his new Secretary of State. But good intentions and sincerity under such conditions cannot be sufficient. The stark truth is that the United States was placed at a tragic disadvantage.

Because of Mr. Churchill's insistence that national elections in England should be held immediately after the conclusion of the war, these elections took place while the Potsdam Conference was actually in progress. The elections resulted in an overwhelming victory for the Labor party, and midway through the course of the sessions Mr. Churchill and Mr. Eden were replaced by a new Prime Minister and a new Secretary of State for Foreign Affairs—Clement Attlee and Ernest Bevin. Fortunately, Clement Attlee's service in the British War Cabinet, and his membership in the British delegation at the San Francisco Conference had familiarized him to a considerable extent with the questions now to come up for consideration. But Ernest Bevin now stood in the place of Anthony Eden and the change was noticeable. In the stead of the courteous and superficially conciliatory Eden, who had for many years played so considerable a part in carrying out the lines of foreign policy laid down by Winston Churchill, the sharply blunt Bevin was from the outset a shock. True, the policies pursued by the representatives of Labor did not diverge noticeably from the traditional policies so long pursued by all British governments, whatever their political complexion. But, inevitably, Mr. Bevin's previous experience in official life had not given him that easy familiarity with every aspect of foreign policy which his predecessor enjoyed to so notable a degree.

The Soviet delegation, headed by Generalissimo Stalin himself, was, as usual, fully prepared and equally decided upon every detail of the objectives that the Soviet government wished to secure. And, because their leaders had dominated the Soviet government since long before the outbreak of the war, they were able to make good use of the advantages they possessed over their British and American associates.

The results of the Potsdam Conference were meager. They included the establishment of a council of the Foreign Ministers of the United Kingdom, the U.S.S.R., China, France and the United States. The announcement provided that the first meeting of the council should be held in London not later than September 1, and that its first task should be the negotiation of peace treaties with Italy, Rumania, Bulgaria, Hungary and Finland. It further provided that the council should subsequently draw up settlements on territorial questions still "outstanding on the termination of the war in Europe," and that the council should further prepare a peace settlement for Germany when a German government "adequate for the purpose" was established.

It was announced that France should participate in the negotiation of the peace settlement with Italy, and that other members of the United Nations would "be invited to participate when matters directly concerning them" were under discussion. The three major powers declared that the preparation of a peace treaty with Italy should be the first task of the new council, indicated their willingness to admit the neutral states, with the exception of Spain, into membership in the United Nations, and deferred any decisive action upon the question of international trusteeships.

While the information was not then made public, the Soviet

government told its allies that it intended to carry out its Yalta commitment by entering the war against Japan within a few weeks.

It is said that President Truman, upon his return from Potsdam, remarked that he had never found a man who was easier to get along with than Stalin. It can hardly be doubted that Generalissimo Stalin and Foreign Commissar Molotov took a more accurate measure of their colleagues. For the arrangements concluded at Potsdam made possible a prompt start in the reconstruction of Europe only if the Soviet government was willing to agree to the kind of peace settlements desired by the other major powers. No start could be made except with Soviet consent. And except for the general agreements reached at Teheran and Yalta, there existed no understanding whatever upon even the general lines of the peace treaties.

However, had American policy then been directed by persons who had the knowledge and vision required, preparations could have been made even after Potsdam so that the September meeting of the Council of Foreign Ministers might at least have advanced the conclusion of European peace settlements in line with the general basic principles that the United States was pledged to support.

For it seems today to be generally overlooked that these "basic principles" were principles that the Soviet Union was equally pledged to support. They were the principles set forth in the Atlantic Charter to which Russia had officially subscribed. They were the principles agreed upon at the meeting of Yalta providing for the establishment in eastern Europe and in the Balkans of freely elected democratic and representative governments. To the achievement of these objectives Russia was solemnly pledged. But at the meeting of the Foreign Ministers of September, 1945, the American delegation appeared to ignore this all-important fact; it apparently failed to realize that the kind of peace the American people wanted could be gained by the implementation of the principles that the Soviet Union as well as the United States had promised to uphold.

There are various reasons for this and the reasons require some analysis.

Mr. Byrnes, who assumed the Secretaryship of State in one of the most critical moments of world history, had only the most tenuous comprehension of the currents and crosscurrents of international affairs. It is true that he had occupied a position of high responsibility in the White House, and that at one period President Roosevelt had depended greatly upon him. His duties, however, were outside the field of activity that had chiefly engrossed President Roosevelt during the last years of his life. He had accompanied the President to the Yalta Conference, but this brief experience was the only opportunity that he had had to familiarize himself at first hand with foreign relations.

He had been successful in domestic policies. But here his activity had been dedicated primarily to smoothing over Congressional controversies and, in particular, to adjusting difficulties that arose from time to time between the White House and the Capitol. It would in any event have been difficult for him at the age of sixty-three to adjust himself to the fact that the foreign policy of the United States could not invariably be a policy of compromise. Occasions must frequently arise when the highest interests of the American people would be jeopardized unless the government knew how to exercise its power and influence to the best advantage to secure objectives upon which the United States could not give way.

Furthermore, Mr. Byrnes, in view of his own inexperience, could not represent the United States with full success in such crucial conferences as those at Potsdam and at London without having at his elbow expert advisers cognizant of all the diplomatic discussions that had taken place during the preceding years, and of all the agreements and understandings previously reached, and competent to see beyond the immediate present and advise him on the long-range policies most likely to be of permanent benefit to the world and to the people of the United States.

Mr. Byrnes continued the nonpartisan approach maintained during the last years of the Roosevelt administration by taking with him to the London meeting Mr. John Foster Dulles. Mr. Dulles was understood to represent the leadership of the Republican party. His abilities had previously been demonstrated, and notably, at the conference at San Francisco. But the expert advice and knowledge Mr. Byrnes needed was not forthcoming from the group of technical advisers with whom he surrounded himself.

Finally, and far more important than these other considerations, between the time that the leaders of the Big Three left Potsdam and the time that the Council of Foreign Ministers assembled in London the atomic bomb had fallen upon Hiroshima.

The realization of the implications in this use of atomic energy spread over the entire world like a poisonous fog. Public opinion became rapidly hysterical. The first reaction within the United States was that the secrets of atomic energy must be closely guarded by the United States, Great Britain and Canada, the three governments responsible for the discovery. An outcry arose that the use of atomic fission should be employed first as a measure of self-defense, and second as a means of bringing pressure upon the other powers. The most violent reaction was from many high-ranking officers of the Army and Navy. It might almost have been thought that the United States was threatened by an impending aggression from the Soviet Union. Only gradually did a more moderate influence become apparent. Later the general public began to understand that there were no secrets in the possession of the three governments other than the manufacturing secrets, and that these could soon be discovered by any government possessing the necessary physical resources. The use of the atom bomb, the prompt surrender of Japan before the Soviet armies had had more than a few days within which to invade Manchuria, and the hysterical reaction of the public in the Western democracies created an immediate gap of suspicion and of misunderstanding between the Soviet Union and the West. This made it all the more essential that the meeting of the Council of Foreign Ministers in London should succeed—and succeed rapidly.—But the meeting in September, 1945, of the Council of Foreign Ministers was one of the most disastrous international conferences of modern times.

The delegation headed by Mr. Byrnes went to London hopelessly unprepared. Not only did the United States have no accurate knowledge of the objectives of the Soviet Union, but it even had no accurate knowledge of what the British government wanted incorporated in so vitally important a settlement as the peace treaty with Italy. As an indication of the failure of our government to determine what its own policy should be, the American delegation upon its arrival in London let it be understood that the United States favored the continued administration by Italy, under the aegis of the International Trusteeship Council, of the former Italian colonies. Within a few days, solely because of British persuasion, the American delegation reversed its position. It announced its desire that Italy should have no control over her former colonies; that their administration should be left to the decision of the International Trusteeship Council.

As is always the case when a democracy like the United States attends an international conference where the delegates of some of the other participating states do not have to be guided by their own public opinion, the American delegation was at a disadvantage insofar as its ability to maneuver was concerned. What the American delegation failed to appreciate, however, was the fact that, had it maintained a firm position with regard to the principles it considered basic, and had it then obtained the support of the American public for those principles, the Soviet government would have been compelled to recognize that the position taken by the United States was based upon a real demand by the American people. It was a moment for "pitiless publicity." The American delegation, however, failed to avail itself of this immense advantage. The American public was kept wholly in the dark even about the nature of the problems coming up for discussion during the course of the conference. Public opinion was consequently unable to make itself felt. The failure of the American delegation to employ the press and the radio to enlighten the American people made it far easier for Soviet propaganda to get across to the American mind. The result, as might have been foreseen, was confusion. The American people had no chance to know what the real issues were, nor to understand what American foreign policy might be.

It must also be admitted that the course of the American delegation was far from clear. Secretary Byrnes, at the outset of the conference, supported the Russian position that the smaller countries should have no voice in the European peace settlements, notwithstanding the Potsdam commitment that they would "be enabled to participate" when matters directly concerning them came up for discussion. The representatives of the British Dominions, under the able leadership of Dr. Evatt of Australia, finally forced an entrance into the conference when the Italian peace treaty was being discussed. But when this resulted in the insistence of the Soviet government that delegates from the two Soviet Republics of Byelorussia and the Ukraine should likewise take part, the situation became so ludicrous that the effort was dropped.

It should, of course, be borne in mind that after the conference Secretary Byrnes told the American public that one of the reasons for its failure was the "insistent demand" by the United States that the Potsdam commitment with regard to the participation of small countries should be carried out.

Throughout the conference the Soviet delegation made it clear that it insisted that the Western powers recognize Russia's right to maintain in Bulgaria and Rumania, as well as in Poland and Hungary, governments established by her fiat. Mr. Molotov insisted upon her right to administer such former Italian colonies as Libya and Eritrea. He refused to consider any settlement with regard to the Dardanelles acceptable to the British and American governments.

After protracted and ever more acrimonious discussions, from which shouting and insult were by no means absent, the Foreign Ministers of the three major powers adjourned the conference sine die. The Chinese delegation remained mute throughout the sessions. The French government, fearing at that stage to commit itself either to the Soviet Union or to the two English-speaking powers, limited itself to an expression of its satisfaction that the United States had urged—although vainly—that France be permitted a voice in the Balkan peace treaties.

As the weeks passed after the end of the London meeting, the international atmosphere became more and more heavily charged with defeatism, suspicion and open antagonism. The question of the control of atomic energy very naturally became an obsession in all the Western democracies. Debates upon the subject took place daily in the press and in the legislative assemblies. The Soviet press periodically announced that it was a question of only a short time before Soviet scientists outrivaled their Western colleagues. Every such assertion gave rise to more heated controversy in the West.

After consultation between Washington, London and Ottawa, President Truman announced that the British Prime Minister, the Canadian Prime Minister and he would meet in Washington early in November to decide on the course that their three governments should take to control atomic energy. On November 15 announcement was made of the agreements reached at this meeting. The three chiefs of government declared that they had met "to consider the possibility of international action: a) to prevent the use of atomic energy for destructive purposes, and b) to promote the use of future advances in scientific knowledge, particularly in the utilization of atom energy, for peaceful and humanitarian ends." They announced their decision that "in order to attain the most effective means of entirely eliminating the use of atomic energy for destructive purposes and promoting its widest use for industrial and humanitarian purposes" . . . . "At the earliest practicable date a commission should be set up under the United Nations Organization to prepare recommendations for submission to the Organization."

It was altogether natural that the Soviet government, excluded from this conference, should have persisted in its suspicion of the ultimate purposes of the Western powers. From the standpoint of all the other members of the United Nations, the implication read into the Washington announcement that the commission to be set up under the United Nations would be subject to the members of the General Assembly, great and small, gave ground for heightened confidence. For, if atomic energy was to be used in the future for purposes of aggression, the smaller powers would suffer just as much as the major powers. They maintained that the control of a discovery by which the entire world might be ravaged could legitimately only be entrusted to all nations. What they most feared was that the ultimate control would be given to the Security Council, where they would have only an indirect voice and where decisions could be blocked by the veto of any one of the major powers.

Shortly after this, an announcement was made that a further conference would be held, this time in Moscow. It was to be limited to the Foreign Ministers of the Big Three.

The Yalta agreement had provided that such meetings should be held every three or four months. The meeting now called for Moscow was in pursuance of that agreement. Secretary Byrnes, Foreign Commissar Molotov, and British Secretary of State for Foreign Affairs Bevin participated. On December 27 the results of this new conference were announced.

The Moscow Conference of December, 1945, appeared to achieve a better understanding and a more cordial relationship between the three major powers. Coming only two weeks before the first preparatory meeting of the General Assembly of the UN, such an achievement was of value. Lamentably, the appearance of harmony was gained solely by a policy on the part of the American Secretary of State that can only be termed one of consistent appeasement in the course of which the most vital principles were sacrificed.

In the Far East, the United States and the Soviet Union reiterated their support of the National Government in China. This increased the probability that the government of Generalissimo Chiang Kai-shek would be able to prevent an interminable civil war and bring about some semblance of internal unity. With regard to Korea, an agreement was reached which, had it been carried out wholeheartedly by the Soviet Union as well as by the United States, might have established a sound precedent for international trusteeships.

In the case of Japan, the United States withdrew from the intolerant position she had previously maintained of insisting upon exclusive control over all Japanese occupation policies. It was agreed that each of the four major powers would have an equal voice in the determination of control policies, and that all the nations interested in the Pacific region, great or small, should be given an opportunity of making themselves heard before long-range policies became crystallized.

Unfortunately, in all the other decisions reached at Moscow the United States disappointed the expectations of those who had expected her to continue to stand firmly for the principles of international democracy and for the rights of the peoples of smaller nations.

The United States joined in the decision that the commission to determine the control of atomic energy should be placed under the authority of the Security Council rather than under the authority of the General Assembly of the United Nations.

With regard to the Balkan peace treaties, the United States flagrantly reversed the position that she had taken at London. She agreed to the exclusion of France from the negotiation of those treaties. What was far worse, she agreed to recognize the Soviet-installed governments of Rumania and Bulgaria provided those governments took in two representatives of "democratic parties not hitherto participating in them." Such a face-saving device was counter to the spirit and to the letter of the Yalta agreements. Its acceptance by the United States constituted a cowardly retreat from the position for which Franklin Roosevelt had stood inflexibly at Teheran and at Yalta in behalf of the creation of freely elected and representative governments throughout Europe as an essential safeguard for future peace. He had secured the agreement of Stalin to that requirement. At Moscow Secretary Byrnes abandoned that great principle. And by its abandonment he destroyed the faith of the peoples of eastern Europe and of the Balkans in the willingness and in the capacity of the United States to defend their just rights, as she was pledged to do. He also paved the way for the immediate consolidation of Soviet domination over eastern Europe and the Balkans, and materially increased the danger that Soviet policy would become one of frank expansion. Finally, he made inevitable the major clash between the Soviet Union and the United States which by his policy of appeasement he had hoped to avoid. That policy is today directly responsible for the failure of Washington and Moscow to reach any understanding upon which a new world order can be founded.

The United States also agreed to postpone the negotiation of a treaty with Italy, notwithstanding the fact that the postponement made it impossible for the Italian people to proceed with the task of political and economic reconstruction, and notwithstanding the commitment at Potsdam that the conclusion of the Italian peace treaty should have priority over all other questions.

Finally, the United States at Moscow gave in to the Soviet contention that the peace of Europe was to be dictated by the three major powers.

The Moscow agreements provided that a peace conference, composed not of all the United Nations, but only of the twenty-one who had actually played some military part in the defeat of the Axis, should be held before May 1, 1946, to agree upon the European peace treaties. But this conference can only be regarded as one of the most cynical devices to which the United States has ever lent herself. For the agreement stated that the peace treaties were to be drafted by the three major powers, and that all the other nations attending the conference would have no power other than to offer recommendations. It was hardly surprising that a few days after the Moscow meeting, the French government officially inquired whether the conference was called merely to ratify the decisions of the Big Three, and announced to the governments of the latter that France "was interested in all important questions concerning Europe or any region whatever of Europe."

The Moscow Conference marks a further occasion when the United States has defrauded the belief of many smaller peoples that they possessed in this government a true champion of international democracy and of individual freedom. It marks a further occasion when the United States proved to be unreliable and inconsistent in her foreign policy. It marked the reversal of the position that the Roosevelt administration had consistently maintained throughout the twelve years when Franklin Roosevelt was President. It marked a moment when the smaller nations of the world had reason to lose respect for the ability of this government, notwithstanding its military power and its material resources, to exercise moral influence.

When the London Conference of September, 1945, broke up in disaster, it was announced that the deputies of the Foreign Ministers would continue with the task of peacemaking. Soon thereafter, however, the deputies departed for their respective homes. But, in part as a result of the "cordiality" established at the Moscow meeting of the Foreign Ministers of the Big Three, at the first meeting of the General Assembly of the United Nations in January, 1946, it was made known that the deputies would resume their interrupted labors.

The deputies made no progress whatever. Committees of experts were designated to report upon territorial and other controversial problems. In every case the result was the same. No joint agreements could be reached.

Suddenly it was announced that the Foreign Ministers of Great Britain, the Soviet Union, France and the United States would meet at Paris the end of April, in order to prepare the ground for the long-awaited peace conference of May.

The program for the Paris Conference implied that the three major powers alone would fix the peace terms for Rumania, Bulgaria and Hungary; that Great Britain and the Soviet Union would fix the peace terms for Finland; that the three major powers together with France would agree upon the provisions of the peace treaty with Italy; and that all the other nations which took part in the Paris Peace Conference would be expected to acquiesce meekly in the terms so fixed. Other members of the United Nations would be given not even the empty privilege of proposing "recommendations" with regard to the peace settlements.

Before discussing the reasons for the additional failure of the preliminary meeting of the four Foreign Ministers in Paris, an analysis must be made of the varying postwar policies of the four major powers toward Germany, of the effect which their total lack of any joint policy had on their ability to agree on peace terms for Germany's neighbors, and on the peace adjustments which should simultaneously have been made in other more distant regions of the earth. For the key to all the peace settlements arising from the Second World War, save those which are exclusively Asiatic, must be found in the decisions of the United Nations with regard to the long-range policy to be pursued toward the German people.

In appraising the course so far pursued by the major powers toward Germany, and the nature of the various controls imposed upon the German people, it is helpful first to recall the situation of the German people at the close of the First World War, and the steps which the Allied nations then took to cope with the possibility of renewed German aggression.

The differences between the autumn of 1919 and the spring of 1945 are clearly apparent. At the end of the First World War, German territory had suffered no invasion since the Russian armies had been rolled back at the very start of the war. The destruction of German cities had been negligible. The physical impact of war had not struck home to the German people.

The terms of the Armistice, drawn under the personal direction of Marshal Foch, and the provisions of the Treaty of Versailles were sufficiently comprehensive to have made possible an effective Allied control of Germany, had they been efficiently executed. They were not efficiently executed.

No real disarmament of Germany was ever enforced. The organization of the German General Staff continued, underground it is true, but nevertheless almost wholly unimpaired. Not only were vast supplies of arms and ammunition retained secretly in German hands, not only was Germany's industrial war capacity permitted to a very great extent to continue unchecked, but large organizations of trained military personnel were permitted under one guise or another to prepare for the day when their services might again be called for by their military leaders. The German people as a whole, therefore, were in no sense suffering from the effects of a defeat that had been brought home to them. Neither were they prevented from immediately taking the first steps in the direction of future aggression and a much vaunted war of revenge.

The reasons the Allied powers failed to make of their **victory** a lasting settlement of the German problem, embodying the real ends for which the war had been fought, became ever more clear as the years passed. These reasons can be very simply set forth.

In the first place, the Soviet Union remained outside the family of nations. The Allied powers regarded her as a dangerous menace in international affairs. Some of the powers, notably Great Britain and France, considered her an even greater danger to their security, in the troubled social conditions which arose after the war years, than Germany herself. The Soviet Union undertook to flirt with the Weimar government, thus giving the Western powers a severe attack of nerves, and thereby making it less likely that any continuing form of Western pressure would be brought to bear upon the Soviet Union. Nor can it be doubted that the earliest dictators of Soviet policy may have believed that Russo-German *rapprochement* might well result in the establishment within Germany of some form of Communist régime closely identified with that of Moscow.

Another major reason for the failure of the last peace was the refusal of the United States to enter the League of Nations and to ratify the Treaty of Versailles, and the beginning of a period of withdrawal by the American people from any share of responsibility in international affairs.

The final, and perhaps the most immediate cause, was the wide divergence between Great Britain and France as to the policy to be applied to Germany in the light of the Treaty of Versailles. Successive French governments emphasized one facet or another of the policy which the French people were united in supporting, but the main lines of that policy remained fixed. France desired the permanent obliteration of Germany as a major power in Europe, the decentralization of German authority, even the political partition of the German Empire, as well as a continuing military control under the aegis of the League of Nations over every form of German activity. Succeeding British governments were bent upon a policy which implied a minimum of controls, military or economic, over Germany, and the speedy resurrection of a greater Germany as a counterpoise to a predominant and militaristic France, as a buffer to a Communist Russia, and as a prosperous market for British exports.

These were the reasons, together with the incoherent reparations policy toward Germany, that made it possible within a brief span of years for the German people to give Hitlerism, when it appeared upon the scene, the popular support and the material help it needed in launching Germany upon the highroad to world conquest.

At the conclusion of the Second World War, almost every inch of German territory had been fought over. The destruction wreaked upon German cities and towns and upon the German people as a whole was unprecedented. The Germans learned for the first time since 1815 the nature of the suffering they had themselves so frequently inflicted upon other peoples. The Allied military control of Germany was absolute. The military agreements of the three major powers gave assurance that the disarmament of the German people would this time be effective and that the industrial disarmament of Germany could readily be carried out.

On the other hand, there were no discernible signs that the German people were at all inclined toward democracy, or toward any form of popular self-government. The Nazi indoctrination had been so efficient and so far-reaching that all German youth would at the most optimistic estimate be poisoned by Nazism for twenty years to come. It was the general consensus among Allied observers that that moral conversion of the German people, which could have been successfully undertaken in 1919 within a brief period, had a joint and intelligently constructed policy been carried out, would now be possible only after a long period of control and of occupation, and through a highly complex indoctrination process.

There are many distinctions which can be drawn between the situation within Germany as it confronted the Allied powers in 1919 and as it confronted the victorious powers in 1945. But the differences which I have listed were salient. They should have led policy makers to certain clear-cut conclusions.

If the failures of the peace made after 1918 were not to be

repeated, and if the advantages to be derived from the military situation of 1945 were to be adequately exploited, what course should the United States, the Soviet Union and Great Britain have adopted?

In the light of the experiences of the past, they should have sacrificed almost every other consideration to reach a joint agreement upon every detail of a long-range policy toward the German people as well as of a short-range military and occupation policy. And this agreement should have been reached at almost any cost before Germany surrendered. Had this been done, every step during the period of military occupation could have been directed toward achieving the general aims of the long-range policy. The ultimate objective, of course, was to make the German people an element in the community of nations that could be trusted to play a peaceful and a constructive part in international affairs.

The underlying essential was the achievement of a united policy so that the German people could see for themselves from the outset that they would not again be enabled to play off one ally against the other as they had so successfully been able to play off Great Britain against France during the years between 1919 and 1925.

The three major powers should likewise have brought about, prior to the defeat of Germany, full Allied agreement on the amount and character of the reparations to be exacted. The agreement should have been premised upon the certainty that the payments could be collected, and that their exaction would not prevent the German people from becoming self-supporting and from achieving individual economic security even before the international controls over their country were lifted. It was equally essential for the three major allies to agree on the joint measures to be undertaken from the very outset of the military occupation to assure the German people of freedom of religion and of freedom of information. The agreement would logically have involved setting up a common standard in the various zones of occupation by which to measure the ultimate fitness of the German people for freedom of expression and local self-government.

The three great powers should have grasped their need to obtain the participation in all such agreements of those European neighbors of Germany which had for so many generations suffered German aggression, and which during the last war had suffered German occupation.

Outstanding among such countries was France. The French people had withstood the rivalry of the Germanic peoples for many centuries. The French Republic had suffered three German wars of aggression within the brief space of seventy years. The ability of Germany to inflict the Second World War upon humanity had proved the accuracy of the French contentions in 1919 as to the nature of the policy that should then have been adopted by the Allied powers.

In varying degree the Netherlands, Norway, Denmark, Belgium, Czechoslovakia and Poland had all been threatened with virtual extinction by the Third Reich. They had all suffered devastation at German hands. They all had to live in the future as neighbors of Germany, in whatever guise the German people might eventually be constituted.

If the ultimate destiny of the German people was to be settled in a way that would prove conducive to the reconstruction and permanent peace of Europe, it would have seemed not only equitable but also a matter of common sense to have given those nations, which after all embrace the greater part of Europe, every opportunity to collaborate in the policy to be adopted toward Germany.

Not one of these steps was taken.

At Yalta the governments of Great Britain, of the United States and of the Soviet Union had officially declared:

We have agreed on common policies and plans for enforcing the unconditional surrender terms which we shall impose together on Nazi Germany after German armed resistance has been finally crushed. . . . Under the agreed plan the forces of the three powers will each occupy a separate zone of Germany. Co-ordinated administration and control has been provided for under the plan through a central control commission consisting of the supreme commanders of the three powers with headquarters in Berlin. It has been agreed that France should be invited by the three powers, if she should so desire, to take over a zone of occupation and to participate as a fourth member of the control commission. The limitation of the French zone will be agreed by the four governments concerned through their representatives on the European Advisory Commission.

It is our inflexible purpose to destroy German militarism and Nazism and to insure that Germany will never again be able to disturb the peace of the world. We are determined to disarm and disband all German armed forces; break up for all time the German General Staff that has repeatedly contrived the resurgence of German militarism; remove or destroy all German military equipment; eliminate or control all German industry that could be used for German military production; bring all war criminals to just and swift punishment and exact reparation in kind for the destruction wrought by the Germans; wipe out the Nazi Party, Nazi laws, organization and institutions . . . and take in harmony such other measures in Germany as may be necessary to the future peace and safety of the world. It is not our purpose to destroy the people of Germany but only when Nazism and militarism have been extirpated will there be hope for a decent life for Germans and a place for them in the comity of nations.

Outside the purely military agreements reached, those provisions embody the accord entered into between the three major powers prior to the surrender of Germany.

There is no need to cavil at the terms of this declaration. Except that they omit the need for the collaboration of the smaller European countries in the determination of policy, and except that they indicate a subsidiary place to be accorded to France, they are wholly desirable and wholly constructive. Further, they show at least an apparent desire on the part of the three major powers to profit from the failures of the peacemaking of 1919.

But here again, as in many other instances in the recent past, people were led to believe that an announced policy, even though couched in general and sweeping terms, would automatically be translated into action. But a policy declaration, such as that made at Yalta, unless it is supplemented by agreements of the most detailed character, meticulously phrased, and implemented in every point, is not in itself sufficient to bring about practical results. It cannot too often be emphasized that the mere announcement to the peoples of the world of desirable objectives does not advance them along the road which leads to those objectives. The announcement of objectives is only the first phase in policy making. Unless a joint announcement of general objectives is simultaneously complemented by detailed agreements upon the manner in which they are to be achieved, disagreements will later inevitably arise not only concerning the interpretation of the objectives, but likewise concerning the precise methods by which they should be attained.

With the final capitulation of the German armies under the new Reichsfuehrer, Hitler's presumptive successor, Grand Admiral von Doenitz, on May 8, 1945, the fatal absence of such detailed understanding became immediately apparent. Events demonstrated not only the lack of a precise and detailed accord between the Allies upon the implementation of general policy, but even a lack of agreement in the purely military sphere.

Chaos reigned within Germany throughout the months of May and June. With a three-way occupation of the defeated country by the national armies of three separate powers, some initial confusion was inevitable. The confusion which resulted, however, went far beyond that which need have been anticipated and sharply impinged upon the realm of power politics.

The zones of occupation, except that to be administered by the French, had been previously agreed upon with geographical precision at the Yalta Conference. Troops of the United States, however, in the first onward sweep of the invasion, occupied an area considerably further to the east of the Elbe River than the Russians considered authorized by the terms of this military agreement. The settlement of this controversy resulted in charges and countercharges which spread far beyond the military sphere.

A far less publicized controversy of the same character took place in Czechoslovak territory.

It was in Austria, however, that the most serious confusion developed. Russian forces not only occupied wide areas supposedly allotted to American and British military forces, but undertook political manipulations that were destined to have serious consequences. The Russian armies occupied Vienna. Both in that capital, as well as in all other parts of Austrian territory that they overran a complete blackout of information was immediately imposed. Every kind of rumor became current. At the height of this crisis, Dr. Karl Renner, an elderly Austrian who had briefly played a prominent part in the first days of the Austrian Republic after the First World War, and who had long been notorious as a fanatical Pan-German, announced the constitution of an Austrian national government. His government was at once recognized by the Soviet Union. It had, of course, been installed by Moscow. Dr. Renner's government immediately requested official recognition from London and Washington, although neither Great Britain nor the United States had previously been consulted or informed of the step thus taken.

Here again the procedure followed necessarily aroused suspicion of the ultimate purposes of the Soviet government. The result was that charges that the Soviet government intended immediately to extend its control, political as well as military, over the whole of central Europe, rapidly gained credence.

The situation in Berlin was comparable. For some time neither the official agents nor the military forces of the British and American governments were permitted by the Soviet authorities to enter the German capital. Here likewise the blackout of information was complete. Here likewise charges were at once circulated that the Soviet troops were perpetrating every variety of atrocity and that the Soviet government intended permanently to exclude Western representatives from Berlin.

While the liquidation of this impasse in Berlin took far less time than it did in Austria, material harm was done to the possibility for close and friendly understanding between the three major Allied powers which should have existed from the moment of Germany's collapse. Even when the Allied Control Commission was finally installed in Berlin, and the sectors of the city allotted to the Western occupation forces were at length occupied, a current of ill feeling persisted which was by no means dissipated by stereotyped statements breathing co-operation issued by General Eisenhower and the other Western commanders.

The friction and ill feeling which arose shortly thereafter between French forces and the American forces of occupation were equally prejudicial and equally unnecessary. The lack of any prior understanding with the French government about which zone the French troops should occupy, and the postponement of this decision until after the Allied Control Commission had met in Berlin, offered an obvious temptation to General de Gaulle and his military leaders to take the initiative in their own hands. Certain sectors of Germany were occupied by French troops not only without the prior agreement of the Allied Control Commission but even against the vigorous opposition of the American Army leaders. The resulting antagonism was hardly ameliorated by the loud and angry claims made within the United States, and even on the floor of the United States Senate, that the French forces of occupation were committing crimes of the most revolting character against the German civilian population.

By the time these conflicts had been to some extent resolved and the French were at length permitted to occupy a small segment of western Germany, it was evident that each of the occupying forces was pursuing an individual and distinct occupation policy notwithstanding their joint commitment that all occupation policy should be laid down by the Allied Control Commission sitting in Berlin.

In the eastern sector occupied by Russia, the line to be followed became at once apparent. The Soviet authorities lost no time in liquidating or in removing not only Nazi leaders and collaborators, but all strongly Democratic leaders as well. Simultaneously they gave vigorous support to those groups in the population which were known to be friendly to the Soviet system. Only a very short time elapsed before hand-picked German Communists, headed by Herr Pieck, were permitted to take over the civilian administration, under Soviet military control. At the same time, even before any agreement on reparations policy had been reached by the Reparations Commission, which in accordance with the terms of the Yalta agreement was now due to meet at Moscow, the Russians were dismantling and shipping to the Soviet Union every available scrap of industrial equipment. The roads to the east were blocked with German livestock and food supplies.

There was no indication, however, that the Soviet authorities intended the German inhabitants within their zone to starve. On the contrary, arrangements for a minimum diet for the population were carried out with considerable efficiency. But the individual German in that area was made to depend upon his Soviet-issued ration card if he wished to keep body and soul together. Such reserves of foodstuffs as individuals had available to them at the war's end were taken from them. The civilian population was compelled to look to the Soviet forces of occupation for its daily bread as well as for its means of livelihood.

With the passage of time, the determination of the Soviet government to extirpate throughout the region of Germany that it controlled every political organization and every political leader not entirely subservient to the Communist party line became ever more clearly marked. Newsprint was made available only to Communist papers. Communist appointees were placed in exclusive control of all radio facilities. At the time that the effort was being made—prematurely as it developed—to compel the Social Democrats in Berlin to accept amalgamation with the Communists so that the latter might secure entire control of such a coalition, every form of pressure was brought to bear upon the leaders of the Social Democrats. The Soviet representatives in Germany insisted, not upon co-operation between Socialists and Communists, but upon fusion.

At Easter, 1946, a conference of Social Democrats and Communists took place at the Opera House in Berlin. The two parties were formally dissolved. Under the orders of Herr Pieck and Herr Grotewohl, the heads of the two parties, not a delegate to the conference dared to register his opposition. A new party, termed the Party of Social Unity, was immediately formed.

But where the Social Democrats were given any chance freely to express their views, as they were in the plebiscite held in those sectors of Berlin not under Soviet control, opposition to fusion with the Communists was overwhelming. And in the Russian zone outside Berlin, Social Democrats at once joined Democratic parties such as the Liberal and Christian Democratic organizations.

Within Berlin, the Social Democrat leaders who promoted

fusion soon had automobiles and extra food supplies. The leaders who were recalcitrant were incarcerated in the concentration camps reopened by Soviet order.

Soviet policy in eastern Germany can only be interpreted as an inflexible effort to consolidate Moscow-dominated German Communism in that area, to fractionize all land holdings, to permit only such nationalized industrial or commercial activities as might fit into the over-all Soviet economic scheme and to constitute the entire region a political and economic tributary of the Soviet Union.

In the British-occupied zone of the northwest, as well as in the American-occupied zone of the south, conditions were chaotic at the outset of the occupation.

As the Russian armies had advanced westward, hundreds of thousands of Germans had fled before them to seek refuge with the British and American forces who, they believed, would accord them more humane treatment. Masses of Poles and other refugees from eastern Europe had fled to the west for the same reason. Innumerable nationals of the occupied countries of western Europe who had been sent to Germany as slave laborers and who had been released at the time of Germany's surrender, blocked every highway in an attempt to return to their homes. Food supplies were totally inadequate to feed these hordes. The wave of anarchy resulting from the presence within western Germany of these masses of refugees was overpowering.

For lack of an organized force of trained personnel to cope with this situation, it was many months before there was any alleviation, before any efficient screening of these floating masses of humanity could be carried out, and before even a minimum of help could be given to that pitiful class of refugees, mainly of the Jewish faith, termed "displaced persons." No accurate record is yet available. But it can be asserted that for lack of effective organization to meet a situation which should have been foreseen, many thousands of innocent persons experienced a degree of tragedy and suffering which was altogether unnecessary.

Many months later, the White House made public the text of

the directive issued to General Eisenhower in April, 1945, which had laid down United States policy for the military government of Germany. At the time of its publication, on October 17, 1945, it was stated that many of the policy statements contained in this directive had been adopted in the Potsdam agreements of August 2, 1945. It was further announced that when this directive was issued to General Eisenhower he had been instructed to urge the Control Council in Berlin to adopt the policy it set forth as the over-all policy to be enforced throughout Germany.

In order to obtain a clear understanding of the United States' course with regard to Germany, consideration must be given to the salient features of that directive.

The directive states that it is an enumeration of American policies relating to Germany "in the initial post-defeat." It says specifically that it is not intended to be an ultimate statement of American policies toward Germany "in the postwar world." General Eisenhower, by the terms of the directive, was vested "with supreme legislative, executive and judicial authority in the areas occupied" by the forces under his command. The American, Soviet, British and French commanders-in-chief, acting jointly, were to constitute the Control Council in Germany, which would be the supreme organ of control, and the authority of this council to formulate policy and procedures and administrative relationships with respect to matters affecting Germany as a whole was to be paramount throughout Germany.

One exceedingly important provision in this directive to General Eisenhower should be quoted in full. It is Section C of Article 3. It reads as follows:

The administration of affairs in Germany shall be directed towards the decentralization of the political and administrative structure and development of local responsibility. To this end you will encourage autonomy in regional, local, and municipal agencies of German administration. The German economic structure shall also be decentralized. The Control Council may, however, to the minimum extent required for the fulfillment of the purposes set forth herein permit centralized administration or establish central control of

a. Essential national public services, such as railroads, communications, and power;

b. Finance and foreign affairs, and

c. Production and distribution of essential commodities.

Further provisions of a general and political character stipulated that the Control Council should bring about the severance of all governmental and administrative connections between Austria and Germany and "the elimination of German economic influences in Austria."

The Control Council should bring home to the German people that they could not escape responsibility for the destruction which they had brought upon themselves; that Germany was to be occupied as a defeatest enemy nation; that the principal Allied aim was to prevent Germany from ever again becoming a threat to the peace of the world; and that essential steps to that end were the elimination of Nazism and militarism, the punishment of war criminals, the industrial disarmament and demilitarization of Germany and "the preparation for an eventual reconstruction of German political life on a democratic basis."

With regard to the economic controls to be imposed upon Germany, the directive stated that, while a program of reparations and restitution was to be enforced, "no action will be taken in execution of the reparations program or otherwise which would tend to support basic living conditions in Germany on a higher level than that existing in any one of the neighboring United Nations."

If the United States should have learned any one lesson from the experience of the First World War and from the tragedies of the years between the two great wars, she should have become convinced that there can be no lasting peace unless the German people are prevented from destroying it by the common action of the great powers and by the continuing supervision of a practical international organization. If peace was to be thus assured, long before the close of the war, while the United States still held the cards in her own hands, she should have secured an agreement with the other major powers upon the main outlines of a long-range German policy and upon the means by which the initial occupation policy might best further the objectives of the long-range policy.

These objectives should have been clear. They were four in number and involved first, the conclusion of a military agreement between the United States, the Soviet Union, Great Britain and France, to serve as a preliminary bulwark until the United Nations organization could function effectively. The agreement should have provided that the four powers would jointly enforce the permanent disarmament of Germany, and assist each other if the German people showed any symptoms of renewed aggressive tendencies;

Second, the permanent political decentralization of Germany, and the full autonomy of the traditional German states;

Third, agreement by the United Nations upon reparations which the German people were capable of paying, but which would not depress German standards of living to such an extent that the individual German could have no hope of economic security;

Fourth, agreement upon the industrial and economic régime which Germany was to be permitted, and upon the nature of the international control to be maintained over it.

The United States failed to insist upon the conclusion of such agreements before the end of the war. It still had the opportunity of pressing for them at Potsdam. But a year later the four major powers were yet further removed from any basis of agreement. The position of the American policy makers could not be more graphically described than by a cable sent from Paris on June 30, 1946, to the New York *Times* by Harold Callender, one of the ablest and best informed reporters of the international scene:

Mr. Byrnes' purpose in insisting upon a discussion of Germany was not to decide here any major question or to fix the date of a peace treaty, but to get the Big Four to agree to study together the whole German problem so that perhaps in about two years an intelligent and practicable plan for a future Germany could be adopted.

It is understood that Mr. Byrnes and his advisers not only have no final plan for Germany, but also are convinced that nobody can have at this time a plan that can be assumed to fit the situation a year or so hence. They believe that it is too early to decide what political shape Germany will take, or what degree of unity or federal decentralization will be desirable and durable.

That report, which is strictly accurate, epitomizes American policy concerning the key to the future of Europe. It has been American policy not to have a plan. It has been American policy to let matters drift and hope for the best. It has been American policy not to control events but to be controlled by events.

Of the accords reached at Potsdam, only one—that upon reparations—spelled out by means of a detailed agreement the way in which these imperative objectives were to be achieved.

The failure of the United States to strike for peace when the moment was propitious for furthering our legitimate objectives is in great part responsible for the cancer that Germany has again so soon become in the European body politic and in the relationships between the major powers. Had such an agreement on long-range German policy been reached at Potsdam, the policies pursued by the four Allied powers would not have been in serious conflict. But under the circumstances, endless misunderstandings were inevitable.

Within the Russian area, Soviet policy became ever more intransigent.

British policy within the British-occupied zone began to provide increasing evidence of being the same policy as that pursued by successive British governments toward Germany after the First World War. There was no indication that the British authorities favored, except in words, either the political decentralization or the economic decentralization of Germany called for in the statement of policy issued by the government of the United States. There was no sign that they were inclined to strip those German industries which were clearly within the category of Germany's war potential. The favor shown to German industrialists, even those classified as presumable war criminals, speedily became notorious.

The least serious criticisms of American policy within the American zone of occupation are that it was incoherent, inefficient and entirely disruptive in its effects. The American military officers entrusted with the major share of responsibility for carrying out occupation policy were well qualified for the military job of winning the war. They were as wholly unqualified by training, by experience or by inclination to administer a constructive policy of occupation.

At the outset of the military occupation only military officers of high rank could have been vested with supreme authority. But not only were they not assisted by civilian advisers properly indoctrinated for the special work required, but they themselves had been given only the most meager opportunity of learning what American policy might be. Furthermore, as the occupation proceeded, the German civilian population commenced to arouse the sympathy of both officers and enlisted men in the American forces of occupation. The American officers in particular were generally strongly opposed to the principles of American policy as set forth in the April directive issued to General Eisenhower. These developments coincided with the recrudescence of the classic British policy that Germany must in the British interest continue to be a major force in central Europe both as a potential buffer against an expanding Soviet Union and as a very necessary market for British exports.

Nor is there anything to be gained by ignoring the fact that the American officers were becoming more and more fearful of the increasing demonstration of Russia's growing influence in Europe.

Above and beyond all these factors, important as they are, every week that passed saw a further decrease of American prestige within Germany, in the eyes of the Allies as well as in the eyes of the German people. For the desire of the American troops to return home was voiced in no uncertain terms by officers and men alike. The clamor arose that with the defeat of Germany no further military control of the country was necessary, but that if our government insisted otherwise, the task should be undertaken by someone else. This attitude made our troops receptive to all those varying forms of propaganda in which the German people are so adept, and which they have learned by experience can easily arouse a sentimental response from the Anglo-Saxons.

What should have been expected in our forces of occupation, namely, a high morale and a reasonable measure of discipline, proved to be wholly lacking. By the beginning of January, 1946, morale and discipline had so completely broken down as to result in the extraordinary and painful spectacle of mass demonstrations of American enlisted men besieging the headquarters of their commanding officers and calling for official action in Washington which would make it possible for them to pull out.

The effect upon the German people was immediately apparent. It could not have been more harmful. But the effect upon the other major powers was even more disastrous.

To the Soviet government, it implied that the United States was reverting, as a result of the pressure of public opinion at home, to her earlier policy of withdrawing from any active share in European affairs and of limiting herself to the exercise of her influence, for what that was worth, at long range.

Among the French people, it accentuated the belief that the United States would once more leave them in the lurch as she had in 1920.

But to the British public what was taking place was even more disquieting. By October, 1945, the great liberal newspaper of England, the *Manchester Guardian* was asking:

How long in the face of terrible pressure for demobilization will the United States be content to keep an occupying force in Europe? Shall we witness again the same spectacle as after the last war? . . . Britain and America want to see Germany in a position where she can be left free, or almost free, from occupying troops and from overseers—a democratic self-governing, economically healthy country that can make a useful contribution to a peaceful Europe. The Russians, and it is to be feared the French, regard Germany as a field to be exploited in their own interests. . . . It is fair to point out what an enormous responsibility rests upon the United States to continue to exert the immense weight of her influence on the side of reason and democratic reconstruction. This she cannot do if she gets out of Europe because of pressure at home.

Here spoke one of the most truly enlightened spokesmen for the British people. Yet even in this case, it was clear that the primary fear was not that by withdrawal from Europe the United States would jeopardize the chances for the continuing disarmament of Germany, and for the transformation of the German people into law-abiding citizens of the world, but rather that by her withdrawal the United States would impede the reconstruction of Germany as an "economically healthy country that can make a useful contribution to a peaceful Europe."

Many factors have combined to make the French policy during the initial occupation of Germany generally antagonistic to the few common policies of the other three occupying powers.

France had been excluded from the decisions reached by Great Britain, the Soviet Union and the United States at Potsdam. Her resentment at her exclusion was naturally profound and entirely justified.

The Potsdam declaration had announced that, while the eastern frontiers of the future Germany would be definitely established in a subsequent peace treaty, the boundaries of the future Polish state abutting on German territory would in general approximate the line of the Oder River. It was properly assumed, in view of this understanding between the three major powers, that the tentative frontier would eventually become the permanent frontier. But at Potsdam no announcement was made of the establishment of any western frontier for Germany.

French insistence increased for the establishment of a western frontier for Germany that would provide the French people with the assurance of security that they had demanded in 1919, and which they had not then obtained. The French government favored in general the political and economic decentralization of Germany. But it likewise demanded in particular the separation from Germany of the Ruhr, the Saar, and the Rhineland, and the establishment of the Ruhr and the Rhineland as an autonomous state to be governed under international control.

To the logical French mind the Ruhr must ever be the chief source of supply for the coal, the power and the steel required for any major German armament program. Consequently, they felt that its separation from the rest of Germany was indispensable if the German people were not again to rearm as they had been permitted to do during the years after the Treaty of Versailles. The failure of the three major powers to agree upon a western frontier for Germany that gave France security was regarded by the French as an indication that her legitimate demands were not going to be met.

As the sole recourse which the French government now saw left to it, the French representative on the Control Council in Berlin was instructed to exercise the French right of veto over all proposals for the economic unification of Germany, since such measures appeared to prejudice the ultimate realization of the French demands.

The issue which thus arose eventually reached a crisis. The deadlock was by no means broken by reiterated threats from Washington that the United States would demand the abolition of the veto right in the Control Council unless France gave way. The French government was hardly likely to take this threat very seriously in view of the notorious insistence of the Soviet Union that each of the major powers must possess a full veto right in all international bodies.

With respect to the lesser powers, the history of the Allied occupation of Germany has demonstrated an almost total disregard for their legitimate right to be heard.

There was not even a semblance of consideration for the Netherlands, the country of western Europe that had suffered most severely at the hands of the German invaders. Dutch industrial equipment, Dutch properties, and, in particular, Dutch livestock had been stolen by the German forces of occupation and had been removed to adjacent regions in western Germany. When, after the surrender of Germany, claims were made by the Dutch authorities for the return of these properties, all of them readily identifiable, the sole response received from the British was that no restitution could be made until a final reparations accounting had been agreed upon.

Similar cavalier treatment was accorded all the smaller allies by the great powers. But the chief damage done arose from the fact that the four major powers failed to recognize that, if an effective German control policy was to be carried out, Germany's smaller neighbors should have been consulted, and that their advice and co-operation would be extremely valuable.

If the German people are to become peaceful members of the community of nations within any foreseeable future, effective measures for the conversion of the German spirit should have been undertaken from the very beginning of the occupation period. The major powers gave but little evidence of recognizing this.

If the German people were to be compelled to realize the war guilt of their nation by the trial and punishment of their war criminals, the trials should have been just but speedy. But the trials of the subordinates who had been guilty of the slaughter of Allied war prisoners or of atrocities against the inmates of concentration camps were desultory. Procedure varied in each occupation zone. It was, however, in the trial of the Nazi leaders that the greatest measure of confusion was present. The International Military Tribunal had not been set up before the end of the war. The major allies did not agree upon its constitution and procedure until after many weary months of bickering and dispute. By the time it began to function, the German people had begun openly to question its legitimacy, and to doubt the ability of the major powers to reach any joint decision as to the guilt of the accused.

Justice Robert Jackson of the United States Supreme Court, serving as the American prosecutor, laid down in an exceptionally brilliant opening address a new principle of international law. He proclaimed the principle that

The ultimate step in avoiding periodic wars, which are inevitable in a society of international lawlessness, is to make statesmen responsible to law. . . . This trial represents mankind's desperate effort to apply the discipline of the law to statesmen who have used their powers of state to attack the foundations of the world's peace and to commit aggressions against the rights of their neighbors. . . . The real complaining party is civilization. . . . Civilization asks whether law is so laggard as to be utterly helpless to deal with crimes of this magnitude by criminals of this order of importance.

A debate immediately arose as to the validity of any new principle of international law which had not been specifically agreed upon by all nations in times of peace. The authoritative answer to that question is that, since every nation of the world had, prior to the war, entered into multilateral agreements outlawing war as an instrument of national policy, there could be no legitimate complaint with respect to the principle now asserted.

Had the International Military Tribunal begun to function

immediately after Germany's defeat, had all the Allied nations agreed upon the principles upon which the trials were to be based, and had it been possible, in view of the new ground to be covered, for the trials themselves to have been carried out with greater dispatch, the reaction of the German people would have been quite different. They would have accepted the sentences imposed as just, and would have regarded the decisions of the court as valid.

Unfortunately, however, the trials dragged on month after month. The German people commenced to question the principles laid down by the tribunal. Frequently the witness stand served as a sounding board for propaganda intended to curry sympathy among the peoples of the Western democracies. There arose a general complaint about the procedure followed and an increasing skepticism of the value of the trials.

In a public statement made more than six months after the trials began, Justice Jackson said, "Some people, especially victims of Nazi terror, wonder why the international tribunal at Nürnberg proceeds in so careful a way. But it is necessary that the justice of the United Nations escape any reproach that we sought revenge rather than justice and truth. If we were not giving the accused every opportunity to justify themselves, it could be taken for granted that within a decade many would accuse us of unfairness." The views expressed by the American prosecutor cannot be challenged, but in the result the trials made little effective impact upon German consciousness.

At best it must remain an open question how much good the trial at Nürnberg actually accomplished. The prosecution had assembled a vast collection of documents, only a part of which was actually used, which bore on the origins of the war, its methods of conduct, and its effect upon civilian populations. By placing these in evidence in the trials, their authenticity was established, for there were present in the dock men who knew whether they were authentic or not and in whose highest interest it would have been to impeach them had they been able to do so.

In the last analysis, so far as the Germans are concerned, it will probably prove that nothing said by the prosecutors discredited the Nazis and their fellow conspirators, the generals and admirals, nearly so much as the statements made by the defendants themselves.

In the first stages of the occupation period, it would have been difficult, if not impossible, to commence an educational program. But what was lacking was a sign that any serious preparation was being made for the future education of German youth, or that the four occupying powers could ever agree on the nature of such education.

In the primary schools some advances were made. During its heyday, however, the Nazi régime had so reduced the period of secondary school attendance, in order to provide time for compulsory labor service, that the scholastic standards of all German youth were unbelievably low compared with the high level attained by the secondary school system under the German Empire.

As for German universities, those in the larger cities were almost wholly destroyed as the result of bombing. Only after eight months were any effective steps taken to obtain non-Nazi faculties for the great German universities, and to complete a sufficient measure of physical reconstruction of the libraries and laboratories and clinical facilities to provide the necessary means for university training. Even then no adequate preparations were made in any of the zones to provide funds with which faculties could be paid, or food and clothing and housing for the undergraduates themselves.

Outside the Russian zone freedom of religion was more rapidly restored. But as was to be expected, granted the basic difference in the occupation policies of the major powers, freedom of information was either wholly lacking, as in the Russian zone, subject to strange and paradoxical restrictions, as was frequently the case in the American zone, or handled solely on the ground of expediency, as in the British and French zones.

In the whole realm that had to do with providing an effective and productive start toward the conversion of the German spirit, not even foundations had been laid a year after Germany's surrender.

After the First World War, no factor contributed more directly to the failure of the Allied powers to unite upon a joint policy toward Germany than the problem of reparations. As a result of agreements reached at Yalta, the Declaration of Potsdam laid down a reparations policy which was an elaboration of recommendations submitted to President Roosevelt in September, 1944, by Henry Morgenthau, Junior, then Secretary of the Treasury.

Reparation in the form of future payments and deliveries should not be demanded. Restitution and reparation shall be effected by the transfer of existing German resources and territories, e.g.,

a. By restitution of property looted by the Germans in territories occupied by them;

b. By transfer of German territory and German private rights in industrial property situated in such territory to invaded countries and the international organization under the program of partition;

c. By the removal and distribution among devastated countries of industrial plants and equipment situated within the International Zone and the North and South German States delimited in the section on partition;

d. By forced German labor outside Germany, and

e. By confiscation of all German assets of any character whatsoever outside of Germany.

In the Potsdam declaration the chapter dealing with reparations was finally elaborated to read as follows:

In accordance with the Crimea decision that Germany be compelled to compensate to the greatest possible extent for the loss and suffering that she has caused to the United Nations and for which the German people cannot escape responsibility, the following agreement on reparations was reached:

1. Reparation claims of the U.S.S.R. shall be met by removals from the zone of Germany occupied by the U.S.S.R. and from appropriate German external assets.

2. The U.S.S.R. undertakes to settle the reparation claims of Poland from its own share of reparations.

3. The reparation claims of the United States, the United Kingdom and other countries entitled to reparations shall be met from the western zones and from appropriate German external assets.

4. In addition to the reparations to be taken by the U.S.S.R. from its own zone of occupation, the U.S.S.R. shall receive additionally from the western zones:

(A) Fifteen per cent of such usable and complete industrial capital equipment, in the first place from the metallurgical, chemical and machine manufacturing industries, as is unnecessary for the German peace economy and should be removed from the western zones of Germany, in exchange for an equivalent value of food, coal, potash, zinc, timber, clay products, petroleum products and such other commodities as may be agreed upon.

(B) Ten per cent of such industrial capital equipment as is unnecessary for the German peace economy and should be removed from the western zones, to be transferred to the Soviet Government on reparations account without payment or exchange of any kind in return.

Removals of equipment as provided in (A) and (B) above shall be made simultaneously.

5. The amount of equipment to be removed from the western zones on account of reparations must be determined within six months from now at the latest.

6. Removals of industrial capital equipment shall begin as soon as possible and shall be completed within two years from the determination specified in Paragraph 5. The delivery of products covered by 4(A) above shall begin as soon as possible and shall be made by the U.S.S.R. in agreed installments within five years of the date hereof. The determination of the amount and character of the industrial capital equipment unnecessary for the German peace economy and therefore available for reparations shall be made by the Control Council under policies fixed by the Allied Commission on Reparations, with the participation of France, subject to the final approval of the zone commander in the zone from which the equipment is to be removed.

7. Prior to the fixing of the total amount of equipment subject to removal, advance deliveries shall be made in respect of such equipment as will be determined to be eligible for delivery in accordance with the procedure set forth in the last sentence of Paragraph 6.

8. The Soviet Government renounces all claims in respect of reparations to shares of German enterprises which are located in the western zones of occupation in Germany, as well as to German foreign assets in all countries, except those specified in Paragraph 9 below.

9. The Governments of the United Kingdom and the United States of America renounce their claims in respect of reparations to shares of German enterprises which are located in the eastern zone of occupation in Germany, as well as to German foreign assets in Bulgaria, Finland, Hungary, Rumania and eastern Austria.

10. The Soviet Government makes no claims to gold captured by the Allied troops in Germany.

After the conclusion of the Potsdam conference a preliminary discussion of reparations by representatives of the three major powers was promptly held in Moscow. This meeting was followed by a further conference held at Paris in which the lesser powers directly interested were likewise represented. An agreement in considerable detail was reached. But six months later, because the major powers could not agree upon any other aspects of a German policy, compliance with the reparations agreement within Germany had entirely broken down. And in the operation of the agreement outside Germany, the results proved to be quite different from those anticipated, owing to the ignorance of Mr. Edwin Pauley, the President's reparations commissioner, of certain notorious aspects of Hitler's activities in the countries which he had ravaged. Mr. Pauley in Moscow blithely conceded all of the Soviet government's demands with respect to its right without qualification to take over all "German assets" in the countries outside Germany which were occupied by Russia. What Mr. Pauley undoubtedly had in mind were bona fide German holdings. Yet it was well known that the Nazi government, after seizing a country such as Austria, had at once placed in German hands every important industry, utility or financial institution which was owned by nationals of that country or of other states. To the Russians these assets were "German." The opportunity was golden, and the Russians made the most of it. The rightful owners of these assets have now been twice robbed. And the result has been that in eastern Austria, as well as in eastern and southern Europe, impoverishment and destitution have been greatly increased, and the burden will in the long run fall equally upon the unfortunate citizens of these countries and upon the Western powers which will find themselves compelled to alleviate the suffering so created.

On July 10, 1946, the United States officially informed the Austrian government that she would herself renounce all claims to German assets in the American-occupied Austrian zone. She further announced she would not recognize as valid the Russian seizure of properties claimed as "German" because of their "forced transfer" to Germans after the Nazi invasion of the republic. This step necessarily increased tension between Moscow and Washington. The entire issue might readily have been avoided had the American reparations commissioner possessed the necessary understanding of the problem when the first reparations conference was held in Moscow.

Obviously, the grave dangers to peace resulting from the totally divergent policies of the major powers toward Germany can be arrested only if the United States, the Soviet Union and Great Britain can still find a way to agree on the basic principles of a joint policy. Yet today, more than fourteen months after the surrender of Germany, the four major powers are unable to agree upon any long-range policy that would implement the Potsdam agreements and provide in a constructive fashion for the political decentralization of Germany and encourage the autonomy of the traditional German states.

There is not yet the semblance of an agreement between them upon the nature of the economic life that the German peoples are to be permitted to enjoy in the years to come.

The agreement on reparations has at least temporarily broken down.

Ten months after Germany's collapse the United States proposed to the Soviet Union, Great Britain and France a twenty-five-year military alliance giving the four powers common responsibility for the continued disarmament of Germany and providing for reciprocal assistance in the event of any new evidence of German aggression. Had that suggestion been put forward before the end of the war or even at the Potsdam Conference as a method of bolstering the United Nations until such time as that organization was able to guarantee the maintenance of world peace, there is every reason to believe that it would been accepted. By the time it was suggested, however, the divergence of policies had reached such a point that it was summarily rejected by the Soviet Union.

The crisis was reached at the meeting of the Foreign Ministers of the Big Four in Paris on July 9.

Mr. Molotov characterized the proposed military alliance as "wholly inadequate in every respect," and announced publicly for the first time Russia's long-range policy toward Germany. He insisted upon the immediate creation of a central German government, and he formally refused to agree to any plan for the political partition or federalization of Germany. The Soviet Foreign Minister made it clear beyond the shadow of a doubt that now that Russia had obtained a part of Germany's territory in East Prussia, and Poland another part, the Kremlin would object to Germany's further "dismemberment." Under Russian protection and inspiration the rest of Germany was to be reconstituted into a unified and centralized state. The tactics employed were exceedingly clever. They would be bound to have a profound effect upon the attitude of the German people toward the Soviet Union.

This failure of the United States to take the initiative when it could has brought with it a chaotic situation in Germany which is threatening to spread throughout Europe.

Today Germany is the scene of a struggle for control between the Soviet Union and the West. The Russians are winning the struggle. Berlin is in the very center of the Russian zone of occupation. Even now the position of the Western allies in Berlin is precarious.

Soviet policy in Germany is dynamic. The policy of the Western democracies is at best only static. The vast majority of the Germans are nationalists. They do not at heart repudiate Nazism; they merely regret, as they did in 1919, their military failure. These are the Germans who are crowding into the Communist party organization, and into the new parties formed under Soviet control. And Germany today is flooded with propaganda based upon Stalin's well-known speech, declaring that Germany's rulers may come and go but that the German state will continue forever.

Every aspect of Soviet policy in Germany points to the eventual turning of the German people to the East.

The security of the entire world depends upon the capacity of the major powers to co-operate. Without such co-operation, not only can there be no peace in Europe, but there can be no peace in the world. Without it the United Nations organization cannot survive.

The task of peacemaking cannot succeed unless the means of

achieving co-operation are still available. Yet the possibility of co-operation, which is now, tragically enough, becoming every day more remote, constituted the very basis of the foreign policy carried on by President Roosevelt until the day of his death.

From the many conversations which I had with him at that time I can without hesitation assert that from the time when Hitler invaded Russia in June of 1941, the President regarded understanding and co-operation between Moscow and Washington as one of the indispensable foundations for American foreign policy.

The President was in an exceptional position to promote that kind of relationship. He himself had been solely responsible for the decision of the United States government in 1933 to bring to an end the situation created by the refusal of the three preceding Administrations to have any official relations with the Soviet government. While he had stood adamant since that time against any infringement by Moscow of its pledge to refrain from any form of interference, direct or indirect, in the internal concerns of the United States, and while he had been vigorously opposed to many manifestations of Soviet policy both internal and foreign, I think it is not too much to say that he sincerely believed that, given a reasonable period of world peace, the sharp distinctions between the Soviet régime and the political régimes of the Western democracies would gradually diminish. He believed it perfectly possible for a stable world order to be created within which our traditional form of Western democracy and the state socialist form of Russian Communism could exist side by side without an inevitable collision. He did not believe that the insistence of the present leaders of the Soviet Union that their Marxist program must ultimately cover the world need necessarily represent the policy of their successors, provided Russian living standards improved, and provided communication between the Russian people and the peoples of the West could be constantly increased.

When one remembers the natural prejudice against Communism which prevailed within the United States, and when one remembers as well the Soviet Union's traditional and by no means unjustifiable suspicion of the Western democracies, the increasingly co-operative relationship that developed between the Soviet and American governments during the war must be regarded as a major accomplishment. It is true that the Soviet government desperately needed the supplies promised by the United States. After the summer of 1941, every effort was made under the direction of President Roosevelt to see that these promises were kept to the letter. On the whole, they were. It is true that at many times during the war the Soviet government seemed unnecessarily cavalier in its acceptance of this help and unduly querulous in its demands for ever greater help, but it can never be forgotten that during the latter part of 1941 and during the major part of the black year of 1942 the Soviet armies were bearing almost the entire brunt of the German onslaught. The long, although inevitable, postponement of the second front in Europe was bound to be construed by all except a few in the highest hierarchy of Soviet officialdom as meaning that the Western democracies intended to permit the Soviet armies to do their fighting and dying for them. In the purely military sphere, however, the relationship between the East and West was surprisingly free from controversy. It was rather in the sphere of high politics that clouds of mistrust remained to be dispelled.

President Roosevelt was a convinced believer in the efficacy of personal contacts between the chiefs of state. He was always confident of his own ability to get on a footing of understanding and trust with men with whom he had to deal, and had long been bent on establishing a personal relationship with Stalin. Notwithstanding innumerable obstacles, physical as well as political, and after many postponements which would have chilled the enthusiasm of any less convinced optimist, his first meeting with Stalin finally took place at the Conference of Teheran. The political results of that conference were even more far-reaching than the military decisions made there.

President Roosevelt had only one further personal meeting with Stalin—the Conference of Yalta in 1945. But in these two meetings the President laid the foundation upon which, so long as he lived, there was being built a relationship between the American and Soviet governments that could never otherwise have existed. He was wholly unwilling to permit any intransigency about details to prejudice the opportunity to attain agreement between the two governments upon broader issues.

He has been criticized for the agreements reached at Yalta that appeared to prejudice the rights of great numbers of people in eastern European countries where the Soviet government was determined to prevent the resurgence of threats to its own security. He has been bitterly assailed for his willingness to admit the Soviet thesis with respect to the eastern frontiers of Poland and the ultimate status of the former Baltic Republics. Superficially these criticisms may seem justified. Yet on the other hand, those who criticize fail to mention the President's unflinching insistence that the United States could not and would not go along in any joint policy with the Soviet government that did not contain specific assurance that in Eastern Europe, as well as in the Balkans, no governments were to be installed save those established through free and uncontrolled elections, and that no governments established through such elections were to be regarded as legitimate unless they remained truly representative. And to those who would point out that the former Baltic Republics constitute an exception, it must be recalled that these states had been an integral part of Russia prior to the First World War, and that they had been reincorporated within Russia long before the United States had entered the Second World War.

Certainly the agreements reached at Teheran and at Yalta having to do with the recognition of the independence and integrity of Iran, as well as those relating to the future of China and of Korea, provided the surest basis for a stable future in those regions that could conceivably have been laid down under the conditions then existing.

Behind it all was the President's underlying conviction that for the sake of world peace, for the sake of the future security of the United States herself, the one great essential was to secure from the Soviet Union the firm commitment that she would continue to co-operate with the United States after the war as a partner in creating and perfecting the new society of nations, the United Nations.

For Franklin Roosevelt in 1945 felt very much as Woodrow
Wilson felt in 1919. It might be impossible to obtain the kind of
agreement on future settlements in eastern Europe, in the Near
East, or even in the Far East, that would represent one hundred
per cent of what the President regarded as equitable or desirable.
But if a United Nations organization could be created, in which
the Soviet Union and the United States would jointly participate
and through which a rule of law rather than a rule of force could
gradually be evolved, that would provide the best opportunity
later to correct such inequities as might exist when the peace settlements were first entered into.

On the essential principles involved, the President had no intention of weakening. He believed that in view of the history of
the years between the two great wars the Soviet Union had a
legitimate right to demand peace settlements that would secure her
from the danger of attack from beyond her borders. He felt that
the Soviet Union could fairly insist that the new political régimes
to be installed in the independent nations adjacent to her frontiers
should be governments that were friendly and that represented
the will of their people. But because of the terms of the Yalta
agreements, the President was equally confident that, if the major
powers abided by their pledge to guarantee democratic and representative government throughout that region, the Soviet Union
would not be able to dominate those weaker peoples solely for her
own aggrandizement.

President Roosevelt could never have foreseen that this moral
obligation assumed by him in the name of the United States would
be weakly thrown away by an American Secretary of State ten
months later.

Any objective appraisal of President Roosevelt's policy toward
Russia must result in the recognition that before his death it had
attained the following objectives. It had established a far closer
and far more understanding relationship between Moscow and
Washington than had ever previously existed. It had committed
the Soviet government to full and loyal co-operation in a future
United Nations. And it had committed the Soviet government
to the principle that the independent nations adjacent to its bound-

aries should be accorded their untrammeled right as sovereign states to enjoy democratic and free governments.

Since the death of President Roosevelt, relations between the American and Soviet governments have undergone a material change. The Soviet leaders, and Stalin in particular, had, as the result of many years of direct dealing with President Roosevelt, finally convinced themselves that the policy he pursued had no ulterior motives. With his death, and with control of American foreign policy vested in new hands, that confidence vanished. At the first meeting between Stalin and President Truman at the Potsdam Conference of July, 1945, a new understanding had to be created at a singularly difficult moment, overshadowed as it was by the announcement of the joint control by Great Britain and the United States of the secrets of the atomic bomb.

The Soviet authorities became persuaded that the United States was now far more under the influence of British policy than she had hitherto shown herself to be.

The showdown came, of course, at the London meeting the following September. The Soviet government made it wholly plain that, as President Roosevelt had long since apprehended, while Moscow was fully disposed to co-operate with the nations of the West through the United Nations organization, provided the international settlements that it believed indispensable for its own security were reached, it was in the contrary event quite prepared to withdraw again from any such form of international co-operation and to undertake to secure these objectives by unilateral action.

Since that time relations between the United States and the Soviet Union have consistently become more strained. Common understanding has all but vanished. Official vituperation has replaced the beginning of a growth of confidence. Haggling on questions of detail has been substituted for the consistent effort made by President Roosevelt to compromise on details but never to abandon principle. And during the past year, when the United States has compromised, it has, unfortunately, been all too frequently upon the question of principle. The situation has reached such a point that the influence of those members of the Soviet

régime who sincerely believe in the need for international co-
operation has been weakened. The Russian leaders who want to
establish a world order dominated by the Soviet system have
been increasingly strengthened.

No such grave problems have arisen in the relations between
Washington and London. It is true that the defeat of Mr.
Churchill and his Conservative government in the national elections of July, 1946, as well as the death of President Roosevelt,
brought about the beginning of a new era in Anglo-American relations. But only a few short days after Mr. Bevin, the new Secretary of State for Foreign Affairs, took office it became clear
that British foreign policy was pursuing its immutable course.
The fact that British foreign policy under the new government
changed so little in objective and even less in method, save with
regard to Britain's colonies, came as a surprise to those who had
thought that the election for the first time of a socialist government with a Parliamentary majority large enough probably to
insure its retention of office for at least five years would mean a
revolutionary change in British foreign policy, as well as to those
who had assumed that the hysterical outpourings of Professor
Harold Laski provided an authoritative interpretation of the
policy of the British Labor party.

It was for wholly different reasons that tension and discord
at least temporarily clouded relations between the two English-
speaking powers. The singularly ill-timed and unhappily worded
announcement by President Truman of the termination of the
Lend-Lease Agreement with Great Britain provided the first
cause. The second was the prompt announcement by the Labor
government of its policies of industrial and financial nationalization which profoundly alarmed many of the more conservative
elements in the United States. The third arose from the prolonged inability of the British and American governments to
agree upon the extent and the terms of the credit from the American government imperatively required by Great Britain if the
British people were to be able to keep their heads above water
during the transition period after the war.

The American public, which had long believed that its internal policy was the most progressive and liberal manifestation of a democratic economy that the Western world provided, and that Great Britain was an example of unrepentant reaction, found the fact that Great Britain had suddenly swung far to the left of the United States hard to grasp. Immediately many voices were heard loudly claiming that the extension of any credit to Great Britain under these circumstances would mean that the American tax-payers were being called upon to help to undermine their own system of free enterprise. The feeling of comradeship and of partnership which had to a very real degree existed during the days of the war was badly impaired by opinions such as these, as well as by the recrudescence in many organs of British Conserva-tism of charges that the United States had resumed her prewar role of Shylock, and that the terms exacted were intended solely to destroy Britain's chance to become once more a great trading nation.

Had these events not taken place at a moment when, because of the course followed by the Soviet government, the international scene was so dark, and the possibility of building any effective and lasting international organization so problematical, the harm done might have been even graver. But in a world where public attention was once more concentrated upon the need for inter-national co-operation if the world was not again to be plunged into a state of total anarchy, these questions of economic policy, basic as they must eventually prove to be, assumed at least for the time being a subordinate place.

A majority of the American people and a majority of the peoples of the British Commonwealth have come to realize that, whatever the disputes which may arise between them, they will probably always be of minor importance if weighed in the balance against the dangers that would result were the members of the English-speaking nations to become fundamentally divided. For temporarily at least the British Commonwealth is weaker and poorer in relation to the rest of the world than it has been since the days when England alone prevented Napoleon from dominat-ing the earth. The co-operation of the United States is indispens-able if the United Kindom is to survive as one of the major powers. The United States, on the other hand, has reached a pre-eminent position in the world of today. But at the same time she cannot fail to perceive that, outside the Western Hemisphere, there is no aggregation of nations from whom she has so little to fear and with whom she has so much upon which to agree—particularly in the ethics of international relationships—as the British Commonwealth of Nations. Together, the English-speaking peoples total some 180,000,000 in population. Between them they control the larger portion of the earth's surface and a preponderant portion of the earth's natural resources. It is obviously to their common interest, until they are assured that a stable and lasting world order has been created and that international organization has succeeded, to work together in the council of nations.

From the larger aspect it cannot be too strongly emphasized that there need exist no root causes that make it impossible for the three major powers in the world to get along together. Yet it is undeniable that the United States and the Soviet Union are today farther apart than they have been at any time since the end of the war.

Tension is daily increasing. Suspicions are continually mounting. Public opinion in the United States and in the greater part of the Western world is rapidly coming to the conclusion that no understanding between the Soviet and the West is possible and that the division of the earth into two major spheres of influence, one controlled from Moscow and one controlled by the Western powers, is inevitable. There is a growing defeatist tendency among the American people to resign themselves to this outcome. There is, however, no corresponding realization of the inescapable conclusion that, if this is to be the outcome, a new war is almost unavoidable.

It is entirely true that after the early winter of 1946 the position taken by the Kremlin has been constantly negative. The Soviet government has repeatedly refused to adopt proposals for international solutions which were made in good faith by the United States and which appear to any impartial observer to be intrinsically wise and desirable. Every proposal made by Washington since February of 1946 looking toward the formulation of a joint policy toward Germany has been rejected by the Soviet Union.

Because of the present intransigence of the Soviet Union, it has become the tendency in the Western world to place the entire blame for the tragic collapse in peacemaking at the door of the Soviet government. It would seem to me far more realistic to admit that the blame for the present disaster should be shared by the government of the United States.

In May, 1945, the United States enjoyed a pre-eminent position among the nations of the world. She had the support of all the smaller nations. She had no ground for controversy or for antagonism with any other major power. She had demonstrated an unrivaled military and industrial strength. And strength, as Winston Churchill has so frequently emphasized, is, above all else, the quality that the Soviet Union most respects. The Soviet government at that time had been given none of the reasons that later arose to feed its appetite and its suspicion.

Had the United States undertaken a foresighted policy of vigorous initiative prior to V-E Day, or immediately thereafter, it would have been infinitely easier to find a basis for agreement with the Soviet Union on a German policy, on the reconstruction of Europe, on international organization, and on those broad foundations for a free world order which in the judgment of the American people were indispensable.

The confusion and timidity of American policy and the increasing chaos which surged over Europe after the Potsdam meeting openly incited a Soviet policy of aggrandizement and of domination. The results are only too plainly apparent. They have been seen in every conference in which the United States and the Soviet Union have participated since Potsdam.

The authority of the Security Council has been dwarfed because the United States and the Soviet Union have been at loggerheads.

When the meeting of the Foreign Ministers of the four major powers took place at Paris in May, 1946, a stalemate occurred. During the weeks between that meeting and the subsequent meeting in Paris on June 15, the tension was accentuated. The questions of detail on which insurmountable differences developed were not the causes for the breakdown of the conference, as Secretary Byrnes appeared to believe. The cause of the breakdown in peacemaking was the failure of the United States long before to find an understanding with the Soviet Union upon the nature of the new world order. And behind that lay the inability of the new directors of American foreign relations to recognize the importance of the time factor in the conduct of foreign policy.

The major points of disagreement in Paris, such as the quarrel over Italian reparations and the control of the former Italian colonies, or the controversy over the future of Trieste and of Venezia Giulia, will be discussed more fully in the next chapter. I cite them here only in order to stress my own conviction that, had the United States arrived at an understanding with the Soviet Union upon the basis of the future would order and especially upon the policy to be pursued toward Germany at the close of the war, there would have been much less difficulty in adjusting such disputes as those which arose at Paris.

After the collapse of the negotiations at the May conference, Secretary Byrnes made three pronouncements.

He declared that whether or not an agreement upon the provisions of the peace treaties with Italy and with the Axis satellites was reached at the June meeting of the Foreign Ministers, the United States would insist that the long-promised peace conference of the twenty-one United Nations be held in Paris in July, so that the conclusion of the European peace treaties might not longer be postponed. He further announced that, should the Soviet Union refuse to agree to the peace settlements that might be formulated at such a conference, the United States would, under the terms of the United Nations Charter, refer any continuing differences to the General Assembly of the United Nations for their determination. Finally, he made public his intention of requesting that a conference of the four major powers be held not later than November, 1946, in order to reach a final decision upon the terms of the settlements to be imposed upon the German people.

It is in my judgment highly questionable whether these public pronouncements, made as they were at a moment of extreme exacerbation in Soviet-American relations, did anything but harm. They were certainly regarded by the Soviet government as evidence that the United States was trying to put direct pressure upon the Kremlin. The intemperate rejoinder of Mr. Molotov made it apparent that the Soviet Union intended to resist such open pressure.

Had indication of American intention been made confidentially, through official channels, it might have proved more efficacious. Nevertheless, it is certainly true that the peoples of Europe should not be permitted to enter another winter without having the assurance that can be derived only from final peace settlements. Certainly the other members of the United Nations, and particularly Germany's neighbors, must be given the chance without further delay to help determine what those peace settlements should be. Certainly the matter must eventually be laid before the Assembly of the United Nations as the one body competent to pass upon the basic issues involved, should the Soviet Union and the West be unable to agree. Finally, it is equally evident that, if the present chaotic condition of Europe persists much longer, economic ruin and political and social upheavals are inevitable and cannot fail to bring about the collapse of what is left of modern civilization.

But the tides are running very swiftly. The Foreign Ministers have shown themselves incapable of striving to achieve that basic understanding which alone holds any hope for the construction of a unified world.

The one last chance of preventing a division of the world into two rival spheres of power and of ideology, with all the tragic consequences, lies in the capacity of the chiefs of the three Western governments to demonstrate a degree of vision and of responsibility that they have not yet shown.

Unless the present impasse can be surmounted at the Paris Peace Conference of the twenty-one United Nations and at subsequent conferences to decide the final policy to be adopted toward Germany, the Soviet Union almost surely will withdraw from the

United Nations and from any further attempt at peaceful collaboration with the Western powers.

The Western powers have votes to spare at a peace conference as well as in the United Nations Assembly. But it is not a question of votes. What is at stake is the creation of a unified world. Should the Soviet Union refuse to continue to take part in the United Nations, international anarchy will loom before humanity.

It seems a far cry from those last lines of the Declaration of Teheran signed in December, 1943:

"We came here with hope and determination. We leave here friends in fact, in spirit and in purpose. Roosevelt, Churchill and Stalin."

CHAPTER III

The Reconstruction of Europe

AFTER every war the victors are granted an opportunity of attaining through peace treaties the fruit of their victory. Three times in the past century and a half war has engulfed the whole of Europe. Three times the victorious powers have tried after their victory to formulate peace settlements which would lay the foundations for a general and lasting peace in Europe.

Whatever its ideological defects, as seen by modern eyes, the peace concluded at the Congress of Vienna in 1815 helped to prevent the outbreak of any general European war for exactly one hundred years.

The peace settlements signed at Versailles after the First World War in June, 1919, resulted in no real or lasting peace. At best they permitted an uneasy and precarious armistice which lasted scarcely twenty years. Europe was then plunged once more into that new and greater conflict known as the Second World War.

Today the United Nations try to find the answer to the same question. What peace settlements can bring about a lasting peace in Europe? What kind of reconstruction of Europe can prevent the resurgence of those conditions which brought about the tragedy which has devastated the whole world and which has, in particular, ruined and prostrated the peoples of Europe?

Every responsible statesman in the United Nations knows that during the immediate future Europe will continue to be, as it has so long been, the part of the world where threats to peace will most frequently arise. They must, consequently, seek an over-all peace settlement through which a new Europe can be constructed, a Europe in which the causes of war, of aggression, of rivalry and of hate can gradually, but consistently, be eliminated. They know that the United Nations possess the military and material power to impose such a settlement. They also realize that its achievement will be impeded or prevented by a clash of conflicting ambitions among the victors, by popular war weariness, and by a lack of vision and of intellectual competence on the part of those entrusted with this stupendous task.

Yet the peoples of the Western democracies at least have begun to see more clearly than ever before what the major objectives should be. What seemed at the end of the First World War an illusory and utopian concept has suddenly come to be regarded as a practical possibility. The ultimate establishment of a federation of Europe is today spoken of by even the more hard-boiled statesmen as a goal which should be sought. It has become plain that a reconstituted Europe composed of a multitude of small states, each insistent upon the ultimate measure of sovereignty, divided one from the other by artificial and often insuperable economic barriers, and refusing to co-operate in the development of natural resources which can only be enjoyed by all the peoples of Europe through such co-operation, can under no circumstances become a Europe in which a lasting peace is possible. What has suddenly become even plainer is that a Europe divided by an iron curtain, dominated to the east by a rigidly authoritarian political and economic system, and composed in the west of a number of increasingly impoverished and unstable democracies cannot long endure.

A United States of Europe is, of course, by no means a new concept. During the past generation Aristide Briand was its leading exponent. It has had no more untiring and eloquent spokesman in recent times than Count Koudenhove-Kalergi. It has had many supporters during the war years in Great Britain and in Scandinavia. It has as yet, however, received no endorsement in any specific form from any of the major powers, and provision for it in the United Nations Charter can only be found by indirection in those articles of Chapter 8 which deal with the creation of regional systems.

In considering the feasibility of establishing a federated Europe, it is useful to analyze the origins and the causes of the wars which have broken out in Europe since the Congress of Vienna in 1815.

It is worthy of special emphasis that no European wars have been brought about in latter years by those smaller European powers where living standards are high and where democracy has been firmly established. The Scandinavian nations, the Netherlands, Belgium and Switzerland are cases in point.

It is worthy of equal emphasis that, since the relatively recent liberation of the Balkan States from the tyranny of the Ottoman Empire, the largest number of Europe's wars have broken out there. It is among the Balkans that the lowest living standards to be found in Europe have prevailed and that representative government has existed chiefly in name, and it is there that racial and religious antagonisms have been strongest.

I have no intention of attempting to draw any hard and fast conclusions from this generalization. However, the objective student gains from the history of modern Europe strong reasons for the belief that, granted the absence of such special conditions as those which have been recurrent in Germany, the truer the form of representative government in the countries of Europe, the higher the standards of living and of education, and the greater the absence of racial and religious discrimination, the less likely it is that war will break out.

It is true that living standards and educational standards were both exceptionally high in Germany, and that local representative government existed in an advanced form, until Hitler's advent. There are several reasons, however, why the Germanic peoples constitute an exception to these general rules.

In the first place national democratic government has never existed in Germany. The Germans could select their municipal governments; they could not decide their national policies. The German peoples have been increasingly subjected since 1848 to the dominant influence of Prussia and to the Pan-German and militaristic doctrines which Prussian leaders have consistently upheld. It must also be remembered that the German people have persistently suffered from a national form of inferiority complex which has been primarily responsible for those obsessions and vagaries in their national conduct which have proved incompre-

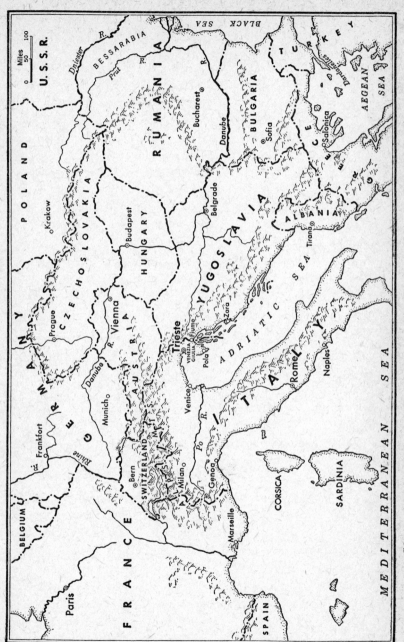

SOUTHEASTERN AND CENTRAL EUROPE, illustrating the strategic position of Trieste

hensible to other Western peoples and which have made them easy prey for the demagogues and the imperialists.

The German mentality is still responsive to Goethe's dictum that "liberty, when crowned with authority, invariably gives rise to oligarchy."

Leaving the Germans as a race apart, European experience seems to show that the best antidotes to war would be democracy, high living standards and an advanced educational level, the solution of those territorial and racial maladjustments which have so long fostered ancient antagonisms, and the reduction of such purely national barriers as hamper regional economic progress and prevent the peoples of Europe as a whole from making use of the natural resources that should be available to all of them. If any regional federation of Europe is to be established under the United Nations organization, the final peace treaties must facilitate, and not impede, its realization.

Democracy cannot be created by the mere signature of treaties in those countries of Europe where representative government has never existed. It requires popular support. It will grow as living standards are raised and as education advances. But it cannot be expedited unless the United Nations adopts, and provides for the enforcement of, a Bill of Human Rights which will insure to all peoples the enjoyment of the essential freedoms of religion, of expression and of information.

A European regional system would have the protection to be derived from the United Nations organization. It could bring about the abolition of the standing armies which have been the chief curse of the smaller nations of Europe. Every government of the lesser European powers could then devote the revenues hitherto employed for the maintenance of those standing armies to social welfare.

Living standards in all the European countries will rise as peace is consolidated, and as those agencies of the United Nations such as the International Bank, the International Stabilization Fund, and the Food and Agriculture Organization are afforded the chance of carrying out their responsibilities. But living standards will be most surely advanced over the years if a regional federation of

Europe promotes industrialization in the more backward countries through the inauguration of co-operative development projects. Regional federation would likewise facilitate the internationalization of railroad, river and air communications under regional authorities, and the elimination of customs and currency barriers.

Obviously this is a long-range program. The great difference in living standards and in the level of civilization between the peoples of western and of eastern Europe makes it improbable that such objectives can be reached within a period of several generations. It may even be that a start may best be made through the establishment of regional groups similar to the Oslo group (the Scandinavian powers, Finland, the Netherlands, Belgium and Luxembourg), each composed of states that have reached approximately the same stage of internal development. But no such objectives can ever be reached save by the creation of some form of European federation.

The United Nations now have the chance to lay a lasting foundation for such a federation of Europe by writing peace treaties that will remove the territorial maladjustments which have provoked international antagonism, and that will solve the so-called "minority" problems which have so frequently been responsible for European strife. Unless these standing causes for controversy and for exaggerated nationalism are wiped out, no regional federation can exist.

The reasons for international suspicions, rivalries and hatreds are infinitely more numerous in Europe than they ever were in the Western Hemisphere. Yet the inter-American regional system could never have been built up had the United States not first proclaimed its new Good Neighbor Policy, and then proceeded as rapidly as possible to remove through negotiation or unilateral act every valid ground for resentment or for hostility on the part of its neighbors.[1]

The United Nations face the same kind of situation in Europe. Before a new structure can be solidly built, the ground must be cleared, and the defects in the terrain corrected.

---

[1] The recent modification of the Good Neighbor Policy by the United States Government has unfortunately jeopardized the inter-American system.

Ideally, every European frontier should be scrutinized to ascertain whether it violates a few simple principles. Does it create resentment on the part of one of the nations which it bounds because it represents a palpable injustice? Does it compel the population within its limits to submit unwillingly to an alien jurisdiction? Does it contribute to economic inequities? Is it, because of its obviously impracticable nature, a factor in perpetuating social, economic or political instability? If the 1936 frontiers of Europe —those which existed before Hitler commenced to remake the map according to his own volition—fall within any of these categories, the present-day peacemakers should try to rectify them so as to obviate their specific defects. Also, the changes made should conform to the Wilson doctrine: "Every territorial settlement must be in the interests of the populations concerned, and not a part of any mere adjustment or compromise of claims among rival states."

There are many such frontiers in Europe. There can be no legitimate doubt that the continuation of some of them would not make for peace.

In my considered judgment the frontiers which the Soviet Union demands as its permanent northern and western boundaries are justified from the standpoint of its security, and justified by the test of the principles enumerated above, provided Moscow agrees to the emigration, with fair compensation, of those nationals of the regions Russia thus acquires who are unwilling to remain under her jurisdiction.

The frontiers insisted upon by the Soviet Union include the rectification of its 1936 boundary with Finland; the incorporation of the former Baltic Republics together with the part of East Prussia that extends as far west as Königsberg; a boundary with Poland corresponding approximately to the Curzon Line of 1920; the incorporation of Ruthenia and of a portion of the Bukowina, and a boundary with Rumania as a result of which Bessarabia will become amalgamated with the U.S.S.R.

Such a new western frontier for the Soviet Union will solve rather than create political and economic conflicts.

In their vast majority the populations thereby passing under

Soviet jurisdiction are not only Slavic; they are likewise desirous of assimilation into the Soviet system. It is only in East Prussia, in Lithuania, and to a lesser extent in Latvia, that any substantial percentage of the population may be fairly considered to be opposed to the change. In Lithuania the problem is complicated by the fact that the Lithuanian people are largely Roman Catholics. In these cases, difficult as the solution is, the only permanent remedy lies in the transfer of populations.

The gravest frontier decisions to be made involve the new boundaries of Germany. The general line of the Oder has been tentatively agreed upon by the four major powers as Germany's new eastern frontier with Poland. This decision, ceding to Poland a substantial part of eastern Germany together with Danzig and the western half of East Prussia, was intended to compensate her for the regions east of the Curzon Line now ceded by the new Polish government to the Soviet Union.

If the peacemakers make this tentative decision a final one, they will perpetrate an injustice and a social and economic blunder which will inevitably make for lasting friction and for European insecurity.

Poland has been deprived of a great portion of her territory by the cessions made to the Soviet Union. The Polish Corridor was a fatal mistake made by the peacemakers of 1919. It cannot be reconstituted. But Poland cannot survive or prosper if she is cut off from the Baltic. The only practical solution is the radical one which lies in the transfer to Germany of the German population of East Prussia, the incorporation of the western half of that region together with Danzig in the new Poland, and the establishment of a new frontier between Poland and eastern Germany which recognizes the legitimate requirements of both peoples.

The Oder frontier would furnish no such recognition. The future Germany must provide a home and the means of livelihood for several millions of Germans over and above its inhabitants before 1936. After the deal made by Hitler with the Kremlin in August, 1939, the Germans who had been residents of the Baltic States were brought back to Germany. Since the end of the last war all the surviving Germans from German-occupied Poland have fled to Germany. The Sudeten Germans who have been expelled from Czechoslovakia and the Germans who have been able to leave East Prussia and Transylvania have also increased Germany's population.

Much of the territory lying between the Oder and the western boundary of the former Polish Corridor is rich farm land. A portion of it at least should be available for German food supplies as well as for German homes. The new German frontier with Poland, if drawn with just regard for the economic needs of the German people, would run considerably to the east of the Oder line.

The new Poland in such event would still be far stronger economically than the Poland of 1939. Racially it will in any case be far more homogeneous. What Poland has ceded to the Soviet Union—the former eastern Poland—was territory occupied in greater part by Slavs desirous of transfer to Soviet jurisdiction. It was the region of Poland where great landed proprietors predominated, and where an impoverished peasantry had small hopes of bettering the condition of life for themselves or for their children. Democracy was unheard of. This cession of eastern Poland, notwithstanding the lamentations of the Polish reactionaries, will make for, rather than prevent, European stability.

The new Poland will have a compact territory inhabited almost entirely by Poles. If discrimination against its Jewish citizens is sternly put down, it will have no minority problem. It will have an extended sea coast, including the large and modern port of Danzig. It will possess all the essentials for a balanced economy, and the opportunity to develop many industrial resources now available to it.

A grave omission in the Potsdam agreements of 1945, and one which will have lasting consequences, was the failure of the Big Three to fix even a tentative boundary for western Germany. The omission has given rise to an extreme chauvinist campaign in France, much searching of the heart in the Netherlands and in Belgium, and has also of course already encouraged many German propagandists to seek to divide the victorious allies by striving to tempt the Soviet Union to take a different line of policy from that pursued by the Western powers.

The more extreme elements in France have demanded the separation of the Ruhr and the Rhineland from Germany and their establishment as an autonomous state under perpetual international control. They demand the transfer of the industrial region of the Saar to France. The justification claimed is, of course, the unquestionable truth that unless the Germans control these industrial regions and their mineral resources they cannot wage any new major wars.

In my opinion the argument is incontrovertible. The United Nations should under no circumstances permit a future Germany to have untrammeled control over industries and resources which alone enable the German people to make war.

Were the major powers unfortunately to decide to reconstitute Germany as a political and economic unit, with a centralized government, the French demands should be granted. France was proven right in the contentions that she advanced in 1919 as to the policy toward Germany that would give her security. This time she must have security. However, a fairer solution—and the only one which could prove lasting—would be the international control, under the United Nations, of the autonomous states of the Ruhr, the Rhineland and the Saar, rather than the incorporation of the purely German population of the Saar within France.

But if, on the other hand, it is finally decided, as I have so long urged, that the future Germany will be decentralized, composed of a number of entirely autonomous states, or groups of states, thus giving political freedom to peoples who enjoyed their independence for many centuries before Prussia and Nazism obliterated their traditional rights, and that this new decentralized Germany will be bound together solely by a customs and currency union, the security of France and of the smaller countries of western Europe will thereby be assured. The German people cannot wage war, nor will the great majority of them wish to wage war, unless they are politically united and politically regimented, and thus susceptible to the leadership of the militarists and of the Pan-German demagogues.

If Germany is decentralized, there will be no valid ground for changing her western frontier from the line confirmed by the Treaty of Versailles, save for minor rectifications which the events of the past thirty years have shown to be required for economic reasons. And except for similar minor rectifications there appears to be no reason to modify her frontiers with Austria and with Czechoslovakia.

I have previously expressed my belief that Italy's frontiers with France and with Austria as they existed at the close of the First World War should not be changed. While there are some ethnic reasons for questioning Italy's continued control over the southern Tyrol, most of the arguments, economic as well as those based upon security, are in favor of retaining Italy's frontier at the Brenner.

It is with regard to the future boundary between Italy and Yugoslavia that one of the most serious and complicated aspects of European reconstruction has arisen. At the close of the First World War, President Wilson did what lay within his power, notwithstanding the secret peace treaties, to bring about an agreement upon a boundary between Italy and the new southern Slav state that would be based upon ethnic grounds and that would be economically sound. To a considerable extent he failed.

During the Peace Conference itself, d'Annunzio with a band of guerrillas seized Fiume, and after Fiume had been later established as an international city, the Fascist régime of Mussolini again gained control of it in 1924.

Apart from the grabbing by Mussolini of regions that were rightfully Yugoslav, the frontier drawn by the treaty of 1919 between Italy and Yugoslavia in Venezia Giulia unquestionably placed many Yugoslavs under an Italian jurisdiction to which they were inherently hostile. The problem is complicated by the fact that the Istrian Peninsula is peopled by Slavs among whom are many enclaves of Italians, particularly along the coastal region. And the city of Trieste is an unmistakably Italian city, inhabited by a population that is Italian by an overwhelming majority. In southern Istria, moreover, the Italians have built up since 1920 a thriving exploitation of the mercury and bauxite deposits, and it is there that coal mines are found from which the Italian people have procured one-third of their coal production.

The frontier between Italy and Yugoslavia, and the final disposition of Trieste, have provided one of the bitterest controversies which have developed between the Soviet Union on the one hand and the Western powers on the other during the discussion of the Italian peace treaty.

At the close of hostilities British and American troops occupied Trieste and the portion of Istria lying to the west of the so-called Morgan line—a temporary frontier which, while based on purely military considerations, approximated the permanent frontier favored by President Wilson for ethnic reasons in 1919. Yugoslav forces under the orders of Marshal Tito, and with the direct approval of Moscow, faced the Western allies across the line to the east.

Every form of propaganda from Yugoslavia, and every form of pressure from the Soviet Union, have been employed to force the Western powers to agree to the cession of Trieste as well as the whole of Istria to Yugoslavia.

Such an agreement would not only be in flagrant disregard of the general principles for the delineation of frontiers which I have listed above, but it would also have consequences of the most far-reaching character in prejudice to the independence of such small states of central Europe as Czechoslovakia, Austria and Hungary.

Trieste, as I have said, is an Italian city. It represents to all the Italian people the climax of the *risorgimento*—their final liberation from Austrian rule. It is the economic and political outpost of Italy against the Slavic world to the east. Were Italy to be deprived of Trieste the Italian people would be submerged by a tidal wave of Irridentism and by a phase of exaggerated nationalism which would long retard their growth into a stable democracy. It would prevent Italy from developing many legitimate economic outlets. It would arouse lasting resentment between the Italians and the Slavs.

But there are other even graver issues involved.

If Italy retained Trieste the port would not be maintained as a political stranglehold over the economy of the states of central Europe, for which it is an economic outlet. But if Yugoslavia obtained Trieste, the traffic through that city would be governed by the political and economic dictates of the Soviet Union. During the fifteen years prior to 1939 fifty-five per cent of Trieste's traffic came from Austria, Czechoslovakia and Hungary. Trieste under Italian jurisdiction represents to those nations the one means by which they can continue to trade freely with the West, and be spared an exclusive monopoly over their commerce by the Soviet Union.

One of the leading statesmen of central Europe sent me word the other day: "Our one remaining hope of independence lies in American resistance to the control of Trieste by the Soviet Union."

If Yugoslavia were to obtain Trieste, the Soviet Union would rapidly secure an exclusive control over the whole of the Danubian basin, over the Adriatic and over the eastern Mediterranean. Greece would be isolated from the West.

The mendacity of Yugoslavia's plea that "Trieste will die without the Yugoslav hinterland" is shown by the fact that during the decade prior to 1939, Yugoslavia contributed exactly nine per cent of Trieste's total traffic.

The only solution which will prove lasting, because it is based on justice and on common sense, will be the retention by Italy of sovereignty over Trieste, with the establishment there of a free port, and the drawing of a frontier along the Wilson line of 1919. In that way the most accurate ethnic line which is feasible will be drawn, and transfers of population can correct the more important exceptions to the rule that Italians should live under Italian rule and Yugoslavs under their own flag. Such a frontier would leave Italy's desperately needed mineral resources in Italian hands, but Fiume and the larger part of Istria would become permanently Yugoslav.

At the Paris conference in July, the Foreign Ministers of the four major powers unfortunately agreed to a compromise proposal which was as unjust and dangerous as it was impracticable. This proposal, advanced by the French Foreign Minister, provided that the city of Trieste should be placed under permanent international control; and that the so-called "French" boundary should be accepted by which Yugoslavia would obtain all southern Istria, including the Italian port of Pola and all the mineral deposits in that area, and in the north the territory running as far to the west as Gorizia and the Isonzo River. Italy would be left with little more than the shipyards at Monfalcone, and the northern coast line of the Gulf of Venice.

Apart from the basic unwisdom, as well as the injustice, of depriving Italy of a purely Italian city of the strategic and economic importance of Trieste, this compromise provides no lasting solution. The world has learned from Danzig how insoluble are the causes for friction and retaliation which such so-called "international solutions" provide. If this decision is permitted to stand it will mean persistent ill will between the Italians and the Yugoslavs, years of agitation and propaganda, and what is most serious of all, persistent pressure by the Soviet Union, as a member of the international body governing the city, to obtain actual, if not open, control of Trieste and over the trade passing through the port.

Apart from the problem of Transylvania, which I will discuss in connection with the question of minorities, the last remaining territorial adjustment of major importance to be listed is one which should be made in respect to the northern frontier of Greece.

The Greek people deserve well of civilization for the part which they have played since they regained their independence at the dawn of the nineteenth century. They made a major contribution in 1942 to the victory of the United Nations. They merit from every standpoint, including the requirements of a stable Europe, the opportunity to live in security and to have brought under Greek sovereignty the Greeks of the Dodecanese and of northern Epirus. For those reasons the northern Epirus should be transferred from Albania to Greece, and a narrow strip of territory lying between the northern boundary of Greece and the Rhodope watershed, and now under Bulgarian jurisdiction, should pass to Greece.

The only true or sound remark which Mussolini made to me in my conferences with him in the spring of 1940, was his assertion that the minority problems had been the curse of Europe, and that until they were solved there could be no hope of any stable peace.

In my belief, the minority problems cannot be solved through frontier and territorial readjustments alone. Populations must be transferred under international control, even though in some cases such transfers may involve a million human beings.

There are many warmhearted, sincere persons who bitterly oppose this. They inveigh against any program which may call for uprooting families from land which may have been in the same line for hundreds of years. But if history, and especially European history has taught us anything, it must have taught us that the minority questions of Europe have been an eternal menace to friendly relations between peoples, a constant stimulant of fanatical nationalism, and a frequent incentive to war. Isn't it better, considering the appalling tragedy in Europe which we now confront, to get through with all the heartaches in this generation, when they may be an inevitable consequence of planning for a peaceful and happier world, and thus prevent new heartaches and tragedies in the generations to come?

Tragic as some of the immediate individual results may be, we should avail ourselves of this moment of world upheaval to effect transfers of population where these are necessary to prevent new conflicts, and thus enable peoples to live under the government they desire, free from racial discriminations.

Where such transfers of population are judged necessary, they should be carried out under the United Nations. They should be conducted with the utmost measure of humanity. The emigrants should receive full compensation for the properties they cannot remove. In the event the emigrants cannot find a new home in Europe, they should be helped by the agencies of the United Nations to settle in those countries overseas which are now already encouraging European immigration as an essential requirement in the development of their national resources.

It should be remembered by the sentimentalists that their

fellows made the same outcry against the transfer of populations between Greece and Turkey in 1920. Yet that enterprise, involving many hundreds of thousands of people, not only proved conducive to far better relations between Turkey and Greece in the years thereafter but also contributed markedly, as both governments now recognize, to the economic prosperity of the two nations.

The tides of war, the aftermath of war, and the unilateral actions of certain governments such as Czechoslovakia, have already brought about an influx of Germans from abroad into every part of Germany. From the ethnic side, the Germans will no longer constitute a problem when Germany's new frontiers are drawn. There are no longer German minorities in Germany's neighbor countries.

In Transylvania, however, the minority problem is so complex that it is wholly impossible to lay down any frontier which conforms to the principles I have mentioned; only by transferring great numbers of persons can a boundary which will prove lasting be determined.

Transylvania is that vast fertile plateau which lies at the eastern end of the Carpathians and which has been the source of interminable and bitter friction between the Hungarians and the Rumanians since the end of the First World War. Before the First World War the greatest part of the region was under Hungarian control. The peacemakers of 1919 awarded the area to Rumania. By the notorious Hitler *Diktat* of 1940 the Hungarians were permitted to reoccupy it. Now the Soviet Union has demanded its return to Rumania. Under ordinary conditions, the present peacemakers might readily lay down a frontier between Hungary and Rumania following ethnic lines and respecting such practical considerations as the best economic interests of the two states and the requirements of available means of communication, as well as the question of just title to the territory.

This, however, is the situation. Transylvania is inhabited by three million Rumanian peasants who under Hungarian rule have been treated as little better than serfs. It is also inhabited by one and a half million Magyars who are determined to remain Hungarians. The Rumanians live in the agricultural areas, the Magyars in the cities. The welfare of the two races is based upon an interdependent economy. To add to this already complicated situation, Transylvanian cities and towns hold a quarter of a million Hungarian Jews; and more than half a million Germans, settled in Transylvania since the twelfth century, are still as wholly unassimilated as they were when the first settlers arrived. They live apart. They became a Nazi *Volksgruppe* as soon as Hitler commenced his march of expansion.

During the years between the wars the Hungarians complained more loudly than any other "succession" state of the persecution and discrimination suffered by their fellow Magyars at the hands of the Rumanians. The latter had by no means forgotten the treatment they had received under Hungarian rule. The two peoples cannot be amalgamated, nor will they become reconciled. There is not the slightest likelihood that the German minorities who have remained will ever be anything but Germans in manner of being and in aspiration.

Religious rivalries cannot be minimized. I remember well how before the war a distinguished group of Calvinists and Unitarians in the United States came to see me at the Department of State to protest against the restrictions the Rumanian government imposed upon their fellow Calvinists and the Unitarian Székelys, an ancient Magyar tribe in Transylvania. The Rumanians are of the Rumanian Orthodox faith, or of the Uniate church; the Hungarians are largely Catholic; some are Calvinist; and the Germans retain the Lutheran form of Protestantism. Religious antagonisms have increased racial hatreds. How can it be imagined that the cession of this entire region, comprising these wholly divergent elements, to either Rumania or Hungary, can ever result in anything but new conflicts, new complaints, new oppressions and a festering sore in the body politic of Europe?

The only practical answer to the question must be found in a surgical operation at the peace table. Transylvania should be divided between Hungary and Rumania by a line which recognizes ethnic principles, but which is drawn primarily for economic reasons. Thereafter populations should be transferred by order of the United Nations so that there will never again be heard the charge that Rumanians or Hungarians are living under a flag that is hateful to them, and that this element or that is suffering oppression or discrimination, whether racial or religious. The Germans should be helped to return to Germany should they so desire. Any solution less drastic than this would merely perpetuate a danger spot which the United Nations are now at length given the chance to eradicate.

Unless the United Nations courageously and constructively confront these territorial and minority problems, there will be no opportunity to build up a new European order which may become that federation of Europe which holds the greatest hope of political stability and peace, and of social and economic progress.

What signs can we see today that the policies and the decisions of the major powers undertaken since Germany's surrender are preparing the way for the establishment of such an order?

We may well start such a survey with a review of the policies of the major allies toward Italy since the conclusion of the Armistice of 1943. By that armistice, Italy became a co-belligerent, rather than the enemy, of the United Nations, and thus her status during the last year and a half of the war was totally different from that of Germany. While the toleration extended to the Italian people after the downfall of Mussolini was grudgingly evidenced, public opinion in all the Western democracies recognized the distinction to be drawn.

The original plans for the administration of Italy had been concerted by President Roosevelt and Prime Minister Churchill long before the termination of the North African campaign. The general scheme was frankly based upon the preponderance of British interests in the Italian theater. It was agreed that in the military as well as the political organization, the extent of American representation should be roughly equivalent to British representation, but that the authority of the United States should be supplementary rather than equal to that of Great Britain. Thus, after the invasion of the peninsula had been accomplished, the highest military authority was the British with the number two man American. In the civilian sphere, the same system was agreed upon.

The details of the blueprint for the so-called "Allied Military Government of Occupied Territory" had been scarcely completed by the time the invasion of Sicily took place. From the outset the system worked badly. It continued to work even more badly as the occupation of southern Italy progressed. By the time Rome was occupied by the Allied governments, the disastrous inefficiency of the system as well as the dangerous implications inherent in it were only too painfully evident.

The agreement at the time of the armistice of the American and British governments, and later of the Soviet government, to recognize an Italian government headed by Marshal Badoglio as the only agency representing the Italian people with which the victorious powers could undertake to deal was justified upon grounds of expediency. The Allied military situation would otherwise have been needlessly jeopardized, and it was improbable that any other arrangement would have resulted in the prompt and orderly surrender of the forces loyal to the Crown and of the remaining units of the Italian Fleet.

But with the occupation of Rome political considerations should have come far more sharply into the foreground. Military strategy, as well as any desirable long-range policy, demanded that the course of the Allied governments should envisage certain ultimate aims. First, to obtain as fully as possible the loyal support and co-operation of the Italian people in the regions of Italy occupied by the Allies, and the fullest participation possible of the Partisans and other resistance forces in northern Italy. Second, to encourage whatever democratic forces might still exist in order to prepare the way for the eventual election of a democratic régime truly representative of the will of a majority of the Italian people. Third, to segregate all the Fascist influences which had gone to cover and ultimately to eliminate them by the will of the Italian people themselves. Fourth, to attain as rapidly as possible conditions which would safely permit local administration in the municipalities and provinces to be turned over to duly elected Italian representatives. Finally, and in many ways the most difficult achievement, to prepare administrative machinery through which relief, food supplies and raw materials could be obtained by the civilian population.

The Allied administrative machine failed to make even a reasonable amount of progress toward these objectives.

As soon as Rome was occupied, the Allied representatives consulted with the leaders of the liberation and resistance fronts. One of two alternatives in the sphere of political action was open to the American and British governments. They could have demanded—and the British in fact long insisted—that Marshal Badoglio continue as Prime Minister, under the monarchy, and that the resistance leaders enter a Cabinet headed by him as the only agency with which the Allied governments would consent to deal.

The other alternative was to insist that a coalition government of the leaders of all anti-Fascist groups be constituted, leaving it to them to choose the Prime Minister.

If the first alternative had been adopted it would have been opposed by all the important anti-Fascist elements, especially those in the north of Italy and would have resulted in a government solely representative of the extreme right.

During the long months before Rome was finally occupied the Romans had feared that their city would either be destroyed deliberately by the Germans, or else be wrecked by the Allied invaders. It was not unnatural, then, that the return of Marshal Badoglio to Rome had aroused popular enthusiasm. His return was to them patent evidence that their immediate trials were ended. But their enthusiasm could at best be only short-lived, for the Italians will neither forgive nor forget that the marshal left them on September 8, 1943, without directives as to the course they should follow when the ironclad occupation of the Germans clamped itself upon them.

The attempt of the British government to force a continuance of the Badoglio government showed little understanding of Italian psychology. It was due partly to sentimental considerations on the part of Mr. Churchill and his Foreign Office arising from the marshal's earlier relations with the British government. It was due still more to the belief that the obligations that the marshal had assumed under the armistice terms and in subsequent agreements were more likely to be respected if he remained in power. But the strongest motive was the desire of the Churchill Cabinet that no step be taken which would in any way prejudice the retention of the House of Savoy.

The adoption of the second alternative was due to the insistence of the United States. This represented the only time when the American government was responsible for the determination of high policy.

This policy resulted in the creation of a new Italian government under the premiership of an elderly Italian politician, Ivanoe Bonomi, a member of the Liberal party who, although he had never faltered in his opposition to the Fascist régime, had nevertheless displayed few signs during his career of possessing the qualities of character and of leadership so urgently required. The Cabinet posts were allotted to leaders of the resistance forces, far too many of whom, however, were of the same vintage as their chief. The Cabinet embraced almost all shades of anti-Fascist opinion. After much debate it was agreed that the so-called institutional question, the question of keeping the monarchy, should be held in abeyance until political stability had been restored and until the freely expressed will of the Italian people could be made known. The King was at length persuaded to abdicate by Enrico de Nicola, now Provisional President but at the time still a private citizen in Naples. A regent, or Lieutenant General of the Realm was designated in the person of the Prince of Piedmont to function as the sovereign authority.

Shifts in the Italian Cabinet took place with great frequency. The Cabinet's authority remained shadowy. No important decision could be reached without the prior approval of the Allied representatives. Even the most urgent measures for relief or reconstruction proposed by the Cabinet were often vetoed for no understandable reason by the British members of the Allied Control Council.

The British government continued to pursue a policy which came to be regarded by the Italian people as primarily vindictive.

Mr. Churchill frequently reiterated those flaming denunciations of Italy which he had been accustomed so eloquently to voice during the period prior to the downfall of Mussolini. British officers lost no opportunity of showing their contempt for the Italian populace. The British information services were instructed to "sell the British way of life" to the Italians, but the results were understandably meager in view of the policies at the top, and the bitterness engendered throughout all Italy by the attitude adopted by the British toward a hungry, unhappy and war-weary people.

There was no stranger evidence of this initial policy toward Italy than the veto imposed by Mr. Churchill upon the selection of Count Sforza as Foreign Minister at a moment of Cabinet reshuffling. Count Sforza had opposed the Fascist régime from the very outset. He had lived in exile for more than twenty years. He had earlier served as Foreign Minister and as Ambassador to France, and few Italians could be considered as well qualified as he to direct Italian foreign policy under the critical conditions then obtaining. During the early war years, while Count Sforza was living in the United States, I had had occasion frequently to deal with him, and I had found him not only resourceful and constructive in his suggestions with regard to the measures to be taken during the war by the United Nations concerning Italy, but also wholly democratic. He was an outstanding example of a liberal Italian patriot.

Yet the anathema hurled against him by the British government, presumably because of his prior refusal to acquiesce in Mr. Churchill's support of the House of Savoy, prevented Italy from obtaining the services of an exceptionally able and experienced man in a post which he was uniquely qualified to fill.

The alignment among the anti-Fascist forces soon crystallized into six principal political parties. Of these, the Christian Democrat, the Liberal, the Socialist, and the Communist were the most powerful. At times, as when Allied policy showed itself to be particularly sterile, the Communist and Socialist parties appeared to grow stronger. At other times both the Christian Democrat party and the Liberal party appeared to gain strength. But a coalition government continued to be necessary since no one of the six parties showed any signs of acquiring a popular majority.

Early in 1945, after the last German forces had been driven out of northern Italy, a new Cabinet was formed which gave far greater promise of vitality than its predecessors. It was headed by Professor Ferrucio Parri, who had won renown and admiration by his underground activities as a resistance leader in northern Italy. But its outstanding member was its Foreign Minister, Alcide de Gasperi.

Dr. de Gasperi had been born in Trento when that city was still under the Austrian flag. In his early youth he had even been elected to the Austrian Reichsrat or imperial parliament. A man of wide experience and of an unquenchable faith in the Italian *risorgimento,* he had helped to create what later became Italy's greatest political force, the Christian Democrat party. This new party, born of the tragedy of the war, is similar in its tenets to the other Catholic Action parties of western Europe such as the Popular Republican Movement in France. It represents primarily the modern liberal element of the Catholic church. In its domestic policies it stands far to the left of center. Its objectives vary but little from those sought by the Socialist party in Italy. But unlike the latter, it comprises no elements which favor any compromise, much less a coalition, with the Communists.

Upon the resignation of Professor Parri in the autumn of 1945, Dr. de Gasperi succeeded him as Prime Minister. And he was destined to remain in office during the dramatic events that led to the abolition of the monarchy and the establishment of the first republic of Italy.

One might suppose that American and British policy in Italy would have been designed to strengthen the prestige of the democratic elements in Italy so that later on, after the peace treaty, a truly democratic government might be elected by the Italian people. It would seem logical, once an Italian government had been formed which included the leaders of the truly democratic parties, to give that government the means of strengthening democratic trends, and of bringing about among the Italian people a realistic appreciation of the tragic harm they had done to them-

selves and to their country by their submission to the Fascist
régime. It would seem natural to give such a government the
fullest measure of authority compatible with the armistice terms
and to help it obtain for the Italian people the food and raw materials, supplies for housing, and transport without which Italy must
suffer a far graver crisis than she had suffered during the days
of German rule.

The contrary was, however, the case. The Allied governments
apparently believed that they had an absolute right to the undying
gratitude of the Italian people for their liberation from Germany.
In order that this gratitude should not lessen, when the Italian
people found themselves without food, fuel, clothing and shelter,
they were given to understand by the Allied authorities that the
blame should be placed upon the Italian government. As a result,
the unthinking began to believe that a democratic Italian government was proving far less competent to provide them with even
the bare necessities of life than the Fascist régime, or even the
German invaders. But the better informed realized quite clearly
that the Italian government was only a front for the Allied Control
Council, and that it was the Allied governments that were
responsible for the increasing plight in which Italy found herself.

If the political approach to the reconstruction of Italy was
primarily stupid, the Allied handling of Italy's economic needs
was grossly incompetent. The Italian people, after the occupation
of Rome, needed food, fuel, raw materials and the means of
transportation for all these commodities, particularly trucks. Only
a small percentage of Italy's food requirements was obtainable
in the country. There were on hand hardly any of the fuel or raw
materials so desperately needed if Italian industry was to recom-
mence, and if employment was thus to be made available.

The Allied authorities charged with the responsibility of providing for the needs of the civilian population, and with the duty of
preparing for the reconstruction of Italy's internal economy
demonstrated their inability to cope with these problems, as well
as an unwillingness to adopt any constructive policy. Time and
again the British authorities who, as has been shown, retained
the ultimate control, opposed extending relief until it had be-

come too late to avert tragedy. Here and there a few individuals among the Americans who held subordinate positions in the Allied Control Council vigorously protested against conditions which were not only causing unnecessary suffering to the Italian people but which threatened to do grave damage to Italian popular sentiment toward the United States. Their voices were invariably silenced in conformity with the order issued from Washington that all American officials, both military and civilian, were to "get along with the British." Before long this order was interpreted to mean that British policy directives were to be blindly obeyed, whatever the effect on long-range American interests.

During the time which elapsed between the occupation of Rome and the final surrender of the German armies, there was only one high-ranking American official who was able stoutly to maintain his position of entire independence as an American representative. By his vision and courage, he not only made it possible to relieve the sufferings of many of the people but likewise preserved for the United States a measure of recognition and of respect on the part of Italian public opinion which otherwise would have been lost.

That figure was Myron Taylor, the President's personal representative to the Holy See. To him was due the establishment of "American Relief for Italy," which, financed by private contributions in the United States, was able, notwithstanding persistent British opposition to ship considerable quantities of relief supplies to Italy. To him also was due the prompt re-establishment, with the support of the American Red Cross, of the Italian Red Cross, which was able to obtain some assistance also from the Italian government and from the Vatican.

Later the relief coming from UNRRA was on a scale vastly greater than that possible to the other two organizations. But the efforts of "American Relief for Italy" and of the Italian Red Cross, undertaken as they were before UNRRA had time to set up any effective organization, provided hope and succor at a moment when the Italian people saw but little light on the horizon. The Italians will not forget the work which those two agencies accomplished at that time, and the evidence which they then were able to give of the desire of the American people to be of help. Their activities have helped to erase many of the sorry impressions created by the deficiencies in the official policy of the Allies in Italy.

In essence, the policy pursued by the Allied Control Council from the first day of the invasion of Sicily to the present time constitutes a record which is shocking in its sterility as well as in the prejudicial effect which it is bound to have upon future relations between the American and Italian peoples.

The paradoxical feature of the situation is that, while the United States has exercised no control over policy, it provided by far the major part of the military effort required in the occupation of Italy. It has contributed almost the entire amount of the relief supplies which have been distributed to the Italian people. Yet the United States, in the minds of most Italians, shares the blame for the mistakes in policy which have been made and for the resentment instilled in the hearts of a people who were generally opposed to the war, and who looked to the American armies as true forces of liberation.

To avoid similar results in other regions where the United States shares the responsibilities of military occupation, it is essential that the American public obtain a true picture of the Italian operation so that it may comprehend how no United States policy, no matter how enlightened and intelligent, could have been enforced under the administrative setup agreed upon for Italy.

The Allied Control Council was originally headed by Major General Joyce of the United States Army, at which time the Allied Military Government was headed by Major General Lord Rennell of Rodd of the British Army. There was no connection between the two organizations. There was unanimous agreement on the part of the original authorities, British as well as American, that the two agencies should continue as separate entities. Yet when Lieutenant General Sir Mason MacFarlane replaced General Joyce as head of the Allied Control Council, he first succeeded in removing Lord Rennell from his position as head of the Allied Military Government, and then obtained the consent of General Sir

Henry Maitland Wilson, who had succeeded General Eisenhower as Commander-in-Chief in the Italian theater, to a merger of the two organizations under his own control.

The new agency then established was technically known as ACC-AMG.

While in the Allied Military Government as originally constituted there was a great preponderance of British officers of senior rank, in the new establishment the preponderance was even greater. Twenty-two subcommissions were set up, of which eighteen were headed by British, and only four, and these of minor importance, by American officers. On the British side a lieutenant general, three major generals, and eleven brigadiers were appointed. At headquarters the senior American officer was a colonel.

Those of the American officers who were not by temperament inclined to be subservient to the British officers with whom they were associated found themselves pushed into the background. They were not consulted when important decisions were made. They were invariably appointed to unimportant assignments; while all important assignments went to their British colleagues. Among the American officers who retained any feeling of independent responsibility, it became a common saying that the Americans were permitted to furnish the money, supplies and transportation equipment for the use of the Allied Control Council, while the British limited themselves to issuing the orders and to furnishing the administrative personnel.

As soon as Lieutenant General Sir Mason MacFarlane had replaced Major General Joyce as administrative head of the Allied Control Council, and had amalgamated the two agencies, he created for himself the title of chief commissioner. Immediately below him came the heads of the twenty-two subcommissions. The person actually in charge of the direct management of the administration of the Allied Military Government was Brigadier Morris Stanley Lush of the British Army, who was responsible solely to Lieutenant General MacFarlane.

Brigadier Lush was a professional civil servant who had had some experience in colonial administration in Africa, and who had seen service in the First World War. He was highly ambitious. He was equally shrewd. He assumed the actual control of Allied policy. He also succeeded in a very brief time indeed in increasing the friction between the American and British officers.

It was solely by chance that, when Lieutenant General Mac-Farlane was suddenly taken ill and compelled to return to Great Britain, the senior vice-president of the organization was an American officer. This was Captain (now Admiral) Ellery Stone of the United States Naval Reserve. Admiral Stone has since served as acting chief commissioner. However, the administrative setup created by Brigadier Lush, under General MacFarlane, had become firmly established, and Admiral Stone did nothing to change it.

Brigadier Lush had himself appointed chief of staff. All administrative papers were routed through his office. All subordinate officers, particularly American officers, have usually been prevented from seeing Admiral Stone or even from talking to him by telephone. He has remained a figurehead.

It would be possible to cite innumerable instances of petty ways in which the British officers in ACC sought to dominate their American colleagues. Once the administrative setup, bad as it was, had been agreed upon, the United States should at least have appointed to the Allied Control Council a senior American general officer, capable of interpreting American policy and of insisting that the essentials of that policy be carried out. What actually happened was that the only American officers permitted by the British to take any part in the organization were either professionals of weak character who were readily dominated, or men from civil life unable to stand up for their country's interests in discussions at the Anglo-American military gatherings.

If the Allied Military Government had remained divorced from the Allied Control Council, the ultimate results might have been better. The basic reason for the creation of the Allied Military Government was sound. The intention was that it should take all the burden of civil government, after the occupation of Italy, from the shoulders of the military commanders so that the latter might devote themselves exclusively to the military campaign. But when the Allied Control Council was unable to provide the

Allied Military Government with the food supplies and transportation so desperately needed by the civilian population, the resulting disorders inevitably put serious obstacles in the way of the military effort.

There existed from the outset a basic cleavage of opinion between British and American officials upon the policy to be adopted toward the Italian people. The American attitude, which accurately reflected American policy insofar as a policy existed, was that the Italian people should be treated with kindness and with humanity. The British attitude reflected accurately the lines laid down by Mr. Churchill in his public addresses. It was not only unforgiving; it was punitive. The British point of view prevailed for the reasons I have indicated, and the interests of the United States have suffered accordingly.

An American businessman, who had been responsible for the creation of one of the largest and most successful industrial enterprises of the United States, and who visited Italy during this period, said to me upon his return:

"As a nation we are proud, and we have reason to be proud, of our capacity for establishing great private businesses which function with model efficiency. We also take pride in the executive and administrative ability of the average American. After looking at the administrative machine which our Government has helped to set up in Italy I am humiliated. It is a disgrace to the United States. The most inefficient country of Europe would be ashamed of it. We have everything needed to make it function in our own interest, and in the best interest of the Italians. So far, notwithstanding all we have put into it, it has done just the contrary."

The Allied Control Council failed to achieve any of the objectives for which the United States agreed to create it. It failed in its handling of political affairs. It failed to provide anything near the amount of food necessary to feed the millions of Italians who were hungry and destitute after the Allied occupation of Rome. It failed to obtain sufficient means of transportation to distribute such food as was available.

The results could not be better summarized than by *Time*

Magazine, when it termed the Allied Control Council "a bumbling Anglo-United States bureaucracy superimposed upon the Italians; composed of four-fifths British brains and four-fifths American supplies—and neither is adequate."

The Italian people, and in particular their leaders, saw only one hope: and that hope lay in an early conclusion of peace.

The failure of the Allied governments to publish the armistice terms gave rise to a hundred conjectures. Their reluctance to agree to publication was due to their fear that the onerous terms, if known, might, by increasing Italian resentment, make the task of the Allied military commanders more difficult. The result showed that these tactics were shortsighted. Italian suspicions, fed by the secrecy maintained and the exaggerated reports which consequently sprang up, were far more harmful in their effect than the resentment would have been if the actual terms had been published after the occupation of Rome. Successive Italian governments urged that the terms be made known. But publication was not permitted until the summer of 1945, long after the war in Europe had ended.

And in the meantime, the hopes of the Italian people for an early peace treaty were repeatedly shattered. The Bonomi Cabinet, the Parri Cabinet, and the de Gasperi Cabinet urged that some recognition be shown the special status of Italy by the negotiation of a separate peace treaty.

At the Potsdam Conference it was announced that consideration would be given to the prompt conclusion of a treaty with Italy. The Soviet, British and American governments declared that the negotiation of such a treaty would be given priority at the meeting of the Council of Foreign Ministers the following September. Failure at London once more postponed to some indefinite future the termination of the increasingly instable situation of the Italian people. After the Moscow meeting of December, 1945, it was again announced that the Italian treaty would be dealt with at the promised peace conference to be held in Paris six months later.

In the meantime, the Italian people were rent with controversies arising from the reports, ever more frequently circulated, of the real intentions of the major Allies.

Reparations was one of the chief problems. The American and British governments announced that, in view of the armistice provisions, they would seek no monetary reparations from Italy. The Soviet government, on the contrary, announced its intention of demanding six hundred million dollars, later scaled down to a sixth of that amount. The government of Tito declared that Yugoslavia would exact the astronomical sum of more than two billions of dollars. The Greek government, representing the people who suffered most from the Fascist régime, and who were most entitled to demand fair reparations from Italy, was at first discouraged from setting any figure, and only later permitted to announce the large figure which it considered just.

But it was with regard to its frontiers and its territorial possessions that Italy faced its gravest uncertainties. Shortly after the collapse of Germany, the Yugoslav régime of Marshal Tito, openly supported by the Soviet government, announced its intention of claiming not only all of Venezia Giulia and the Istrian Peninsula, but the city of Trieste as well. For a brief period Yugoslav forces actually occupied that historic city. Only after a grave crisis, were the Yugoslav troops withdrawn and the city occupied by British and American contingents. Istria was then divided along the Morgan line, drawn by the Western powers in accordance with military consideration. The western half, inhabited predominantly by Italians, was occupied by the forces of the Western powers. The eastern section, where Yugoslavs were in a majority, was occupied by Tito's armies. For many months the opposing forces faced each other across a narrow "no man's land."

In Italy, the demand arose on all sides for assurance that under no circumstances would Trieste be wrested from her.

The bitter feeling was increased by the early declarations made by Italian Communists that the Italian people should gladly cede Trieste and the whole of Istria to their "democratic" friends in Yugoslavia, as a sign that they possessed a "broad, rather than a narrow, outlook." This odd appeal that the Italians blithely renounce a region which for generations had been the symbol of the *risorgimento*, and where half a million Italians lived, was met by street riots and by denunciation from even the most liberal quarters. Before long the Communists changed their tune. Even then, however, they limited themselves to admitting merely that "Trieste was undoubtedly an Italian city."

To the impartial observer, the difference between the fair claims of the southern Slavs in 1919 and the flamboyant and mendacious pretensions in 1945 of the cohorts of Marshal Tito was notable. At the conclusion of the First World War, the spokesmen for the Yugoslavs had been Messrs. Trumbitch and Pashitch. It would have been difficult to find two more diverse personalities than the dour and patriarchal Pashitch and the jovial and ebullient Trumbitch. But they possessed one opinion in common. They both recognized that if the new Yugoslav state was to be secure, its frontiers must not create lasting resentment between the southern Slavs and the Italians. They also had an accurate perception of the imperative need of the Serbs, Croats and Slovenes for future stability in eastern Europe.

Marshal Tito and his associates have been held back by no such considerations of realistic statesmanship. To them the sky is the limit.

And behind Tito stands the Kremlin. So far the Soviet government has shown itself determined to dominate the Balkans, and in particular to secure by means of its satellite state of Yugoslavia entrance to the Adriatic through the port of Trieste.

There is a diverting account of a conversation which took place recently between an exceedingly influential Senator—who has had much to do with problems of foreign policy—and a prominent Italian official. The latter urged that the United States must in its own interest, in the interest of world peace, as well as on the ground of principle, refuse to permit Trieste to be severed from Italy. The Senator remarked that he simply could not understand why the Italians were so upset about Trieste. It seemed to him a very insignificant matter. "Why," he said, "Trieste only twenty-seven years ago was an Austrian city. What real difference does it make if you now lose it?" When the Italian replied that apart from the broader questions of policy involved, Trieste was a city of Italians, and that the Senator might have forgotten that not so long ago—in 1866 to be precise—Venice had also been under Austrian rule, the Senator expressed the opinion that the Italian was mistaken, for he was sure that Venice had been continuously under the Italian flag for many centuries!

It has in fact been surprising how the American press has belittled the issue of Trieste; it has regarded the question as one whose intrinsic importance would never justify any impasse in the peace negotiations if the Soviet Union continued to demand the cession of the city to Yugoslavia.

Yet Trieste has become the last free outlet for the trade of Austria and of the smaller countries of eastern Europe such as Czechoslovakia. The control of Trieste by the Soviet Union would seal their doom as independent nations.

If the pernicious compromise providing for international control of Trieste to which the United States agreed in Paris in the summer of 1946 is maintained, it will mean that Russia will find the way through her participation in the control government not only to dominate the former Italian naval base of Pola, now to be turned over to Yugoslavia by this compromise, but also the shipyards of Monfalcone, where the greatest shipbuilding facilities in the whole of the Mediterranean are located. For this great Italian industry is dependent for its operation on power plants located in territory now to be transferred to Yugoslavia. It will imply Russian control of the Adriatic, and the beginning of Russian domination of all the eastern Mediterranean.

Unless Trieste and the Italian populated areas of Istria and of the rest of Venezia Giulia remain under the Italian flag, not only will a new Alsace-Lorraine problem arise to plague Europe, but the possibility of building up a free and peaceful Europe will be gravely diminished.

The Italians since the beginning of the century have feared Russia's entrance into the eastern Mediterranean. The possibility that she may now dominate their own Italian city of Trieste has become a nightmare. The disastrous decision of the Foreign Ministers at Paris to cede the Italian areas of Briga and Tenda to

France pales into insignificance in comparison with the portentous nature of their decision with regard to Trieste.

The policy of the Soviet Union regarding Trieste, as well as her original insistence that Italy be stripped of all of her prewar colonies, and that these be placed under Russian administration, created widespread popular antagonism throughout Italy. The relatively poor showing made by the Communists when national elections were at last held may be in part attributed to this fact.

Italy has been usually a poor colonizer. Probably only a nationalistic dictatorship, such as the Fascist régime, would consider the retention of such remote provinces as Italian Somaliland and Eritrea a vital issue. But the two near-by North African territories of Cirenaica and Tripolitania, more generally known as Libya, fall into a different category. The Italian government, after Italy's liberation, undoubtedly voiced the belief of the Italian people when it asserted that Cirenaica and Tripolitania should not be regarded as colonies but rather as integral parts of Italian territory, as Algeria is considered a part of metropolitan France.

In a total population of seven hundred thousand in Libya, one hundred and twenty thousand are Italians. These form an integral part of a mixed population which includes Jews, Arabs, Berbers and Negroes. These North African territories were acquired by Italy long before the establishment of the Fascist régime. They have become to a very considerable extent essential to Italy's national economy. Furthermore, successive Italian governments had invested very considerable sums in their development. Trade with the Italian homeland was continually increasing. Except by the Senussis of Cirenaica, there had been no charges that the Italian administrators were dealing unjustly with the native population.

The official position was thus stated by the Italian government:

The title deeds to the acquisitions were legal in all respects from the international standpoint, and at home the will of the majority, repeatedly and freely expressed in Parliament, showed that they had the approval of a majority of the country.

The consent and encouragement given by leading European powers to this expansion of Italy in Africa were also the recognition of an essential need arising from the steady growth of her population. These reasons still continue to exist and will no less unavoidably exist tomorrow.

The United States had at first intended to agree, as the Italian government desired, that Libya should continue to be administered by Italy after the conclusion of a peace treaty, subject to the authority of the International Trusteeship Council of the United Nations.

It was the Soviet government which blocked this solution, at the London meeting on September of 1945. The Soviet government not only demanded that Italy be permanently deprived of these territories as well as of the territories of Eritrea and Somaliland, but also that the Soviet Union be designated the sole administrator for Libya and for Eritrea. The British government favored British administration of Eritrea and Somaliland, with Libya to be placed under the direct control of the International Trusteeship Council, and immediate independence for Cirenaica—this last proposal being due to the wartime commitment made by the British government to the Senussi chieftains that their country would not be returned to Italian control. France supported continued Italian administration of all the colonies.

During the succeeding months the position of all the major powers, except for France, on the disposition of the Italian colonies changed repeatedly. And at the Paris meeting of the Foreign Ministers in June, 1946, they at length agreed to put off any final decision for a year, thus leaving the issue to become a football of Italian politics and a constant incentive to exaggerated nationalism in Italy.

The story of the intervening months offers an opportunity to form an illuminating estimate of the consistency and firmness of principle of the major powers. The United States had modified its original position. But the Soviet Union had so changed its own original position that at the end of a series of conferences it warmly espoused the very proposals that the United States had at first offered, and that the Russian delegation had at that time so vigorously combated.

From the standpoint of common sense, and with a due regard

for the best interests of the native populations in these four Italian colonies, the ideal solution would unquestionably be a direct administration of Eritrea and of Italian Somaliland by the International Trusteeship Council, and the administration of Libya by Italy under the supervision of the International Trusteeship Council until the inhabitants are prepared for independence.

To the many people in the United States and to the even larger number in Great Britain who have believed that the Italians were a decadent people, incapable of understanding and much less of practicing democracy, the events of the spring of 1946 must have proved surprising. In the national elections of June 2 the vote for the abolition of the monarchy carried by twelve million to ten million. The Christian Democrat party, which polled the largest vote, gained two hundred and seven seats in the Constituent Assembly. The Socialists and the Communists together elected only two hundred and twenty delegates, with the Communists obtaining a popular vote of only a little over three million. The Socialists made a far better showing. But the significance of the elections was enhanced by the fact that some of the smaller parties, like the Liberals and the Republicans, gained enough seats in the Assembly to assure an absolute majority of the purely democratic parties when the constitution was finally adopted. Communism thus was proved to have made little headway. The Italian electorate, with women voting for the first time, had demonstrated its determination to adhere to the principles of liberal democracy.

The Assembly elected as Provisional President of the first Italian Republic Enrico de Nicola, of Naples, Italy's foremost constitutional lawyer. Already sixty-eight years of age, he had held public office during the pre-Fascist period, but had firmly refused to accept any post under Mussolini. It is not yet widely known that it was Dr. de Nicola, as a private citizen, who personally directed the negotiations that led up to the abdication of Victor Emmanuel III, and that thus made possible the installation of a popular government, since the democratic party leaders would have refused to serve so long as the King remained upon the throne.

The fall of the House of Savoy marks the end of the initial

period of the modern history of Italy. The constitutional monarchy would have remained as an institution had it not been for the blind obstinacy of the old King and of his son, Umberto.

In the summer of 1943 the leaders of the democratic and resistance groups had negotiated at Brindisi, through spokesmen whom they had selected, with Marshal Badoglio. The marshal was then heading the Cabinet appointed by the King, after the downfall of Mussolini, to negotiate the Armistice.

The democratic spokesmen pointed out that both the King and the Prince of Piedmont must share in the responsibility for Italy's tragedy. They could not obtain popular support if they remained in the Quirinal. But the young son of the Prince was not so tarred with obloquy, and the democratic parties agreed to support the House of Savoy provided the King and his son both abdicated and a regency was established under Marshal Badoglio until the young Prince attained his majority.

The marshal agreed wholeheartedly to this suggestion. A devoted monarchist, he saw in this solution the one assurance of a continuation of the House of Savoy. He at once communicated with the King, urging his consent to the proposal. The reply was abrupt. Not only would the King refuse to abdicate, but he accused Badoglio of disloyalty and of seeking to advance his own interests at the expense of the Crown.

Thus, because of the stupidity of Victor Emmanuel III, the little-lamented royal family—whose predecessors had been so truly beloved by the Italians for the part they had played in the unification and liberation of Italy—fled into exile.

There can be no question the influence of the Vatican and of the Pope himself are far stronger in Italy than they have been for many decades. The fall of the Fascist régime, after its persistent efforts to undermine the standing of the Vatican with the Italian people, has added to the prestige of the Holy See. The courageous resistance to the German invaders and to the Fascist gangsters so often demonstrated by the parish priests, as well as by some of the Italian hierarchy, added to the moral strength of the church. Finally, the stalwart position maintained by the Supreme Pontiff himself, and the realization of the Italian populace that it was owing primarily to the Pope's own efforts that the Holy City had been saved from destruction, greatly enhanced his popularity and influence.

In the political crystallization which took place after the end of the war, these facts assumed practical importance. The constantly increasing strength shown by the Christian Democrat party cannot be regarded as a phenomenon altogether divorced from renewed popular confidence in the church.

I have undertaken this somewhat detailed analysis of the Italian scene in recent times because it offers not only a typical example of the trends in western Europe in the immediate post-war period, but likewise an indication of the salient aspects of the American approach to the problem of European reconstruction.

To further the legitimate interests of the American people, the United States should have adopted a policy consistently designed to hasten the political and economic reconstruction of Italy, so that the Italian people might as rapidly as possible become again a constructive and democratic factor in the European community of nations. The advance that the Italian people have made has been achieved in spite of, and not because of, American policy.

The United States has permitted Great Britain to lay down the course to be followed in Italy. We have far too often supinely followed. We have rarely led. Instead of helping the Italian people to rebuild a free, progressive and democratic Italy, we have risked her political, economic and social collapse. Only by the unaided efforts of the Italians themselves has that collapse been averted.

The story of what has taken place in eastern Europe and in the Balkans since Germany's defeat constitutes a tragic record of human misery. It is all the more tragic because it was made possible only by the incapacity of the statesmen of the Western powers. The pattern was drawn as a result of the failure of the United States to insist that the peace settlements throughout Europe should be agreed upon before the end of the war and that a provisional agency of all the United Nations should execute these agreements from the first moment after Germany's surrender. Had that been done, all the United Nations, and not the

Soviet Union alone, would have had the means as well as the authority to insure the return of free democratic government to the peoples of Poland, Austria, Hungary and the Balkans.

Had that been done, the incentive for Soviet expansion would have been far less, the grounds for controversy between the East and the West would have been much smaller. The iron curtain which shrouds eastern Europe would not have been raised. The foundations for a free order in Europe would already be under construction. The peoples of Europe would have seen adjustment after adjustment being made in accordance with a fair and constructive plan prepared beforehand by the spokesmen for the United Nations. All they see today is a welter of conflict, of cruelty and of confusion.

The explanation for what is now taking place is to be found in part in the understanding reached between Generalissimo Stalin and Mr. Churchill during their first stormy meeting in Moscow. Great Britain recognized the predominant interest of the Soviet Union in Poland, Czechoslovakia, Hungary, Rumania, Yugoslavia and Bulgaria. Reciprocally, the Soviet Union recognized the predominant interest of Great Britain in Greece. Both powers agreed to refrain from undertaking unilaterally to control Austria.

It was subsequent to this understanding that Mr. Churchill threw Great Britain's support in Yugoslavia to Tito and his Partisans, and permitted General Mihailovitch and the Chetniks to go to the wall. There is no question that the Churchill Cabinet believed that this maneuver would ultimately preserve British influence in Yugoslavia and thus prevent any Russian domination of the eastern shore of the Adriatic, even after the Combined Chiefs of Staff, over Mr. Churchill's violent opposition, had abandoned all idea of invading Europe through the Balkans.

It was a foolish gamble on the part of the British since Tito was wholly under Soviet control. Necessarily, it failed. It represents what is probably Mr. Churchill's greatest mistake in political tactics during the period he served as Prime Minister.

The agreements reached were tacitly accepted by the United States at Moscow in October, 1943, and at the Teheran Conference in the following month. They were, of course, recognized at the conference at Yalta in 1945.

At Yalta, President Roosevelt obtained the Three Power commitment that the peoples of eastern Europe would be guaranteed free elections and representative government. This was the one means by which the harm already done could have been rectified. Had this pledge been carried out, the evils of the moment and those which the future holds, could have been avoided. The good faith of the United States was at stake. But at Moscow in December, 1945, the word of the United States and the rights of the eastern European peoples were both disregarded by Secretary Byrnes in his search for appeasement.

The Churchill-Stalin understanding was tantamount to the recognition by the two Western powers of the right of the Soviet Union to establish its influence over independent peoples who had been recognized by the Treaty of Versailles as entitled to an untrammeled sovereign freedom. It established a precedent for a world order based upon a system of continental spheres of influence, each dominated respectively by one great military power, rather than for a new order founded upon law and justice, and upon the principle of the equality of sovereignty of all states, great or small.

It has been claimed that this understanding was no more than the admission by the Western powers of Russia's right to safeguard her future security by preventing these smaller countries from again becoming, as they had so often in the past, a springboard for aggression against her by some other major power.

It would patently be impossible for any peaceful world order to be established if the community of nations were to permit these smaller and generally turbulent countries of eastern Europe to be controlled by governments hostile to the Soviet Union and used as pawns against her. Russia had the undoubted right, as an outcome of the victory which she had done so much to win, to demand that the peace settlements, and the new international organization to which she was already pledged, should provide her with adequate guaranties against any repetition of the aggressions she had so often suffered in the past. It cannot be too often reiterated

that there can be no lasting world peace until Russia obtains legitimate security.

But security is one thing, and imperialistic expansion is another. The safety of the Soviet Union in Europe would be last-
ingly assured by the establishment of free and democratic governments in all the countries of eastern Europe, and by the
gradually increasing living standards of their people. But neither
the safety of the Soviet Union nor the safety of the peoples of
western Europe can be assured through the imposition of Russian
control over many millions of people who will not long submit to
any form of alien domination. The history of the Serbs, the
Poles, the Magyars and the Czechs makes this only too clear.

Except in Poland, the course followed by the Soviet Union in
the countries which she occupied was everywhere much the same.
As soon as the German troops had been driven out or captured,
the Russian armies took over entire control of every activity.
A rigorous and all-embracing blackout of all information about
what then took place was immediately imposed. It continued for a
protracted period. As soon as this obscurity began to lessen
slightly the same phenomena were in each case apparent. A general
liquidation had taken place, not only of the Fascists and their
puppets, but also of most of the leaders of the political parties
known to be unwilling to serve the ends of Communism. Control
of all key positions in the Army and the police, in finance and
industry, in agriculture, and in communications and the press had
been placed—subject, of course, to the control of the Soviet military authorities—in the hands of local Communists. *De facto*
régimes, termed "purely democratic," had been set up. These were
composed of members of the Communist party or of its affiliates.

In Bulgaria the liquidation in terms of human life was far more
considerable than in Rumania. But in Rumania, partly because of
the greater measure of industrialization in that nation's economy,
the dispersal of property and the distribution of lands was far more
considerable than in Bulgaria where the greater part of the agricultural area had long been owned by the small farmers and
peasants.

Propaganda blared out every day that the iron dictatorship of

a small minority was "true democracy." Yet every informed
European knew that a great majority of the people in the Balkans
and in eastern Europe was unalterably opposed to Communism
and that even to such leaders of proletariat parties, as Maniu, the
chief of the Rumanian Peasant party, and George Dimitroff, the
head of the Bulgarian Agrarian party, the tenets of Communism
were anathema.

When the doors were at last slightly opened, and American
press correspondents and official agents of the United States
were permitted entry, except for those who were notoriously subject to Soviet influence, none were able to report the slightest
ground for hope that either those free elections or those democratic and representative governments promised in the Declaration
of Yalta would be forthcoming.

In Yugoslavia the story is essentially the same. After the
original agreement between Mr. Churchill and Generalissimo
Stalin the British government forced the royal Yugoslav government-in-exile, then established in London, to accept Marshal Tito
as its official delegate in Yugoslavia. The so-called coalition
Cabinet, established as the result of British pressure, dominated
from the outset by Communist elements, soon eliminated the Liberal elements which had passed over to it from the government-
in-exile. The next steps were inevitable. Under Communist
auspices a new constitution was established, the Crown was
abolished, and a Yugoslav Republic was proclaimed. The new
government, with Marshal Tito as its head, operated from the
outset as a facade for an administrative oligarchy directed from
Moscow.

The utter prostration resulting from Fascist and Nazi devastation, as well as from the desperate civil war which ravaged every
part of Serbia, Slovenia and Croatia has as yet prevented any
overt evidence of popular resistance. It is also unquestionable
that the Tito government has far more popular support than
have the governments installed in the other occupied countries.
Yet I believe that, unless the Soviet government intends to force
Yugoslavia into a closely integrated Sovietized structure and eventually to liquidate great numbers of the population, the régime

now set up cannot last long. If there is any people of Europe who have repeatedly proved their unwillingness to submit to foreign rule and their capacity to overthrow alien domination, it is the Serbs.

We too often think of Yugoslavia as a homogeneous entity. It is of course anything but this. During the years between the great wars the Serbs dominated the Croats and the Slovenes and neither of these had secured any real measure of local autonomy when the Second World War broke out. The federated kingdom barely existed except in name. The bitterness was so great that large numbers of the Croatian and Slovenian people refused to lift a finger to help the Serb-dominated government of General Simovitch resist the German invasion. It was only with great reluctance that the Croatian leader, Machek, agreed to take part in that government. General Mihailovitch was a Serb. It was he who led the only forces of resistance to the Axis until after the German invasion of Russia and the creation, with Soviet support, of Tito's Partisan bands. The later war between the Chetniks and the Partisans, the capture of Mihailovitch, his so-called trial and his liquidation, were all due to the fact that Mihailovitch was first of all a Serb, as well as a strong monarchist and a violent anti-Communist. Tito's supporters were mainly Croats and Slovenes. It is upon their support—and not upon Serb support—that the present Yugoslav régime is based.

The inner working of this régime is typical of all the governments of the Soviet-dominated countries from Poland through to Bulgaria. The efficiency of the system is remarkable. It is worthy of a detailed analysis because it has already become standard throughout the region which the Soviet Union claims as her sphere of influence.

Nominally, Yugoslavia has become a federation consisting of six peoples' republics. Each of the six republics is granted cultural autonomy. Diversity in culture and in language is officially encouraged but no such autonomy is dreamed of in the realm of politics. Under none of the dictatorships which existed in Yugoslavia from time to time before the Second World War were the different peoples of Yugoslavia governed by a more centralized

régime. Never before have they been compelled to be so subservient to a single center in Belgrade as they are to that which
exists today.

The nominal government of Yugoslavia does not govern. The
so-called National Front, comprising nearly a dozen political
parties, does not undertake the political direction of the country.
The real government of Yugoslavia is vested in the seven-man
executive committee of the Communist party which in turn takes
its orders directly from Moscow. The political parties which make
up the National Front have less than ten per cent of the representation in Parliament. Their identity is submerged in an organization
directed exclusively by the Communists.

No legal opposition exists. The last non-government newspaper
—which aptly enough was named *Democracy*—was suppressed
just before the so-called general elections of November, 1945.

The Communist party controls all the political activity
sponsored by the National Front as well as the so-called "mass
organizations" like the Women's Anti-Fascist League, the Anti-
Fascist Youth, the United Syndicates, and the Alliance of Co-
operatives. These organizations include every citizen of Yugoslavia. They are subdivided into national, regional, district,
county, municipal, ward, block, street and even apartment units
and every one of these thousands of units is headed by an administrative "activist." It is the activists who have the power
to confer or annul such vital necessities as ration cards and identity
papers.

The Yugoslav Army has been completely reorganized. All officers have been named by the Communist party.

The government has decreed regulations which insure stereotyped popular unity. This unity is enforced by many agencies,
but in particular by the recently established secret police known
as OZNA—"The Section of People's Security"— which has, of
course, been established on the model of the Soviet NKVD.

An auxiliary agency has been created in a system of public
attorneys, officially termed "The Eyes and Ears of the Government." These agents are distributed through every government
agency, factory or public organization. It is their duty to report

all citizens who express any opinions in opposition to the government.

Can it be cause for surprise, in view of these controls, that Tito's government claimed an eighty-nine per cent victory in an election in which no opposition was represented?

The Communist system of economic controls, however, has proved to be even more effective than the police and political controls in bringing about an enforced unity. The economic controls have made the Yugoslavs entirely dependent upon the government for their means of livelihood. A form of state socialism quite as thorough as that which has been developed in the Soviet Union has been introduced in Yugoslavia. While the constitution of January, 1946, theoretically recognizes the right of private property, this right is so restricted and so subject to rigid state control that today it exists only in theory.

The Tito government inherited from the prewar governments a monopoly over railroads, mining, salt, matches, tobacco and other products. It has further enlarged the economic activities of the government by resorting to the direct confiscation of land and industries either on the grounds that the former owners were "pro-Fascists" or war profiteers. Over a million acres of land have already been confiscated, half of which has been kept by the government and the other half distributed to Partisan followers of Tito. A portion of this land, it is true, had belonged to the German minority in Yugoslavia.

All transportation is in government hands, including not only the merchant marine, but even privately owned automobiles.

Only government-sponsored banks do any business.

Industry is being steadily nationalized. One hundred per cent of the metal industry and fifty per cent of the food industry in Serbia has been expropriated and is now being operated by the government. A few of the former owners have remained on as employees in their own factories, but most of them have either fled or been liquidated by "Courts of National Honor." The once exceedingly influential class of businessmen has been obliterated. The white-collar employees and industrial workers are today entirely dependent on the state as their sole possible employer.

The Tito government has now established chain stores throughout the country.

The objectives set forth in the constitution of 1946, namely, government nationalization of industry and ownership by government-sponsored co-operatives as the mainstays of the state, have very nearly been achieved. The entire population, except for the peasants, has been relegated to the status of a proletariat dependent for its living upon the government. The peasants themselves, long the most truly independent factor in the political structure of Yugoslavia, are being subjected to an increasing number of government controls. They are now being told precisely what and how much to plant as well as where and how to plant. They are forced to produce so much government-obtained seed and are heavily fined if they fail. They are compelled to sell their wheat only to the government at government prices. The once highly individualistic Yugoslav peasant today enjoys the doubtful privilege of serving as a state agent on his own land. There is no escape for him from the meshes in which he is caught—agrarian reform laws, farm co-operatives, seed procurement, government tractor stations and ceiling prices. Over and above this entire intricate system of economic controls and political unification is the all-powerful Federal Planning Commission which is the direct tool of the Soviet government.

It is not without interest that UNRRA has directly contributed to this program of state socialism. UNRRA has supplied for relief purposes 2,500 tractors and 11,000 American trucks. With this equipment, the Yugoslav government can wield complete control over all agricultural production in the country.

Foreign trade is a tight monopoly of the government. If an American businessman, for example, wishes to have any dealings in the Yugoslav market he can do so only with the direct authorization of the Yugoslav Foreign Trade Ministry. All foreign concessions in Yugoslavia have already been abrogated.

During the years immediately following the end of the First World War, Yugoslavia relied primarily on France and Great

Britain in its financial and economic life. During the years immediately preceding the Second World War she was reluctantly but of necessity forced to depend upon the Axis powers. Since the war, she has been compelled to become an integral part of the Soviet system, to cut all her former financial and economic ties with the West, and to orient her entire economic life to the Soviet Union. The people of Yugoslavia today are as much under the Soviet political and economic system as if they had become an integral part of the Union of Soviet Socialist Republics. The same condition very largely obtains in Poland, in Rumania, in Albania, and in Bulgaria, and the tide in Hungary seems to be moving inexorably in the same direction.

The recent history of Greece presents the outstanding example of the reverse side of the picture resulting from the failure of the United Nations to create before the war's end some provisional political agency representative of all the Allied powers. As has been shown, the Churchill-Stalin understanding provided that, in return for British acquiescence in the predominance of Soviet influence east of the Stettin-Trieste line, the Soviet Union would recognize the supremacy of British interests in Greece. The British part of the bargain was generally observed. Observance by the Soviet Union of its share of the compact was purely nominal. Soviet support of the Greek extremist coalition, known as the EAM, and its affiliated ELAS bands of armed revolutionaries, has been notorious.

The Greek people deserve recognition from all the Allied powers for the valiant help they rendered to the Allied cause. The war left their country prostrate. But since the end of the war the Greeks have been forced to endure a constant clash between the monarchists, the middle-of-the-road Republicans, and the extremists of the left wing. Greece has been suffering what is equivalent to a civil war.

From the first moment of the German evacuation, British troops, dispatched with the consent of the Greek government-in-exile, have endeavored to maintain order, to prevent outrages upon the civilian population, and to put an end to civil strife. Every kind of charge has been leveled from the left against the British occupation. This campaign at length ended with the formal accusation brought by the Soviet government at the meeting of the Security Council of the UN in February of 1946. Moscow declared that the continued presence of British troops in Greece constituted a menace to world peace. This charge was later permitted to lapse.

Under the conditions that have obtained since the German armistice, Greece has become a testing ground of the relative strength of Great Britain and of the Soviet Union in the Middle East. For effective Soviet domination of the Balkan Peninsula, as well as control over the Dardanelles would be impeded if the Greek people were able to set up a government that would maintain the traditional relationship between Greece and the West. Only Soviet control of Trieste could eliminate the difficulties so created.

The constant effort of Russian propaganda to force the withdrawal of British troops from Greece before the elections were held, and the Russian refusal to participate in Allied supervision of the elections as a means of bringing about the withdrawal of the other major powers from any part in their supervision, can only have been intended to promote an open warfare in which the far more cohesive, better disciplined, and better financed elements of the leftist minority would have had a good chance of gaining supremacy. However, when the Western powers stood firm, and free elections were held, the Communist-inspired coalition admitted its weakness by refusing to participate.

The crimes and excesses of one kind or another which have been perpetrated in Greece during the period of British occupation have mounted steadily. Some of them are unquestionably due to the right. But objective observers, even those who are sympathetic to left ideology, have been compelled to admit that by far the major portion of the crimes are due to left wing elements. Throughout Greece, outside of the large cities, armed bands have continued to terrorize the civilian population and even the local authorities. In the north the ELAS revolutionaries have received assistance from the Macedonian autonomists as well as from the Communists in Albania.

Under such conditions the appointment of a regent in the person of Archbishop Damaskinos, the temporary withdrawal of the King until a plebiscite can be held, and the election of a monarchist-inclined government have naturally done little to encourage stability or to put an end to what is close to internal chaos. It may readily be admitted that the British have carried out their responsibilities with little finesse, and that the action of the British military forces has often lent color to the charges of their undue partiality for the Conservative parties.

Until some global settlement has been reached between the Kremlin and the major powers of the West, there can be no solution of the dilemma which will make it possible for the Greek people to begin the task of establishing political and economic stability.

To the observer of European events in the years after the First World War there were few more profoundly interesting contrasts than that offered by the differing courses taken by the two neighboring peoples of Hungary and Czechoslovakia. The Hungarian Magyars are intensely nationalistic. They have enjoyed independence or autonomy for well over a thousand years. Czechoslovakia was a new and an artificial state, composed of widely divergent racial elements between whom there was no natural affinity. Yet the trend in Czechoslovakia, notwithstanding the almost insuperable obstacles arising from the rivalries between Czechs and Slovaks, and Czechs and Sudeten Germans, was steadily toward an advanced and progressive social order. They created one of the truest democracies in Europe. The trend in Hungary, on the other hand, was almost equally steadily backward towards a social order which had long since passed in the rest of Europe.

In Hungary, the regent and the Hungarian governments attempted the impossible task of trying to solve Hungary's basic problems through a policy that retained the essentials of medieval feudalism. It is true that concessions were made to the twentieth century in the form of a thin veneer of political reform. But of concessions to the demands of modern economy there were none. None of the real social or economic ills of the country were squarely faced. The great estates of the Hungarian landlords were left precisely as they had been for many centuries. The system of taxation, notwithstanding the assistance rendered by the highly competent experts appointed by the League of Nations, was not reformed in any fundamental. No effective effort was made to further industrialization. In short, the economy of the country remained largely static. It continued to be the economy of a hard-working but backward agricultural people where the standard of living of all but a small percentage of the population remained pitifully low.

With but few exceptions political leadership was less than medi-ocre. The chief effort of successive Hungarian governments was to arouse public sentiment against the Treaty of 1919 by which Hungarian nationals had been placed under Rumanian sovereignty. The outstanding issue for twenty years was Hungary's territorial claims.

It is quite true that from the standpoint of European stability, the Hungarian people were dealt with both unfairly and unwisely in the peace settlements of 1919. Their economic progress was hampered rather than encouraged by the terms of the peace treat-ies. But with all due allowance for the injustice to which they had been subjected, the record of the Hungarian people between the two world wars was one of almost complete sterility.

When Hitler launched the Second World War, the feeling within Hungary against Nazism and all that it represented was strong. The strenuous efforts of the German government to incul-cate Nazi doctrines in Hungary and to create a vigorous Hun-garian Nazi party had largely failed. So far as the average Hungarian was concerned, there was never at any period in the country's long history any love lost for the Germans. The military and economic pressure brought to bear upon Hungary by the Third German Reich was bitterly resented, for the Hungarians are a valiant and a stubborn people. But fear of Russia and of Com-munism was infinitely greater. That fear was the chief reason for the ignominious and unworthy role which Hungary was forced to play in the war.

With the collapse of the Axis, Hungary was occupied by Rus-sian troops. Then followed the customary protracted blackout. A

Hungarian Republic was proclaimed. Elections were held in which the Communist candidates were overwhelmingly defeated. The Soviet authorities had had insufficient time in which to perfect their customary occupation machinery. But the government then established by the Smallholders' party was compelled to include Communists in key positions, and the democratic party organizations were further obliged to eliminate from their political lists all individuals to whom the Communists objected.

By Soviet direction, even before the present Republican régime was installed, a Russo-Hungarian trade agreement had been concluded which vests virtual control of Hungarian economy in Soviet hands. Under present conditions political developments will automatically depend upon the decisions reached at Moscow. The Hungarian Republic has, however, been officially recognized by the United States and by the other major Western powers.

There can be no question that certain of the results of the Soviet occupation are to the benefit of the masses of the Hungarian people. The great landed proprietors have vanished or been displaced. Their enormous holdings are already being distributed to the peasants and small farmers. Various forms of industry are already being fomented by Russian initiative. But in the wider sense, there can be no reason to anticipate that the steps so far taken will advance the lasting reconstruction of eastern Europe. The Hungarian people throughout their history have made it clear that they will not submit to any Slav overlordship. Their manner of being as well as their religious tradition makes it improbable that they will voluntarily adopt Communism. Unless they are subjected to such a régime of liquidation and of forced emigration as that imposed by the Soviet government upon the Cossacks during the earlier years of the Soviet revolution, there is little likelihood that they will long suffer Russian control. The only way in which the Hungarian people can be encouraged to become a positive, rather than a negative, factor in the structure of eastern Europe is by the rapid conclusion of a peace treaty which is just rather than punitive. Their speedy admission to the United Nations organization, an opportunity for self-determination, and incorporation in an economic federation of eastern

Europe, will prove to be the surest means of promoting their reconciliation with their neighbors, and of securing progress and political stability in their neighborhood.

To any foreign observer who visited both Hungary and Czechoslovakia some years after the close of the First World War, the contrast could only occasion unbounded admiration for the achievements wrought by the Czechoslovak people.

It is too often forgotten that the founders of Czechoslovakia in the initial years of the new republic confronted problems which were far more complicated and far more difficult to solve than those which faced the officials of any other "succession" state. The country was almost incapable of any military defense if a greater Germany were once more permitted to grow up. The nationals of the new republic were Czechs, Slovaks, Ruthenians and Sudeten Germans. It would be difficult to conceive of any collection of races less easy to weld into one truly national whole. Yet the inheritance of the Czechs was not limited to their entrancing land of wooded mountains, of small green farms, of clean and tidy small towns and of thriving local industries. Their heritage also included a passionate desire for freedom and a quality of will which will not be denied.

The leadership in Czechoslovakia was, of course, assumed from the outset by the Czechs. They are a dour, hard-working, intensely patriotic, and stubborn people. But among the convictions that they hold most dear is an unshakable faith in human equality. The republic was founded upon that concept. Much unnecessary pity has been wasted upon the alleged discrimination shown by the Czechs against the Sudeten Germans. From the first days of the republic the latter possessed precisely the same civic rights as those enjoyed by all the other racial groups in Czechoslovakia. It is true that a policy was adopted which prescribed a national language and a national culture for all Czechoslovak citizens in order eventually to bring about a more homogeneous nation. To that end, German was no longer taught in public schools or used for official purposes. But such policies represent neither persecution nor unjust discrimination. Had the Sudeten Germans possessed any loyalty for the new country of which they had become citizens, their abilities, their industrious habits and their many other good qualities would have secured for them an important share in the determination of all national policies. Their loyalties, however, as the months prior to the year 1938 made so tragically clear, were given solely to their country's deadly foe.

Can there be any ground for just criticism of the Czechs because they have demanded the elimination of this cancer in the body politic of Czechoslovakia by the expulsion to German territory of all the Sudetens who betrayed their country to the Nazi invader?

The founders of the Republic of Czechoslovakia in 1919 were Dr. Thomas Masaryk and Dr. Eduard Beneš. To them more than to any others was due the final liberation of the Czech people from Austria. The first President of the republic, Dr. Masaryk, died in 1936. His successor in the Presidency, and his own Foreign Minister, Dr. Beneš, survives. He has again done more than any other Czech to bring about his country's resurrection after its martyrdom in 1939. There has been no European leader between the two world wars who has demonstrated a greater quality of statesmanship.

I was near the German frontier in the early days of September, 1938, just prior to Munich, and I heard over the radio that hysterical diatribe of hate and of rage which Hitler launched against Dr. Beneš to the Reichstag. I can still hear the gross insults leveled, as by a drunkard or a maniac, against that small, composed figure who was the President of the neighboring state. Deserted by France and by England, Dr. Beneš was forced to resign his office a few weeks later. First, he took refuge in the United States where he served as a professor in the University of Chicago. Then, when Great Britain and the United States finally agreed to recognize the Committee of Liberation which had been set up in London as the legitimate government-in-exile of Czechoslovakia, Dr. Beneš became its Provisional President.

I talked with him often in Washington in those years. His faith in Czechoslovakia's eventual liberation and in the opportunity that would be afforded its people once more to take up the task of self-government never blinded him to the magnitude of the new problems which Czechoslovakia would face after the victory was won.

To Dr. Beneš, Czechoslovakia's only salvation lies in her ability to remain free from the domination of the powers of either western Europe or of eastern Europe, and in being permitted to pursue a policy which is based on equally close relations with both the East and the West. During the years before the end of the war, Dr. Beneš pursued that objective with consummate ability. In 1943, notwithstanding the opposition of the British government, he proceeded to Moscow. There he concluded a treaty which provided the necessary basis for an equitable relationship between the Soviet Union and Czechoslovakia after the defeat of Germany. Had that agreement not been reached at that time, and had Dr. Beneš not proved in all his acts that the policy which he intended to pursue was predicated upon real friendship with Moscow, the results of the Russian occupation of Czechoslovakia after Germany's defeat might have been far different.

As it is, Dr. Beneš has been obliged by the force of circumstances to make many concessions. Ruthenia has been ceded to the Soviet Union. The occupation has involved inevitable conflicts of jurisdiction which created great difficulties for the government after its return to Prague. The Soviet armies still utilize Czechoslovak territory. The exercise of Russian influence is persistent.

But in the national elections held in the spring of 1946 the people voted freely. There was no restriction upon the freedom of the press nor upon legitimate political activities. In Bohemia and Moravia the Communists and Socialists obtained a majority of fifty-five per cent. In Slovakia the Centre triumphed. In the republic as a whole the right and Centre polled forty-nine per cent of the votes. The new Cabinet was headed by a Communist. But in the National Assembly Dr. Beneš was once more elected President by a unanimous vote. So long as he remains at the helm, Czechoslovakia will retain her independence and follow a course of national democracy.

The history of the western European powers contains few pages so humiliating as those which set forth their sacrifice of Czechoslovakia in 1939. The Czechoslovak people are deserving of such recompense as can be offered. But we further owe them a great debt of gratitude for what they now represent. For in the troubled and uncertain Europe of today they constitute a truly democratic, progressive, peace-loving and moral force which can greatly contribute to the ultimate establishment of a new and better order.

The history of the Austrian people in the years between the two wars was one of the most tragic in Europe. They could have obtained economic security, even within the confines of the tiny new republic left to them in 1919, if the League of Nations and the other "succession" countries had permitted them to take part in some form of economic federation with the Danubian states or with all the countries of eastern Europe and thus continue the commercial and financial interchange with the other parts of Austria-Hungary that they had enjoyed during the days of the Hapsburg Empire.

The *Anschluss* with Germany was vetoed, and legitimately vetoed, by France. But the major European powers made no effort to foster the economic federation of eastern Europe, without which the Austrian people were doomed to eventual inanition, and without which the new Austria would always be a tempting prey to the Pan-Germans.

After the first years of their prostration the Austrian people abandoned hope. In no country of Europe was there greater apathy. What Count Ciano, the Italian Foreign Minister, said to me in the spring of 1940 was unquestionably true: "The great majority of Austrians would even today rather be a part of Germany than have to live the life of starvation and of progressive exhaustion they are forced to lead in independent Austria." There was some excuse for the acquiescence of the Austrian populace in Hitler's rape of their country.

Unfortunately, there seem to be as yet few signs that the major powers have formulated any policy which will result in greater benefit to the Austrian people than that which the Allies adopted in 1919. As a result of the agreements reached at Yalta, Austria was subjected to a four-power military occupation. Friction between the Russians, the British and the Americans developed from the outset. Quarrels arose over the lines of the zones of occupation allotted to each occupying power. Vienna and eastern Austria were subjected to the bitter experiences which Russian occupation has entailed for all the occupied peoples.

When Vienna emerged from its initial blackout, a provisional Austrian government had been constituted, headed by Dr. Karl Renner. The men associated with him in the provisional government were for the most part Communists, even though certain of them were by no means free from the suspicion of having served the Nazis after the *Anschluss*. This provisional government, recognized by the Soviet Union without prior consultation with either London or Washington, was for some time denied official recognition by the Western powers. After some semblance of order had been restored, national elections were held. To the surprise of many observers, the Communists succeeded in electing only four delegates out of 169 to the Austrian National Assembly.

The Allied Control Council set up for Austria was similar to that established in Berlin, but it was forced to operate within a far smaller area. The record of the Allied occupation of Austria is one of utter confusion, of hopeless inefficiency, and of a tragic disregard for every just right of the Austrian people who had been promised their freedom and independence at Moscow in 1943.

Austria, like Germany, was divided into four military zones. Vorarlberg and the Tyrol were held by France; Upper Austria and Salzburg by the Americans; Carinthia and Styria by the British, and Lower Austria by the Russians.

Economic interchange between the four zones was long nonexistent. Austria has always been an exporter of salt, but Vienna was for months without salt, because it was produced only in the American zone. Oil produced in the Russian zone is unobtainable in Upper Austria. Transport has become increasingly difficult. Ten thousand Austrian freight cars have disappeared into that part of eastern Europe behind the "iron curtain."

The Austrian government until now has been helpless to make any start toward reconstruction. It can have no conception of the assets that may still be left in the country, for under the Potsdam agreement the Russians were handed over all "German" assets in the territory occupied by the Soviet Union outside Germany, and these, in the Russian interpretation, included all Austrian as well as foreign properties which Hitler had taken.

After the *Anschluss* the Nazis had ruthlessly seized all Austrian industries and financial institutions. The Danube Steamship Company, for example, was absorbed by the Hermann Goering Werke; the Creditanstalt and Länderbank of Vienna were taken by the Deutsche Bank and the Dresdner Bank; the oil fields of Zistersdorf were developed by the Nazi government itself. All these enterprises or properties, and many others as well, are located within the Russian-occupied zone of Austria. The Soviet government claims them all as "war booty." Factory after factory has been occupied by the Red Army, and the machinery exported to the Soviet Union. Austria has been largely deindustrialized. Yet all these assets were legitimately Austrian before they were looted by the Nazis.

The maladministration of the occupying powers has also prevented any distribution of the food supplies which Austria produces. Hunger has spread throughout the country. In midsummer of 1946 the average diet was only 1300 calories.

Not until then were the rigid lines of demarcation between the zones of occupation relaxed so that commercial traffic within Austria could be resumed. At the same time the occupying powers agreed that legislation enacted by the Austrian government could be vetoed only by the unanimous votes of the four members of the Control Council, instead of by the single vote of any one member as had previously been the case.

But these decisions were far too late. The harm had all been done. Austria was utterly destitute and her people starving. The Austrian people have been treated as a conquered and not as a "liberated" nation.

Yet Austria is the key to Europe. It must be the keystone in any arch of European federation which may later be built. The blind stupidity of the policy pursued by the major powers of the West in their treatment of Austria passes comprehension.

There are only two alternatives which the United Nations can adopt if the Austrian people are to be given the opportunity to survive.

The first alternative, the participation by Austria in an economic federation composed of all or part of the eastern European and Balkan countries, will obviously meet with the vigorous opposition of the Soviet government unless that federation is dominated by Moscow. But such a federation, dominated neither by the East nor the West, would bring about a rapid rise in the living standards of all the eastern European peoples, and a consistent increase in their political independence.

The other alternative, one which is already openly favored by many South Germans as well as by many Austrians, is the creation of a new political and economic federation composed of Austria, Bavaria and other autonomous South German states. Such an alternative must, however, necessarily be regarded as dangerous to the future peace of Europe. The underlying menace is of course the possibility that, should a greater Germany be authorized by the United Nations in the future, the entrance of Austria into a German bloc would greatly strengthen Germany's position and increase the incentive to renew Pan-Germanism.

At the present moment the possibility seems remote. Such a possibility seemed equally remote twenty-five years ago. And any step that tends toward the centralization of government in Germany rather than toward decentralization must be regarded as fraught with menace for the future peace of the world.

Russia's fear of any peace settlements that would result in the establishment of what it regards as a "cordon sanitaire" in eastern Europe will not be dispelled. Her policy is already directed toward the economic absorption and the political domination of the peoples of eastern and southeastern Europe. Yet unless policies which during the unhappy months since the end of the war have proved to be irreconcilable can still be reconciled, there is no practical solution for Austria's dilemma. Her people will be condemned to the same fate as that which they faced in 1919. Austria provides the test case of whether the Soviet system and the Western system can still be reconciled in Europe.

One must look at the peoples of the smaller countries of western Europe, overrun by the Germans in 1940, and suffering under German occupation until the close of the war, with renewed admiration for their vitality, their courage and their amazing recuperative capacity.

In Norway, Belgium and Luxembourg, the physical destruction resulting from the occupation and from the ravages of the war which was fought upon their soil was less than in most of the other European countries. Yet even so there is hardly a corner of any of these countries that cannot show some evidences of the bitter struggle. The spirit of resistance in all of them has fortunately carried over into the period of reconstruction.

The political transition in Norway and in Luxembourg which took place when the governments-in-exile returned was very brief. In neither country was there any question of the desire of the majority that the constitutional monarchy be retained. When national elections were held, governments were elected which were similar in political complexion to the governments that had held office at the time of the invasion.

In Belgium, it is true, King Leopold III was prevented from returning to Brussels by strong opposition from the left, but the opposition was rather to the person of the monarch than to the monarchy itself. When national elections were held in Belgium, the Communists were shown to have made but small gains, the traditional political parties retaining an overwhelming popular support. The economic condition of Belgium was gravely impaired, but by no means disastrously so. The Belgian people have concentrated upon reconstruction far more than upon politics. To the intense surprise of many foreign observers, the Belgians have proved apathetic to politics, and neither the Socialist nor the Communist leaders have demonstrated any ability to change this indifference. Even the most controversial question of all, the question whether King Leopold should or should not be restored to his throne, aroused but little interest.

The people of the Netherlands have reacted to their liberation in a manner which is wholly distinct. Public opinion in the United States has failed to realize that the Netherlands have suffered in proportion to their size a far greater measure of material damage and a far greater loss of life than any other country of western Europe. No western European nation has a greater right to the assistance of its major allies in the task of reconstruction, and in securing just compensation from the German people for the destruction for which they are responsible.

The loyalty of the Dutch people to the House of Orange has again been demonstrated. But with that exception, the political life of the Netherlands will be wholly different in the future from what it has been in the past. The provisional government of the Netherlands, installed immediately after the evacuation of the Germans, was a government composed of resistance leaders. It has been succeeded, after the national elections, by a government of the same character. The Centre party and the moderate elements of the left are both strong. In the Netherlands the same trend has been seen as in every other country of western Europe where national elections have been held. The people have voted for parties that stand for advanced social reform in internal policy. But they have opposed by a great majority parties that favor the subordination of all individual liberty to the state. The Communists, here as elsewhere in the West, have made but slight gains.

The Netherlands government is confronted with two major problems. These are the claim which the Netherlands government has decided to make at the Peace, Conference for a part of Germany's territory, and the bitterly controversial issue arising from the demands of the people of Indonesia for independence.

Before the conclusion of the war the Dutch government-in-exile announced that as compensation for the flooding of Dutch agricultural lands by the Germans it would demand that some form of servitude be imposed upon an area of Germany adjacent to the Dutch frontier in order that, until the Netherlands could produce its prewar quota of food, these supplies might be grown within Germany for the account of the Dutch people. With the election of a new government this claim was changed to ask for the transfer to Dutch sovereignty of an area on the eastern border of the Netherlands, running from Maastricht south to the neighborhood of Duesseldorf, and from there to the Ems River and the North Sea. It was one of the most intensively industrialized areas of Western Europe.

The claim of the Netherlands government for full compensation for the losses which the Dutch people have suffered is not open to question. It is wholly just. It cannot rightfully be denied. But whether the kind of compensation now claimed would redound to the benefit of the Dutch people in the long run is open to serious question. The proposal earlier advanced for compensation in kind through the imposition of a temporary servitude upon a given area of Germany would be less likely to retard European reconstruction.

The importance of what France represents to the interests of the United States can hardly be exaggerated. The existence of a free and democratic France on the eastern bounds of the Atlantic is an assurance of great strategic value to American security. France is politically of preponderant importance in western Europe. She must continue to be, as she has so long been, a major factor in the councils of the nations. Commerce between France and the United States has long represented an item of major importance in the trade relations of this country. Even more than that, the French throughout the independent life of the United States, by reason of their devotion to the principles of democracy as we have understood them and by their dedication to the ideal of human liberty, have, with the exception of the British, been more closely identified with the American manner of being than any other western European people.

Granted these truths, it had long been evident that intimate collaboration between France and the United States in the postwar period would be of outstanding value if our government was to secure strong European support for the adoption of its European reconstruction policy. As the war drew to a close, the fact that the French people were prostrate, facing rapidly impending bankruptcy and suffering from so shattering a blow to their morale that it might well presage a radical social and political transformation, would have seemed to make it desirable that the objectives of American foreign policy should have been:

To help the French people in every practicable way to speed their political recovery and their return to constitutional government.

To agree with the French provisional government before the close of the war upon a program of measures through which the United States could take the initiative, after Germany's defeat, in expediting France's economic and financial reconstruction.

To support the claim of the French provisional government that France be restored to a position of equality with the other major powers, and to insist upon her inclusion in any international conferences where French interests were to be considered, particularly Allied meetings in which questions affecting French security were to be determined.

Finally, to make friendly allowance in all official negotiations for the extreme—almost psychopathic—sensitiveness of French public opinion on all questions where France's national dignity was involved, especially those in which her interests overseas were concerned.

American policy has unfortunately pursued none of these objectives. It has generally failed even to envisage them. It has been at best vacillating and haphazard in its approach to French problems. That relations between the two nations are as good today as they are is owing far more to the innate common sense of the French people and to the wisdom of some of their present leaders than to American policy.

With the final recognition, after interminable shilly-shallying, of General de Gaulle as the head of the French provisional government, the United States at last canalized relations between the two countries into official channels. Our government's treatment of General de Gaulle had not only been unfortunate, it had been stupid. Whatever the suspicions of his ulterior motives, however difficult his peculiar temperament might have made him to deal with, events long before the end of the war had obviously made him, at least for the time being, the indispensable man in France. He represented to a majority of the French people a personification of French resistance and a symbol of the soul of France.

Acting from the standpoint of practical international politics, the British government had from the autumn of 1940 persistently backed General de Gaulle for political leadership in France. Mr. Churchill might from time to time lose his temper and loudly complain that the heaviest cross he had to bear was the Cross of Lorraine, but that by no means implied any deviation in the line of British policy. Washington and London could not have afforded any longer to follow divergent policies with regard to France.

In the national elections held under General de Gaulle's provisional government in the autumn of 1945 to select a constituent assembly, the results were precisely what objective observers familiar with the French scene had for some time been predicting. The greatest political party of the Third Republic, the party which represented the great French middle class, the Radical Socialist, was almost swept out of existence. The parties of the right elected a scant handful of deputies. The Communists increased their strength. So did the Socialists. A new party, the Mouvement Republicain Populaire, a resistance group consisting principally of Liberal Catholics, elected approximately as many deputies as the Socialist or the Communist parties. These three parties secured more than three-fourths of the total number of seats in the National Assembly.

The first government was a coalition of these three parties. As might have been anticipated, the Communist leaders consistently tried to control the government. Partly because of this difficulty, General de Gaulle in January of 1946 resigned as Provisional President, and was succeeded in the Presidency by the Socialist Félix Gouin.

With the appointment of a new Cabinet it became clear that the Socialist party was assuming major responsibility in the government. The control of foreign policy remained, as it had been under General de Gaulle, in the hands of Georges Bidault, the leader of the Popular Republicans. The Communists temporarily accepted minor portfolios. The issue upon which General de Gaulle ostensibly resigned was the refusal of the National Assembly to approve the military credits which he demanded. But the real issue was more far-reaching. The real issue was whether in the Fourth French Republic the legislative or the executive branch of the government should possess the greater share of power. General de Gaulle, not only because of the military traditions in which he was steeped but also because of his sincere conviction that the downfall of the Third Republic had been due chiefly to the weakness of the French Executive, demanded that in the new constitution this error of the past should be corrected. A majority of the French people, impressed with the evils of the authoritarian systems where the legislative branch had been relegated to the role of a rubber stamp, insisted that the representatives of the people, the members of the legislative assembly, must continue to possess ultimate control, in particular, the right to override or even to displace the head of the executive branch of the government.

In the United States and in the other Western democracies it was assumed that General de Gaulle's resignation implied that the Communist party had maneuvered its way to control, and that France was headed for Communism. The events of the next few months showed how mistaken these assumptions were.

The growth of Communism in France during the war had, in fact, been much less than might have been expected. There was little evidence that the backbone of France, the farmers, and the French men and women who live outside the larger cities, had been in any sense allured by Communist propaganda. Quite the contrary.

Under the procedure proclaimed by the provisional government, the Constituent Assembly elected in the autumn of 1945 was obligated to complete the drafting of a new constitution for submission to the French electorate by May of the following spring. The constitution so drafted represented to a very large degree the political theories of the left. While supported by the Socialists, it was largely of Communist inspiration. It eliminated the second legislative chamber of the Third Republic, to which the Socialist leaders as well as the Communists were strongly opposed, and for all practical purposes placed the control of government exclusively in the hands of a majority of the members of a unicameral legislature. To most of the French people it was apparent that such a constitutional system would make it possible for any strong and well-disciplined minority, like the Communists, to secure control of the government by its ability to dominate the legislative body.

There was, however, a widespread belief that because of the growing desire of the masses of the people to end the uncertainties of a provisional government, and to get back as quickly as possible to a constitutional status, a majority might vote in the plebiscite in favor of the constitution as drafted rather than risk an indefinite prolongation of their provisional régime.

But the French once more demonstrated their essential sanity. The draft constitution was rejected by a very large majority, and as a result of the new national elections which were consequently held a month later, the political picture was radically changed. The Popular Republican Movement replaced the Communist party as France's strongest party, and the smaller parties of the right and Centre materially increased their representation. Such old-time political figures as Edouard Daladier and Paul Reynaud returned to parliamentary life, and the Radical Socialists under Herriot's leadership regained some of their former strength. Georges Bidault, while retaining his position as Foreign Minister, replaced the Socialist, Félix Gouin, as Provisional President.

There can be no question that the electoral results were in part due to the unwillingness of a majority of the French people to tolerate control by a party that, in the judgment of many of them, took its orders from Moscow and that stood for a political system that implied the gradual obliteration of the personal liberty so dearly prized by the highly individualistic French citizenry.

The French people are giving every evidence that, unless Europe suffers new disruption, they will rapidly return to constitutional democracy.

Economically, the United States might have arranged to help France during the transition postwar period in two primary ways. After the German occupation and the manipulation of French currency by the so-called financial wizards of the Reich, French popular confidence in the franc could only have been restored by radical measures. The most effective measure was obviously an American credit to France similar to that finally negotiated with Great Britain. The other indispensable measure of assistance would have been an assurance to the French government that during the initial transition period the food supplies urgently required by the civilian population, which France could not yet produce, would be furnished either by the United States or some other agricultural exporting country, and that the materials needed by French industry for reconstruction would also be supplied.

The United States, however, took no such initiative. No broad program was even discussed. Little economic assistance was given save in the shipment of a small percentage of the coal and cereals needed, and in the extension of a small Export-Import Bank credit.

By the early spring of 1946 a crisis in France was imminent. National bankruptcy was hanging over the French people. The orthodox conservatism of the coalition government proved utterly ineffective in stemming a rapidly uncontrollable inflation. The printing of currency reached the fantastic total of one billion francs a day. The only remedy, increased production, was impossible because the French government was unable to secure any considerable amount of industrial equipment or raw materials.

Almost all of France's industrial equipment was worn out at the end of the German occupation. The Germans had worked it overtime. No modern tooling could be obtained in Europe. French dollar credits had been exhausted and, unless exports could be shipped overseas, there was no way to secure new equipment. The private foreign assets of all French citizens had been blocked. But even had the French government seized these assets as a means of procuring additional foreign credits, the amount so obtainable would have been hardly sufficient to meet French needs for more than a few months.

The deflationary policy decreed by the Gouin government was bound to be ineffective unless France could obtain sufficient credits from the United States to put her once again in a position to intensify her production and resume her export trade.

At the last moment the American government, which had been under the strange delusion that a credit to France would work to the advantage of the Communists—when the contrary was, of course, self-evident—permitted the French government to send a mission to Washington, headed by the brilliant and magnetic leader of the Socialists, Léon Blum, to discuss the terms of the long-deferred credit. After some weary weeks of negotiation a credit was authorized through the Export-Import Bank. It was received in the nick of time to prevent disaster.

It is perhaps in a third and equally important objective that American policy toward France has failed most disastrously and inexcusably. The United States should have realized in its own interest that France's return to the councils of the major powers would secure us the co-operation of a people generally inclined to share our beliefs about world reconstruction. Moreover, if the United States had generously taken the initiative in furthering France's return, French public opinion would rapidly have lost that sullen suspicion of the United States so sedulously aroused by German and other alien propaganda.

The conference at Potsdam, from which France was excluded, dealt with the future frontiers of Germany. There is no single question in the reconstruction of Europe that more directly and vitally affects France. Yet the United States made no real effort to secure her admission to this conference. France was thereafter confronted with the official announcement of the United States, the Soviet Union and Great Britain that Germany's future frontiers had been established in the east, but that no settlement had been reached with regard to Germany's western frontiers.

At the meeting of the Foreign Ministers in London in September of 1945 France was represented. But not only was she prevented from participating on a basis of equality in the discussion of the issues which arose, but she was confronted with the public announcement that the only European peace treaty in the determination of which she would be permitted to take part was the treaty with Italy. Yet none of the United Nations could attempt to deny that France possessed vital interests in eastern Europe, particularly in the Balkans, and that no equitable European settlement could conceivably be undertaken unless her interests were consulted, and unless she was given an opportunity to have an equal voice with the three other major powers.

France's demands for an equal voice in determining the European peace settlements are not due solely to considerations of national prestige. They stem equally from French fears that the treaty with Germany will be similar to that laid down at Versailles, and will fail to grant her the security against Germany upon which her survival depends. Until she is given final assurance that Germany can never again use the industrial and mineral resources of the Ruhr, the Rhineland and the Saar to make war against her, she will not co-operate effectively with the other major powers in the reconstruction of Europe.

The United States has failed to make just allowances for psychological factors in Franco-American relations. Time and time again American officials both in Washington and in Europe have publicly voiced their belief that France was "finished," have shown petulant irritation because France continued to speak as a great power, and have blusteringly asserted that the French government would have to do what Washington desired.

American policy toward France has not only been generally negative and far too often sterile, it has been unrealistic and uncomprehending. The highest interests of the United States demand that the people of France recover as rapidly as possible their former political and economic strength, that they be assisted in establishing firm relations of friendship with the East as well as with the West, and, above all else, that they be given the practical assurance that their future security against any German aggression will be regarded as a matter of vital concern to the United States herself. The proposal for a four-power military alliance, made public by Secretary Byrnes in May, 1946, has to some extent relieved French anxieties on this latter point.

At this moment the iron curtain still conceals all of Europe east of the Stettin-Trieste line. To the west the struggle to agree upon the basis for peace is still going on. So far the few agreements reached by the Foreign Ministers of the Big Four give no indication that the opportunity to build a new order for Europe, which will establish peace because it has eliminated the causes of war, will be realized.

The clash of the Soviet system and of the free system of the West has become intensified. Europe is on the brink of being divided into two competing and antagonistic spheres of influence. Yet the chance still remains that a reconstruction of Europe may be in the making behind the present clouds of suspicion and of controversy. If that reconstruction is to endure it must of necessity provide for one Europe and not two. It must establish the foundation for a new and as yet untried federation of the European nations, merging their individual sovereignties to the extent that the general welfare of the peoples of Europe demands.

CHAPTER IV

The Inter-American System Is in Jeopardy

THREE years after I entered the foreign service of the United States I asked to be transferred to a post in Latin America. It was not difficult to secure compliance with my request, but it was hard to prevent my superiors from entering a notation upon my efficiency record that my judgment and mental stability should receive especial scrutiny. In those remote days assignment to Latin-American posts was usually reserved for those who required disciplinary action, or for those who had proved themselves misfits or incapable.

The Assistant Secretary to whom I made my request, and who had been invariably helpful to me, asked me why I wished to waste several years of my life in a remote region where little of interest to this country would be going on, after I had already served in the Far East and, by departmental custom, would certainly be considered for assignment to a "first-class" post in Europe.

At that time, thirty years ago, the Department of State was still largely influenced in this opinion by the point of view in London or in Paris. There the Latin-American Republics were still considered as *petits pays chauds*, where only trade, and not much of that, could come up as a subject for official negotiation.

But the convictions which I had reached as a very young man have strengthened with every year which has since passed. They are based upon the belief that except for the establishment of a successful international organization, no objective within the field of foreign policy is of more vital significance to the United States than the maintenance of the unity of the Western Hemisphere and the achievement of relations of real friendship and understanding with its neighbors of the New World.

The security of the United States depends upon the attainment of that objective. That has been proved by the Second World War, if proof was needed. By its attainment the prosperity of the American people can be greatly enhanced, as a majority of those American interests concerned in foreign commerce have long since learned. If it is achieved, foreign nations will know that the United States speaks in the councils of the world as a partner in a system that comprehends an entire continent, and a continent that is united.

For the better part of thirty years, the pursuit of that objective, whether I was in or out of government, has been my chief interest. Even when in more recent years my time has necessarily been devoted to many other urgent problems, that interest has never been secondary.

When Franklin Roosevelt became President, he gave me an opportunity to play a part in making those ideals a fact. Under his guidance and under his inspiration the "Good Neighbor Policy" became a living thing. For the first time in the history of the New World the vision which Bolívar upheld to the American peoples one hundred years before became, through the determination and the wisdom of a President of the United States, a reality. An inter-American system of one for all, and all for one, existed.

True, it was still, when he died, only in its formative stage. Certainly, it still possessed many weaknesses and required a vast amount of implementation. But the foundations had been solidly laid. They were renunciation by every American Republic of all action which involved, directly or indirectly, intervention in the sovereign concerns of its neighbors; common agreement to resolve all inter-American difficulties by the peaceful means provided in a series of multilateral pacts; agreement to consult together and find common methods of defense whenever any danger from without threatened the hemisphere, or any one of the republics; and agreement to co-operate in all practicable ways in order to advance the well-being of the peoples of the Americas.

The modern world has seen no more enlightened nor practical foundation for international understanding, whether regional or universal, than that established by the series of treaties and agreements entered into by the American Republics between 1933 and 1943.

The Good Neighbor Policy had created an inter-American system—a regional system of sovereign states, sovereign in all that affected their purely internal affairs, but prepared to mold their external relations in such shape as would best advance the common welfare of their peoples.

Gone were the grounds for that bitter hostility toward the United States which had inevitably stemmed from this country's insistence during many generations upon utilizing the Monroe Doctrine to impose its will by fiat upon the weaker nations of the hemisphere. Gone were the reasons for the deep-rooted suspicions among the Latin-American peoples that the great power of the North was in reality bent upon a policy of imperialistic expansion. Gone was the justification for their outraged indignation at each act of military intervention in their independent countries. Gone was their belief that the government of the United States was only a front for the great financial and commercial interests, regarding the common man solely as an object destined for indefinite exploitation.

For the New Deal had become quite as much of a symbol of positive democracy in Latin America as in the United States itself, and knowledge of its existence had checked a defeatist popular trend toward authoritarianism. Franklin Roosevelt had come to be regarded not only as the leader of the hosts of democracy, but in a very real sense as the friend of the forgotten and of the downtrodden.

And had not Franklin Roosevelt officially declared that his government did not wish "one additional inch of territory"? And had not his administration agreed to solemn treaties, ratified by the United States Senate, pledging the United States never again to interfere "directly or indirectly" in the internal concerns of its neighbors? Had not the United States reversed its earlier economic policy, seeking now by the personal directives of its President to find new markets within its own territory for the products of its neighbors? Had it not created agencies, such as the Export-Import Bank, to help the other American Republics start their programs for industrialization and to help tide them over the recurrent economic crises of the uncertain postwar world?

The peoples of Latin America had for many generations listened to empty phrases about Pan-Americanism; now they were seeing the accomplishment of deeds. A wholly new spirit of co-operation sprang into being. For the first time in a hundred years hemispheric solidarity actually existed.

In the narrower and more purely selfish sense, the United States had thereby gained a means of security which was of incalculable value. Had that solidarity not existed when the attack upon Pearl Harbor took place, the Panama Canal would have unquestionably been the object of sabotage or of aerial bombardment; the invasion of North Africa could not have been undertaken; and this country would have been compelled to retain at home a great percentage of the forces ultimately sent overseas in order to be prepared to meet airborne armies of the Axis whose entrance into the Western Hemisphere could readily have been facilitated by populations prepared to welcome them.

I am frank to admit that when I left the government in the autumn of 1943 I was confident that the basis for the new inter-American system was so solidly laid, and that the advantages of that system to all of the peoples of the Americas, and in particular to the people of the United States, were so generally recognized by public opinion as well as by official circles that it could not be undermined. I would have regarded as ludicrous a prediction that within two years it would reach a stage of advanced disintegration, that the whole of the hemisphere would again be shot through with suspicions and animosity toward the United States, and that the American Republics would be threatened with a division into two opposing blocs, one dominated by the United States and one spearheaded by Argentina. Yet that is precisely what has occurred.

It is because of my ineradicable conviction that the safety of the United States, the highest welfare of all of the other American Republics, and in a larger sense the survival of democracy and the peace of the world depend upon the restoration of the inter-American system as it once was, that I am writing this chapter in blunt terms. The issues involved are too grave to permit of euphemisms.

Any accurate analysis of the history of inter-American relations between 1943 and 1946 must be based upon an objective appraisal of the policy pursued by the United States toward Argentina during those years. For the results of that policy shaped all recent developments within the hemisphere. They have been directly responsible for the resurrection of suspicions and antagonisms which it had been hoped had permanently disappeared with the consolidation of the inter-American system. That policy has promoted discord within the American family of nations, gravely undermining the inter-American solidarity which proved itself at the time of Pearl Harbor and grew stronger during the months when the New World became involved in war. It has shown itself to be a factor of such corrosive force that its work of disintegration, even if now arrested, may leave its traces for many years to come.

It is necessary, however, before undertaking any detailed account of this policy or any comprehensive evaluation of its results, to review in broad lines Argentine developments in modern times. For there can be no correct appreciation of this recent chapter of hemispheric history and of this extraordinary episode in United States policy without an accurate comprehension of Argentina's place in the continent and of the recent political and economic development of the Argentine people.

Argentina is a country which is in many ways unique. Throughout her independent life, she has been one of the richest agrarian nations of the world, with only a recent spurt toward industrialization, and yet more than two-thirds of her nearly fourteen million inhabitants live in large cities. Buenos Aires alone has more than three million citizens. Her per capita wealth places her among the five wealthiest countries of the world. Ninety-eight per cent of her people are of European stock. Her ability to assimilate immigrants rapidly and transform them into true nationals is equaled only by the United States.

Her railroads and other communications systems were British-built and British-financed. So were a majority of her public utilities. While great capital investments have been made by Dutch, French and other European interests, the preponderance of Great Britain in her finance and commerce is still very large.

Her foreign trade has been the highest per capita of any country on earth. But of her exports only ten per cent have been shipped in normal times to the United States, and of her imports only some fifteen per cent came from this country.

These facts help to explain why Argentina has always regarded herself as far closer to Europe than to the rest of the Western Hemisphere. Her cultural and racial ties are with Europe and she has looked to Europe for her export markets and her major capital investments.

There is a no more vigorous and assertive people of the New World, nor is there a more adult people in the Americas. Pride of nationality and faith in the destiny of the Argentine nation are so powerful that the second-generation Spaniards and Italians who comprise the bulk of recent immigrants are just as devout exponents of "Argentinidad"—the privilege of being a part of the life of Argentina—as are the descendants of the colonial pioneers.

Like all Spanish-Americans the Argentine people are exceedingly individualistic. But beyond all others they are given to an exaggerated nationalism. This quality stems in part from the heritage of Spanish civilization which colors every aspect of Argentine life and in part from their belief in their special star as well as from their remembrance of the valor and determination with which in the earlier decades of their national history they successfully repelled all attempts at alien control, whether Spanish, French or British.

If we in the United States recall accurately what our own national characteristics were during the period between the age of Jackson and our emergence as a world power—the fierce national pride we displayed, the arrogance we demonstrated when it seemed that our nation's honor was at stake—we can better comprehend these traits as they exist in the Argentine of today.

During the last decades of the nineteenth century and the first years of the present century the government of Argentina was under the exclusive control of a small oligarchy representative of the great landholders. While the Argentine Constitution more nearly approximated the Constitution of the United States than that of any other American republic, the election laws were manipulated in such a way as to make the perpetuation of the landholders' oligarchy inevitable. Free elections, genuinely representative of the will of the majority, were unknown. A truly feudal system had been created. Finally, owing to the courage, the vision, and the democratic faith of a member of the landholding class, Dr. Roque Saenz Peña, an election law was enacted while he was President of the republic which made popular government possible.

In 1916, at the first national elections held after the passage of the Saenz Peña law, Dr. Hipólito Irigoyen, the candidate of the Radical party, was swept into the Presidency by an overwhelming majority. President Irigoyen was the first President of Argentina who satisfied the aspirations of the masses of the Argentine people. His administration endeavored to give the Argentine middle classes, as well as labor and agriculture, an Argentine New Deal.

There were, unfortunately, three major obstacles which made any considerable measure of success impossible. Hipólito Irigoyen was a mystic. The legend had it that he had inherited this quality from a Turkish grandfather. He had received his political training from his uncle, Leandro Alem, the first great leader of the Radicals, but he possessed none of the customary attributes of the successful politician or of the demagogue. He was inarticulate. Even in office he operated instinctively as the clandestine revolutionist. Upon the rare occasions when he spoke in public he read from a verbose and almost incoherent text which bore many symptoms of hallucination. He loved concealment and lived, while in the Presidency, in a modest apartment, inaccessible to the throng and far from the Presidential palace. He had neither glamour nor charm nor approachability.

Yet he possessed a strikingly compelling personality. Upon the rare occasions when he received me upon official business, as Chargé d'Affaires of the American Embassy, I never failed to be impressed with a quality of innate force and inherent greatness of character, which his peculiar physical characteristics—a pine-apple-shaped head, a Mongolian mask with straggling threads on each side of his mouth which did service for a mustache, and an evasive gaze—could not dispel.

Throughout his first Presidential term he retained a hold upon the rank and file of the Argentine people which no other Argentine President has ever approached. He was idolized. But his complete lack of executive gifts and of administrative capacity constituted the first obstacle to his achievement of the political objectives he hoped to secure for the people who had placed him in office.

And the second obstacle was his bad judgment of men and the dearth of experienced personnel within the Radical party to whom he could turn for administrative or legislative support.

With few exceptions, the men whom he appointed to his Cabinet or to whom he looked for advice were wholly deficient in the qualities needed. The march toward reform consequently was not only halting but often led along paths which ended in confusion or disaster.

The third obstacle arose from the fact that this wholly democratic government of Dr. Irigoyen took office during the middle of the First World War. The Irigoyen foreign policy was one of fanatical neutrality, of essential isolationism and of consistent antagonism to any attempt by the United States to force the other American Republics to join the Allied cause. But at the same time, this democratic administration held office at a moment when every Argentine was prospering as a result of the war. During the First World War, as well as during the Second World War, the agricultural production of Argentina was stimulated to the highest degree. Prices received for Argentine meat and grain soared to new high levels. To the average Argentine, not only did the Irigoyen administration mean recognition, for the first time in Argentine history, of the rights of the hitherto "forgotten man," but Argentine isolationism and Argentine neutrality became identified as policies of the Radical party and associated with the thought of great material prosperity.

The importance of this fact—that as a result of the experience of the First World War, Argentine opinion tended to identify isolationist nationalism with domestic democracy and domestic prosperity—cannot be overemphasized in any fair appraisal of the events of more recent years.

After completing his constitutional term of six years, President Irigoyen was followed by his chosen successor, Dr. Marcelo Alvear, and in 1928 was elected for a second term. The corruption and administrative confusion which were notorious in the first Irigoyen administration were far graver in the second, for Dr. Irigoyen was by now in his eightieth year and wholly incompetent to assume the burdens of the Presidency. His second administration coincided with the world depression. The economic life of the country came to a standstill, and there appeared to be no hope of any remedial action from government. Conditions became so intolerable that even the Constitutionalists—and the Argentine people were in their majority firmly wedded to constitutional government—began to favor any change which promised action as against governmental inertia.

Those conditions gave rise to the tragic precedent for the military revolt in 1943.

In 1930 a military coup d'état, headed by General Uriburu, took place; Dr. Irigoyen was arrested and imprisoned and his government was turned out. The ensuing military dictatorship lasted for a protracted period. Argentina's first experiment in liberal and popular democracy was halted.

When the 1931 elections were held, the Conservative elements, joined by the right-wing Radicals, nominated as their candidate for the Presidency one of the latter, General Agustín P. Justo. The left-wing Radicals, representing a vast majority of the party and loyal to the policies of Irigoyen, refused to vote. At the conclusion of his term of office in 1938 President Justo was succeeded by Dr. Roberto Ortiz, his Minister of Finance.

Dr. Ortiz, like his predecessor, had been a member of that wing of the Radical party which had been opposed to President Irigoyen. His election was undoubtedly manipulated. There can be no question, however, that he was determined to reunite all the various elements within the Radical party as the majority party of the republic. It was equally his intention, I am confident from my own conversations with him, to restore free elections to the Argentine people.

In the field of foreign policy, President Ortiz vigorously opposed either isolationism or neutrality in the face of the increasing menace of Hitlerism. He was a sincere democrat. And he was outspoken in declaring for a new and co-operative relationship, instead of the traditional antagonism, between the United States and Argentina as the best means of insuring the safety of the New World. His determination on this point had been greatly influenced by the visit of President Roosevelt to Buenos Aires in 1936.

With his inauguration the prospects for a return to liberal democracy became bright. He vigorously eliminated the officials primarily responsible for the provincial electoral frauds of the previous election, and the chances for an honest administration constantly improved. The warring factions within the Radical party were reunited. Popular support swung to the President.

But simultaneously the Conservative oligarchy which had favored his election took alarm at his display of courageous independence. The old-time bosses sought means of checking a policy which would bring the Radical party back to power. The opportunity was at hand. President Ortiz, a diabetic, suffered partial blindness in 1941, and soon after was compelled to resign. A few months later he died.

No more tragic misfortune could have been inflicted upon the Argentine people. Dr. Ortiz not only could have averted the internal crisis of 1943, not only could have brought the Argentine people back into the paths of democratic and representative government, but he could also have prevented the course which the Argentine nation followed during the Second World War. Roberto Ortiz may not have possessed outstanding qualities of statesmanship, but he did possess true vision of where the interests of his country lay and saw clearly that only through wholehearted identification with the United Nations and with the cause of hemispheric solidarity could Argentina obtain assurance that her independence and security would be safeguarded.

He was succeeded by the Vice President, Dr. Ramon S. Castillo, who, as is not infrequently the case in republics where the Vice-Presidential candidates are nominated for reasons of political expediency rather than because of their abilities, was the complete antithesis of President Ortiz.

Dr. Castillo was a native of the Argentine interior and had never set foot outside his own country. He was a narrow-minded, reactionary member of the Conservative party, wholly devoid of the qualities required for the Presidency in a critical moment in Argentina's history. He was the tool of the corrupt influences which gained control of his administration. He was uninterested in international affairs. Because of his conviction that it was good politics as well as because of his own inclinations, he insisted that from Argentina's standpoint no difference was to be perceived between the issues presented by the Second World War and those that had arisen during the first.

Once when I was talking with President Roosevelt of the difficulties brought about by Argentina's attitude subsequent to the Rio Conference of 1942, and was speaking of the problem presented by President Castillo's narrow nationalism and lack of knowledge of the rest of the world, President Roosevelt interjected to say: "He is really an Argentine Coolidge!" No more apt comparison could have been made.

President Ortiz had publicly announced his conviction that the Argentine Republic should not and could not remain neutral in the struggle between totalitarianism and freedom.

Dr. Castillo made it very plain that he would vigorously oppose the policies urged upon his countrymen by his predecessor.

President Castillo had exceedingly strong support for this position. He was backed by all the reactionary elements of the church, and the contrary views expressed by so truly eminent an Argentine cleric as Bishop de Andrea were little heeded. The great majority of the army and of the navy leaders, the financial and commercial interests—even the British interests doing business in Argentina—and a large percentage of the landholders, all demanded neutrality.

It is true that the great newspapers, the intellectuals and a considerable number of the members of the liberal parties, stanchly battled for a policy of open support for the Allied cause. But these efforts were more than counterbalanced by the growing power of the ultra-nationalists and by the effective propaganda and subversive activities of Fascist and Nazi agents.

There can be no question that the sympathies of the rank and file of the Argentine people were strongly aligned against the Axis. But Argentina was prosperous, and their experience of neutrality under President Irigoyen in the First World War had convinced them that neutrality meant a continuation of prosperity.

Then came the attack upon Pearl Harbor. I have already related elsewhere in considerable detail the history of the Inter-American Conference at Rio de Janeiro in January, 1942, and the position there taken by the Argentine delegation.

By February of that year all the American Republics, with the exception of Chile and Argentina, had taken action to align themselves with the United Nations. Chile broke relations with the Axis in January, 1943, and Argentina thus became isolated from all the other American Republics.

Notwithstanding the vehemence of ultra-nationalist groups and the potent influence of the Nazis and Fascists, a popular feeling began to develop within Argentina that the country should follow the example of Chile and implement the agreements into which she had entered at the Conference of Rio de Janeiro by breaking all political and commercial relations with the Axis powers.

What was more effective in its immediate results, however, was the disquiet occasioned among the army and navy leaders by the fact that military and naval material was being supplied to the other American Republics by Lend-Lease. The Argentine generals were especially exercised by the assistance of this character rendered Brazil by the United States.

Speaking for this government, I had made it plain to the Argentine government upon repeated occasions that Argentina would receive no such assistance unless she were willing to bear her share of the burden of defending the Western Hemisphere from Axis aggression. To an Argentine naval and military mission which came to Washington in the winter of 1943 I had made it emphatically plain that unless Argentina complied with the obligations into which she had entered at the Rio de Janeiro Conference the provisions of the Lend-Lease Act alone would make it impossible for us to consider supplying her with material which was desperately needed by our allies.

The conflict of opinion within Argentina became acute. When the Western Hemisphere had been drawn into the war, President Castillo had declared martial law. Under the authority thus obtained censorship was imposed upon the press and the radio. All public criticism of his neutrality policy was stifled and the Congress was prevented from assembling. The political reaction was bitter.

The Argentine Army, honeycombed as it was with the subversive propaganda of German agents headed by the German Military Mission of Instruction, was divided into two camps. A lesser group favored an immediate break with the Axis and an arrangement with the United States which they hoped would result in their securing Lend-Lease equipment. A much larger group demanded a continuation of the neutrality policy. But this group, inspired by committees of younger officers, in which Colonel Juan D. Perón had long been active, regarded the constitutional government of President Castillo as incompetent to cope with either the internal or the external crisis. These committees were first of all nationalist, but they had become imbued with the belief that Argentine democracy was decadent. Their ideal was an authoritarian and militarized Argentina powerful enough to dominate South America.

The precedent created in 1930 by General Uriburu's military revolt had not been forgotten. It inspired the army leaders with the belief that they were warranted in overthrowing a constitutional government which had proved unable to carry out its functions, and with confidence that they themselves were fully capable of assuming the government and that in so doing they would meet with popular support.

The climax came on June 4, 1943. A military uprising, originally headed by General Rawson, who was, however, immediately succeeded by General Ramirez, overthrew the Castillo government.

The situation was confused. It was at first believed that the men favoring an immediate break with the Axis, like General Rawson, were in control of the movement, but it soon became apparent that General Ramirez himself possessed no real authority and that, unless he could obtain support for such a policy from the other leading generals in the Army and, far more important, support from the colonels led by Colonel Perón, Argentina's international position would remain unchanged. Internally, the situation had gravely deteriorated because of the immediate abrogation by military fiat of all constitutional rights.

At the instance of the United States, the governments of the other American Republics immediately consulted together about the attitude they should jointly adopt toward the new Argentine régime. There was no difference of opinion. The belief that relations should be established with the new régime, since it was obviously a *de facto* government in effective control of the republic, was unanimous, and diplomatic relations were resumed after the lapse of only a few days. The Brazilian government, in particular, expressed the strong conviction that it would be far easier for all the other American Republics, identified as they were with the cause of the United Nations, to exercise a favorable influence upon Argentina's foreign policy if official relations were maintained.

During the summer and early autumn of 1943 President Ramirez repeatedly informed American Ambassador Norman Armour, who handled the situation with consummate ability and tact, that he had obtained sufficient support from his army leaders to enable his government to break relations with the Axis powers. Twice he named precise dates for such action. Each time, however, a sudden shift of the military line-up prevented the commitments from being carried out. The position of the figureheads in the régime became more and more precarious. Their only nominal authority was still further weakened when at the end of 1943 it became known that various key members of the Argentine dictatorship had taken a prominent part in the preparation of the revolution which broke out at that moment in Bolivia.

When the rest of Latin America learned of this intervention in Bolivia, a storm of indignation was aroused. The Argentine dictatorship was all the more concerned since the Inter-American Committee on Political Defense[1] had recommended, and all the American governments except Argentina had agreed, that no new American government that came to power by force during the war should be recognized until the other American Republics were in accord that it was of purely native inspiration and willing to comply with inter-American defense agreements. Argentina feared that her complicity in the Bolivian revolt might be publicized and that, as a result, her position vis-à-vis the other American countries would be worsened.

An act of appeasement was at length determined upon. Believing that he had sufficient public and military support to warrant the decision, General Ramirez on January 26, 1944, announced a rupture of all relations with the Axis. Telegraphic communications with the Axis powers came to an end, and various steps were taken to eliminate subversive agencies and Axis financial and commercial activities in the republic.

This brought an immediate crisis. The ultra-nationalists screamed to high heaven, and the Nazi sympathizers pulled every wire available to them, but the real pressure came from the Army. The more authoritarian-minded of the "colonels" headed by Colonel Perón, and the frankly pro-Nazi military elements coalesced. Within three weeks of the announcement of the rupture with the Axis powers, General Ramirez was forced to sign his resignation and was succeeded as President by his Vice President, General Farrell. However, Colonel Juan Domingo Perón emerged as the strong man of the dictatorship.

What had in reality taken place? It is essential that the answer to this question emerge with some clarity from beneath the obscurantism of the official diagnosis offered by the State Department in Washington.

[1] Established by the Rio Conference, the Inter-American Committee of Political Defense was then sitting in Montevideo under the able leadership of that sturdy Uruguayan statesman, Dr. Alberto Guani.

What had really happened was that the men controlling the Argentine Army had replaced one puppet, General Ramirez, by another puppet, General Farrell. The fundamental situation resulting from the overthrow by the Argentine Army of a constitutional Argentine government was in no wise altered.

The same influences which had brought the military dictatorship into power still remained in effective command of the situation behind the governmental façade they had set up in the Casa Rosada. The real dynamic force behind the military coup d'état was the coalition of younger officers bent upon securing control of the government. That some of them admired Nazi power and German military efficiency there can be no doubt. That they used the avowed pro-Germans among the higher military and naval officers for their own ends is unquestionable. But they were primarily fanatical nationalists intent upon cleaning the Augean stable of the Administration seized from the Castillo government. Some of them were entirely sincere in believing that they were accomplishing an act of patriotism. Others were guided by selfish ambition. All of them, however, were ignorant of the facts of inter-American and of international life. They could have been educated more safely and more readily had the régime which they had established remained in official relations with the other governments of the Americas.

The Department of State, for reasons which must now be analyzed, decided not to recognize the new façade which Argentina's army leaders had erected in Buenos Aires.

The reasons for this decision were as follows. Argentina had long been a "pain in the neck" to the three or four members of the Department of State who were then determining the hemispheric policy of the United States. The constitutional governments of President Justo, of President Castillo, and even of President Ortiz had, at a succession of inter-American conferences, frequently opposed United States delegations on questions of policy. This had brought about injured susceptibilities and a very personal resentment on the part of the guiding influences in the Department of State. The feeling of hostility toward Argentina was notorious and had been made increasingly apparent.

In addition to this, a major part of the American press and many radio commentators, upon the plausible assumption that developments in Argentina were identical with the course of Nazism and of Fascism in prewar Europe and with bland disregard of the fact that military dictatorships of one kind or another had, unfortunately, been the rule rather than the exception in many parts of Latin America for well over a century, were ever more loudly clamoring for a policy of open coercion toward all of those Latin-American countries in which purely democratic governments were not in power.

The Department of State at that time was peculiarly susceptible to pressure of this kind because of the policy it had pursued toward the Franco government in Spain and the Vichy government in France. There must also be considered the pressure resulting from the valid and entirely legitimate resentment of a great portion of the American public at the failure of successive Argentine governments to carry out the commitments made at the Rio Conference to curb the subversive activities of Axis agents, to sequestrate Axis financial and commercial interests, and to co-operate with the other American governments in hemispheric defense.

The Department of State, having reached its own conclusions, then communicated its determination to the Foreign Offices of the other American Republics. If its decision had been based exclusively on the intervention of the Argentine military dictatorship in Bolivia, that decision, whether expedient or inexpedient, would have been regarded by the other American Republics as based upon defensible and moral grounds. But the attitude of the government of the United States was based officially only upon the failure of the military dictatorship to take effective action against the Axis powers, although relations with the Axis had been severed by the Ramirez government, and this decision had been maintained by the Farrell government.

The immediate reaction of the other American Republics was that before the United States arrived at her final conclusion in this matter, and before she summarily requested the other American Republics to follow suit, an opportunity for inter-American consultation should have been afforded in accordance with both the spirit and the letter of existing inter-American agreements. The agreement specifying obligatory consultation between the American Foreign Ministers whenever the vital interests of the hemisphere are jeopardized had been framed to provide for precisely such contingencies. But Washington permitted no consultation. The other American governments were curtly informed that Washington desired identical action on their part. When arguments or requests for fuller consideration were advanced, peremptory admonitions resulted and every form of pressure was brought to bear.

The majority of the other American Republics fell into line, although three, Chile, Bolivia and Paraguay, continued official relations with the Farrell government.

The Good Neighbor Policy had suddenly undergone a woeful transformation. It had become unilateral and overbearing. So it continued for the better part of a year.

The Department of State obviously labored under the impression that the attitude which it had adopted would bring about a rapid overturn of the Farrell government. When this did not immediately happen, it used coercion. Financial and economic sanctions were tried out. The gold deposits of the Argentine government held in the United States were frozen. Announcement was made that American merchant vessels were no longer to proceed to Buenos Aires. Minor and exasperating commercial restrictions, bearing chiefly upon the civilian population, were put into effect. The initiative was invariably taken by the United States. The governments of the other American Republics were then requested to follow her lead.

If it were possible to contend that the existing inter-American agreements and the Good Neighbor Policy conceivably permitted the employment of acts of unilateral coercion by the United States against some other American republic—which they do not—the procedure followed could only have been justified if it could have been expected to bring about practical results. The stupidity of the policy adopted lay in the fact that financial or economic coercion by the United States could never be effective in weakening the

national economy of Argentina or in creating a financial or
economic crisis unless the other American Republics were disposed
to co-operate in the imposition of such economic sanctions, and
unless Great Britain was willing to take similar action.

The commercial relations between the United States and
Argentina, although materially increased as a result of the war,
represented only a minor fraction of Argentina's trade with the
rest of the world. Those American Republics that depended to
a large extent for the maintenance of their own national economy
upon trade relations with Argentina were unable to agree to an
economic boycott. What was far more important, the British
government bluntly refused even to consider any stoppage of
Argentine imports. The need of the British people and of the
British armed forces for the meat, vegetable oils and cereals produced in Argentina was so great that the British government
could not even consider such a possibility unless the commodities
coming from Argentina were replaced by United States substitutes.
This was clearly out of the question. Furthermore, the British
government was unwilling to take any action that might jeopardize
its vast investments in Argentina by incurring retaliatory action
by the Argentine government.

In an unusually vigorously worded communication, the British
government not only informed the Department of State that it
was unwilling to co-operate in a boycott of Argentina, but it likewise plainly told the United States Government that, if what the
United States sought to achieve in Argentina was a greater
measure of co-operation against the Axis powers, the Department
of State was pursuing a sadly mistaken policy.

Simultaneously, United States authorities commenced to issue
a series of provocative and condemnatory statements, directed
against the dictatorship in Buenos Aires, in the belief that they
would provoke popular reaction in Argentina against the military
government and arouse public support in the rest of Latin America
for the position taken by Washington.

The policy of the State Department misfired in every particular.
It created the impression throughout the hemisphere that the
United States was determined to go the limit, no matter how far

that limit might extend, in bringing pressure to bear upon Argentina in order to overthrow the military régime.

Among the great majority of the Latin-American peoples, to whom the kind of military government installed in Buenos Aires had been originally decidedly unsympathetic, the course followed by the State Department aroused a revulsion of feeling. The peoples of Latin America are accustomed to military dictatorships. All of them have from time to time suffered from such régimes. The Ramirez or Farrell governments constituted in their judgment merely a further example of a military régime, although of an exceptionally unsavory variety. Intrinsically, however, they could see but little distinction between the Farrell government and the Uriburu government, which had installed itself in Buenos Aires some fourteen years before, and which eventually under the pressure of public opinion had gradually given way to a return to constitutional government.

The issue was, therefore, not so much the fact that the military dictatorship in Buenos Aires was objectionable and reprehensible but that the United States was beginning once more to show signs of an intention to use its overwhelming power to dictate to the people of a sovereign American state what they should and should not do about their internal concerns.

That the United States had for almost twelve years consistently refrained from even the semblance of such interference had brought about a very general and sincere belief that the Good Neighbor Policy was there to stay. The present signs to the contrary created widespread consternation. The new trend gave rise to an incipient doubt of the sincerity of the United States, as well as a suspicion that the Good Neighbor Policy might have been employed primarily to procure support for the United States at a time when it feared aggression from abroad. It further aroused the inevitable reaction created when a smaller nation is subjected to pressure by a larger power, and in this case sympathy was the more easily aroused since the smaller nation was a member of the Spanish-American community.

So rapidly did this revulsion of feeling take place that before many months had passed the Argentine flag would be greeted by loud cheers when it appeared upon the screens of moving picture houses in Spanish-American countries, while the persons believed to be responsible for the policy of the United States would be even more loudly booed.

The reaction of the Argentine people was naturally far more intense. Public opinion in the United States overlooks the fact that no Latin-American people are prouder of their sovereignty than the Argentine people, more wholly unwilling to tolerate any form of foreign pressure, and more traditionally unimpressed by the United States. The Argentine people as a whole are strongly democratic in their manner of being. They have always evidenced an even exaggerated individualism. But if American public opinion had been familiar with the history of Argentina, it would have learned how upon several occasions the mass of the Argentine nation has rallied in support of a ruthless and brutal dictator rather than permit the national government to be subjected to foreign coercion.

Throughout the period of their independence, relations between Argentina and the United States have at the best been frigid. At times the resentment of the Argentine people at the overbearing attitude of the United States has been intense. The caustic phrase of President Irigoyen when he declared that the Argentine government would never *ir a la zaga*—follow in the wake—of the United States represented accurately Argentine popular feeling. The geographical distance between the two countries impeded until recently any reciprocal popular understanding. Cultural relations scarcely existed, and Argentina's commercial interests were centered in Europe where United States tariff legislation inexorably compelled them to remain.

Politically the two peoples had much in common. But it was not until Franklin Roosevelt became President that this was felt by the Argentine people. Roosevelt became to them the symbol of democracy; the real friend of the underprivileged masses of the people. His visit to Buenos Aires marked the first moment when there was created in Argentina any genuine and spontaneous mass cordiality toward the United States. Even today, at a moment of unparalleled bitterness of feeling, Franklin Roosevelt's memory is honored and cherished by the Argentine people.

But this cordial feeling toward the United States vanished as a result of the change of policy begun by our State Department at the beginning of 1944. By its new course the Department of State not only brought about a violent popular reaction against the United States, but also materially increased popular support for the dictatorship. By intensifying blind nationalism, it undermined the attempt of the democratic parties to create a cohesive body of public opinion in opposition to the dictatorship.

Nor should it be overlooked, as the State Department did overlook it, that the Castillo government had been notoriously corrupt, hopelessly reactionary and flagrantly inefficient. It had ignored all of the many legitimate complaints of the white-collar workers, as well as of industrial and agricultural labor. The younger army leaders, under the inspiration of Colonel Perón, were not so shortsighted as to fail to realize the popularity that could be derived from recognizing the justice of the demand of a great majority of the population to share in the benefits accruing to the country during a period of unprecedented prosperity.

By the summer of 1944 the inter-American situation had degenerated into what was currently regarded as a duel between the United States and Argentina. The other American governments for a time sat back to await the result of this trial of strength. By a series of singularly maladroit maneuvers our Department of State tried to create the impression that the life of the Farrell government would be short. But as time went on and as the authoritative information available clearly demonstrated that the Farrell government was becoming stronger than ever in its hold on the country, the Latin-American countries, and in particular those closest to the Argentine problem, became more and more uneasy. From the broader standpoint this increasingly tense antagonism between the northernmost and southernmost American Republics threatened to destroy permanently all semblance of inter-American solidarity and to disrupt the inter-American system upon which they had grown increasingly to depend. From the narrower point of view, it became obvious that such republics as

Chile, Brazil and Uruguay, who had common frontiers with Argentina, and whose economic life was inextricably linked with hers, would suffer material prejudice if they were compelled to take sides between the two opponents. Also rumors by the hundred were spread by elements of the extreme Left in various parts of the hemisphere that the "colonels' government" had military designs upon Argentina's neighbors.

The Latin-American governments began to exchange views between themselves and increasingly to urge the need for a prompt composition of the quarrel.

In the autumn of 1944, after consultation with several other Latin-American governments, the Argentine government made a move which was both clever and legitimate. It addressed a communication to the Pan American Union formally requesting a consultative meeting of the Foreign Ministers of all the American Republics, in order that the Argentine government—to disprove the frequent allegations of our State Department—might have the opportunity fully and publicly to explain its position and to specify the concrete steps which it had taken to comply with its inter-American commitments.

This well-timed Argentine proposal was received with consternation by the Department of State. The request for consultation was in accord with the letter and spirit of existing inter-American agreements. No government could officially deny that the controversy between the United States and Argentina jeopardized the welfare of the entire continent and threatened the security of the hemisphere while the World War was still being waged. There can be no question that the failure of the United States openly and frankly to meet the challenge of the Argentine government to prove or disprove its charge at an inter-American consultative meeting was a major error of policy.

The State Department first tried to influence the other American governments to refuse to agree to the meeting requested by Argentina on the ground that her present government was not officially recognized by a majority of the other American nations. This effort, however, proved fruitless. For it is the time-honored tradition of the Pan American Union that every member republic has a continuing right to representation in the Union whether or not its government is recognized by the sister republics.

The Department's uneasiness was increased by frank statements from several of the larger South American governments that if an inter-American conference now took place they would find themselves unable to support the position of the United States.

Many Latin-American governments informed the Department that from their standpoint the continuation of the situation was intolerable. In their judgment the sterile policy of nonrecognition insisted upon by the Department had placed the security of the entire hemisphere in jeopardy. Some practical and immediate step would have to be taken to meet the emergency.

However, at successive meetings of the governing board of the Pan American Union, the Department was able to postpone action upon the Argentine request. Another solution of the dilemma in which it had involved itself had now been suggested.

Some months before the Mexican government had urged a consultative meeting. This suggestion had been sharply rebuffed. The Department adopted the attitude that it alone would decide what the relations of the rest of the hemisphere should be with Argentina. When the Ambassador of a great South American state ventured the opinion to the official in the Department most responsible for the policy then being pursued that his own country could not continue to boycott indefinitely a nation with which it had a common frontier and with which commercial relations were imperative if the civil population was to maintain itself during the existing war stringencies, he received the scarcely reassuring reply, "Argentina can go to hell!"

Soon afterward the determination of the Department's inter-American policy passed into the hands of Messrs. Stettinius and Rockefeller. It was soon apparent that they wanted to repair the damage to hemispheric solidarity which had been done during the preceding year, and to find some equitable solution for the Argentine impasse. They enthusiastically agreed that a special conference of all the American Republics "co-operating in the war effort" be held at Mexico City in the early winter of 1945, with the understanding that the conference would result in an agreement upon some face-saving device through which the Argentine government could resume official relations with the rest of the American family of nations.

Before the conference met in Mexico City in February, 1945, the new régime in the Department sent a special mission to Buenos Aires. In the ostensibly secret conversations which there took place with Colonel Perón, Dr. Juan Cooke, and other actual leaders in the Argentine government, it was agreed that if Argentina implemented her hemispheric defense commitments contracted in 1942 at Rio de Janeiro and accepted the opportunity to re-enter the fold of the American nations which would be held out to her after the Mexico City conference, the United States would abandon its coercive attitude and cancel all the restrictive measures which had been imposed on economic relations between the two countries. It was clearly understood that military matériel would no longer be withheld. While the suggestion was made that it would be eminently desirable for the military dictatorship to turn the government over to the Argentine Supreme Court until national elections could be held, the suggestion was not pressed, and Colonel Perón steadily refused to make any commitments about what he claimed were purely internal questions.

The Latin-American governments, to whose vision and initiative alone the conference was due, were determined that it must accomplish three major objectives: First, the conclusion of an inter-American agreement which would insure the commitment by the United States that it would join in repelling armed aggression, whether from without or within the hemisphere, against some other American republic so long as the World War continued. Second, the positive assurance that the United States would commit itself to continue this obligation after the end of the war by a treaty to be ratified by the United States Senate. The Latin-American Republics further insisted that the treaty must likewise include all the salient obligations entered into by the United States in the inter-American agreements concluded during the years of the Roosevelt administration, and specifically the obligation to maintain the principle of nonintervention by the United States in the domestic concerns of the other American nations. Third, the achievement of some understanding that would end the open breach between Argentina and the United States and restore inter-American solidarity.

These objectives were fought tooth and nail by a majority of the State Department functionaries, who objected to any attempt to strengthen the regional inter-American system. It was their set purpose to destroy entirely the inter-American structure erected during the preceding eleven years. They gave as their pretext their desire that the American Republics take no step that would make for a regional rather than a universal international order.

A smaller group within the Department headed by Assistant Secretary Rockefeller opposed this attempt on the more clear-sighted ground that, while the regional system of the Americas must necessarily be subordinated to the over-all authority of the coming United Nations organization, it should nevertheless be strengthened and consolidated so that it might, in fact, become a strong pillar of the United Nations organization.

The new Secretary of State Stettinius, who arrived at the conference the day it opened, knew but little of inter-American affairs. Fortunately the delegation included Senator Connally, the chairman of the Senate Foreign Relations Committee, and Senator Austin, an outstanding Republican member of the committee. Largely because of their own convictions and because of the ability with which they enforced them, the two Senators made possible the realization of the altogether desirable objectives of the Latin-American governments.

The chief accomplishment of the conference was the Act of Chapultepec. By this agreement the American Republics declared that any attempt, whether by an American state or by a non-American state, against "the integrity or inviolability of the territory or against the sovereignty or the political independence" of an American republic, should be regarded as an act of aggression against the others. They agreed to consult in order to fix the measures to be undertaken in such event. The resolutions called for an inter-American treaty to replace the declaration as soon as the war ended, and provided for the creation of a permanent military staff committee to propose the necessary measures to

insure hemispheric defense. They also provided for the maintenance of certain standards of democracy and of individual liberty
in the hemisphere, and reaffirmed earlier pledges to respect the
principle of nonintervention.

The conference also placed in the hands of the Inter-American
Juridical Committee[2] the responsibility for co-ordinating and
consolidating all the existing hemispheric peace machinery, provided for consultative meetings of the American Foreign Ministers every year, and regular Pan-American conferences every four
years; and agreed upon enlarged powers for the Pan American
Union as well as upon measures of reform in its attributes and
functions.

With regard to Argentina—a subject excluded from the official
agenda of the conference—the delegates agreed that if Argentina
would subscribe to the Act of Chapultepec, declare war upon the
Axis and give evidence that she would tighten up restrictions on
Axis activities, all the American Republics should resume official
relations with her. The United States individually further gave
assurance that if these steps were taken it would exercise its
influence to the fullest extent to bring about Argentina's entrance
at the outset into the United Nations.

Argentina promptly declared war upon the Axis and signed the
Act of Chapultepec. Progress was made in eliminating Axis
agencies and financial interests in Buenos Aires. Recognition of
the Farrell government followed.

By the salutary initiative of the Latin-American governments
and because of the vision and ability of leaders of the Senate
Foreign Relations Committee, the solidarity of the New World
had been at least nominally restored. A good start had been made
in repairing the damage done by the disastrous performance of
the State Department during the preceding year. The stage was
now set for the United Nations Charter meeting at San Francisco.
And the republics of the Western Hemisphere now at least possessed the assurance that they could take part in that meeting in
some semblance of unity, rather than as a disrupted and divided
group of states.

The course pursued by the United States at the Conference

[2] This committee was established by the Conference of Panama of 1939.

of Mexico City did much to reassure Latin-American public opinion. It was clearly a long step in the right direction.

The United States had now helped to bring about a united attempt to enable the Argentine dictatorship to maintain the dignity of the Argentine nation while making good in practice, as well as in words, its commitments to take effective action against the remnants of the Axis organizations operating in Argentine territory, and to restore such individual rights as freedom of expression and freedom of information.

There was no valid reason for the State Department to have gone further than that until all the American Republics had been satisfied that the Argentine government had, in fact, fulfilled, in spirit as well as in letter, the agreements which it had signed at Mexico City. The Department, however, went much further than this. Having reversed its former course, it was apparently incapable of moving slowly on its new course, as any reasonable measure of prudence would have dictated.

There was little justification for the United States to pledge itself to bring about any immediate admission of Argentina as a member of the United Nations. The Argentine government in power at that moment was the exact opposite of the democratic type of government which it was supposed the new world order would set as a standard. Both the last constitutional Argentine government and the military dictatorships which had succeeded it had at first refused to comply with their inter-American obligations and subsequently, after finally breaking relations with the Axis, had failed notoriously to implement the rupture. Furthermore, and at that moment an even more weighty reason for going slowly, the dictatorship was limiting those political rights of the Argentine people which it had undertaken to restore at the Conference of Mexico City.

The story of the antics of the United States delegation at San Francisco, insofar as the basic issues of inter-American policy are concerned, would afford material for a slapstick farce had they not resulted in developments that have already had, and promise to have many more, consequences of tragic import for the United States, and for the welfare of the entire New World.

In its handling of its relations with the other American Republics during the San Francisco Conference the United States suffered from two material handicaps in addition to the resentment and friction occasioned by the Argentine problem.

The first of these was of its own making. Throughout the years when the pristine principles of the Good Neighbor Policy were being maintained, the Latin-American Republics had been led consistently to believe that in all world issues the United States would co-operate closely with its American neighbors and would consult them prior to embarking upon any major policy. They had been given to understand that the United States viewed its own interests in the community of nations as inseparable from the interests of the rest of the hemisphere; that, while the only world power of the New World, it nevertheless remained a partner in the American family of nations, and did not consider the rest of the American Republics merely an appanage.

There was consequently very deep resentment occasioned throughout Latin America by the failure of the United States to consult the other republics and to obtain their views and recommendations before participating in the Dumbarton Oaks meetings where the preliminary draft of the United Nations Charter was agreed upon by the four major allies. The Latin-American states did not expect an invitation to take part in these meetings. They did expect—and rightly—an opportunity to learn the opinions of the United States regarding world organization and to discuss these opinions with her before the final conclusions of the Big Four were reached. And it would obviously have been of immense advantage to the United States had the rest of the world known that when the United States spoke at Dumbarton Oaks she interpreted the aspirations of the two hundred and fifty million citizens of the twenty-one free nations of the New World.

This opportunity was deliberately spurned. It was rejected because of timidity and because of the childish petulance of individual officials in the Department who were disgruntled by the failure of the Latin-American governments to adopt without question the State Department's wishes concerning hemispheric affairs.

Ignored by the United States, the other American Republics

held many purely Latin-American negotiations in order to construct that kind of purely Latin-American front which had not even been thought of for ten years. And the feelings aroused as a result of our attitude were by no means pacified by the pedagogical efforts of some officials of the Department, after the Dumbarton Oaks meeting, to disguise as "consultations" the lectures which they delivered to Latin-American diplomats upon the meaning of the tentative United Nations Charter.

The other obstacle encountered by the United States delegation was the growing fear and suspicion of the Soviet Union which began to be rampant in many Latin-American countries as the Russian armies advanced into central Europe, and as evidences of Soviet postwar policy became clearer.

The contemptuous attitude displayed toward the Latin-American delegates at San Francisco by Mr. Molotov accentuated this feeling. His insulting reference to that distinguished statesman, Mexico's Foreign Minister, Dr. Ezequiel Padilla, at the first meeting of the Steering Committee at the opening of the conference, when he insinuated that the Mexican Minister's remarks had been dictated by the United States, infuriated all the Latin-American delegations. The bitterness so engendered was largely responsible for what followed.

At the Yalta Conference, to offset the Soviet obsession that the British Dominions were subservient to Downing Street and that the Latin-American Republics blindly obeyed the behests of Washington, President Roosevelt had agreed that the Soviet Republics of Byelorussia and the Ukraine should be permitted to become members of the future United Nations organization. The Latin-American governments, when later informed of this commitment had acquiesced upon the understanding that Argentina should be simultaneously admitted.

Without warning the Soviet Foreign Commissar demanded that the representatives of the two Soviet Republics take part in the San Francisco Conference itself.

At a secret meeting of the Foreign Ministers of the Big Four, attended by the Foreign Ministers of Brazil, Chile and Mexico, the Russian demand was debated. Secretary Stettinius, after some efforts to get out of the moral pledges made at Mexico City, finally sponsored the Latin-American insistence that if the Russian demand was granted a similar invitation be extended to Argentina. After much angry debate Mr. Molotov declared: "I will support the admission of Argentina, but only if the United States will invite the Polish government of Lublin in addition to the republics of Byelorussia and the Ukraine."

Both the British and American governments had theretofore refused to agree to the admission of the Polish government. Secretary Stettinius reiterated the opposition which this government had expressed to Molotov when the Soviet Foreign Commissar had visited Washington on his way to San Francisco.

The Soviet Foreign Commissar then rejoined that in such event he was not sufficiently familiar with the Argentine situation to make it possible for him to support Argentine admission without further deliberation. (It was unknown as yet to the Department of State that at a meeting in the Brazilian city of Sao Paulo, in progress at the very moment that the San Francisco Conference was in session, Argentine and Soviet representatives were agreeing to a basis for diplomatic relations, and to a tentative series of trade agreements.)

The United States delegation found it difficult to persuade the Latin-American delegations to agree to vote for the admission of the two Soviet Republics in view of the attitude of Mr. Molotov. At first they persistently withheld their consent. Their agreement was forthcoming only in return for the firm promise by the United States that, should they consent, the American delegation would take such steps as might be necessary to insure the admission of Argentina.

At the meeting of the Steering Committee the following day the Latin-American delegates voted for the admission of the two Soviet Republics. The Soviet delegate voted against the admission of Argentina.

And at the subsequent plenary session of the conference, Mr. Molotov, although defeated in his attempt to exclude Argentina, triumphed all along the line by the public furore he created by his attacks upon the Argentine régime, by his references to the scathing terms in which that government had been denounced by former officials of the United States and by the emphasis he gave to the undeniable inconsistencies of American policy.

No incident during the conference created greater uproar in the American press. Not only the Communist-line papers, not only the extreme left organs, but the overwhelming majority of the press throughout the country, whether liberal or conservative, attacked the position taken by the United States delegation as destined to provoke a conflict with the Soviet Union and as intended to force into the United Nations a Fascist state which it was alleged had no right to admission.

Notwithstanding his presumable lack of experience in dealing with an uncontrolled public opinion, Mr. Molotov had succeeded brilliantly in distracting public attention from the real issues and in obtaining popular support for the Soviet aims. The public mind was focused exclusively upon the delinquencies—real or alleged—of the Argentine government. It gave no heed to the lack of true sovereignty of Byelorussia or the Ukraine. It paid no attention to the fact that the Polish government was wholly subservient to Moscow and that the liberties of Polish citizens were immeasurably less than those of Argentine citizens. It did not even know that the Soviet Union had agreed to vote for the admission of Argentina if Poland was admitted. And, what was even more important, it could not know that only a year later Soviet Russia would enter into official relations with the Argentine government which Mr. Molotov so vehemently denounced!

Granted that the chief political objective of the United States at San Francisco should have been to work out with the Soviet Union a charter of the United Nations of which both countries could approve, there is no shadow of justification for the failure of the United States delegation to tell the American people the actual facts. The issue was far from being that contest between democracy and Fascism which the Soviet delegation so successfully made it appear. It arose exclusively out of the peculiarly unsavory maneuvering by various powers and groups of powers to strengthen their position within the United Nations. If the American people had known the facts they would have formed an accurate appraisal. As it was, the wrath of public opinion was turned against Argentina. And the bitter prejudice so created has been in no small degree responsible for the latest blunders in American official policy.

Press and radio criticism stampeded the American delegation. Of the chief delegates only Senator Connally and Senator Vandenberg kept their heads. When Secretary Stettinius, in a state of abject panic, agreed, upon Soviet insistence, to scrap the entire inter-American regional system, it was Senator Vandenberg who stood like a rock behind the Latin-American delegations. He insisted that the charter must make provision for the existence of regional systems with full authority in a time of emergency to take steps in self-defense, subject to the ultimate over-all authority of the United Nations organization.

The efforts of the two Senators were on the whole successful. But the final adoption of the United Nations Charter left the Latin-American governments uncertain of the extent to which they would in the future be justified in depending upon the United States. They lacked confidence in the consistency of American policy toward them.

Within a few weeks' time the benefit resulting from the change of policy undertaken by the United States at the Inter-American Conference at Mexico City was obliterated. Public opinion in Argentina, as well as in many other parts of South America, was exasperated by the renewed press and radio attacks against the Argentine government. In the United States the basic issues involved were completely submerged. Hemispheric policy and inter-American relations were ignored.

The inter-American policy of the United States was further complicated by the fact that immediately after the San Francisco Conference the Secretary of State, Mr. Stettinius, was removed from office and replaced by James F. Byrnes.

Mr. Byrnes assumed his duties at one of the most critical moments in the history of the United States. The Potsdam Conference was about to be held. American public opinion was concentrating upon the rapid deterioration in relations between the Soviet Union and the United States and upon the multitudinous problems which were arising in Europe as a result of Germany's defeat. The war against Japan was still continuing. Immediate problems of foreign policy which were mounting in the Far East were as serious in their import as those in Europe or in the Near East. The new Secretary of State was neither able nor inclined to undertake any personal direction of inter-American policy. He had had no previous connection with inter-American affairs. Also it must be frankly stated that he evidenced no understanding of their intrinsic importance to the United States. His chief desire was that some official take this burden off his shoulders and undertake the direction of inter-American policy in such a manner as to cause the least amount of trouble to the Secretary of State himself.

That someone was soon found in the person of Spruille Braden, who had been sent as American Ambassador to Argentina upon the urgent recommendation of Nelson Rockefeller a few months before. Mr. Braden had displayed in past years many admirable qualities. He had for many years had close connections with Latin America. He had demonstrated vigor and understanding as the United States representative on the Chaco Commission which had finally brought about an end to the Chaco dispute between Paraguay and Bolivia. He had served with equal energy as Ambassador to Colombia, and his personal activity had been in no small part responsible for Colombia's realization of the danger to her internal safety and even more to the security of the Panama Canal from the German aviation interests operating in that country. Subsequently, as Ambassador to Cuba, Mr. Braden had displayed even greater activity. In this case, however, it must be frankly admitted that a large section of the Cuban people felt that his activities as American Ambassador directly impinged upon their domestic concerns at a time when political passions were high; and the reiterated requests for his recall made by the Cuban government, while evaded by the State Department, indicated the resentment occasioned in official circles by his interpretation of his mission.

Throughout his official career Mr. Braden had been tireless in his efforts to promote the security of the hemisphere and the

safety of the United States by finally eradicating every semblance
of Axis activity in the New World. The question which must
legitimately be raised is whether his methods were destined to
secure the desired results, and whether his attitude and the course
he followed were not inevitably bound to arouse wholly unnecessary resentment toward the United States by creating the un-
mistakable impression that the American government was not
only laying down the law to the other American peoples, but
also violating its official inter-American engagements by interfering directly in their sovereign and internal affairs.

These questions were sharply raised during the brief months
when Mr. Braden served as Ambassador in Buenos Aires. At the
moment when he arrived in Argentina, Colonel Perón was openly
directing the Argentine government. Both the Argentine press
and the foreign correspondents were being intimidated as well as
censored. The democratic parties opposed to the dictatorship were
at odds. They were deprived of all constitutional guaranties. Not
only the leaders of the hitherto unrecognized Communist party,
but also the leaders of such traditional political parties as the
Socialist and Radical parties, were imprisoned on any trivial
pretext. The evidences of sympathy given by Mr. Braden, as the
Ambassador of the great democracy of the North, to the democratic groups in Argentina, and his effective insistence that proper
freedom be given to the foreign press representatives were most
valuable. They were likewise legitimate. Had he limited himself
to such proper diplomatic activities, he would, in my judgment,
have accomplished far more to strengthen the cause of democracy
than he did. He would have lessened the rapidly growing belief
that the United States intended to dominate the Argentine nation.
Instead he increased it by creating the impression that his activities were intended to bring about the overthrow of the Argentine
government and its replacement with one more satisfactory to
Washington.

Mr. Braden almost immediately engaged in a bitter personal
feud with Colonel Perón. He then commenced a series of public
addresses in the capital in which he scathingly denounced the
officials in power, and made a tour of the interior of the republic

where he repeated the process. It became difficult at times to know whether a political campaign had not already commenced in which the United States Ambassador was one of the candidates. Mr. Braden began to be considered throughout Latin America merely as the personal antagonist of Colonel Perón. A growing audience watched the spectacle from the sidelines. The contest began to be regarded not as a contest between the forces of New World democracy and a dictatorship which had shown no few evidences of Fascist inspiration, but rather as a contest between the representative of the United States and the representative of a weaker power.

I know of no instance in the relations between the United States and the Latin-American Republics where any lasting benefit has been derived from a United States Ambassador's undertaking to insult, to decry and patently to urge the overthrow of the government to which he has been accredited. Some of the citizens of a country who are opposed to the government in power may momentarily welcome any kind of attack upon it, no matter whence it may come, but to the masses of the people national pride comes first. To the average Argentine, no matter how much he may have deplored the dictatorship imposed upon him, and no matter how much he may have desired its replacement by a constitutional government, the vehement attacks made upon his government by the representative of the United States became the cause of deep-rooted resentment.

The average Republican during the Roosevelt administrations may have vigorously detested every manifestation of the New Deal. He may have wholeheartedly wished the replacement of the Administration. But had a foreign ambassador in Washington undertaken to tour this country and publicly inveigh against the Roosevelt administration, accuse it of every form of dereliction, and invite the people of the United States to bring about its defeat at the next elections, even the most fanatical of the Roosevelt haters would have joined with the supporters of the government in demanding the ambassador's immediate dismissal.

The Argentine people are no more disposed to stomach flagrant interference in their internal concerns by foreign representatives in their country than are the people of the United States. They are far more infuriated by such activities when undertaken by a United States ambassador than by the representative of another nation because of that deep-rooted antagonism to the United States which had only begun to disappear when the Second World War broke out.

It has been assumed by the interventionists and by the starry-eyed international reformers in this country that the great majority of the democratic elements in Argentina welcomed the activities of Mr. Braden. All evidence is to the contrary. A few opposition leaders acclaimed him when he first commenced his campaign, but long before the national elections took place these signs of approval had vanished in a general chorus of protest from all the liberal elements against foreign intervention.

Because of the acts of anti-Semitism in which a number of Perón's henchmen engaged, it has also been assumed that the Jewish community in Argentina regarded Ambassador Braden as their savior. There is no vestige of proof for that assumption.

Mr. Braden's short career as Ambassador in Argentina had these results, most of which will have far-reaching effects:

Extreme nationalism in Argentina was greatly strengthened by the popular belief that the sovereignty of the nation was menaced. Mass support for the political aspirations of Colonel Perón rapidly increased by reason of the appeal he could make on the ground that the Argentine Republic was being coerced by the United States. The rank and file of the old-line democratic parties are resenting the interference of the United States Government even more bitterly than they did at first, because they are convinced it was the direct cause of their frustration. The mass of the Argentine people will for many generations remember not that this interference on the part of a United States ambassador was intended to bring about the restoration of their political liberties, but solely that a United States ambassador, with the full support of his government, intervened in the purely domestic concerns of the Argentine nation and openly assailed the Argentine government to which he was accredited.

It was in the light of these circumstances that Ambassador

Braden was recalled to Washington by Secretary Byrnes to replace Nelson Rockefeller as Assistant Secretary of State, and to be charged with the almost untrammeled direction of the policy of the United States towards its American neighbors.

It is believed in Washington that pressure for Mr. Braden's selection for this office came from two chief sources. The first consisted of those individuals who had been responsible for the "cracking-down" policy toward Argentina undertaken by the State Department prior to the short Stettinius-Rockefeller interlude and who hoped to justify their own record by a further application of the same nostrum, only in even larger doses. The second was composed of those groups in the United States that were striving vigorously to have this government adopt a policy of open intervention in the internal concerns of the other American Republics, ostensibly for the purpose of removing all governments that were not, in their judgment, truly "democratic," and replacing them with governments of which these groups approved. The most effective political agency spearheading this second source was the C.I.O.'s Committee on Latin-American Affairs, of which Jacob Potofsky and George Michanowsky[3] were the exceedingly active chairman and executive secretary.

Two developments marked Mr. Braden's first days in office, both of them disastrous in their effect upon inter-American understanding and in the reaction of the other American Republics toward the policy of the Department of State under its new dispensation.

[3] The following excerpt from a speech delivered by Senator Wherry on the floor of the United States Senate on the legislative day of Monday, July 29, 1946, as printed in the *Congressional Record* for Wednesday, July 31, 1946, is not without significance in this connection:

"It so happens that the executive director of this Latin-American committee of the CIO is George Michanowsky, born in Yalta, Russia, who arrived in the United States from Panama in 1940. He was not a United States citizen, and he registered as an alien on December 17, 1940.

"Mr. Michanowsky served for a while with New York's *PM*, in 1942. Now this same man has moved into the select circle as advisor to our Secretary of State and as a molder of American public opinion. I want to enter into the record a copy of a letter written to Secretary Byrnes on August 6, 1945, which is startling, to say the least, and is self-explanatory:

"'(JACOB S. POTOFSKY, CHAIRMAN; GEORGE BALDANZI; L. S. BUCKMASTER; LEWIS B. CLARK; JOSEPH CURRAN; SAMUEL J. HOGAN; O. A. KNIGHT;

The first had to do with Brazil.

Getulio Vargas had been President of Brazil for fifteen years. Even in its most repressive moments, his administration could have been classified only as a benevolent dictatorship. It was wholly national in character and devoid of any similarity to the authoritative dictatorships of Europe.

MARTIN C. KYNE; DAVID J. McDONALD; MILTON MURRAY; JOSEPH P. SELLY; WILLARD TOWNSEND; GEORGE MICHANOWSKY, EXECUTIVE SECRETARY)

PHILIP MURRAY   JAMES B. CAREY
PRESIDENT   SECRETARY-TREASURER

COMMITTEE ON LATIN-AMERICAN AFFAIRS
CONGRESS OF INDUSTRIAL ORGANIZATIONS.
NEW YORK, N. Y., AUGUST 6, 1945

Hon. James F. Byrnes,
    Secretary of State, Department of State,
        Washington, D. C.

Dear Mr. Byrnes:

Please permit me to congratulate you on your magnificent achievements at the Potsdam Conference. I also wish to thank you very much for your kind letter of July 5.

At this time I should like to acquaint you, on a confidential basis, with a very important matter I have dealt with during your absence from this country: In order to offer maximum support to United States Ambassador Spruille Braden's admirable activities on behalf of democracy in Argentina, we have engaged in a campaign on his behalf both in this country and in the lands to the south of us. We have specially publicized Mr. Braden's fine record, deserving the confidence of business and labor, among Latin-American workers, organized and unorganized. This step was particularly important since there was a chance that propaganda campaigns emanating from certain quarters and calculated to resuscitate the moth-eaten cry of "Yankee Imperialism" threatened to make some headway and to confuse the situation in various countries, especially in Argentina.

An inspired Associated Press story describing how admirable a stand you had taken on the Argentine question and reaffirming in detail our full and unqualified support of Ambassador Braden created a sensation in Latin America and made the front page of Argentina's biggest newspapers. Hard on the heels of this story and certain other actions originating with me, the Under Secretary of State Joseph Grew was happy to announce on August 2 that representatives of Argentine labor unions had called on Ambassador Braden in Buenos Aires to express their disapproval of the recent campaign of defamation directed at the Ambassador and obviously inspired by certain elements.

Since I know how limited your time is, I shall confine myself today to giving you only this sketchy outline of some of the things I have done during your absence to assist United States foreign policy and the cause of democracy. It will be a great honor to hear from you on this subject at your convenience. At your request, of course, I shall be glad to elaborate on any of these points.

                                          Very sincerely yours,
                                          George Michanowsky.' "

The support given to the United States by the Brazilian government under President Vargas and his brilliant Minister for Foreign Affairs, Dr. Oswaldo Aranha, even before the attack upon Pearl Harbor, had been wholehearted and spontaneous. President Vargas had personally informed the Japanese emissaries before the Japanese assault upon the United States that, if Japan declared war upon this country, Brazil would regard such action as hostile to herself. Notwithstanding grave internal obstacles, President Vargas had insisted, as soon as the United States was drawn into the war, that Brazil must immediately as a first step, break all relations with the Axis powers. This step was taken in January, 1942. Before six months elapsed, Brazil had declared war upon the Axis powers. Not only did President Vargas offer all Brazil's naval facilities to the United States, but the Brazilian Fleet at once co-operated with the South Atlantic Squadron of the United States. What was far more decisive was President Vargas' immediate grant to the American air forces of all the airfields and other installations required to establish bases in the northern portion of Brazil.

It was the utilization of these airfields that made it possible for the United States to invade North Africa in the autumn of 1942. As a result of personal conferences between President Roosevelt and President Vargas, the Brazilian government agreed to take part in such operations in Europe as were believed by the United States to be indispensable to the success of the North African campaign, notably those that were planned in 1942 for the contingent occupation of the Azores. The Brazilian government later sent an expeditionary force to Italy where Brazilian troops fought at the side of the United States divisions. At no time throughout the course of the war did the United States possess a more loyal ally than Brazil.

President Vargas had decided that as soon as the war was over the Brazilian people must return to a constitutional form of government. He believed that the ill effects of the corrupt and inefficient régimes which had preceded his own administration had been largely obliterated by his administrative policies. The disintegration of the great sprawling republic which threatened

when he seized office and the trend toward selfish and narrow
regionalism had been checked. He believed that a solid foundation had been laid for equitable participation in the national
prosperity by Brazilian labor and agriculture and he was convinced
that the transition from the war dictatorship which he had been
directing to constitutional democracy could be effected without
serious hindrance.

Upon the defeat of Germany he announced that national elections would be held six months later, and that he himself would
under no conditions be a candidate for the Presidency.

Two major parties crystallized. The first nominated as its
candidate General Eurico Dutra, who had been Minister of War
in the Vargas Cabinet. The second nominated General Eduardo
Gomes who had been one of the ablest figures in the Brazilian Air
Force and possessed an admirable record. A third party, the
Communist party, was led by Carlos Luis Prestes, one of the most
brilliant figures in present-day Brazil.

By early autumn the political campaign had become intense. At
the elections to be held on December 3 the electorate was to vote
not only for Presidential candidates but also for Senators and
Representatives, who were to compose a national assembly charged
with the duty of drafting a new national constitution.

President Vargas had made it clear that, while his government
would keep hands off, he hoped his supporters would vote for
General Dutra. The supporters of President Vargas commenced
openly to demand that the elections be limited to the selection of
the members of the National Constitutional Assembly and that
the election of the future President be postponed until after the
new constitution had been adopted. This issue became the crucial
issue in the political campaign. Those who favored elections for
a Constitutional Assembly were regarded as favoring the temporary retention of President Vargas in office, while those who
insisted that the elections be carried out as originally proclaimed
were the supporters of General Gomes.

The question involved was solely an internal political dispute
between two factions of the Brazilian people and possessed no
international aspects.

At that moment Mr. Braden arrived in Rio de Janeiro on his way to Washington to assume his new duties. The American Ambassador to Brazil, Dr. Adolph Berle, showed Mr. Braden a speech he wanted to make at a large meeting of the members of the Brazilian press which was to take place within a few days at Petropolis.

In this speech Dr. Berle expressed in the most emphatic terms his conviction that the Brazilian elections should take place as originally planned and his belief that there was no reason the selection of a Constitutional Assembly should interfere with the simultaneous election of a Brazilian President and Congress.

Mr. Braden expressed his enthusiastic approval. The speech was delivered as planned. The adherents of General Gomes immediately insisted that the speech constituted a clear-cut indication that the United States wished President Vargas to withdraw from the Presidency and that he no longer possessed the friendly confidence of Washington. Those opposed to General Gomes, on the other hand, even more vociferously claimed that the Ambassador's speech infringed the sovereignty of Brazil and was a clear-cut evidence of interference on the part of the United States. A tempest arose. Disorder threatened in Rio de Janeiro.

It became known that President Vargas was seriously considering changing the election proclamation. At the same time he replaced the chief of police in Rio de Janeiro with his own brother. A rapid movement within the Army resulted; army leaders demanded the President's immediate resignation, which was promptly forthcoming. No bloodshed or civil strife resulted. The former President left immediately for his home in the State of Rio Grande do Sul, and his place as Chief Executive was taken by the Chief Justice.

The incident had far-reaching consequences. The Brazilian people, like all the Ibero-Americans, are intolerant of any infringement of their national sovereignty. Even those leaders who for political reasons made use of the Ambassador's intervention privately condemned it. Brazilian labor, which had greatly benefited from the measures enacted by the Vargas government, assailed the action as gross ingratitude on the part of the United

States toward a government which had loyally supported it when it was under attack by the Axis. The great body of Brazilian public opinion of all political shades felt that the nation had suffered an indignity at the hands of the United States.

Throughout the rest of the hemisphere the incident was played up as further evidence that American policy had changed, that the Good Neighbor Policy was vanishing and that American intervention was once more a thing to be feared.

When the Brazilian national elections finally took place, General Dutra, the candidate supported by former President Vargas, was elected President over General Gomes by a majority of two to one. Although he was not a candidate, President Vargas was elected to the National Senate by the states of both Rio Grande do Sul and Sao Paulo and as a deputy from almost every other one of the Brazilian states.

This whole unhappy history had a material effect upon the very real friendship and understanding which had existed for many years, and especially during the war years, between the Brazilian people and the people of the United States. Anti-American demonstrations, which had been hitherto unknown, took place with some frequency.

The second unfortunate development which took place after Mr. Braden's return to Washington was the State Department's postponement of the inter-American conference planned for the autumn of 1945 in Rio de Janeiro to negotiate the hemispheric defense treaty envisaged in the Act of Chapultepec. The United States was officially committed to participate. All the governments of the American Republics wanted this consultative meeting held without delay, regarding it as essential for their own security now that the war against the Axis had been won.

Because the State Department was unwilling for any inter-American conference to be held at which the Argentine government would be represented and because it refused to consider the conclusion of an inter-American defense treaty in which the existing Argentine régime would take part, it abruptly informed the Brazilian government on October 20 that it wanted the conference postponed. In view of the troubled situation which then existed in Rio de Janeiro, the Brazilian government agreed. Only then were the other American Republics notified. They all were indignant that their own wishes had been over-ridden and that they had been given no opportunity to express their views before the conference was postponed. Fortunately, indignation was even more openly expressed by the Foreign Relations Committee of the United States Senate. Senator Connally, Senator Vandenberg, and Senator Austin of the Committee on Foreign Relations had previously been invited by the Department of State to attend the conference at Rio de Janeiro in the same capacity as that in which they had so ably served at the conference at Mexico City. The first these members of the legislative body knew of the postponement of the conference was when they read of it in the newspapers. Mr. Braden was promptly summoned to a session of the committee at which the members of the committee made known in no uncertain terms their insistence that in the future the Department of State live up to the spirit and letter of the inter-American agreements into which the United States had entered and refrain henceforth from taking unilateral action in questions affecting all the American Republics. The confirmation of the appointment of Mr. Braden as Assistant Secretary of State was held up for some weeks by the Senate as an expression of its determination that the policy which it had now laid down be complied with in the future.

The action taken by the Foreign Relations Committee was in the highest degree salutary. It accomplished much in persuading public opinion in the other American Republics that even if the Department of State proved to be derelict in its interpretation of the Good Neighbor Policy and of existing inter-American agreements, the Senate of the United States not only possessed clear understanding of such obligations but also intended to see to it that these were carried out.

Within a few weeks, however, added ground for controversy between all of the American Republics was created. The Minister for Foreign Affairs of Uruguay, Dr. Rodriguez Larreta, officially communicated to the governments of the other American nations a series of recommendations, obviously intended to apply to the Argentine situation. The essential provision in these recommendations was contained in the words which read:

> Nonintervention must be used on the basis that it is not a shield behind which crimes may be perpetrated, law may be violated, agents and forces of the Axis may be sheltered and binding obligations may be circumvented.

In essence, the Uruguayan proposal urged that whenever a "government of force" comes into power in any American republic and deprives its citizens of their political liberties, such a régime *ipso facto* becomes a menace to the security of the rest of the hemisphere and its existence a legitimate reason for the other American Republics, after consultation and agreement, to take what measures of intervention they may consider necessary in order to restore democratic and constitutional government in that country.

At the particular moment when this Uruguayan proposal was communicated to the other American governments, no project could have been more controversial. There existed among the twenty-one American nations only a minority of governments that could have been regarded as democratic and constitutional. Furthermore, the policy pursued during the preceding two years by the Department of State toward Argentina had given rise to the conviction in many parts of the New World that the United States was already intervening in the internal concerns of that republic. Recent events in Argentina and in Bolivia, where the United States had for many months insisted that the other American countries should not recognize a government which had come into power through a revolution, had increased the suspicion that the United States was reverting to a big stick policy.

The Uruguayan proposal, notwithstanding repeated denials in Washington, was widely regarded as inspired by the United States. This impression was naturally increased by the fact that the Department of State publicly announced its enthusiastic endorsement "in principle" of the Uruguayan proposal before it had even been digested in the other Foreign Offices to which it had been sent.

Moreover, there still remained in the minds of all Latin-American statesmen the memory of the period not so long ago when it was the announced policy of the United States to interfere directly in the domestic concerns of all the smaller Latin-American nations and when this interference all too frequently ended in such use of armed force as in the tragic military occupations of Nicaragua, the Dominican Republic and Haiti.

For all these reasons, evidences of violent disapproval of the Uruguayan proposal became manifest in almost every American republic. Leading statesmen of the Americas, none of whom could be regarded as hostile to the United States, condemned the proposal as contrary to the basic principles of the inter-American system. Nine American governments, among them those of Mexico, Brazil, Colombia, Chile, Cuba and Ecuador, which carry great weight in the councils of the American family of nations, officially replied to the Uruguayan government by stating that they could not support a recommendation that envisaged the possibility of any form of intervention in the domestic concerns of an American nation.

The controversy continued to flare and its intensity was increased by repeated pronouncements from the Department of State that unanimous inter-American agreements were outmoded, and that action such as that suggested by Uruguay should be taken whenever a "substantial number" of the American Republics considered it necessary. Such pronouncements naturally enough increased the suspicion that the United States was once more planning, under another guise, urged on it by inter-nationalist groups, to embark upon Theodore Roosevelt's policy of "cleaning up" Latin America. For no responsible Latin American could be oblivious to the fact that this country, through the crippling economic pressure it could bring to bear, could control a "substantial number" of the smaller American Republics should it at any time wish to bring about some form of ostensibly "collective" intervention in one of the larger American Republics.[4]

[4] The utter inconsistency of the course pursued by the Department of State concerning this vital issue was later graphically demonstrated. On July 17, 1946, the governing board of the Pan American Union, composed of representatives of all the American Republics, unanimously approved a draft for a "Declara-

At this critical moment the Argentine national election campaign entered its final stage. Colonel Perón had obtained the support of a wing of the Radical party in addition to that of his recently created National Labor party. His opposition, composed of the bulk of the Radical party, the Socialist party, and the now legally recognized Communist party, had joined forces to nominate as their presidential candidate Dr. Tamborini, a highly respected Radical leader. While the Conservative party did not officially take part in this "popular front," its leaders all supported Dr. Tamborini and contributed to his campaign. The Democratic candidates had not only all the financial assistance they could require, but the support of all the press, which was not restricted during the campaign.

Until just before the close of the campaign the State Department indulged in that type of agreeable delusion caused by wishful thinking. It felt confident that the election results would justify its "cracking-down" policies, which had been so enthusiastically applauded by most of the American press. It was encouraged by the reports sent from Buenos Aires by American press correspondents who continued to insist that Colonel Perón could not possibly be elected if anything approaching fair elections were held. It stubbornly refused to see the plain facts, for the unvarnished truth was that Colonel Perón's popularity among the poorer classes of the Argentine people had been growing by leaps and bounds.

For many months Colonel Perón had maintained that he was the friend of the downtrodden and of the underprivileged. But he had not limited himself to appealing to the Argentine masses to join him in a triumphant "social revolution"; he had given them very practical evidence of the benefits which his election would bring them. At his behest the military government had enacted a series of decrees, all of them contributing substantially to the

tion of the Rights and Duties of the American Republics." This draft contained the provision: "Intervention by any one or more states, directly or indirectly, and for whatever reasons, in the internal or external affairs of another state, is inadmissible." The official approval given by the Department to this hemispheric declaration completely reversed the position it had taken only a few months before. Fortunately it constituted a reversal in the right direction.

improvement of labor conditions and raising materially the wage scales previously in effect. One decree in particular had secured him overwhelming support. It provided a yearly bonus for each worker, equivalent to a regular month's salary.

As I have already stated, the Argentine social and economic system still had many feudal characteristics. For the first time since the earlier days of Irigoyen, the great masses of the Argentine people believed that a political leader had arisen who would prove to be their friend and help them to better living conditions, which in many cases were truly desperate. When they saw that this popular idol was under attack by the United States their ardor for his cause was redoubled.

Only a few weeks before the date of the elections, February 24, 1946, the Department of State began to take alarm. Reports were now received that the triumph of the opposition might not be so certain after all. When these reports became altogether alarming the Department suddenly decided upon an amazing gamble.

For many months the Department had been tabulating intelligence reports on Axis activities in Argentina, especially on Axis connections with Argentine officials. These reports had increased as a result of facts learned after the Allied occupation of Germany. In the fatuous belief that the publication of this information would defeat Colonel Perón, the State Department published its files in the form of a "Blue Book" just two weeks before the elections.

There can be no possible denial of the truth of the official charge, later made by the Argentine government, that the publication of the Blue Book, by its timing and the manner of its release, constituted "a lamentable interference in the internal political affairs of Argentina." It was a clear violation of the treaty commitment entered into by the United States at Montevideo in 1933, and reaffirmed in several subsequent inter-American agreements to abide by the principle of nonintervention.

But from the standpoint of practical expediency alone the step thus taken by the United States represented an almost unbelievably crass blunder.

Had the Blue Book been published prior to Mr. Braden's mission to Buenos Aires, it is conceivable that the charges contained in it, a majority of which I believe are well founded, might have had a conclusive effect upon Argentine public opinion. Published at the very height of a passionate campaign, it inevitably had an effect precisely the opposite of that intended. It increased popular support for Colonel Perón. It even more greatly stimulated ultranationalism. It raised general hostility to the United States to a fever pitch.

It was not surprising that in Colonel Perón's only newspaper, when the votes daily counted were tabulated after the elections in parallel columns, the photograph that adorned the column of votes cast for Dr. Tamborini was not that of the candidate, but instead that of Mr. Braden. When the elections finally took place even the opposition was compelled to admit that they were entirely free of fraud and of coercion.

Colonel Perón had triumphed by the greatest electoral college majority ever known in Argentine history, and by a very substantial popular majority as well. He had swept with him into the Senate and the House of Deputies huge majorities of his supporters, and his candidates triumphed in twelve of the fourteen provinces.

As a result of the policy that the United States had pursued toward Argentina during the preceding two and a half years, this country had received at the hands of the Argentine people the worst diplomatic defeat it ever sustained in the Western Hemisphere and had suffered a loss of influence and of prestige in South America that will not be forgotten for many years to come.

But this was not all. Twelve hours before the Blue Book had been published, the State Department had summoned Latin-American Ambassadors in Washington to hand them copies of the document. Most of them knew that it was already in the hands of the press for later release. This was the kind of "consultation" undertaken by the Department on a question that involved the highest interests of all the peoples of the Americas, and that unquestionably justified a joint, rather than a unilateral, approach.

To the majority of the other American countries, the opportunity of expressing their official views concerning the policy of the United States toward Argentina was more than welcome. In their communications to the United States all the leading Latin-American governments have in unmeasured terms condemned the policy pursued and have made it clear that they will refuse to countenance the continuation of such a policy.

The considered point of view of Latin-American democracy was well set forth in an editorial appearing on March 22 in *El Tiempo*, a leading newspaper of one of the hemisphere's truest democracies, the Republic of Colombia, when it said:

We are confronted with a reality which we must analyze serenely and dispassionately, interpreting it in its purely democratic significance as the result of a popular plebiscite which was carried out honestly and normally, as the parties which took part in the election have announced. That reality stamps the victory of Colonel Perón, not as an act of force, but as the free and sovereign expression of the Argentine nation. And it is in that sense that we must confront this reality from the American point of view.

Those who are even superficially familiar with the history of the Argentine nation and who are more or less familiar with its evolutionary process, and especially those who are acquainted with the nature of its social-economic structure, will not have the slightest difficulty in interpreting the electoral success of Perón as an express protest on the part of the Argentine people against conditions which were not far different from those of a kind of feudal organization. Argentina, as a nation of great land holders and of powerful industrialists, was beginning to suffer from social trends which were an anachronism, in many aspects unfortunate, and in almost all aspects unjust. Perón can signify in the present century a reaction against feudalism, and perhaps the secret of his success consists primarily in his having taken advantage—as an opportunist and certainly as a demagogue—of a situation which was already intolerable in order to bring about what he himself has called his "triumphant social revolution."

Nevertheless what appears to predominate in the political doctrines of what we might call Peronism is the nationalist sentiment which has been gaining strength in Argentina in recent years.

We do not try, because it does not interest us, to justify Peronism, but only to explain the phenomenon of his triumph, and for that reason we interpret that political movement as the expression of a certain social-economic moment in the life of Argentina. But to these factors must be added other factors which have contributed to the growth of this phenomenon. Among such factors is the stimulation which the nationalist sentiment in Argentina received as a result of the mistaken policy of the State Department in Washington in relation to the government of Buenos Aires.

The very publication of the Department of State's Blue Book may not have been intended to be, but in reality certainly appeared to be, an act of intervention in the Argentine elections which took place at the very moment when the political struggle in Argentina was at its most acute phase.

The policy pursued was mistaken because it violated one of the principles most dear to the peoples of the American continent, the principle of non-intervention, consecrated in an inter-American pact to which all the nations of the Hemisphere subscribed with rejoicing because they believed it to be a great triumph of the international law of the New World.

It would, consequently, not be paradoxical to say that this policy of the State Department helped very considerably to elect Colonel Perón. It is possible that without such intervention Perón might have been elected for the reasons to which we have already referred. But from every point of view the policy of the Department of State served strongly to assist Perón in his election campaign, since it aroused the nationalist sentiments of the Argentine people and in particular exacerbated the anti-Yankee feeling which has traditionally existed in Argentina, because, among other reasons, of the influence of certain European powers.

But once the triumph of Perón has been brought about, and brought about as the result of fair elections, it makes little difference what the reasons for that triumph may have been. We believe that it is necessary to accept this result, to recognize this result, and to respect this result as the sovereign act of an independent people.

Nothing would be more fatal for the future of the inter-American policy than any attempt now to isolate the Government of Perón. If that Government, we repeat, had been born of a coup d'état, and was clearly opposed by the democratic desires of the Argentine people, there would be justification for the nations of the Continent to consult together with regard to the desirability or the nondesirability of recognizing that Government. But since that Government has been elected in accordance with the Constitutional procedure of the Argentine Republic and as a result of elections surrounded by guaranties, and consequently wholly fair, the Governments of the American Republics have no other course than to accept the Government of Perón without reservations as to its nature, since the nature of that Government is a question solely within the competence of the Argentine nation. Any contrary course would result in the violation of one of the most honored principles of the Atlantic Charter and one of the most elementary foundations upon which international relations must rest.

Finally, those of us who believe in democracy must accept democracy with all its risks. And what has taken place in Argentina is purely and simply democracy.

Colonel Perón's election resulted in a feeling of intense exasperation toward the State Department among the leading members of both parties in the Senate Foreign Relations Committee. Such outstanding leaders as Senators Connally and George on the Democratic side, and Senators White, Vandenberg and Austin on the Republican, had already made it plain at the time of Mr. Braden's nomination that they strongly disapproved of the Department's policy, both because they believed it entirely at variance with the principles of the Good Neighbor Policy and because they did not believe it could work. They had been put off with the assurance that Mr. Braden would not be a "policy-making official," and that since Dr. Tamborini would unquestionably be elected President, all reasons for continuing the controversy with Argentina would soon end. Now Colonel Perón had been triumphantly elected, the prestige of the United States had suffered a serious collapse throughout the hemisphere, and the American government appeared to have entered a one-way street from which extrication promised to be not only difficult but painful as well.

The Senate leaders promptly forced a showdown. The Secretary of State soon announced that a new ambassador, George Messersmith, was being sent to Buenos Aires. President Truman, in his Army Day address in Chicago, took occasion to state that the United States was prepared to enter into an inter-American defense treaty with "all" the American Republics, thus expressly disavowing the previous policy of the State Department which had repeatedly proclaimed that the United States would "never" enter into any inter-American defense pact to which an Argentine government headed by Colonel Perón was a party. The State Department behind a screen of verbiage intended to persuade public opinion that its previous policy remained unaltered, was compelled to prepare to embark upon a new course.

The question is, in view of the history of the past three years of Departmental policy, how much of the inter-American system still remains to be salvaged, and what elements are there in Argentine-American relations that can be used to construct a new and better understanding between the two peoples.

The answer to this question depends primarily—granted a fundamental change in the policy of the United States—upon the intentions of Colonel Perón and upon the policies of his new government.

What manner of man is Perón? To the American people he has been depicted almost exclusively as a dyed-in-the-wool Fascist, as a new edition of Hitler, as a corrupt tyrant, and as a ruthless antagonist of democracy, surrounded and inspired by Nazi agents.

One need not be an admirer of Colonel Perón to question the accuracy of this portrait, nor to suspect that much of the impression of him created in the United States has been the result of propaganda—part deliberate, and part unintended. And in the latter category must be placed a large amount of the information sent north by a few American press correspondents in Argentina. Their individual point of view has been so biased that they have been unable to report on men and events during the turbulent days which have passed in Argentina with any reasonable degree of objectivity.

First and foremost Juan Perón is an "Argentino." He is an extreme nationalist—proud of his country, and convinced of its superior position in the inter-American world. He is a typical product of his own soil. Coming from the middle classes, he has spent the whole of his adult years in the restricted and disciplined life of the Argentine Army. By dint of calculating ambition and of exceptional energy he succeeded in advancing himself into a position of dominating influence over his fellow officers, senior as well as junior. He has ever had an eye to the main chance. When the opportunity came to enlarge the sphere of his activities he was not slow to grasp it.

In this endeavor he was aided by an unusually attractive personality. Fifty-one years of age, he seems much younger. From the standpoint of the Argentine masses he possesses much that makes for popularity. He is both *guapo* and *muy macho* in Argentine vulgar parlance—physically brave and very masculine.

Of the experience or breadth of education that would qualify him for the Presidency, he has none. But he has the capacity to learn with almost incredible rapidity.

His frankness in his attempt to grapple with the facts of international life can best be indicated by a confidential letter which he addressed to President Truman through an emissary two months before the elections. In this communication he bluntly stated that for fundamental reasons Argentina and the United States should reach an understanding based on mutual good will. He urged that the Argentine government's blocked funds held in the United States be released so that Argentina would be in a position to buy American goods and start a two-way trade between the two countries which would be reciprocally beneficial. He expressed the conviction that such a step would make it possible for a new and better epoch to commence in the relations between the two nations, and put an end to the misunderstandings which had already done so much damage. He referred to the cordial and satisfactory agreements reached at the time of the mission headed by Ambassador Warren and General Brett, sent to Buenos Aires the preceding year by Secretary Stettinius, and to the wide understanding arrived at covering economic relations as well as military, naval and aviation co-operation in the defense of the continent. All this had gone by the board, he stated, as soon as Mr. Braden had entered the scene. Should he reach the Presidency, he concluded by declaring, it would be his firm intention to pursue a policy of true and loyal co-operation based upon the agreements reached with the Warren Mission.

This letter was unanswered. By the ordinary standards of diplomatic procedure a candidate for the Presidency does not address a letter to the President of another republic dealing with official matters or giving assurances as to his policies if he is elected. But granted the exceptional circumstances which existed, this action would hardly warrant the continued insistence of his innumerable detractors in the United States that the position taken by this government toward Colonel Perón was justifiable on the ground of his stubborn unwillingness to agree to effective measures of hemispheric security.

Colonel Perón has undoubtedly been close to German influences. But so were the great majority of the officers in the Argentine Army. People here forget too readily that the Argentine Army has for many decades been trained by German instructors. Likewise, Colonel Perón has certainly never demonstrated any belief in our own form of democracy. But it must also be remembered that throughout the larger part of his life what was termed democracy in Argentina was in reality a feudal form of government designed to maintain the grasp of the privileged classes upon the Argentine fleshpots, and that, with one exception, the elections in which he himself was elected President were the first that the Argentine people had ever known that were free of fraud and coercion.

He is undoubtedly an opportunist and a demagogue, as the democratic press of Latin America has called him. But so have been a host of other politicians of the Latin countries who have later accomplished much for the benefit of their fellow men.

Juan Domingo Perón has the inherent capacity and the chance to make of his promised "social revolution" a New Deal for the Argentine people.

The greatest problems with which President Perón's new government is confronted are the question of agrarian reform and the method by which the state can best protect and stimulate industrialization.

Argentine economy is founded upon the production of agricultural exports. While industry has largely increased during the war, supplying a half of the nation's income, it chiefly involves the processing of farm products, and even so still totals only one-tenth of the national exports.

More than two-thirds of Argentina's arable land is cultivated by tenants or landless labor. Perón has promised to abolish the system which has so long prevailed, and to turn laborers and tenants into proprietors. Should the issue be pressed by the new government it seems hardly probable that the Radicals, Socialists and Communists can fail to lend their support.

The industrial problem is more complicated. The nationalization of public utilities, particularly the British-owned railways, offers but one aspect. The new industries are pressing for protection by high tariffs, and the program which President Perón has formulated for workers' benefits may depend for its fulfillment upon some compromise upon tariff protection between the new government and Argentine big business.

But the danger to the Perón administration in such event will arise from the fact that artificial tariff barriers to the importation of foreign-manufactured goods will inevitably cut down the ability of foreign countries to buy Argentina's agricultural exports, and thus strike at the heart of the Perón project for agricultural reform.

President Perón requires the best economic and agricultural talent available to advise him in the intricate problems with which he must rapidly deal. There is so far little evidence that such able advice will be forthcoming from the inexperienced and largely unknown men whom he has appointed to his Cabinet. President Perón's ultimate success will depend upon his ability to procure a continuation of the support which a majority of his fellow citizens have so far been willing to give him and in perpetuating the democratic freedom under which his administration commenced. But it will also depend upon the readiness of the United States to do its part in drastically changing its own policy and in making that much-talked-of, and never implemented, co-operation between Argentina and the United States a reality.

In this discussion of the reasons for the present collapse of the inter-American system I have concentrated almost entirely upon the political aspects of the problem, because the collapse has been chiefly due to our own disastrous handling of the political relations with our neighbors of Latin America. But there are many other contributing factors, largely economic, some social. And some with which I have dealt previously arise from Nazi and Fascist activities designed to disrupt the hemispheric solidarity which had existed to so notable a degree at the time of the entrance of this country into the Second World War.

When the Western Hemisphere was drawn into war it became

evident that all the American Republics would suffer a severe shock to their national economy. This shock would be even more severe during the immediate postwar period.

The European market was essential to their economy. After 1939 nearly one-half of their exports and imports was automatically cut off. With the involvement of the United States, our need for strategic materials resulted in procurement contracts which, together with the joint Allied requirement for agricultural commodities produced in Latin America, prevented the economic dislocation from having any immediately prejudicial effect. Production continued at a high level.

It was clear as early as 1942 that if the United States were to pursue a constructive economic policy in its inter-American relations, and make its assurances of co-operation something more than mere words, it must be prepared during the first stages of the postwar period to assist in practical ways in helping its Latin-American neighbors to tide themselves over the appallingly difficult period of economic readjustment with which each would be faced. For they all would confront the prompt termination of procurement contracts; they all would face a slump in the world price of their chief exports; and they all would have to solve the situation created by the resumption of imports which competed with consumers' goods produced locally by industries established during the war. Moreover, for a while at least they would have great difficulty in obtaining essential imports from overseas.

Unfortunately, the government of the United States has failed completely to render any efficient assistance to its neighbors in meeting this crisis.

Instead of tapering off procurement contracts, and using the strategic materials so purchased after the war to create much-needed stock piles in this country, it terminated its contracts abruptly. At the Mexico City conference the United States had pledged herself to consult with the governments concerned whenever contracts were terminated in order to find means of lessening the shocks thus created. This pledge was ignored.

At the Conference of Rio de Janeiro in 1942, by authorization of President Roosevelt, I had officially assured all of the Latin-

American governments that in the allocation of goods in short supply Latin-American civilian needs would be treated on the same basis as our own. The moment the war ended this policy was scrapped. Notwithstanding the assurances given at Mexico City to the contrary, the Latin-American Republics were left to fend for themselves in the United States market, and as a result the citizens of the other American Republics were unable to obtain in the transition period after the war as large a quantity of goods in short supply as they had before. Replacements in the industries used to help the United Nations win the war were unobtainable.

Inflation has set in in all the American Republics. In many it has already reached fantastic figures. Because of the failure of the United States to render any practical help, and to see the need for a continental program of mutual assistance, many American governments will resort to artificial controls which it will take long to eradicate, and which will raise many barriers to that freer flow of international trade which this government has pledged itself to promote. The apparent indifference of Washington to its neighbors' difficulties and the unquestioned failure of the Department of State to live up to some of the commitments on economic policy which it made have created additional and serious ill-feeling toward the United States.

What is, however, more immediately disquieting is that the economic dislocations will result in social and political upheavals in many parts of the Americas. At this critical and uncertain moment of the world's history such disturbances occasion muddy waters in which those who regard with strong antipathy the maintenance of continental unity would delight to fish.

Until the world has been brought to a state where a true peace prevails, and until the United Nations has given evidence that it can actually fill the requirements for which it was created, it must be recognized that Soviet policy will not be employed in the New World for the purpose of strengthening inter-American solidarity and thereby increasing the security of the United States and the tranquillity of mind of the citizens of this country.

The more divided the Americas become, the greater the antagonism to the United States within the Western Hemisphere, the weaker the influence of the United States in other parts of the world.

It can hardly any longer be alleged that the Soviet government is motivated by purely ideological principles now that it has entered into official relations with the Argentine government which Mr. Molotov so vigorously condemned on ideological grounds a year ago at San Francisco. Nor can it be taken lightly for granted that the Soviet government believes its future trade with Latin America can be so great as to warrant solely for that reason the dispatch of some of its ablest diplomats, surrounded by innumerable assistants, to the Latin-American Republics.

To those who have been observing recent trends in Latin America it has come as no surprise that the Communist party throughout the American Republics is now once more, after a lapse of some years, pursuing the familiar line of inveighing against American imperialism, and taking every advantage derived from recent United States policy in order to arouse suspicion and hostility among the masses against the American people.

If inter-American unity is to be restored there is only one way in which it can be done. That is for the United States to abandon totally the policy toward Latin America that it has followed during the past two and a half years.

It should at once revert to the true principles of the Good Neighbor Policy which, in act although not in word, it has discarded in recent times.

It should, in the matter of the recognition of new governments, adopt the procedure of automatic recognition and abandon its disastrous effort to use the act of recognition as a means of bringing pressure upon its neighbors.

It should, in every aspect of its policy, abide by its treaty commitment to refrain from interfering in the internal or external affairs of the other American peoples.

It should abide by its pledge, whenever questions arise which affect the welfare or the security of the New World, to seek through common and co-operative inter-American effort the necessary remedies. It should refrain from unilateral action.

It should seek to strengthen the inter-American system within the legitimate sphere assigned to it by the United Nations Charter.

It should further the rapid conclusion, as an integral part of that system, of an inter-American defense treaty, and the subsequent establishment, by virtue of such a treaty, of an inter-American Military Staff Committee.

It should utilize existing machinery, such as the Inter-American Financial and Economic Advisory Committee, for the purpose of maintaining a practical, reciprocal program designed to make possible true economic co-operation between the United States and the other American Republics.

It should, in its domestic policy, make provision for the support of such an economic program.

It should encourage, through private as well as official channels, the rapid industrialization of the other American nations as the best means of improving living standards in those countries and in consequence of increasing trade between the Americas.

It should undertake a far greater measure of official activity in promoting labor and cultural co-operation between the United States and Latin America.

The unity of the Americas proved to be the greatest element of safety that the United States possessed at the time of the attack upon Pearl Harbor. That measure of security will vanish unless these steps are taken, and taken rapidly.

Chapter V

Shadows over the Near East

AVIATION is eliminating time and space. During the Second World War many hundreds of thousands of the men in our armed services lived and fought in the countries of the Moslem world. They came to know the peoples of Morocco, of Algeria, and of Tunisia. They were stationed for long months among the Egyptians and other Arab races. They sweltered in the steaming ports of the Persian Gulf.

Consequently, there is fermenting in the consciousness of the American people a yeast of understanding and of knowledge which will ultimately destroy misconceptions that have prevailed for many generations.

But to the average American, the Near East, that region where East and West meet in opposing tides, remains merely a shadowy realm inhabited by backward peoples incomprehensible in their language, their writing, their tendencies, their religion and their culture. It is a region still so remote and so alien that the idea of any development within it creating any impact upon the vital interests of the United States seems utterly incredible. No concept would be more dangerously mistaken. If the precarious peace of the moment is to be shattered, the immediate origins of war will arise in the Near East.

The Near East may be defined as the area which comprises Turkey and Iran, the independent or autonomous Arab states of Egypt, Saudi Arabia, Iraq, Transjordania, Yemen, the Lebanon and Syria, the protectorates and colonies of the Persian Gulf, of Arabia, and of the Red Sea, the former Italian colony of Libya, and the presently mandated territory of Palestine.

This vast region, for so long the theater of conflicts of interest between the imperial powers of Europe, is today more than ever the area in which a gigantic contest has commenced between imperial forces which have for a century and a half proved to be inherently irreconcilable.

In this area Great Britain has long maintained preponderant control. This part of the world still constitutes the vital link between the British Isles and the British Empire of the Far East. The intrusion of any other major power in that area threatens the English life line, which in the past has been menaced in turn by France, Germany and Russia.

Today British supremacy is again threatened by Russia. Russian determination throughout the nineteenth century and nearly half of the twentieth to break out from the Black Sea through the Dardanelles to the Mediterranean and to achieve hegemony over the Persian Gulf has represented an intolerable threat to every British statesman from Palmerston to the more recent Curzon and Winston Churchill. But the threat today is far greater than it ever was in any past years. It has fallen to the lot of the Labor government of Clement Attlee and of Ernest Bevin to face that crisis.

We are witnessing a clash of empires. That this clash is coincident with a conflict of ideologies—a conflict between Soviet Communism and Western democracy—and that it is attended by an immediate rivalry between the Soviet Union and the Western powers over oil and communications, cannot obscure the basic fact that the fundamental issue is the antagonism of opposing empires.

Every manifestation of Soviet policy during the postwar period has made it clearer that the Soviet government of Stalin is pursuing precisely the same objectives that were envisaged by Nicholas I and Alexander II.

The Soviet government has already secured a preponderant position in the Balkan Peninsula through the control which it has gained over the governments of Rumania, Yugoslavia, Bulgaria and Albania. Its vigorous onslaught at the first meeting of the United Nations General Assembly upon the position precariously held in Greece by Great Britain, and the tactics of the Moscow-inspired Greek EAM have made it obvious that Russia seeks control in Greece as well. Moscow's policies toward Turkey, intrinsically a war of nerves backed by recurrent threats, have shown that the Soviet Union seeks to achieve not only the cession of such Turkish regions on the Black Sea as Kars and Ardahan, but what is far more important, a sovereign and fortified control over the Dardanelles. The Soviet willingness at Paris in July, 1946, to agree to the cession in the Italian Peace Treaty of the Dodecanese Islands to Greece does not mean that Russia does not still hope to secure hegemony over these strategic outposts of the Dardanelles through a concession from some later and more "friendly" Greek government than the one presently in power. Her much debated and thoroughly ventilated activities in northern Iran have furnished another indication that the Soviet Union is no longer disposed to tolerate British participation in determining the course that the Iranian people are to pursue. The early and exacting demands of the Soviet government for sole administration of the former Italian colonies of Libya and Eritrea add conclusive contributory evidence that the Kremlin is determined sooner rather than later to supplant Great Britain as the predominant power in the Near East.

Were the Soviet Union to succeed in attaining all its presently revealed objectives in the Near East, it would effectively control the eastern Mediterranean, the passage through the Red Sea, the territories adjacent to the Persian Gulf, and would be enabled to cut off with the utmost facility all sea and air communications between Great Britain and such of her Far Eastern possessions as she may hold at the end of the present transition period.

Were Great Britain to be forced to acquiesce in the decisions taken by the Soviet Union, not only would she be rapidly divested of any means of control over those of her Far Eastern possessions that desired to remain under British sovereignty, but she would be deprived of that freedom of access to overseas Dominions, such as Australia, New Zealand and the Union of South Africa, which her centuries-old mastery of the seas has so long preserved.

The issue for Great Britain is, consequently, vital. The outcome will determine whether Great Britain and the British Commonwealth of Nations are to remain one of the three major units in

NEAR EAST, where Russian and British interests conflict; showing spheres of influence in Iran

the world of nations of the future, or whether the era of Great Britain as a major power has ended.

It is primarily in the Near East that this decision will be made.

If it be remembered that in 1940 Great Britain was at her weakest and was fighting alone against a triumphant Axis to which the Soviet Union was still bound by the pact of August, 1939, it is easier to understand the reasons for the policies pursued by London since that time in the Near East. British prestige, as a result of an unrelieved series of military defeats, had sunk to a low level in the Arab world. The British government sought to procure support by catering to Arab prejudices and desires and thereby to preserve a framework of British power in the Moslem world.

But the Soviet Union saw each new evidence of British policy in this regard as additional proof that the primary British objective was to organize the Arab peoples against the Soviet Union. To the Russian leaders, British efforts to weld a close union between the Arab chiefs and between the more reactionary elements in the Near East polities could only be interpreted as an intention to forge an anti-Soviet front.

The history of British policy in the Near East during the war period is dramatic. It constitutes a strange amalgam of great ability and ingenuity dedicated to the pursuit of objectives that were already anachronistic and that would inevitably become unattainable in the postwar world.

The romantic dreams of Colonel Lawrence still dominated the thinking of the permanent officials of Whitehall, who appeared to be convinced that Great Britain could still constitute herself the benevolent patroness of the Arab world and the only protecting power that the Arab peoples would recognize. They envisioned a new caliphate inspired from London.

The prologue was delivered by Anthony Eden. The British Foreign Secretary graciously announced that any movement for Arab unity would be approved by the British government.

The first act was staged in Syria. The campaign against the Vichy French afforded the British government an admirable opportunity to eliminate French influence in the Levant and to support Arab nationalist aspirations by sponsoring the absolute independence of Syria and of the Lebanon. For many months that brilliant and adept personage, General Spears, headed the corps of British officials who consistently stimulated nationalist movements in the Levant states.

The second act took place in Egypt where the British Ambassador, Lord Killearn, compelled King Farouk—in much the same tutorial manner as that displayed by his great predecessor, Lord Cromer—to appoint as Prime Minister Nahas Pasha, the leader of the Wafd, the strongly nationalist but equally strongly anti-Axis party. The pupil rebelled; tanks surrounded the royal palace; the new Prime Minister was named. But what was significant was the immediate devotion to the ideal of Pan-Arab unity of a hitherto uninterested Egyptian political leader.

The third act also was set in Egypt. As a result of Egyptian initiative, the chiefs of government of Iraq, Saudi Arabia, Transjordania, Yemen, Syria and the Lebanon signed a protocol in Cairo in the autumn of 1944 providing for the creation of an Arab League. The final treaty was signed in the spring of 1945. From the outset the Arab League commenced a campaign of ultra-nationalism. It instigated a series of offensives against the Jews of Palestine, including a boycott of all Palestine exports. It hurled charges against the French in the Levant. It even laid down a barrage against the United States in the belief that this would forestall any official measures sympathetic to Jewish aspirations.

The last act which has so far been presented contains several scenes.

The French have been eliminated from the Levant.

Turkish resistance to the Soviet Union has been stiffened by British support.

Transjordania has been declared independent, subject to the terms of an alliance with Great Britain.

Egypt and Saudi Arabia have become allies.

Iraq and Turkey have entered into a new pact of mutual support.

But the final act is yet to be played. There can be no question that the Arab League possesses some aspects of reality. The Arab peoples are intrinsically nationalists. They are traditionally anti-foreign and they are drawn together by the realization that they are endangered by the clash of mighty forces impinging upon them. But of what use to Great Britain can such an Arab League really prove to be?

The Arab peoples are poor. They have no military resources. They are torn by religious and political feuds. They have no underlying motive that would induce them to support Great Britain in preference to any other power that could furnish them with more tangible benefits. In the long run, would it be surprising, once their desperately impoverished masses have learned the meaning of independence, if the Soviet Union could seem to offer more real hope of freedom from grinding exploitation and an illusion of a higher living standard?

The tides of Pan-Arabism are rising. They were given impetus by Whitehall, but today it seems likely that these tides will be harnessed by Moscow rather than by London. Should that prove to be the case it will not be long before they are flowing strongly against the West.

In order to obtain an accurate over-all understanding of the way in which the realization of Russia's present objectives would transform the political and economic structure of the entire Near East and thereby affect the interests of the United States, it is necessary to emphasize certain aspects of recent history.

With the outbreak of the Second World War, Turkey's position was critical. This time there existed none of the inducements that had persuaded Turkey to join the central powers in the First World War. As a result of the transformation wrought by Atatürk, Turkey's sympathies on the whole were far more inclined toward the Western democracies than toward the Axis powers. But on the other hand, during the first two years of the war, until the British and American forces had finally made effective headway in North Africa against the German and Italian invaders, Turkey found herself strategically and politically isolated. Her isolation was emphasized by the circumstance that the close understanding forged by the Treaty of 1921 between Turkey and the Soviet Union had lapsed and the Soviet Union, until June of

1941, was identified with the Axis powers. Turkey was in a vise from which there seemed no escape. At best, therefore, her course could only be that of precarious neutrality. As victory seemed gradually to veer toward the side of the United Nations, this original neutrality underwent successive stages of transformation. The supplies of chrome which Turkey had originally furnished to Germany were at length stopped. Political relations with the Nazi government were eventually severed. Finally, during the very last stages of the war, Turkey declared war upon the Axis.

As victory approached, the relations between Turkey and the Soviet Union, however, were marked by increasing friction. Moscow denounced her pact with Turkey, who experienced mounting evidences of Russian pressure. Fortunately for the sake of Turkey's people, the Turkish government continued to be headed by that exceedingly shrewd and flexible intimate of Atatürk, earlier known as Ismet Pasha and now respected by the Turkish population as President Inonü. Furthermore, Turkish economy had suffered relatively little from the war strain. An unprecedented degree of internal unity existed among the great majority of the elements in the Turkish population.

With the termination of the war in Europe, signs and portents emanating from Moscow made it apparent that the Soviet Union was trying to achieve that traditional objective of the czarist governments—that objective which had for so long and so successfully been combated by Great Britain—domination over the Turkish people.

Evidences of these ambitions were not absent from the recent negotiations between Stalin, Roosevelt and Churchill, at Teheran and at Yalta. Nor was the Turkish government unaware of the precise form they were taking.

But the first overt indications of a major war of nerves against Turkey were recognized by Western public opinion when two relatively unknown Georgian professors published in Russia a document in which they vigorously demanded annexation to the Soviet Georgian Republic of that part of the Black Sea coast line of Turkey which the professors alleged had previously belonged to the Georgian people. This demand was played up in all the effective ways so well known to Soviet propaganda. For a considerable period the official press and the official radio broadcasts within the Soviet Union vehemently admonished the Turkish government to negotiate forthwith the cession of these areas to the Soviet Union. The strip of Turkish territory coveted by the Soviet Union comprises the district of Ardahan and the Province of Kars and extends from the present Soviet frontier as far as Trebizond on the Black Sea.

The history of these areas is of some interest. Long a part of the Turkish Empire, they were hypothecated to Russia by the terms of the Treaty of Berlin of 1878 to insure the payment by Turkey of the war indemnity imposed upon her, and remained under Russian jurisdiction until the close of the First World War on the ground that the indemnity was never paid. They were then returned by Lenin to Turkish sovereignty. The Treaty of 1921 concluded between the new Turkish National Government and the Soviet government terminated all treaties that had been concluded between imperial Russia and imperial Turkey. In a plebiscite held in Kars and Ardahan at that time and recognized as valid by the Soviet authorities, an overwhelming majority of the inhabitants voted for Turkish nationality.

The basic issues were set forth clearly and unequivocally by Turkish Prime Minister Saracoğlu in the autumn of 1945. Referring to the Russian propaganda which alleged that the Province of Kars and Ardahan under Russian sovereignty would become a home for Armenians dispersed throughout the world, he said:

The whole world knows that there is not a single Armenian living in these territories.

We have confidence in our own Armenian citizens living in other parts of our country, the majority in Istanbul. . . . . By the treaty of Kars, signed with the Soviets, our eastern frontiers took their definitive form as they are today, and ethnological realities were thus preserved with the free consent of both parties.

Certain newspaper dispatches claim that Kars and Ardahan were taken by Turkey at a time when the Russians were weak. First of all there is nothing that can be described here by the words "to take" or "to be taken." It is a question of the reintegration of a population in its whole form within the motherland as indicated by their own free will and vote. Secondly, in the days when they claim Russia was weak, Turkey was almost non-existent. Faced with such evident truth, such a statement is absolutely unjust.

It is also clear that these (Soviet) professors of history do not know history, past or present. At most they are trying to interpret Hitler's "lebensraum" or are victims of a disease which requires spilling of blood of innocent people once again so that they can record it for use in classroom lectures.

At the same time the Soviet pressure for the abrogation of the provisions of the Montreux Convention of 1936 regulating passage through the Dardanelles and restoring to Turkey the right of fortification became increasingly strong.

It will be remembered that the secret agreements of 1916 entered into between Great Britain and France and the last czarist government provided that victory over Germany should bring with it Russian control of Constantinople. This secret agreement was publicly denounced by the Soviet government shortly after the revolution of 1917 as an iniquitous creation of imperialism, as indeed it was.

However, there would seem to be no question that today the Soviet government is determined to secure sole control over the outlet from the Black Sea to the Mediterranean, and to abrogate the sovereign control over that all-important waterway which Turkey exercised for so many centuries. Repeated official declarations that Turkey is prepared at any time to participate in a new international conference to consider the modification of the Montreux Convention and the recent fumbling efforts of the United States to propose international control over all international waterways have been met with stony silence at the Kremlin.

Since his retirement from office, Mr. Churchill has revealed what has hitherto been a closely guarded secret in Washington and London—that the Soviet government proposes to demand of Turkey the cession of strategic sites in the Straits upon which to construct Russian fortifications and air bases. Should such sites be granted, the Soviet Union would of course control not only the Dardanelles and the Black Sea, but the Aegean as well.

These two major questions involving the sovereign rights of

Turkey remain in uneasy abeyance. For the moment Soviet propaganda has diminished in intensity. We must assume, however, that the Soviet Union has merely prepared its position for a renewed diplomatic offensive when the moment seems opportune.

Relations between Russia and Iran have naturally received far more prominence during recent months. After the German onslaught upon Russia in the summer of 1941, Iran suddenly became of vital importance to the Allied military effort. The country offered the only route by which armaments and other supplies could be safely transported to the Soviet Union by the United States and Great Britain. This route ran from Basra on the Persian Gulf through the heart of Persia, across the Caspian Sea to Russia's southern cities.

In order to secure this vital means of communication the three Allied powers obtained from the Iranian government an agreement permitting Russia to send forces of occupation to northern Iran, Great Britain similar forces of occupation to the southern Iranian provinces, and the United States forces sufficient to insure the safety of the roads over which Lend-Lease supplies were to be shipped from the Gulf.

In view of past history, the government of Iran very naturally became increasingly anxious that the occupying powers make some firm commitment to withdraw the forces of occupation at the end of the emergency. After the conference of Teheran in the autumn of 1943, and on the resolute initiative of President Roosevelt, a special declaration was issued in the name of the United States, Great Britain and the Soviet Union, in which the three governments pledged themselves as being "at one with the government of Iran in their desire for the maintenance of the independence, sovereignty and territorial integrity of Iran." As a result of later negotiations, the three governments pledged themselves to withdraw all their armed forces from Iran not later than March 2, 1946.

At the start of the war, Iranian political, social and economic structures were already in an advanced stage of decomposition. The old Shah, Reza Shah Pahlevi, who had seized power twenty years earlier and imposed a brutal military dictatorship over the

Persian people, was deposed by the Allies in 1941. His successor, his son, Mohamed Reza Pahlevi, had none of his father's force of character.

The parliament, or Majlis, was honeycombed with agents of foreign powers. The public administration was not only chaotic, but notoriously corrupt. German intrigues and German propaganda had disrupted what little national cohesion existed within the government.

With the commencement of the shipment of Lend-Lease supplies to Russia, the nation's transportation system was wrecked, which meant that the means of distributing the home-grown food supplies were blocked. But the government could obtain no help from the Allied governments in securing food from abroad, nor trucks with which to distribute food. I can well remember the urgent pleas addressed to me by the Iranian Minister at that time imploring some help from the United States. But the military exigencies of the moment were so great that the relief afforded was tenuous in the extreme.

Famine broke out. Food riots raged in many cities, especially in Teheran. To cap the climax, the Russian forces of occupation in the north prevented the shipment of any food supplies from the Province of Azerbaijan, which they held, to the stricken southern provinces of Iran, so that the contentment of the inhabitants under their régime should shine in comparison with the dissatisfaction of the residents of the regions under British control.

The economy of the entire nation became chaotic. The foreign advisers appointed by the Iranian government were helpless to procure any remedial action. As so often had happened in the past, the Persian people suffered as a result of the traditional contest between Russia and Great Britain for control of their country.

Throughout the period of occupation the Russian authorities in northern Iran rigidly excluded even official agents of the other major powers from the districts that they occupied. They assumed increasingly a position of supreme authority, prohibiting officials of the Iranian government from exercising their legitimate functions. Finally, in the late autumn of 1945, the Soviet military authorities not only took no action to prevent a Separatist revolt which broke out in Tabriz, the capital city of Azerbaijan, and which was held by the Communist-inspired Tudeh, or proletarian party, under the banner of "autonomy and separation" from Iran, but they even refused to permit the government at Teheran to send troops to the area to repress the revolt.

It is useful to remember that the Persian province of Azerbaijan has often been a disturbing element in the Persian body politic. It lies between Turkey and Russia, and possesses long-standing affinities with the adjacent regions in those two countries. When the Bolshevik revolution was triumphant in 1917, the Georgians, and the Armenians of Van, proclaimed the creation of a Republic of Azerbaijan, and announced that its capital would be at Baku.

The Persian province contains something less than two million inhabitants. They are by no means homogeneous. They have none of the national sentiment displayed by the residents of the other provinces of Persia. They are far more stalwart in their general type and far more independent of the sporadic controls emanating from Teheran. Their capital city, Tabriz, is the greatest city in Persia. Their racial make-up is part Persian, but with a preponderance of Turkish, Kurdish and Armenian stock.

There can, however, be no question that the revolt in Azerbaijan, like the rebellion of the Kurdish tribes in Iraq, as well as in Iran, was inspired from Moscow. The Persian officials within the province who had been removed from their posts by the Russian authorities were replaced with hand-picked appointees. One of these, Pishavari, had been employed as a Soviet agent in Persia as far back as 1921. In the intervening period he had been given some employment within Russia. Now, when the moment was opportune, he was taken out of his pigeonhole and dusted off, and emerged as the leader of the Tudeh party in Azerbaijan. And it was soon notorious that the ostensibly native demand for autonomy was inspired by Russian propagandists trained in the Tashkent "School of Oriental Studies."

This direct intervention in the internal affairs of Iran, which clearly jeopardized her integrity and which portended the amalgamation of Azerbaijan and the other northern provinces, under one guise or another, with the Soviet Union, resulted in frantic appeals by the Iranian government to the Western powers.

When the Security Council of the United Nations was at length installed in London in February, 1946, the appeal of Iran came before it. After a bitter dispute between the British and Soviet delegates, the council sanctioned direct negotiations between Moscow and Teheran, with the specific understanding, however, on its part, that the council reserved the right to request information at any time on the progress of these direct negotiations.

March 2, 1946, came and went. The American troops in Iran had long been withdrawn. The British occupation forces were removed. The Russian forces remained, the Soviet government sullenly refusing to give any explanation of this clear violation of its contractual obligations to Great Britain and the United States, as well as to Iran, and further declining to give any indication of when its forces would be evacuated.

The Security Council was due to meet late in March in New York. When it became certain that this violation by the Soviet Union of its charter commitments, as well as of its specific agreements, would be brought before the council by Iran, the Soviet government declared that it would require until the tenth of April to prepare its case, and requested that the council hold no sessions until that date. This request was rejected.

What then transpired appeared superficially to be as follows. The council met upon the date originally fixed. The Soviet representative announced that he would attend no sessions at which the Iranian question came up for discussion on the grounds that his government's request for postponement had not been accepted and that an agreement between Iran and the Soviet government covering all the points at issue already existed. To this the American representative, Secretary Byrnes, rejoined that the information he had received from Teheran indicated that no such agreement had been entered into. At that moment the Soviet delegate announced that he would attend no further meetings of the Security Council at which the Iranian question was debated and solemnly stalked out of the session. For the time being the council was flabbergasted. Continued Soviet abstention could paralyze the council. Upon the initiative of Secretary Byrnes, the council then determined to hear the representative of Iran, her able and enlightened Ambassador in Washington, Hussein Ala. By instruction of the government in Teheran, headed by Prime Minister Ahmed Ghavam, the Ambassador declared that no agreement with the Soviet Union existed.

Events then moved rapidly. The Soviet government announced that all Soviet troops would be withdrawn from Iran by May 6, provided no "unforeseen circumstances" arose.

The Security Council addressed a communication to both Moscow and Teheran requesting a reply by April 3 to its inquiry as to the status of the negotiations between the two governments and as to whether the announced withdrawal of Russian troops was "conditioned upon agreement on other subjects."

There was much speculation whether, in view of its previous attitude, any reply would be forthcoming from the Soviet. But answers were received from both governments within the time set.

The Russian answer stated that all Soviet troops would be withdrawn from Iran within five or six weeks, and that any proposals under negotiation between Moscow and Teheran were "not connected with the withdrawal of Soviet troops." The Iranian government announced in its response that in view of Russia's promise to withdraw her armed forces it would not press at that time for consideration of its complaint that the Soviet government was interfering in the internal affairs of Iran.

The council thereupon adopted a resolution, submitted by the American Secretary of State, deferring further consideration of the Iranian appeal until May 6, and calling upon both governments to report at that time whether the evacuation of the Russian armies had then in fact been completed.

The actions of the council were received with wide acclaim. Little attention, other than sour, was paid to the statements made by the Australian delegate upon the council, Colonel Hodgson, who had been alone in opposing the council's resolution. He was generally regarded as a killjoy.

And yet the statements made by Colonel Hodgson went straight to the heart of the problem, far below the superficial semblance of reality with which his colleagues and public opinion in general seemed to be so enchanted. For to these the fact that an immediate crisis in the relations between the Kremlin and the Western powers had been averted appeared to be all that mattered.

Colonel Hodgson pointed out that the official statements of the Soviet and Iranian governments as to whether any negotiations between them had succeeded were entirely at variance. The council had failed to undertake any impartial investigation of this point. The council had dealt solely with the matter of troop movements. It had wholly failed to deal with Iran's original complaint, namely, that Russia had flagrantly interfered in her internal concerns. Finally, Colonel Hodgson bitterly assailed the precedent created by the council in seeking compromise solutions of the basic questions involved behind closed doors and in failing to deal with these issues in official and public sessions of the council; and declared that this course would gravely weaken the prestige and authority of the council.

Rarely have such complaints proved more rapidly to be well founded.

Before twelve hours had passed Teheran announced that the Iranian and Soviet governments had concluded an agreement establishing a joint stock company for the exploitation of Persian oil. It was immediately assumed that other agreements, more far-reaching in their scope, had also been reached.

It was at once clear, therefore, that the council had simply whitewashed a Persian concession to the Soviet Union which had been previously declared unconstitutional by the Persian Prime Minister himself. It was equally evident that the agreements had been concluded at the very moment that the Iranian government solemnly announced that no agreements of such a character were even contemplated, and had been negotiated under the pressure resulting from the presence of Soviet troops upon Persian territory.

The council had upheld the principle that every state, no matter how small, should possess the right to state its complaints before the council. That was an achievement of permanent value.

But in the case of Iran the council had permitted itself to be wholly outmaneuvered. The violation of the Soviet government's commitment to withdraw its troops by March 2 was palliated. The flagrant intervention of the Soviet Union in Azerbaijan was disregarded. And the announcement by Moscow that its troops would be withdrawn within five or six weeks "unconditionally," was at once discovered to be "unconditional" only because Moscow had already obtained all the concessions from Iran that it desired.

It was soon discovered that these concessions placed the actual control of northern Iran in Soviet hands. For the agreement to grant to the Soviet Union fifty-one per cent of the stock in the projected Russo-Iranian oil corporation would vest in the Soviet government the means of determining the political and economic destinies of the region over which the corporation exercised its powers. The stipulation that a future Persian parliament, to be elected June 7, must approve these terms was obviously a pure formality, since under existing conditions of Soviet pressure in Iran the Iranian government would unquestionably obtain a majority in the parliament. And the ominous news that the Soviet agreement with Ahmed Ghavam further provided that the Iranian Prime Minister would negotiate a settlement of the Azerbaijan issue with Pishavari, the Russian-schooled leader of the Tudeh party in that province gave unquestionable evidence that Russian supremacy in Azerbaijan was now to obtain official Iranian sanction.

What became startlingly clear was that the Iranian Premier had used the Security Council for his own purposes in negotiating with the Soviet Union as a means of getting the best terms he could.

It was not surprising that on April 8 the Kremlin announced that the Soviet representative on the Security Council had been instructed to demand that the Security Council abandon its decision to reopen the Iranian question on May 6, on the ground that full agreement had been reached between Teheran and Moscow, and to characterize the previous actions of the council with regard to Iran as "not right and illegal," and as contrary to the United Nations Charter.

Soviet policy toward Iran is, in my belief, based far more upon strategic and political factors than upon economic considerations. At both the Teheran and Yalta conferences, President Roosevelt made it plain that the United States favored an equitable partici- pation by the Soviet Union in the oil resources of Iran. Stalin, however, gave no indication that that issue was of immediate concern to his government. The Soviet government has now deter- mined to take over the concessions for the exploitation of oil in northern Iran primarily to prevent any other foreign interests from operating in that vital region. The issue is first of all one of security.

The Persians have alternated between hatred for Great Britain and hatred for Russia. They are, in the eyes of the Soviet leaders, a weak, disorderly and antagonistic people. With Russian control over oil development in northern Iran, the Soviet government can fill Azerbaijan and its four adjacent provinces with technicians and other agents who can readily propagate pro-Russian leanings among the inhabitants. And most of all it can prevent the activi- ties there of foreign emissaries who could threaten the safety of Russia's great oil operations around Batum. Finally Russian pre- ponderance in Azerbaijan affords a constant means of exercising pressure upon Turkey's weakest flank.

An agreement upon the internationalization of the oil resources of the Near East is doubtless the fairest and the most practical method of ending the long intrigues of the oil-seeking powers, which have repeatedly engendered such dangerous feuds and so gravely prejudiced the legitimate rights of the Near Eastern peoples. But it seems doubtful that such a solution would in any sense meet Russian desires. It is undeniable that the vast expanse already controlled by the Soviet Union is rich in oil resources. The Soviet Union is not an oil-hungry power like Great Britain, and as the United States must soon become. The objective sought by Moscow is control of the Near East. It views the British- American oil agreement negotiated by former Secretary Ickes on September 24, 1945, as a new and menacing method by which the Western powers will clamp additional controls over vast stretches of the Near East. The continuation of the concession of the British-dominated Anglo-Iranian Oil Company, which controls about one-sixth of the entire area of Persia, is regarded as an obstacle to Russia's political plans in the Near East, which must be brushed aside.

The agreements reached with Ahmed Ghavam while the Security Council sat in judgment in the Bronx upon the Iranian problem mark another step in the realization of the Soviet program of replacing British influence in Persia.

The Arab governments, as distinguished from the masses of the Arab peoples, are by no means blind to the present trends of Soviet policy. Their fear grows with every new manifestation of Russian imperialism. Equally they are united in their determination to rid themselves of all evidences of British control, short of sacrificing the support of Britain and the other Western powers against any overt evidence of Soviet aggression.

But they are still reft with jealousies and traditional rivalries among themselves.

The British government has announced the termination of its mandate over Transjordania, and the grant of full independence to that country, subject to a treaty of alliance. The action taken is open to grave question, inasmuch as the territory accorded to the government of Transjordania is in reality part of the Palestine mandate, and the decision presupposes that everyone involved, including the other powers that authorized the mandate, would consent to such a partition.

This step had also a strangely disruptive effect upon the slender ties that had developed between the members of the Arab League. The British announcement, which was coincident with the negotiation by the governments of Transjordania and of Iraq for a federal union, brought sharply into the foreground the jealousy of the lesser Arab states resulting from accumulating evidences that Saudi Arabia and Egypt were assuming the leadership of the Arab world. The leaders of Iraq and of Transjordania consider that Arabian hegemony should be vested in the Hashimite dynasty, of which King Feisal, the glamorous figure of the First World War, has been the most eminent member, and to which the ruling houses of both Iraq and Transjordania belong.

A crisis arose with the demand King Ibn Saud made to

the British government that a cession of Transjordan or of Iraqi territory be made to Saudi Arabia so as to provide Saudi Arabia with a common frontier with Syria. The creation of such a corridor linking Saudi Arabia with Syria would permanently separate Iraq and Transjordania, and would enable King Ibn Saud far more easily to dictate the policies of the Syrian government. It would, of course, permanently eliminate any future opportunity for the creation of that federation, so often proposed in recent years, of Transjordania, Syria, the Lebanon and Palestine, a federation which would greatly facilitate the economic development of those four states and materially promote the welfare of their inhabitants.

But if there are factors that draw the Arab states apart, there is one issue that above all others draws them together. That issue is Palestine. They are as one in their fanatical opposition to the establishment within Palestine of a commonwealth in which the Jewish people would be afforded any measure of authority, and to which the tragic Jewish refugees of Europe could turn as to a homeland.

In this fanaticism the dominating figure of the Arab world, King Ibn Saud of Saudi Arabia, has been foremost. Before considering the complexities and the intricacies of the Palestine problem, it would be easier to understand the background against which any negotiated settlement of that problem must be reached by a brief survey of Saudi Arabia and an appraisal of the point of view of its omnipotent ruler.

Saudi Arabia and Yemen are the most backward of the Arab states. Except in the isolated oil centers, and in a few of the ports where signs of modern progress can be seen, the life of the population has changed but little in the past five hundred years. The rule of Ibn Saud is both spiritual and temporal. It is that of an absolute dictator. There is probably no potentate of the modern world who possesses more complete authority within his domain. The rigidity of the tenets of the puritan sect of Mohammedanism to which Ibn Saud adheres tends to prevent the assimilation of Western ideas, and to consolidate as well the paternalistic control of the dynasty which Ibn Saud has forged.

The territory over which Ibn Saud rules comprises the major part of the Arabian desert. Recent surveys conducted at his request by officials of the United States Department of the Interior and of Agriculture have proved that many portions of these desert areas could be profitably developed by intensive irrigation. But apart from the revenues obtained from the pilgrims of the Mohammedan world when they make their periodical visits to the holy places, the sole important source of revenue in Saudi Arabia lies in its oil resources.

The Standard Oil Company of California first commenced its operations in this area in 1930. Three years later Ibn Saud granted to the Arabian-American Oil Combine, owned half by the Standard Oil Company of California and half by the Texas Company, a large concession extending over a considerable portion of Arabian territory. In 1939 the concession was extended to cover all the remainder of Saudi Arabia. The rentals and royalties already derived by Ibn Saud have been considerable. In addition, King Ibn Saud obtained during the war sizable loans granted by the companies on advance royalties.

Ibn Saud has long been fully aware of the interest shown in his territory by the imperial powers. He is intimately informed of the play of international politics. He has been determined that the development of the oil resources of the kingdom should not be utilized as a means of extending the political power of any of the major powers over his own domains. Before the Second World War insistent demands by British agents for concessions within his territory were abruptly refused. Similar approaches from Mussolini's government were rejected. Immediately prior to the outbreak of the war exceedingly lucrative proposals for oil concessions from both Germany and Japan were bluntly turned down. Rightly regarding the United States as the one major power which had no political interests in the Near East, Ibn Saud was determined that only American interests should be utilized in developing the national resources of Saudi Arabia.

In 1943 President Roosevelt, upon the suggestion of Secretary Ickes, first favorably considered the proposal that the Government of the United States finance the construction of a pipeline to bring oil from Saudi Arabia to a Mediterranean port, preferably one in Palestine, primarily for the use of the United States Navy. Public opposition within the United States to this proposal was so loud, because of the implication that government funds would be used in an operation that would be highly beneficial to private interests, and the hostility displayed by both the British and Russian governments was so intense, that the proposal was temporarily abandoned. However, the project is still under consideration by the Arabian-American Oil Corporation as a private operation. The successful construction of such a pipeline, would, of course, bring the United States for the first time into open competition in the eastern Mediterranean with those European powers which possess vital interests in that region.

The Near East represents to the European nations their chief source of oil, except for the oil resources of Indonesia, and except for their participation in the exploitation of oil in northern Latin America.

The British government-controlled Anglo-Iranian Oil Company's concessions in Iran are estimated to comprise more than one-fourth of the oil reserves of the Near East. In Iraq, the British government possesses a preponderant interest in the oil reserves, although United States, Dutch and French groups have a minor share in that area. Syria is known to have very large oil reserves, and one of the chief reasons for the persistent reluctance of the French government to terminate its mandate over Syria lay in the fact that it feared it would then abandon its right to have a predominant voice in the exploitation of these reserves.

One of the most vicious aspects of the concessions obtained by the Western powers for the development of the oil resources of the Near East is that the share of the oil revenues accruing to the governments granting the concessions has either passed into the control of individual rulers or of the ruling oligarchy. The peoples whose national resources have been sold have obtained no benefits. The royalties have already been immense. They will increase during the postwar period. Had the governments of the Western powers insisted that the concessions obtained by their companies must provide that a major part of the royalties should be devoted to the improvement of sanitation and of education, to the development of agricultural and irrigation projects, and to the economic betterment of the masses of the people, the standard of living in all the Near Eastern countries would already have been notably improved.

From the standpoint of American policy it is clear that such an improvement would have resulted in increased markets for American exports, and in an interchange between the United States and the countries of the Near East which could only have proved beneficial to American interests in that great area of the world. But as it is, the revenues derived have been primarily devoted to the aggrandizement of a handful of the privileged, or have found their way into the customary channels of official corruption.

The importance of oil in its bearing upon the question of Palestine and upon the solution of the Palestine problem is, unfortunately, immediate. King Ibn Saud is by far the most forceful personality among the rulers of the states comprising the Arab League. He is likewise the most recalcitrant of all the Arab leaders in his attitude toward the creation of a Palestine commonwealth. He has placed himself squarely at the head of Arab opposition. Consequently, the powerful American interests concerned in the development of the oil resources of the Near East have brought increasing pressure to bear in order to discourage the Government of the United States from adopting any course with relation to the Palestine problem which might lead King Ibn Saud to revoke existing American concessions and transfer the rights granted to American interests to the nationals of other countries. That pressure will continue until a final solution has been reached.

There can be no question that the problem of Palestine has become the immediate political issue of the Arab world. However, there can also be no question that Arabian opposition to all reasonable or fair settlements of the Palestine question has been artificially stimulated. Few Arabs possess any natural antipathy for the Jews. The Jewish people have lived among the Arabs for many centuries without molestation and with relatively little friction. The recent wave of anti-Semitism which has swept the Arab world, and which has been peculiarly virulent in Egypt and in

Iraq, undoubtedly had its origin in the Axis propaganda of the war period. Even today it is being artificially kept alive. It has been stimulated by the British policy of appeasement of the Arabs. It has been fostered because many Arab leaders have seen in anti-Semitism an easy way to further their individual ambitions and to strengthen their hold upon their people. But it has been rendered especially violent because of the astute appeal made to the fanaticism of peoples peculiarly prone to fanaticism by propagandists who are working in the interest of the Soviet Union.

President Roosevelt had long believed that the most desirable method of attempting to obtain a fair solution of the Palestine problem would be direct negotiation between Jewish and Arab leaders. He hoped to find the way by which King Ibn Saud might be persuaded to favor this step. During the years prior to the outbreak of the Second World War he had not only individually made various moves in this direction, but had given specific approval to the conduct of such negotiations, without publicity, under the direction of Dr. Chaim Weizmann. The outbreak of the war prevented any progress being made in that direction.

The President had by no means, however, abandoned the idea. He had, with complete justice, great faith in his own ability as a negotiator. At the conclusion of the Crimean conference in the early winter of 1945, the opportunity presented itself for him to have a personal conference with King Ibn Saud. The latter came to the Mediterranean for that purpose and the conference took place on the American warship upon which the President was traveling on his return to the United States.

There has been much misinterpretation and much deliberate distortion of what took place during this conference. I talked frequently with President Roosevelt about the solution of the Palestine question. After his mind was originally made up upon this subject I never knew him to vary one iota in his beliefs. He always favored the establishment of an independent Commonwealth of Palestine as a National Jewish Homeland. He always believed that the most desirable means of bringing this about would be an agreement reached by representative leaders of the Jewish people with representative leaders of the Arab states. He never believed that Great Britain, the United States or any other major power could unilaterally impose a solution by force upon the Arab world.

He believed that the Arab leaders could be shown and could be convinced that an equitable solution of the problem of Palestine, achieving the objectives in which he himself believed, would prove politically and economically profitable to the Arab peoples. He was certain that material arguments could be advanced which would encourage the needed conviction. However, if negotiations failed after a reasonable trial, he was equally convinced that the future international organization must assume the responsibility for a settlement that would establish a Commonwealth of Palestine secure from all possible aggression from neighboring states, and protected by the police power of the international trusteeship granted jurisdiction by the international organization.

I am wholly confident that President Roosevelt took no position in his conference with King Ibn Saud that was in the slightest divergent from these views. The correspondence which he had with King Ibn Saud upon his subsequent return to Washington was purely formal. The health of the President at that time had already deteriorated to such a point that the official letters dispatched to King Ibn Saud and signed by him were dictated for him. But even so, the assurances contained in the communications signed by the President were in no sense at variance with the principles he steadfastly maintained.

However, President Roosevelt most certainly did not believe that the Arabs or Christians who were residents of Palestine should be deprived of their equal political or religious rights as a result of the creation of a Palestine commonwealth in which the Jewish people might eventually become preponderant. Nor did he believe it possible that the establishment of an independent Palestine would *ipso facto* solve the entire Jewish problem. He saw it merely as a great contributory factor in alleviating the sufferings of the Jews, and as an act of essential justice.

What President Roosevelt envisaged was the establishment of an independent Commonwealth of Palestine, a National Jewish Homeland, in which Jewish refugees from Europe, or voluntary

Jewish immigrants, could find a refuge; where Jewish immigration would be restricted only if economic conditions within the country required it and where a democracy could be established capable of affording individual liberty and security to all residents of the country whether Jewish, Arab or Christian.

With the death of President Roosevelt and the retirement of Winston Churchill as British Prime Minister, the two leading advocates of a prompt and equitable solution of the Palestine problem on a basis such as that outlined were removed from the political scene. President Truman, while officially sympathetic to the plight of the Jewish people, has neither the experience, the intimate knowledge, nor the direct interest in the furtherance of such a solution possessed by his predecessor. Although the British Labor party was officially on record as favoring the establishment of the Commonwealth of Palestine, the new British Foreign Secretary, Mr. Bevin, displayed a bias in his attitude toward Palestine wholly at variance with the sympathetic interest so long manifested by Mr. Churchill. While the Soviet government refused to take any official stand in the matter, Zionist leaders both in England and the United States were satisfied that Moscow would not oppose a just solution of the problem along the lines favored by the more moderate Zionists.

Unfortunately, the policy assumed by the United States after Mr. Truman had succeeded to the Presidency proved neither constructive nor helpful. The pronouncements coming from the White House and State Department can only have been made because of the belief that they would be politically advantageous in their effect upon the Jewish communities in the United States.

In the latter part of the summer of 1945 President Truman publicly announced that he was urging the British government to permit the immediate entrance into Palestine of one hundred thousand destitute Jewish refugees from Europe. The impact of such a declaration upon the British government and upon British public opinion at a moment when British resources were at their lowest ebb, and when there was no indication that the United States was prepared to do more than offer moral advice, was far from helpful.

The iniquitous Palestine White Paper issued by the government of Neville Chamberlain in 1939, and nominally still in effect, announced that the British government, as mandatory power, would, after five years, prohibit all Jewish immigration into Palestine unless the Arabs agreed that it should continue. The White Paper was an act of abject surrender undertaken in the fallacious belief that the British government could purchase tranquillity at the price of the sacred rights granted the Jewish people by the Balfour Declaration. No one has more truly characterized this betrayal than Winston Churchill when he assailed it in the House of Commons as "an act of repudiation: a plain breach of a solemn obligation."

During the war the British government had, it is true, upon occasion relaxed the provisions of the White Paper to permit the entrance into Palestine of small numbers of European refugees.

But, iniquitous as it was, the White Paper of 1939 still was in effect at the time of President Truman's sudden pronouncement. From the British standpoint the American gesture implied a demand that the British government abrogate its official policy at a moment when Arab reaction to such a step would be exceedingly violent. To the British public, as well as to the British government, it looked as if the United States were prodding Great Britain into a course that would be exceedingly dangerous to a weakened and much beset England, without assuming any responsibility for seeing that the people of Palestine were safeguarded against dangers which the British government believed would at once arise as a result of such a move.

After much violent backstage recrimination between London and Washington, a compromise was eventually found, and announced on December 10. The American and British governments proclaimed that they had determined to establish a joint Anglo-American committee of inquiry on Palestine and European Jews for the following purposes:

1. To examine political, economic and social conditions in Palestine as they bear upon the problem of Jewish immigration and settlement therein and the wellbeing of the peoples now living therein.
2. To examine the position of the Jews in those countries in Europe where they have been the victims of Nazi and Fascist persecution and

the practical measures taken or contemplated to be taken in those countries to enable them to live free from discrimination and oppression, and to make estimates of those who wish or will be impelled by their conditions to migrate to Palestine or other countries outside Europe.

3. To hear the views of competent witnesses and to consult representative Arabs and Jews on the problems of Palestine as such problems are affected by conditions subject to examination under Paragraph 1 and 2 above, and by other relevant facts and circumstances; and to make recommendations to the Governments of the United States and of the United Kingdom for ad interim handling of those problems as well as for their permanent solution; and

4. To make such other recommendations to the Governments of the United States and of the United Kingdom as may be necessary to meet the immediate needs arising from conditions subject to examination under Paragraph 2 above by remedial action in the European countries in question, or by the provision of facilities for immigration to and settlement in countries outside Europe.

The terms of the announcement further provided that the report of the committee which was composed of six American and six British members must be rendered within four months of the time when the inquiry commenced.

The inherent weaknesses in such a move were not overlooked by Zionists nor by impartial observers who believed that an expeditious settlement of the question of Palestine was imperative if peace was to be maintained in the increasingly critical period confronting the Near East. Commissions of investigation in Palestine have been legion since the mandate commenced. Their reports have been sterile.

The report of the new commission could prove productive only if the members chose to use this opportunity to make radical and far-reaching recommendations of a constructive nature which would provide for the prompt solution of the Palestine controversy. It could prove positively beneficial only if the British government gave concrete evidence that it would abide by the recommendations of the commissioners, and carry them out. Otherwise the report finally rendered would be of no more practical value than all the previous reports gathering dust in the pigeonholes where they had been deposited.

In view of the gravity of the situation so rapidly developing in Palestine, and in view of the appalling tragedy of the homeless, bereft and destitute Jews of Europe, the knowledge that in any event four vitally important months would now pass without alleviation of the conditions within the camps of the "displaced persons" in Europe, while a commission of inquiry again made a report which could at best have no immediate result, was devastating in its effect. Instead of tranquilizing the Jewish people, it embittered their spirit.

Furthermore, Great Britain retained sole authority in Palestine, unless the United Nations questioned the control over Palestine vested in her by the League of Nations. The United States' participation in the new commission gave her a measure of moral responsibility but without the slightest degree of actual authority to improve the situation of the Jews in Palestine through remedial action, or to relieve the suffering of the Jewish refugees in Europe by procuring for them the means of finding a refuge in Palestine.

The White House had believed that the announcement of the creation of the Anglo-American Commission would avert all further action in the Congress in behalf of the establishment of a Palestine commonwealth. Leaders of both parties in the Senate and in the House, however, refused to be overridden by the executive branch of the government, as they frequently had been in previous months. By a large majority the Congress adopted a concurrent resolution couched in the following terms:

Whereas the Sixty-Seventh Congress of the United States on June 30, 1922, unanimously resolved "that the United States of America favors the establishment in Palestine of a National Home for the Jewish people, it being clearly understood that nothing should be done which may prejudice the civil and religious rights of Christian and all other non-Jewish communities in Palestine, and that the holy places and religious buildings and sites in Palestine shall be adequately protected"; and

Whereas the ruthless persecution of the Jewish people in Europe has clearly demonstrated the need for a Jewish Homeland as a haven for the large number who have become homeless as a result of this persecution; and

Whereas these urgent necessities are evidenced by the President's request for the immediate right of entry into Palestine of one hundred thousand additional Jewish refugees; and

Whereas the influx of Jewish immigration into Palestine is resulting in its improvement in agricultural, financial, hygienic, and general economic conditions; and

Whereas the President and British Prime Minister have agreed upon the appointment of a joint Anglo-American Committee of Enquiry to examine conditions in Palestine as they bear upon the problem of Jewish immigration and the Jewish situation in Europe and have requested a report within one hundred twenty days; Therefore Be It Resolved:

That the interest shown by the President in the solution of this problem is hereby commended and that the United States shall use its good offices with the mandatory power to the end that Palestine shall be opened for free entry of Jews into that country to the maximum of its agricultural and economic potentialities, and that there shall be full opportunity for colonization and development, so that they may freely proceed with the upbuilding of Palestine as the Jewish National Home and in association with all elements of the population establish Palestine as a democratic Commonwealth in which all men, regardless of race or creed, shall have equal rights.

The position taken by the legislative branch of the government was firm, tonic and enlightened. As has so often been the case in recent months, the Congress favored a foreign policy that was far more positive than that of the Executive, and far more likely to further a healthy world reconstruction.

To stem to some extent the bitter reaction created by the appointment of a new time-consuming commission at a moment when the tragedy of the Jewish refugees in Europe lay heavily upon the public conscience in all the English-speaking countries, the British government announced its intention of attempting to persuade the Arab leaders to agree to a monthly immigration into Palestine of some 1,500 refugees.

At a time when the press was filled with eyewitness reports of the appalling situation confronting the European Jews who had barely escaped with their lives from the mass liquidations of Hitlerism, and when every expert survey made it unmistakably clear that these so-called "displaced persons" numbered several hundred thousands at a bare minimum, the announcement that an endeavor would be made to admit a trickle of 1,500 a month into

Palestine was little more than a cynical travesty. It seemed intolerable that the surviving Jews of central and eastern Europe, wasting away both spiritually and physically in improvident concentration camps, should be forced to await for an indefinite period an opportunity to start life anew in the homeland of their fathers.

To every believer in the moral values for which the United States has fought, the right of every individual to live safely, without fear and without discrimination, in the land of his birth must be safeguarded as one of the essential foundations upon which a free world can be constructed. Many of us have consequently maintained that once this right was assured there would be no need for the Jews of Europe to find a new home in Palestine, or in any other alien refuge. But those of us who have this logical and intrinsically righteous conviction have, sadly enough, been fundamentally mistaken. We have had no personal experience of the poisonous cloud of anti-Semitism which hangs over Europe, and no individual knowledge of the intensity of the Hitler-fostered hatreds which still linger in almost every corner of the Old World. These cannot be eradicated by official fiat. Nor can we realize—unless we have talked with the refugees—how few of the "displaced persons" are willing to face the horror of returning to their former homes, where memories of the bitterest of all conceivable personal tragedies would arise at every turn, and where the vision of death and of destruction would constantly be present. The refugees long for peace and safety. They long above all for a place of refuge where they can be sure they "belong." Palestine represents that ideal.

Even the stanchest of the anti-Zionists who have visited Europe since the war, and even those American members of the Anglo-American Commission who were originally more than lukewarm in their belief that Palestine was a necessary haven, but later talked with the Jewish refugees in Europe, now confess that the opening of Palestine to the pitiful Jews who have survived the tragedies of the past ten years is an imperative obligation which confronts humanity.

While the British government finally announced that it would permit the entrance each month of 1,500 Jews into Palestine even before receiving the report of the Anglo-American Commission of Enquiry, the agreement of the Arab leaders was never forthcoming. In fact, some of the most prominent officials of the Arab League vehemently denounced the decision of the British government and protested that it was in flagrant violation of commitments previously made to them. An Arab boycott of all exports from Palestine was declared. Anti-Jewish riots broke out in Egypt and North Africa. Unfortunately, these were in turn followed by assassinations and uprisings on the part of Jewish extremists in Palestine itself. The British authorities finally declared martial law.

As might have been anticipated, this action was at once denounced by Zionist leaders, who insisted, in the words of the Joint Chairman of the American Zionist Emergency Council, that Palestine as a whole was being governed "as one large prison with its Jewish citizens treated like a band of criminals, stripped of elementary human and civil rights."

When the report of the Anglo-American Commission was finally made public in the spring of 1946, it was met with an outburst of violent recrimination in all the Arab states as well as in the rest of the Moslem world, and with more restrained, but nevertheless bitter, disappointment on the part of the Zionist leaders. The commission recommended that 100,000 certificates be authorized immediately for the admission of Jewish refugees into Palestine. It further recommended some desirable and enlightened steps, notably in connection with the problem of land tenure. But at the same time it strongly recommended that Palestine should not become a Jewish state. Furthermore, while recommending that an international trusteeship under the United Nations be established over Palestine, the commission made it clear by implication that it believed that the sole administering power should continue to be Great Britain. The wording of the report further made it evident that the committee favored the policy of restricting Jewish immigration that the British government had for so long pursued once 100,000 refugees had been admitted.

President Truman immediately endorsed that part of the commission's recommendations which had to do with the admission into Palestine of 100,000 refugees. He refrained from commenting upon the balance of the report.

The British government on the other hand officially stated that it must have American military and financial assistance if this provision of the committee's recommendations was to be carried out. Furthermore, both the British and American governments soon announced that before any action was taken they intended to consult both Arab and Jewish leaders.

The net result of the appointment of the commission was that insofar as the basic questions were involved the situation remained precisely what it had been eight months previously.

The belief spread among many of the Jewish people, even elements. not identified with the more extreme Zionist groups, that Palestine was rapidly becoming the base for British imperial policy in the Near East. British troops were stationed in Egypt, Libya and other parts of North Africa, as well as in the Lebanon, in addition to Palestine. British divisions were still in occupation of Greece and Italy. Military detachments were likewise placed at such strategic points as Sicily, Crete, Cyprus and the Dodecanese Islands, in addition to the permanent garrison at the British base of Malta. The concentration of British power, however, was shifting to Palestine. The port of Haifa was being enlarged as a major naval base and the construction of air bases in southern Palestine was being rushed. By the beginning of 1946 British armed forces concentrated in Palestine approached the astonishing total of 100,000.

In view of the tension so rapidly developing within the Near East between the Soviet Union and Great Britain, it was not unnatural that many Jews saw in Great Britain's reluctance to further a just solution of the Palestine problem a clear indication that the British government now that it was compelled to withdraw from Egypt intended at all costs to maintain its own control over Palestine as a strategic necessity for the protection of the Suez Canal, to the exclusion of the establishment of any autonomous commonwealth.

There has been no phase of its handling of foreign policy in which the British Labor government has bungled more flagrantly than in its dealing with the Palestine question.

It is now an open secret that the American members of the Anglo-American Commission objected to various provisions of the report and finally agreed to make the report unanimous only because of the positive assurance given them from highly authoritative sources that the British government would place in operation all of the recommendations of the commission, including those the Americans regarded as imperative.

Months have now elapsed since the report was rendered. The British government shows not the slightest intention of carrying out the most urgent recommendation of all, that 100,000 refugees from Europe be given a haven in Palestine. Once more British officials announce that without American help nothing can be done. Worst of all was Mr. Bevin's cruel and unjust reflection upon American public opinion in his singularly ill-considered reference at Bournemouth to the Jewish citizens of New York.

The way in which the British Cabinet has attempted to deal with the mounting tide of opposition to British policy within Palestine has been equally crass. Its attempt in midsummer of 1946 to cow the Jewish spirit by arresting two thousand Jewish leaders and by putting the Jewish Agency in Palestine out of operation was justly characterized by Dr. Chaim Weizmann as an "assault by the Mandatory Government on the Jewish people of Palestine."

The old Zionist leader, broken in health, but still indomitable in his struggle for the Jewish Homeland to which he had dedicated so great a part of his life, was in Palestine at the height of the crisis.

A British subject, and an outstanding scientist, Dr. Weizmann had contributed greatly to the British war effort in both world wars. There was a note of deep pathos in his words when the crisis arose: "The Jews have helped Great Britain in two world wars. Now, Amin el Husseini, the Grand Mufti of Jerusalem, a war criminal and sworn enemy of Britain sits in a palace at Cairo, while Moshe Shertok of the Jewish Agency, who raised an army of 25,000 Jews in Palestine to fight shoulder to shoulder with

Britain in World War II, is imprisoned in a British detention camp."

And, farsighted statesman as Dr. Weizmann has always proved to be, he added: "I believe the British have missed a wonderful chance to bring the Arabs and Jews together. If the British wish, the Jews and the Arabs can come together."

Those last words of Dr. Weizmann epitomize what Great Britain might have done in the past—might have done until very recently.—But the chance for Great Britain alone to find any solution for the most critical problem of the Near East has now, after many long years of opportunity, slipped from her grasp.

It seems to me that the controversial subject of Palestine must be analyzed with entire frankness if any final and equitable solution is to be found in the foreseeable future. Much harm has already been done by the unwillingness of statesmen, in the Western democracies in particular, to speak bluntly concerning some of the basic issues involved. Public opinion in the United States has all too often been persuaded that the difficulty is primarily one of antagonism between the Arabs and Jews. It has been inclined to believe that this bitter predicament can be settled through sleight-of-hand. It has far too often been led by vote-seeking politicians to think that this crucial, tragic problem is going to be solved by pious expressions of sympathy on our part, or that the appointment of commissions will necessarily produce results.

President Edouard Beneš of Czechoslovakia, one of the most truly enlightened and liberal democratic leaders in Europe during the past thirty years, touched upon an essential truth when he recently said, "The establishment of a Jewish Home in Palestine is a necessity for all nations because anti-Semitism is a regrettable but practically inevitable social phenomenon."

I, myself, cannot regard anti-Semitism as "practically inevitable," but I do know that it confronts us.

Whatever the reasons for anti-Semitism may be, and however inexplicable and shocking anti-Semitism may appear to our hearts and minds, the men and women of the democracies who wish to contribute toward its permanent eradication make no contribution by denying that it exists and that it still spreads. The poison of anti-Semitism was disseminated throughout the Western world as a result of the cataclysm launched by Hitler upon our civilization. It represents one of his greatest crimes against his fellow men.

The establishment of an independent Commonwealth of Palestine, offering the Jewish people a chance to find a true home is far from being a final answer to the Jewish problem. But it will make the final answer affirmative and remedial. The rest of the answer lies in the capacity of moral opinion to make a reality of the ideals for which the United States joined in the contest with the Axis. They strove to secure for men of all creeds and of all races equal rights and equal opportunities. From the practical standpoint those ideals will not be achieved within any immediate future. They may be established by the letter of the law, but their ultimate realization depends upon a change of heart and mind in men and women throughout the world.

An independent Palestine, carrying out development projects to the extent pronounced feasible by such outstanding authorities as Dr. Lowdermilk, can absorb a very large Jewish immigration. The lives of many hundreds of thousands of human beings would be saved were they permitted refuge there. It would lessen the evil tensions of the present. It would give the homeless and the unwanted a home where they are wanted, and where they could become happy and prosperous citizens of a country that could well become a model in the community of nations.

Earlier Jewish immigration and investment in Palestine have transformed a poverty-stricken and sparsely settled area into a region that is in many ways an example of modern and progressive civilization. The Jewish people in Palestine have demonstrated what intensive and diversified farming can do in that area. Industries of many kinds have given employment and prosperity to an increasingly large number of the inhabitants, Jews and Arabs alike. The geographical location of Palestine tends to make the region a commercial link between the East and the West. The report of the British Royal Commission on Palestine has made it clear beyond the shadow of a doubt that the Jewish development of the region has been beneficial not only to the Jews but to the Arabs as well. If further proof were needed, the fact that the Arab-speaking population of Palestine has increased from 600,000 to 1,200,000 within the quarter of the century during which the modern Jews have been developing the resources of Palestine is sufficient evidence.

There is no fundamental difference between the Jews and the Arabs. There is no hostility that has any basic reason for existence, once an equitable solution of the Palestine problem has been found, and the Arab world learns that the United Nations will insist that that solution be maintained.

As the recent Joint Resolution of the United States Congress has made clear, the Government of the United States has long been officially committed to the establishment of a Jewish National Home in Palestine. Furthermore, both the Democratic and Republican parties have endorsed this policy at their National Conventions.

There has been much debate both in England and in the United States as to the proper interpretation of the original Balfour Declaration of 1917, and specifically as to whether it implied that the Jews were to have no right to be anything more than a perpetual minority in Palestine.

The most authoritative British statesmen, including Mr. Winston Churchill, who were members of the government which originally endorsed the Balfour Declaration, have repeatedly asserted the contrary. But perhaps Mr. Lloyd George, who was Prime Minister at the time, may be regarded as speaking with the greatest authority on this matter. Mr. Lloyd George has stated, "There has been a good deal of discussion as to the meaning of the words 'Jewish National Home' and whether it involved the setting up of a Jewish National State in Palestine. . . . There could be no doubt as to what the Cabinet had in their minds. It was not their idea that a Jewish State should be set up immediately by the peace treaty without reference to the wishes of the majority of inhabitants. On the other hand, it was contemplated that when the time arrived for according representative institutions to Palestine, if the Jews had meanwhile responded to the opportunity afforded them by the idea of a National Home, and had become a definite majority of the inhabitants, then Palestine would thus become a Jewish Commonwealth. The notion that Jewish immigration would have to be artificially restricted in order to insure that the Jews should be a permanent minority never entered into the heads of anyone engaged in framing the policy. That would have been regarded as unjust and as a fraud on the people to whom we were appealing."

The fact that subsequent British governments pursued a policy wholly at variance with the policy envisaged by Mr. Lloyd George and his collaborators cannot change the fact that the Balfour Declaration at the time it was announced unquestionably offered the Jewish people an opportunity to make of Palestine not only a National Jewish Homeland, but likewise an independent Jewish commonwealth. That ideal, an independent Jewish Commonwealth of Palestine, represents today to many millions of Jews in all parts of the world a symbol of the beginning of the end of their martyrdom.

If the Government of the United States, in accordance with its repeated pledges, intends to assume a practical, as well as a moral leadership in settling the dangerous controversies which threaten world peace, it must without further delay assume leadership in solving the problem of Palestine. If our recent vacillations and procrastination continue, the hope of any peaceful solution will become increasingly remote. Not only is the artificial hostility engendered among the Arab leaders becoming more acute, but Palestine threatens to become a scene of increasing contention between the Soviet Union and Great Britain.

As I publicly stated not many months ago, "The commonwealth will come into being only when the United Nations decides, as it must, that the establishment of a Jewish commonwealth in Palestine is essential to world peace and to world stability. Unless the International Trusteeship Council of the United Nations is charged with the obligation of carrying out such a decision the Commonwealth of Palestine will continue to be an ideal and not a reality. Only the United Nations itself, representing the concerted determination of the free peoples of the world, will possess the necessary authority to achieve a final solution of the Palestine problem.

The British Government should under Article 77 of the United Nations Charter transfer its mandate over Palestine to the International Trusteeship Council.

From the moment the Council assumes jurisdiction the United Nations should make available whatever armed force may be required to give assurance of security to all inhabitants of Palestine.

The Council should thereupon summon representative Jewish and Arab leaders for consultation as to the most desirable solution.

Should it prove impossible for the International Trusteeship Council after full consultation with both Jewish and Arab leaders to obtain their agreement to whatever solution it considers most equitable and desirable, the United Nations should nevertheless decree that its decision be carried out.

Once this step has been taken, the International Trusteeship Council should set up a broadly representative provisional government in Palestine and entrust it with all necessary authority until such time as free elections can be held and an independent and democratic government can commence to function.

As soon as the Council is entrusted with a Trusteeship over Palestine, unrestricted immigration should be permitted. Immigration should thereafter be interrupted only if the International Trusteeship Council or the future Government of Palestine decides that such restriction is temporarily required for economic reasons.

As a result of the various factors to which I have already referred, the present Arab opposition to the creation of an independent Palestine, into which Jewish immigraiton would be unrestricted, has assumed in the minds of the Western peoples an importance which is at variance with realities.

Should the United Nations take such action as that urged in the preceding paragraphs the Arab states would be unable to oppose it. Arab threats of violence are as empty as they are preposterous. There are no military forces of any size in any Arab state. Such forces as there are are devoid of any modern military equipment, and entirely unprepared to engage in armored or air warfare. The forces that the United Nations might have to send to Palestine to preserve order during the first stages of an independent commonwealth need be very small indeed.

There is no basis for the repeated assertion made in official circles in the United States—as when President Truman said in August, 1945, that he would not "like to send 500,000 American troops to Palestine"—that American support for an independent Palestine means the obligation to send there large bodies of American soldiers. The utmost that might be anticipated would be local disturbances among the Arabs within Palestine.

American policy with regard to Palestine, and in a broader sense with regard to the Jewish people, has for many years past been hag-ridden by domestic politics. It has been frequently ignominious. It has been bereft of any enlightened moral leadership save during the years when Franklin Roosevelt was President of the United States.

President Roosevelt's courageous initiative in 1938 in forcing the other governments of the world which were lining up against the Axis to share in the responsibility for finding a refuge for the Jewish people of Europe resulted in the creation of the Inter-Governmental Committee on Refugees. The committee could have been responsible for an outstanding humanitarian achievement prior to and during the war years, but notwithstanding the tireless work of such representatives of the President as Myron Taylor, the final results amounted to little more than zero. The Government of the United States itself permitted the committee to become a nullity.

The United States is today confronted with the same opportunity. It should immediately assume leadership within the United Nations in having the organization accept the responsibility for finding a permanent and just solution of the Palestine issues. That opportunity will now be presented at the meeting of the General Assembly in the autumn of 1946. For unless all of the major powers share that responsibility Palestine may well become the spark which will light a vast conflagration.

No people in the history of mankind have suffered more grievously than the Jewish people. The peoples of the Western democracies cannot wash their hands of their responsibility for this tragedy. If a free and peaceful world is to be within our grasp, the Jewish people must receive something better than illusory promises and hollow assurances of sympathy.

Two years ago in *The Time for Decision* I wrote:

That a practical solution can be found, I am firmly convinced. I am equally persuaded that it will be found along the lines proposed by Dr. Judah Magnes, President of the Hebrew University of Jerusalem. He suggests a union of Jews and Arabs within an autonomous Palestine and a federative system, political as well as economic, comprising Palestine, Syria, the Lebanon, and Transjordania.

It seems to me that for practical reasons such a federation should be an integral part of any general federative union which may be set up in the Near East.

I still believe that that solution is the most desirable. It is the most likely in the long run to prevent lingering antagonism between the Arab and Jewish peoples. It is the most likely to prove conducive to the rapid rise of living standards in the Near East. But if the United Nations assumes its rightful responsibility in the establishment of a trusteeship over Palestine, it must permit the immigration into that country of those who desire to settle there and whom the economy of Palestine can support. In such event, Palestine will in the future in all probability have a majority of citizens of Jewish faith.

The final achievement of independence by the peoples of Syria and of the Lebanon may encourage this solution of the problem. While these two new republics are members of the Arab League, they must appreciate the direct benefits they could derive from a pooling of the resources of the four states of Syria, the Lebanon, Transjordania and Palestine, to insure the hydroelectric and agricultural development of the region.

The world of tomorrow, if peace is maintained, will be a world in which countries like the United States must ever seek new markets for the profitable disposal of their industrial production. The Near East is a region that through an increase in living standards and through an enlightened program for the development of its natural resources, can provide a vast market for exports from the Western democracies.

What do all these divergent factors and problems add up to?

This is the summary as I see it. It is a summary fraught with valid reason for concern to every American citizen.

The Near East threatens to become a vast battleground for the conflicting interests of the Soviet Union and of the Western powers. There is no reason why such a conflict should ever take place. The interests which are now shaping themselves so dangerously are not irreconcilable. There is more than sufficient economic opportunity in the Near East for any legitimate requirements of the major powers for generations to come. The immediate and the dangerous issue is one of power. Not of economics.

If she is willing to assume the responsibility, this nation has the opportunity to formulate a policy of international co-operation through the United Nations and thus to avert the threatening conflict. For such far-reaching problems as the future status of Palestine and the allocation of the oil resources of the Near East can only be settled if all the members of the United Nations realize that the failure to settle these questions and to settle them justly spells an immediate threat to every one of them.

But, above and beyond even such critical questions as these, looms the increasing menace to the future of the world arising from the apparent intention of the Soviet Union to seek her own kind of security by extending her domination into the Mediterranean and over the southern reaches of the Near East.

It is here that the United States can prevent the catastrophe. It so happens that the United States is the only major power that has no political interests in the Near East.

She is today the only world power comparable to the Soviet Union. She has no grounds for political rivalry with that nation. She does have every legitimate reason for assuring herself that the present Soviet concept of security should neither disrupt the United Nations nor annihilate the independence and the sovereign rights of the weaker peoples of the Near East. She has a further right to assure herself that the economic potentialities of the Near East should become available to all foreign countries on a basis of strict equality of opportunity.

These fair objectives cannot offer now or ever any threat to the safety of the Soviet Union or to her opportunity to develop to the fullest possible extent her program for the betterment of her people.

Is it conceivable that the policy of the United States cannot be so shaped as to procure an understanding between the world's two greatest powers that is based upon these truths? Such a policy of co-operation can be commenced without delay. It can be founded on the opportunity afforded both countries to work together in the Social and Economic and Trusteeship councils of the United Nations and thus before it is too late solve controversies which, if they are permitted to grow, will develop into power politics at its most dangerous. For unless such a policy is undertaken and undertaken successfully, the clouds that now hang low over the Near East will break into a storm which will sweep all before it.

CHAPTER VI

The Nationalist Surge in Asia

WITH the truer perspective that future generations will possess, it may well be that of all the developments brought to pass by the Second World War, the most significant will be seen to be the awakening of the peoples of Asia.

During the years between the great wars the West only occasionally gave heed, and that but scant, to the accumulating signs that the Asiatic peoples were becoming politically conscious. The evidence was forced upon our attention here in the United States by the increasing demand of the people of China for the abolition of extraterritoriality; by sporadic outbursts of anti-foreign feeling; by the more sensational features of the campaign for self-government in India which once in a while made the front pages in the American newspapers; by an occasional mutiny against the Dutch authorities in Indonesia; and perhaps most directly by the negotiations for the grant of full independence to the Filipino people. But by and large, the West has regarded the hundreds of millions of men and women in Asia as people of little account, of small importance except as consumers of our cheaper exports, and in their overwhelming majority as people who would for an indefinite period remain passively under the control of the Western powers which had for so long dominated and exploited them.

Even to the few who paid any heed, the problem inherent in this growing political consciousness in Asia seemed to be of no urgency. For it was generally believed that the low standard of living and the abject conditions which characterized the toiling masses of the Far East made it highly improbable that any movement among them to end their political and economic subjection to the West could prove successful. What made the problem seem even less urgent was the general assumption that the Filipinos, the Indonesians, the Indians, the Burmese and the Chinese would for a long time to come think and act solely as nationals of their own countries or, more accurately, as members of their own communities, and that any coherent conception of Asia as a region within which there existed a community of purpose and an identity of objective could not by the nature of things even exist.

These Western assumptions would probably have proved fallacious even had the Second World War never taken place. Most of the leaders of the Asiatic people had received an excellent education in Western universities and had assimilated the best that Western civilization has to offer. They had returned home not only with a strong national pride and a burning desire to benefit their fellow nations but with the full consciousness that the problems of their countries were the same as those of their neighbors; and they were in frequent communication with their progressive colleagues throughout Asia.

I remember that Manuel Quezon told me in a conversation which I had with him before the Second World War that his contacts with the younger Nationalist leaders in the Netherlands East Indies and in India had existed over a period of many years. He was intimately familiar with their plans, with their failures and with their accomplishments. He told me that when he finally convinced himself that the actual independence of the Philippines would shortly become an accomplished fact, he felt that this achievement would be not only the realization of the ideal which Filipino patriots had so long pursued, but also a great opportunity for the Filipino people to further by their own example the chance of other subject peoples of the Far East to attain their independence. He considered that the Filipino people had a responsibility to demonstrate that self-government and independence should be rapidly conceded to the colonial peoples of Asia.

Paradoxically enough, it has been the rapacious government of Japan during the years of the Second World War that has most greatly spurred the nationalist movement in the Far East. To the Western mind, the Japanese slogan of "Asia for the Asiatics" and the proclamation of a Japanese new order in the Far East were nothing more than blatant propaganda undertaken solely for the purpose of weakening the influence of the Western powers. ·It seemed incredible that the rule of the Japanese militarists could offer any inducement even to an uneducated Asiatic, or seriously weaken the hold over Asia of the Western democracies. But to a great part of Asia the onward-sweeping tide of Japanese victories during the early stages of the war implied primarily the end of an epoch of alien subjugation and of alien exploitation, and, perhaps even more, the opportunity finally to obliterate Western contempt.

The much vaunted concept of the superiority of the white race ended finally with the surrender of Singapore and the capture of the Philippines. For the first time since the defeat of Russia in 1906 and the capture of the German garrisons in China in 1914, the East had triumphed over Western power. Now an Asiatic nation had apparently defeated the combined forces of all of the Western powers.

There can be no question that almost everywhere the Japanese forces of invasion were at first hailed as liberators. It was only after the Japanese armies of occupation had shown themselves to be far more ruthless in their domination and in their exploitation of the local populations than the Western powers that opinion underwent some transformation. But everywhere the Japanese invaders, as an integral part of their program of exploitation, encouraged nationalist movements. The leaders were generally representative of groups that had long been pledged to national independence and to a complete severance of all ties with the colonial powers.

In every part of Asia today the tides of nationalism are rising more and more rapidly. The developments which have taken place since the surrender of Japan are merely symptoms of a profound change which cannot be arrested. There exists in the world of today neither the armed force nor the economic power to arrest it.

China is more nearly a cohesive whole than it has been in thirty-five years. However bitter and prolonged the struggle between the Nationalist Government and the Communists may be, the Chinese people have become nationally conscious. How-

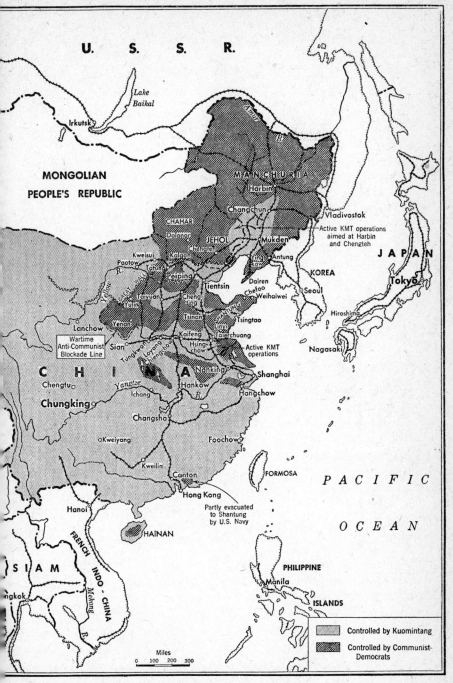

CHINA, showing Kuomintang and Communist areas

ever deep the distinctions and the barriers created by religion, by class and by tradition between the component elements of the subcontinent which we call India, the Indian people are commencing to regard themselves as a nation. However filled with obstacles their road to autonomy or independence may still be, there is awake within the peoples of Indonesia and Burma a spirit of nationalism which had previously made itself felt only spasmodically. However reluctant France may be to abandon the strangle hold that she has maintained for so many decades over the peoples of Indo-China, the autonomy of Indo-China cannot long be postponed.

The outstanding question has been whether the major powers would realize that the period of Western domination in Asia had inevitably come to an end and would be prepared, upon the conclusion of the war, to agree upon a program to enable the colonial peoples of the Far East who were ready for self-government to achieve it as rapidly and peacefully as possible.

In an address which I delivered to the Foreign Policy Association of New York on October 16, 1943, I said:

More than a hundred years ago the moral force of public opinion in Great Britain compelled the British Government to abolish slavery within the territories of the Empire and a great British Prime Minister led a valiant and successful fight for the abolition of the international slave trade. Eighty years ago, the American people proved the eternal truth that this Nation could not survive half slave and half free. Can the peaceful, the stable, and the free world for which we hope be created if it is envisioned from the outset as half slave and half free?—if hundreds of millions of human beings are told that they are destined to remain indefinitely under alien subjection? New and powerful nationalistic forces are breaking into life throughout the earth, and in particular in the vast regions of Africa, of the Near East, and of the Far East. Must not these forces, unless they are to be permitted to start new and devastating inundations, be canalized through the channels of liberty into the great stream of constructive and co-operative human endeavor?

We all of us recognize that it will take many generations for some backward peoples to be prepared for autonomy and self-government. But I am persuaded that any International Organization should establish the basic principle that no nation has the inherent and unlimited right to govern subject peoples; that all nations which possess jurisdiction over other peoples must recognize in effective fashion that such control is to be exercised primarily for the purpose of preparing these alien races to undertake the responsibilities of self-government as soon as they are capable thereof; and that until they are fitted for autonomy the administering power, as a trustee, must hold itself responsible for its administration to world public opinion as represented in the International Organization.

The right of all peoples to their liberty must be confirmed as the moral force of public opinion long since established the right of man to his individual freedom. I do not believe in the doctrine of a superior race. The enjoyment by peoples of the right of self-determination is not limited by Divine warrant, nor for that matter by the Atlantic Charter, to the White race. Peoples capable of autonomous government should be possessed of that right whether they be yellow or brown, black or white.

For several years, no such program was forthcoming. The major colonial powers, influenced in no small part by the adamant unwillingness of Mr. Churchill to "preside over the liquidation of the British Empire," were wholly unwilling to take any steps which might diminish their imperial rights.

The Government of the United States, which before the end of the war had the influence necessary to bring about the establishment of some constructive program, proved altogether timid and vacillating in its approach. The Soviet government took the lead, it is true, as a spokesman for the interests of dependent peoples. But its leadership could hardly fail to be interpreted as due primarily to a desire to weaken the influence of the British Empire.

With but scant preparation, consequently, the United Nations Conference at San Francisco was confronted with the opportunity and responsibility of establishing within the United Nations Charter the mechanism, as well as the principles, by which all dependent peoples would be permitted to obtain or to prepare for self-government.

The results are before us. In Chapter 11 of the United Nations Charter it is provided that, "Members of the United Nations which have or assume responsibility for the administration of territories whose peoples have not yet attained a full measure of self-government recognize the principle that the interests of the inhabitants of these territories are paramount and accept as a sacred trust the obligation to promote to the utmost, within the system of international peace and security established by the present Charter, the wellbeing of the inhabitants of these territories."

This declaration of principle is, so far as it goes, unassailable.

But in Chapter 12 of the Charter, by which the International Trusteeship Council is established and the international trusteeship system is specified, it is merely provided that "the United Nations shall establish under its authority an international trusteeship system for the administration and supervision of such territories as may be placed thereunder subsequent to individual agreements."

It is, of course, clear that until and unless the present colonial powers enter into "individual agreements," they are under no obligation to grant to the dependent peoples now under their control either self-government or independence, and are bound merely, by the very broad principles set forth in Chapter 11.

The British Labor government has now undertaken in its relations with the peoples of India and in its negotiations with the Egyptian government a policy entirely distinct from that maintained by preceding British governments. By its dispatch to India in the spring of 1946 of a Cabinet mission to draw up an agreement with Indian leaders upon a constitutional form of government for India, and by its official announcement made at the same time that the Indian peoples would receive complete independence, should they insist upon it, Great Britain has at last shown with finality her realization of the rapidly moving current of events in the Far East. By her dealings with Egypt, she has further made clear her recognition that the Egyptian people are no longer reconciled to remaining as wards of the British government. But at the same time, she has shown no indication that she intends to expedite agreements with the International Trusteeship Council. The other colonial powers have shown even less evidence of an intention to hasten this solution. When the United Nations Assembly meets in New York in September, 1946, it will then be seen whether the International

Trusteeship System is to be enabled to perform the salutary duties for which it was created.

Any attempt to relate the history of the developments in Asia in recent months and to evaluate their effect on our hopes for a peaceful world order must be made in the light of this overwhelming fact—that many of the peoples of Asia will no longer be denied their right to political and economic independence. Any lasting integration within the United Nations organization of the West and the East depends upon the recognition today—not tomorrow—by the Western powers that this demand for freedom must be accepted, not rejected.

It is easier to visualize the component parts of the new Asia which is being born before our eyes in their proper relation if we start with the vast area of China. China represents the oldest continuing civilization the world has known. It comprises the largest mass of human beings living within the confines of any sovereign country. For more than a century it has been the arena within which the great powers of the West have contended for the advancement of their imperial aims, and it is likely that it will continue to be. From the standpoint of the future, the Chinese people can become the greatest stabilizing factor in the Far East, provided they are helped to maintain the independence and integrity of their territory and to achieve internal unity.

It is the tendency of a certain type of well-intentioned but foggy-minded liberal in the Western democracies to think of China as an integrated nation where democracy as it is practiced in the West can be instituted within a relatively brief time and where so-called Chinese public opinion truly represents the thinking of the Chinese masses. Nothing, of course, could be farther from the truth. The patient, toiling masses of China's population are living today as they have lived for a thousand years. They have nothing to say concerning their own political determination. Their lives are spent, like those of their forefathers, in a ceaseless struggle to keep body and soul together and to make it possible for their children to survive to undertake the same struggle in the face of suffering and adversity. That is not to say that the prospects for the advancement of political responsibility and for the improvement of the living standards of the hundreds of millions of souls who are China have not been vastly bettered as the result of the ideals and efforts of the leaders of modern China such as Sun Yat-sen and Chiang Kai-shek. But it does mean that those prospects will not materialize unless the world makes it possible for the Chinese people, by their own unimpeded efforts, to attain the objectives which these leaders have laid down for them. It does mean that the China with which the Western world must deal today is a China which speaks with the voice and as a result of the decisions of a handful of men around the Generalissimo or in the headquarters of the Communist leaders of Yenan.

When Japan surrendered, China had suffered fifteen years of almost continuous aggression. Her richest provinces had been occupied by the Japanese. All her seaports and nearly all her major cities were in Japanese hands. Millions of her citizens had died in the course of the war or had been forced to flee before the Japanese armies into the far interior. Her government had been cut off from almost all outside contacts throughout the duration of hostilities. The large measure of financial assistance rendered by the United States and British governments had proved no effective bulwark against the mounting spiral of inflation. The Chinese people as a whole were suffering more and more from an inflationary process which affected increasingly the individual life of every one of them. The Chinese government was shot through with corruption from top to bottom. The Generalissimo and his most loyal supporters appeared wholly unable to do more than undertake occasional palliative measures.

The military alliance against Japan between the National Chinese Government of Chungking and the American and British governments had been replete with violent discord which the wartime censorship generally succeeded in concealing but which occasionally broke out into public notoriety. The perhaps tactless, but highly courageous, insistence of General Stilwell that the help given by the American government be put to effective use against the common enemy rather than used in domestic strife resulted in the general's recall. The continuing antagonism between the Generalissimo and the agents of the British government was known throughout the East.

Yet notwithstanding these undeniable weaknesses in the Chinese National Government and notwithstanding the almost insurmountable obstacles which he confronted, Chiang Kai-shek proved himself a successful war leader. He succeeded in maintaining sufficient unity within China throughout the long period in which he has held supreme authority to make it possible for him to aid in the defeat of Japan. Thus far he has contended successfully with both his foreign and his domestic enemies.

Chiang Kai-shek has had to face every conceivable obstacle in his epic and interminable struggle as head of the National Government and as chief of the Kuomintang to save his country from foreign domination and to urge it ever onward to national unity. He has demonstrated qualities of statesmanship and of vision that were not apparent in those years now long since past when he served under Sun Yat-sen. He has been untiring in the pursuit of his country's interests as he has seen them. His resiliency has been superhuman. That he will go down in history as one of the great figures in the construction of a new Asia cannot be questioned.

He has been greatly assisted by the outstanding capacity of many of those with whom he has surrounded himself in his government. I have known no modern statesman more notable for his grasp of fundamentals, for his ability to negotiate and for the rapidity of his mental processes, than the able Dr. T. V. Soong, the Generalissimo's brother-in-law and present Prime Minister.

But there can unfortunately be no question that Chiang Kai-shek has shown little administrative or executive capacity. Corruption and inefficiency have saturated every branch of the public administration. Austerity in office has been the exception, and graft the rule. And with the end of the war the long-latent opposition of the rank and file of the Chinese people to the indefinite continuation of the existing form of government has been making itself felt more strongly every day. This growing popular opposition has necessarily made it far more difficult for Chiang Kai-shek to obtain the vigorous public support which he required in order successfully to cope with the crisis brought on by the Communists after the surrender of the Japanese.

The Chinese Communist party of today commenced its independent political life when the Kuomintang party, as it had been created by Sun Yat-sen, split in 1927 into two parts.

For some years the Chinese Communists were blockaded by Kuomintang armies in southeast China. They then undertook their amazing trek to the remote provinces of the northwest. Under the leadership of General Chu Teh, the Red armies, then numbering only two thousand men, marched from Kiangsi through the rich province of Szechwan and the impoverished and war-ravaged provinces of northern Shensi and Shansi, until they finally established themselves in Yenan. By that time the continuous accretion of new recruits had brought the Communist forces to a total of one hundred thousand. Today they number at least half a million.

From that time on the Communists have been blockaded by the armies of the Kuomintang. Yet the wartime policy of the Communist leaders was undeviating. It was represented by their slogan, "Chinese must not fight Chinese," and after 1939 they refused to permit any clash with the Kuomintang which might precipitate that Chinese civil war which was Japan's major objective.

The three chief leaders of the Communists have long been General Chu Teh, the Commander in Chief, Mao Tse-tung, the leader of the party, and Chou En-lai, Secretary General of the Communist party and its chief negotiator.

All three are of peasant origin. Chu Teh's great gifts as a lightning strategist and as a ruthless and untiring leader in the field are belied by his heavy, awkward build and his kindly, smiling face. There is nothing about him reminiscent of the severe, inhibited and harassed figure of Chiang Kai-shek.

Of the three it is Mao Tse-tung who is outstanding, however. What has always been closest to his heart has been the improvement of the conditions of life for that eighty per cent of China's people who farm the land and among whom he was born. He is wholly sincere in his conviction that Marxism represents the one sure means for relieving China's ills. He recognizes that the Chinese people are not yet ripe for Communism, and that they must pass through many intermediate stages of evolution before they come to it. But he is determined that China's new political structure must be so built as to facilitate rather than retard the development of Communism.

In Yenan he has organized the peasants into co-operatives, and he has already undertaken successfully the establishment of local industries under party control.

A tall, quiet, enthusiastic man of some fifty years of age, with a high forehead and a keen gaze, Mao Tse-tung looks more like the schoolmaster which he originally prepared himself to be than the most powerful Communist leader of East Asia.

His present purposes are clearly set out in a speech which he delivered in April, 1945:

> After victory in the war of resistance, a National Assembly based on broad democratic foundations should be called to form a democratic coalition government, embracing all parties and groups, as well as non-party representatives. The Government should be a coalition no matter whether the Communists are a majority or a minority in the National Assembly.
>
> As soon as the new democratic coalition government and a united high command are formed, the troops in China's liberated areas will be handed over to them at once. But all Kuomintang troops must also be handed over to them at the same time.

That has been the basis for negotiation between the Communists and the National Government during the months of 1946. And in the political strategy so proclaimed it will be seen that the Chinese Communist party has pursued precisely the same line as that laid down for the Communists throughout the world—from Chile to Cuba, and from the Netherlands to Italy.

The chief political and military problem with which the National Government has had to contend has been the fact that in the north the Communist leaders of Yenan were to all intents and purposes maintaining a separate and sovereign government within China. For some time before the end of the war the Soviet government had ceased to provide the National Government with the armaments and military supplies which it had at one time furnished. There was much reason to believe that Moscow was giving the Communist leaders every advantage in order to make it possible for them to maintain an attitude of stubborn intransigence. The Communist leaders had effective publicity throughout the West in the propaganda which had long been current in their behalf. Nor was this propaganda by any means without foundation. In the regions controlled by the Chinese Communists the peasants had actually been given a real voice in local government. The distribution and reclamation of land had actually been carried out. Industries had been created out of thin air. The morale of the Chinese people under their authority was infinitely higher than that of the Chinese still subject to the authority of Chungking.

The more extreme reactionaries in the National Government made every effort to make sure during the latter stages of the war that no compromise should be reached between the two régimes. Chiang Kai-shek himself made certain that neither Lend-Lease supplies nor armed contingents should be sent as help to the Yenan government. It was not strange that, as a result of the controversies which had persisted for nearly twenty years, a large part of the Chinese military contingents under the command of the National Government were employed to watch the Communist armies rather than to assist in the prosecution of the war against Japan.

There is no advantage to be gained in this brief survey by reviewing in any detail the sordid history of the constant haggling which went on between Chungking and Yenan during the war against Japan. It is sufficient merely to emphasize that all efforts prior to V-J Day ended in failure. The visit of General Patrick J. Hurley to Yenan when he was American Ambassador to Chungking, and the visits to the national capital of the Communist negotiator, Chou En-lai, produced no results. Consequently, when the United States Government demanded that arrangements be made for accepting the surrender of the Japanese troops in Chinese territory, the National Government refused to authorize the Communist authorities to have any part in arranging for the surrender, because of the opportunity which that would afford them of securing arms and military equipment still in the possession of the Japanese armies.

The result was utter chaos. The Communist authorities naturally enough forced the surrender of the Japanese troops wherever they were in a position to do so. The armies of the National Government attempted to prevent this wherever they could undertake any resistance. The American military authorities and their occupation forces were placed in the unsatisfactory position of finding themselves in between the two contending factions. Civil war broke out. It was attended by loud outcries within the United States from those who sympathized with the Communist faction, demanding the immediate withdrawal of every American soldier from China. It was met with equal virulence on the part of those who sympathized with the National Government, and who believed that Moscow was utilizing the Chinese Communist armies to establish its own immediate control over China and thereby to overthrow the National Government.

In an evaluation of the situation, a situation which for reasons to be shown vitally affects the national interests of the United States, two general aspects must be clarified. The first involves the relative position and importance in the Chinese polity of the Kuomintang party, of which the National Government is the mouthpiece, and the Communist party, of which the Yenan leaders are the authorized spokesmen.

The other, inextricably woven into the internal structure of China today, is the international aspect which derives from the agreement reached at Yalta between the United States, British and Soviet governments and the treaty subsequently signed at Moscow between the Russian and Chinese National governments, which was in turn predicated upon the Yalta agreements.

There can be no question that advanced liberal opinion in the English-speaking countries has become strongly prejudiced in recent times against the Chinese National Government. This prejudice is in part due to the recalcitrant attitude which Chiang Kai-shek has so consistently displayed toward the Communist party of Yenan. It is perhaps in greater part due to the fact that the

Kuomintang, of which he is the recognized leader, has stood for one party rule in China. It is apparently forgotten by the bulk of liberal opinion in the United States at least that the one party rule of the Kuomintang was devised by the most advanced leader that China has ever possessed, Dr. Sun Yat-sen, as a temporary measure to continue only until an efficient government could bring order out of the total chaos into which China had been plunged by the interminable civil wars of the early years of the past century. It seems to be equally forgotten that the Soviet government, so much admired by a large percentage of these exponents of liberalism, is likewise a one party government created for precisely the same purposes as those for which the Kuomintang was originally designed. It is also overlooked that with the end of the war the Generalissimo announced the intention of the Kuomintang to abandon its monopoly of government, and his own desire that during the year 1946 preparations should be concluded for the establishment of a government representative of the free decision of the Chinese people.

The term "the Communist government of Yenan" is, strictly speaking, an anomaly. The Chinese Communists have exercised unquestioned authority within the area they have controlled and have undoubtedly carried out measures that have resulted in benefit to the masses of the Chinese people rather than to the favored few. But the region which they have held in unoccupied China comprises no large cities. Their reforms have related very largely to a purely agricultural population. The structure of authority which they have erected like all Communist governments, is essentially a dictatorial régime consisting of quite as small a handful of men in proportion to the total population of the area as that represented by the Chungking government itself.

The treaty signed at Moscow between the Prime Minister of the Chinese National Government, Dr. T. V. Soong, and the Soviet Foreign Commissar regulates the present relations between China and the Soviet Union. When it was made public, it was acclaimed almost universally as an agreement which insured Russia's recognition of the full rights of the Chinese people to complete independence, to the territory that Japan had taken from them during the preceding generation, and to the integrity of the remainder of Chinese territory. It was regarded as official proof that the Soviet government not only intended to support the National Government rather than the Communist leaders of Yenan, but likewise would abstain from any effort to control the internal affairs of the Chinese people.

While it had long been rumored, it was not officially made known until February 12, 1946, that the agreements of Yalta had included a hitherto unpublished accord by the three major powers which provided for the Sino-Russian Treaty. The Yalta agreements thus very definitely shaped the destinies of the Chinese people for them.

It will be remembered that this agreement was signed by President Roosevelt, Prime Minister Churchill, and Generalissimo Stalin on February 11, 1945, six months prior to Japan's surrender. It will also be remembered that by the Preamble the Soviet Union agreed to enter the war against Japan after Germany's surrender on the following conditions, accepted by the two major powers of the West:

1. The *status quo* in Outer Mongolia (the Mongolian Peoples Republic) shall be preserved;
2. The former rights of Russia violated by the treacherous attack of Japan in 1904 shall be restored viz:
   a. The southern part of Sakhalin as well as all the islands adjacent to it shall be returned to the Soviet Union;
   b. The commercial port of Dairen shall be internationalized, the pre-eminent interests of the Soviet Union in this port being safeguarded and the lease of Port Arthur as a naval base of the U.S.S.R. restored;
   c. The Chinese Eastern Railroad and the South Manchurian Railroad which provides an outlet to Dairen shall be jointly operated by the establishment of a joint Soviet-Chinese company, it being understood that the pre-eminent interests of the Soviet Union shall be safeguarded and that China shall retain full sovereignty in Manchuria;
3. The Kurile Islands shall be handed over to the Soviet Union.

It is understood that the agreement concerning Outer Mongolia and the ports and railroads referred to above will require concurrence of Generalissimo Chiang Kai-shek. The President will take measures in order to obtain this concurrence on advice from Marshal Stalin.

The heads of the three great powers have agreed that these claims of the Soviet Union shall be unquestionably fulfilled after Japan has been defeated.

For its part the Soviet Union expresses its readiness to conclude with the National Government of China a pact of friendship and alliance between the U.S.S.R. and China in order to render assistance to China with its armed forces for the purpose of liberating China from the Japanese yoke.

There are three points in this agreement that should be stressed. The first is that the provisions that secure for Russia joint participation in the operation of the Chinese Eastern Railroad and the South Manchurian Railroad give her a predominant voice in the economic development of Manchuria. So long as the Russian government is able in this manner to control the shipment of imports as well as regulate the distribution of local products, Soviet commercial interests will in practice necessarily be given preferential treatment.

The second point to be emphasized is the fact that through the recognition of the "pre-eminent interests of the Soviet Union" in the port of Dairen and through a new lease of Port Arthur as a naval base, Russia is restored to the predominant position in Manchuria that she occupied prior to the war with Japan in 1904.

The third point and the most important point of all is to be found in the penultimate paragraph of the Yalta agreements. The agreement of the three powers that the Soviet's claims are to be "unquestionably fulfilled" made it clear that Russia was to obtain these rights whether or not the Chinese National Government was willing to grant them.

There can in my opinion be no legitimate objection to the return to Russia of southern Sakhalin and of the Kuriles. Russian possession of them is essential if the Soviet government is to obtain security for its Siberian provinces. Both territories were torn from Russia by Japan. The internationalization of Dairen and the grant of permanent autonomy to Outer Mongolia have a considerable measure of justification. However, the restoration to Russia of the right formerly possessed by the imperial Russian governments to dominate Manchuria through the control of the Chinese eastern and south Manchurian railroads, and the lease of Port Arthur as a naval base, necessarily fall into a different category. These concessions, which will make it altogether impossible for a new unified China to exercise full sovereignty within Manchuria, are all the more objectionable in view of China's absence from the conference table where they were decided. The willingness of the United States to sanction them can be extenuated only on the ground that at the time they were fixed there was as yet no imminent prospect of Japan's defeat. To President Roosevelt at Yalta, the need for Russia's participation in the war against Japan as a means of hastening the victory must have loomed larger than any other considerations involved.

The terms of the Yalta agreements were, of course, accepted by the Chinese National Government. Granted the all-powerful position which Russia would occupy in northeastern Asia after the defeat of Japan, and granted that Russia was likewise in a position, through assistance to the Communist leaders of Yenan, to plunge China into a prolonged civil war, the Chinese government had no alternative, in view of the unequivocal support given to the Russian demands by the two major powers of the West. The treaty concluded at Moscow was merely the overt recognition of the inextricable dilemma into which the Chinese government had been forced.

With the final defeat of Japan it had become more and more apparent to every thinking American that the outbreak of civil war in China would immediately endanger the long-range interests of the United States, as well as her short-range interests, because of the presence there of relatively large bodies of American troops. From the broader point of view, it was also unmistakably plain that a Chinese civil war would immediately bring into juxtaposition the interests of the Soviet Union and the interests of the American government. The Soviet government was determined to restore Russia to the position that imperial Russia had enjoyed in the Far East prior to the war with Japan, and to do so would use every means that lay within its power. Civil war would inevitably mean that under one pretext or another the Soviet government would extend its influence within China far south of the Manchurian province.

For reasons of strategy as well as for reasons of legitimate economic interest, the United States could not agree passively to acquiesce in the establishment of a Soviet-dominated China. For forty-five years she has been foremost in insisting on the policy of the Open Door in China, as one of the foundations of American foreign policy; and the preservation of it had been one of the causes of the conflict between the United States and Japan. The position of the other Western powers, notably Great Britain, would inevitably be similar to the position of the United States. A Chinese civil war would create an immediate danger of such a clash between the Soviet Union and the Western powers as to eliminate any reasonable prospect for the successful establishment of the United Nations or for the construction of a world order upon which lasting peace could be built.

The departure of General Patrick J. Hurley from the official scene as American Ambassador to China and the confused charges that he hurled at the Department of State obscured to a considerable extent the real issues which confronted the American government.

General Hurley had unquestionably made every effort to further the objectives of the United States as he construed them. He had acted with transparent sincerity. He had attempted on repeated occasions, by conferences with the Chinese Communist leaders, to remove the grounds for acute friction between the Communists and the National Government and thus lessen the chances of civil war. He interpreted his mission primarily, however, as a responsibility which placed upon him the obligation to see no evil nor weakness in the National Government to which he was accredited, and to see no strength nor good in the Communists opposing that government. The junior members of the American foreign service who had made a more realistic appraisal of the true Chinese picture, and who recognized the admirable qualities of many of the Communist leaders and realized the great hold which they were beginning to have upon a large percentage of the masses of the Chinese people, became anathema to their chief. The struggle within the State Department between the two opposing tendencies had been simmering for many months before it broke into newspaper headlines with the announcement of the Ambassador's resignation and the publication of his diatribe against the officials of the department who had refused to adopt his views. The dispute did nothing to advance American interests nor strengthen American prestige at a singularly delicate moment. For the long-awaited clash between Chiang Kai-shek and the Communists now seemed imminent. It may be said without hesitation that the action taken by the President and by the State Department at the time of General Hurley's resignation was by far the most constructive and vigorous step that has been recorded in the field of American foreign policy during the past two years.

On December 15, 1945, President Truman issued a public statement setting forth United States policy toward China and simultaneously appointed General George C. Marshall, former Chief of Staff, as the new American Ambassador to the National Chinese Government.

The President's statement was intended far more to have a determining effect upon the Chinese leaders than to enlighten American public opinion. It contained two key sentences:

It is the firm belief of the United States Government that a strong, united, and democratic China is of the utmost importance to the success of the United Nations Organization and for world peace. . . . The United States recognizes and will continue to recognize the National Government of China and cooperate with it in international affairs.

The President's statement urged the Communist leaders to abolish their "autonomous armies" and to agree to their integration into the Chinese National Army as soon as a broadly representative Chinese government had been established. It also urged the National Government to abolish its one party system and to include within the new coalition government a fair and effective representation of all other political elements in China.

The clear-cut, realistic and vigorous policy thus outlined by the Government of the United States, which was of course predicated upon the recognition by the Chinese National Goverment that the desperately needed assistance which the United States could furnish would not be forthcoming unless the terms of American policy were complied with, achieved prompt results.

No better emissary could have been found for the task of carrying out this policy than General Marshall. His knowledge of China was at best superficial. While he was necessarily fully conversant when Chief of Staff with the backstage difficulties encountered by all American representatives, diplomatic as well as military, in their dealings with the Chinese government in Chungking, he had, however, no intimate familiarity with the political scene. But he brought to his mission an impartial and objective point of view, and his great and deserved prestige within the United States was of inestimable value in gaining influence for him with each of the opposing factions. He possessed, moreover, great tact and patience, an exceedingly lucid mind, the ability to estimate relative values with unusual rapidity and an unfailing grasp of the essential realities which were involved in what had already become a most ominous situation. General Marshall had been in China only a few days when it was officially announced that he had been requested by both factions to serve as mediator between the representatives of the Chinese National Government and representatives of the Communists. A tentative agreement seemed later to be reached. A truce brought an end to the bitter fighting which had been going on for many weeks between the National and Communist armies. So-called "truce teams" of American officers were appointed to make sure that the terms of the truce were respected by both sides. The National Government announced its plans for the broadly representative government required by the President's statement and Chinese unity appeared for the first time in twenty-five years to be imminent.

Unfortunately, these bright prospects were almost immediately clouded by the position taken by the Soviet Union.

In the final stages of the campaign against Japan, the Soviet armies had occupied Manchuria and had there accepted the surrender of the Japanese divisions in that region. During the weeks when civil war seemed almost inevitable, the Chinese National Government had requested the Soviet military authorities to remain in Manchuria until the duly authorized representatives of the National Government could assume jurisdiction over the territory formerly occupied by the Japanese. The Russian government had agreed to this request, but had announced its intention of evacuating the whole of Manchuria by February 1. When the date for their withdrawal arrived and the Russian military authorities gave no indication of leaving, it was discovered that they were not only constructing new military installations but were demanding of the Chinese National Government economic concessions far greater than those stipulated in the Yalta agreements and in the subsequent Sino-Russian Treaty of Moscow. It further became known that not only were Chinese National troops being given no opportunity to assume jurisdiction over the province but that Chinese Communists, as well as so-called "Union Communists" arriving from Russia, were demanding joint control over the province. Finally, it became known that Chinese Communists were making preparations to create an "eastern Mongolian autonomous republic" which would include not only the province of Jehol but also a very large portion of Manchuria itself.

To the members of the Chinese National Government as well as to some of the Communist leaders themselves, these developments could only imply that the Soviet Union was determined to exercise a far greater control over Manchuria than that provided by the Yalta agreements. Manchuria contains three-fourths of China's heavy industries, which under Chinese sovereignty would constitute the very key to her capacity to reconstruct and to defend a unified country.

In any such eventuality the United States could not remain merely a passive spectator. The rape of Manchuria by Japan in 1931 had touched off the spark which eventually led to the Second World War. By consenting to the provisions of the Yalta agreements, President Roosevelt had intended to establish the foundation for a treaty relationship between China and the Soviet Union that would insure the integrity and independence of China. He had committed himself to obtain China's consent to those provisions, which was reluctantly given. Were the terms agreed to by Russia to be wholly disregarded, and were she now to follow a policy that might soon place her in the very position that Japan

had attempted to secure—in actual control of the whole of China—
the vital interests of the United States would be as clearly jeopardized as they had been by Japan. What was equally important, the
Government of the United States through President Roosevelt
had assumed a moral obligation to the Chinese people which would
be flagrantly violated were the Soviet Union to persist in the
course upon which it appeared to be embarked.

The ever-mounting tension which has unfortunately been evident in the relations between the Soviet Union and the United
States during the months which have since elapsed has inevitably
been reflected in the increasingly grave impasse which the United
States confronts in China.

The initial success of General Marshall in paving the way for
an apparent approximation of the Kuomintang and Communist
interests soon was seen to have been short-lived. The more
reactionary of the followers of the National Government frequently sabotaged his efforts. But as relations between Moscow
and Washington deteriorated one could not avoid seeing that
the attempts of the representatives from Yenan to find solutions and to adjust differences with Chiang Kai-shek became
progressively more feeble. By midsummer an armed conflict between the Nationalists and the Communists seemed at hand.
General Marshall's efforts at mediation were generally believed to
have failed.

The United States was placed in a highly awkward dilemma.
The American government had recognized that the outbreak of
a new civil war in China would involve the immediate risk of a
major clash between the United States and Russia. The history
of the Spanish civil war and of Soviet participation in it was fresh
in the minds of officials in Washington. The United States could
not acquiesce in the control of China by the Soviet Union. Yet if
renewed civil war came about and the Communists obtained active
support for the Red armies from Moscow that would undoubtedly
be the outcome unless Chiang Kai-shek received American help.
For the Nationalist armies were in no condition to resist by
themselves a Communist attack which was aided and abetted by
the Soviet Union.

The American government had within China troops stationed there for the ostensible purpose of helping the Chinese National Government to take over and disarm the Japanese forces remaining on the mainland when Japan surrendered. These American troops remained. If they were withdrawn from China the last physical means of checking a Communist attack upon the National Government or of discouraging any major act of Russian intervention in China would be eliminated. The Communists, who had at first publicly acclaimed the efforts of the United States to promote Chinese unity and had offered their full co-operation to General Marshall, now began to claim that the United States was trying to maneuver Chiang Kai-shek into a position where he could dominate his Communist opponents. By July, 1946, the mediation proceedings had broken down so completely that in a public proclamation the Communist leader, Mao Tse-tung, bitterly assailed American help to the Kuomintang as well as the maintenance in China of any American troops. He demanded their immediate withdrawal.

Mao Tse-tung's appeal to Chinese popular hatred of foreign intervention could not but have a prompt and far-reaching effect. It threatened a rebirth of the Communist-inspired xenophobia which had been rampant in the early 1920's. It obliterated the storm of popular protests against Russia when the Soviet forces were not withdrawn from Manchuria.

The United States was now forced into a corner where it would be damned if it did, and damned if it didn't. If it obeyed the Communist warning to get out, it would destroy its own influence and prestige and gravely weaken the position of Chiang Kai-shek. It would risk the probability that Soviet influence would soon become supreme in China. If it refused to heed the Communists it would afford a plausible pretext for violent agitation against the Western powers, and especially against itself, and thus likewise bring about a weakening of the National Government which was supported by the United States.

The reasons for what has happened can probably best be summarized in this way. The decision to send General Marshall to China to compose differences and to prevent civil war was courageous and wise. Had the Soviet government desired that a real agreement be reached General Marshall would have succeeded. But it must be admitted that his efforts were also impeded by the fact that the manner in which American troops were frequently employed too often gave color to the Communist charges—whether just or unjust—that the United States military officials were more concerned in seeking strategic advantages for the Central Government than in limiting themselves to insuring the terms of the truce between the two factions.

There is also to be added a further and deep-lying element in the problem which could not be better expressed than in these words written to me recently by an American press correspondent now in China:

The continuation of American military assistance to the Central Government will and has worsened the chances for a true political settlement of outstanding problems; will and has increased the dangerous possibility of efforts to resolve China's impasse by military might.

I don't see how we can expect two unequal boxers to negotiate peacefully if, behind their backs, we're filling the gloves of one with lead slugs. It seems to stand to reason that when the smaller sees he's being out-talked, two to one, the least he can do is rise up and stalk away, and gird up his loins to continue a battle which he's been fighting for nineteen years and through which he's become so adept and cunning that he *had* to be asked to sit down and negotiate in the first place.

If he hadn't been such a good fighter he wouldn't have been invited to talk; and he wouldn't have been such a good talker, either.

I think it is now apparent that the way in which the policy adopted by the United States has been interpreted or implemented by the American military commanders in China is one of the chief reasons for our present dilemma. But the dilemma itself can hardly be dispelled unless the over-all relationship between the United States and the Soviet Union undergoes a major change for the better.

It is hard, at best, to see how China's internal situation can be solved, except by an uneasy and distrustful truce, within a generation.

In their uprooting of family ties, in their regimentation of entire masses, in their defamation of religion, in their concentration—to the exclusion of every other value—on materialistic science, lies the chief obstacle to the rapid sweep of the Communists' doctrines throughout the peasant masses of China. That obstacle will, however, be greatly diminished if anti-foreign agitation flames once more over China. It is in permitting the incurrence of that danger that American foreign policy with regard to China has notably failed.

Except for the Declaration of Cairo, announced in the late autumn of 1943 by President Roosevelt, Prime Minister Churchill, and Generalissimo Chiang Kai-shek, and in which the Soviet government did not participate, the major powers made no public announcement before the defeat of Japan on the nature of postwar settlements in the Far East.

The Cairo declaration satisfied a major part of the legitimate objectives of China, gave much-needed assurances to the Korean people that they would ultimately secure their liberty and independence and announced the general nature of the terms to be imposed upon Japan. Necessarily, however, the declaration was couched in general terms. It could not at that time have contained, particularly in view of the abstention of the Soviet Union, any detailed blueprint of the precise method and the details to be provided in each final Far Eastern peace settlement.

Insofar as Russia's presumed objectives were involved, these, as has already been shown, were covered in the agreements of Yalta and in the subsequent Moscow treaty between the National Government of China and the Soviet Union. But the major powers made no effort later to reach between themselves any specific and detailed agreements covering the manner in which such difficult problems as the liberation of Korea and the restoration of Siam to her prewar status should be undertaken.

The inevitable result has been not only confusion but a form of confusion which has given rise to wholly unnecessary friction and dangerous misunderstandings between the major powers most directly concerned in the Far East.

The question of Siam is a glaring instance of this lack of preparation and of prior agreement. Siam, of course, had become a puppet state under Japanese control. Her boundaries had been modified and her territory enlarged at the expense of her neighbors. The whole structure of Siamese political and economical life had been surcharged with Japanese officials and Japanese collaborationists.

Two months after Japan's surrender, at a moment when the whole region south of China was in a chaotic state owing to the continued presence there of Japanese armed forces with no competent authorities of the United Nations to whom they might surrender, and owing to serious revolt by many of the native populations against any attempt to restore them to the jurisdiction of the prewar colonial authorities, it became known that the British government had presented the Siamese authorities with a series of far-reaching demands. The British insisted that the whole of Siam's national economy be placed in British hands, that the whole of Siam's civil administration be placed under British authority, that all Siamese exports be regulated solely by the British government, and in general and until such time as Siam might eventually be received into the membership of the United Nations, that Siam become a British protectorate. Naturally enough, these demands not only were vigorously objected to by the leaders of the Siamese people but they were also vigorously denounced by the Chinese government and less openly but equally firmly condemned by the Government of the United States.

As a result, an exceedingly unfortunate and unnecesary storm of controversy arose which was finally stilled only with the signature of a treaty of peace between Great Britain and Siam at Singapore on January 1, 1946, which safeguarded Siamese sovereignty. The treaty provided that the Siamese government must restore to their rightful owners all the territory as well as all the properties that it had obtained after Siam's entrance into the war on the side of Japan. The treaty, however, further provided that for the time being the Government of Siam should forego all her normal exports, tin, rubber, teak and rice "except in accordance with the recommendations of the Combined Boards in Washington or any successor body." The treaty could only be construed as reasonable and essentially fair. The regulation of exports insured that Siam's co-operation with Japan would not give her an unfair advantage over such neighboring states as Burma and Malaya, where Japanese destruction would for some time to come prevent any resumption of the export of similar commodities. The treaty likewise obligated Siam to restore stolen property. It did not, however, impair the sovereignty or the legitimate territorial integrity of the Siamese people.

It is scarcely necessary to point out that the terms finally contained in the Siamese treaty with Great Britain would readily have been approved by the other major powers had proper preparatory agreements been reached prior to the end of the war.

The subsequent dispute which arose between France and Siam belongs within the same category. In the spring of 1946 French troops from within French Indo-China invaded Siamese territory. The French declared that the clash occurred as a result of depredations committed by Siamese bandits. The Siamese maintained that the incident was far graver. They insisted that the French were attempting to secure by force territory which was rightfully Siamese and which had been the subject of dispute between the two countries. The controversy was fortunately submitted to the Security Council of the United Nations. But the fact that it could arise at all presented a glaring evidence of the lack of any detailed agreements upon postwar settlements in the Far East between the major powers.

In the case of Korea, the lack of any prior agreement was far more disastrous. The Cairo declaration gave notice to the world that the United States, Great Britain and China "mindful of the enslavement of the people of Korea were determined that in due course Korea shall become free and independent." Generalissimo Chiang Kai-shek had strongly supported those phrases with the statement that, "If Korea is not independent, not only Chinese independence cannot be complete, but the peace of east Asia cannot be secure."

It must have been clear to any impartial observer that Korea, wedged as she is between the Asiatic provinces of the Soviet Union and the northern regions of China, would once more rapidly become the scene of constant rivalry between the neighboring powers, if the nations of the world did not take every practical measure to insure that she remain wholly free from the preponderant influence of any major power. The integrity and complete independence of Korea is essential to the maintenance of a stable and peaceful order in the Far East. Through the latter decades of the nineteenth century and the first years of the present century Korea was martyrized in consequence of the rivalry of China, Russia and Japan, each one striving to control the government and the economic resources of the country. The lessons to be drawn from that experience cannot be gainsaid.

Yet beyond the announcement made at Potsdam immediately prior to Japan's surrender, assuring Korea of independence after a preparatory five-year trusteeship period under the Soviet Union, the United States, Great Britain and China, no plans for her liberation or eventual reconstruction were devised.

As a purely military measure, the Soviet Union and the United States agreed to divide the country at the thirty-eighth parallel of north latitude, Russian forces occupying the northern half and the United States in occupation of the south. The dividing line became an insurmountable barrier. The southern part of Korea is largely agricultural while all her industrial resources are located in the north. Any attempt at economic reconstruction would be wholly impossible under such conditions.

There has been no more deplorable example of lack of proper preparation and of general ineptitude than the United States occupation of southern Korea. At first the Japanese administrative officials were confirmed in their posts by the highest American military authorities. When this step resulted in a loud and angry outburst from the Koreans as well as from the American people, American civilians wholly untrained and wholly unqualified for the posts which they were to occupy were pitchforked into the positions left vacant by the departing Japanese. American officials who in private life had made honorable records as bookkeepers or as accountants were suddenly confronted with the need to formulate banking and currency policies for the Korean nation in a moment of acute crisis.

An absolute military dictatorship was set up which undertook not only to deal with economic problems, with which it proved wholly incapable of dealing, but also to dictate to the Korean people the political course they should follow.

It was still more serious that as a result of the lack of any detailed over-all agreement between the Soviet government and Washington, the military authority in each of the two halves into which Korea had been divided began to suspect the other of propaganda and of devious activities directed against its legitimate interests. The Tass News Agency in Moscow charged that the American authorities in southern Korea were deliberately carrying on anti-Soviet propaganda directed at Soviet representatives throughout the Far East. These charges not unnaturally brought forth angry denials from General MacArthur's headquarters at Tokyo with the corollary of a *tu quoque*. The Korean people, at first enraptured by their liberation from the forty-year-old domination of the Japanese, soon turned violently against both the Soviet and American forces of occupation. Korea became within a brief space of time a seething cauldron of political and economic confusion. No progress was made for many months even in initiating any reasonable system under which the trusteeship period could be inaugurated, the barriers between the north and south removed, and the Korean people be given the chance to prepare themselves for the responsibility of independence.

As a result, conditions in Korea have become desperate. Under the Moscow agreements of December, 1945, a United States-Soviet commission was appointed and was instructed to consult with the Korean democratic parties for the purpose of establishing a provisional Korean government. When the Joint Commission finally met, its meetings proved to be completely futile. The Soviet authorities flatly refused to consult with any Korean political leaders who had opposed the terms of the Moscow declaration with respect to the installation of a trusteeship over Korea. Had the Russian views prevailed, the provisional government which had been envisaged would necessarily have been composed exclusively of the Korean Communists operating within the Russian zone of occupation who had proved themselves willing to follow the party line laid down by Soviet agents. After pro-

forces of Japan should have been clouded by senseless domestic bickerings in the United States over the steps that were being taken and by the bitter resentment of the Soviet government over its exclusion from any real participation in occupation measures.

As a means of allaying Allied suspicion of the ultimate intentions of the United States and as a means likewise of assuaging injured susceptibilities, the Government of the United States announced the establishment of a Far Eastern advisory commission to sit in Washington with the power to advise the American Commander-in-Chief of the occupation forces in Japan, but with no power to determine policy. The Far Eastern Advisory Commission was composed of representatives of the United States, Great Britain, France, the Netherlands, Canada, Australia, New Zealand, China, India, the Philippines and the Soviet Union. The Department of State was fully aware that the Soviet government would not be represented at the initial meeting because of its bitter resentment at its exclusion from any real measure of control. The sessions of the Far Eastern Advisory Commission were made wholly ludicrous by continued announcements from the American Secretary of State that Soviet representatives undoubtedly would attend, although the other governments knew that the Soviet government would not attend, and the entire world knew that unless it did the commission would be entirely pointless.

This stalemate continued for several months, during which the Soviet government quite legitimately held aloof and the members of the commission occupied themselves by passing futile resolutions and by undertaking sightseeing tours to Japan. The matter was not clarified until the meeting at Moscow in December between the Foreign Ministers of Great Britain, the United States and the Soviet Union, when a partial agreement was finally reached as a result of which Russia's vital interests in the Far East and her right to play at least a nominal part in the determination of occupation and control policies in Japan were recognized. The Far Eastern Advisory Commission at Washington was continued but with the word "Advisory" stricken out of its title, and an Allied control council was established in Tokyo composed of the United States, the Soviet Union, Great Britain and China.

Nominally, therefore, the United States had finally recognized the application in the Far East of the principle of joint interest and of joint responsibility. However, these agreements were greeted in the United States with an outburst of denunciation condemning any weakening of the supreme authority of General MacArthur. The failure of the national administration to enlighten the public was almost wholly responsible. In order to palliate public criticism, Secretary Byrnes repeatedly gave it to be understood that the new agreements did not really change the existing situation and that in all important matters the United States and General MacArthur would in reality remain in supreme control. Such statements as these once again aroused the justifiable resentment of the Soviet government. It was not only impracticable, it was in the highest degree unfortunate for the United States Government to attempt thus to carry water on both shoulders since, if the agreements were valid, the United States would be compelled to share its authority and its responsibility in Japan, whereas if the agreements did not mean precisely what they said, they were worse than valueless.

During the four months of American occupation before the Moscow agreements, the United States had treated the occupation of Japan as a private monopoly. But even so, American public opinion was sharply torn as to the wisdom of the measures that General MacArthur was carrying out. He was bitterly criticized for not having immediately worked the miracle of transforming a Japanese government and a Japanese administration of the most bureaucratic character, which for many long years had been wholly under the domination of the most highly militaristic influences within the Japanese Empire, into a modern and progressive government composed of farsighted and liberal Japanese democrats. The Department of State, upon whom the sole responsibility lay, subject to the approval of the President, for the elaboration of the political aspects of the occupation policy and for the failure of the United States to have reached a satisfactory working arrangement with the other Allied powers providing for joint participation in the occupation, became vocal in its criticisms of the wisdom of the steps taken by General MacArthur. It cannot be denied that it has been the tendency of General MacArthur, throughout his long and exceptionally brilliant career to seek to assume all responsibility, and to possess the sole determination of the policies which he is to carry out. But in this case General MacArthur was faced with a situation where he had to be prepared to act, and act immediately. The lives of the men under his command depended upon his willingness to act. If he was not furnished with a policy formulated in Washington, he can hardly be justly criticized for making his own policy, or for refusing to permit the representatives of other governments to tell him what that policy should be.

Some time later the State Department announced to the American people what the United States policy toward Japan would be. It did not seem to realize that its policy should have been made known as soon as the military occupation of Japan had been consolidated, or that the agreement of the Allied powers was a primary requisite.

General MacArthur has been accused of many faults by liberal elements in the United States and particularly in Great Britain, as well as by Soviet authorities. When the final record of his administration of Japan is written, however, it will be seen that it has, from a military standpoint, been in the highest degree efficient, in the highest degree effective, and that, notwithstanding the inordinate and unnecessary obstacles which he has been forced to encounter, he has moved steadily and progressively toward the democratization of the Japanese people and toward the total elimination of the political and economic factors that had made it possible for the military caste so long to control the destinies of the Japanese people and to prove a menace to the welfare of other peoples.

Within six months from the time American troops landed in Yokohama, Japanese war criminals had been arrested and the men chiefly responsible for Japan's wars of aggression had been removed from all participation in Japanese affairs. The Emperor had renounced his divinity; state Shintoism, built up through the connivance of Japan's militaristic leaders, had been destroyed; and freedom of religion had been proclaimed. The old and corrupt political caste had been removed from all influence or control. The large business monopolies had been obliterated; distribution of land to the small farmers had begun; relief to the needy and homeless had been efficiently provided; and a free press and free speech had been established.

The earlier Cabinet of Prince Higashi-Kuni had given way to a Cabinet headed by Baron Shidehara. I have known Baron Shidehara for thirty years. When I was first in Japan he was serving as Vice Minister of Foreign Affairs under Count Ishii. Subsequently Ambassador in Washington, he held office later as Foreign Minister at the moment when Japan's first measures of aggression were being carried out. Under the utmost difficulties, Baron Shidehara, while a believer in the destiny of a great Japanese Empire, proved himself a liberal of the old-fashioned Japanese kind. That represented the nearest approximation to a democrat, in the Western meaning of the term, that Japan has produced. So long as he held an official position, he unfalteringly opposed the course toward aggressive warfare and expansion by conquest upon which the military clique had decided. But he proved quite powerless to stem the current.

He was now seventy-three years of age, and by the nature of things he could do no more as Prime Minister than serve as a symbol in this bitter moment of transition during which the Japanese people were being afforded the chance to lay the foundations for a representative and liberal constitutional system.

After the national elections which were held in the spring of 1946, Baron Shidehara was succeeded as Prime Minister by Shigeru Yoshida.

There was little difference in the background or point of view of the two men. Mr. Yoshida had been, like his predecessor, a professional diplomat. He had been prevented by the Army from serving as Foreign Minister in 1936 on the charge that he was too liberal in his opinions. He was then sent as Ambassador to London.

During the months prior to the elections new political parties had been formed. The appearance within these parties in positions of great power of men who were proved guilty of complicity with

the militarists added materially to the difficulties of the new Prime
Minister in forming a Cabinet. He himself represented the Liberal
party, which had polled the largest popular vote. Yet he had only
been elected chief of the party by his fellow Liberals because
the earlier President of the party, Hatoyama, had been disqualified
by General MacArthur from holding office. In the same way his
original selections for the Agriculture and Justice portfolios had
also been disqualified.

Of the twelve Ministers in the new Cabinet as finally constituted, six were Liberals, three independents, and the remainder—
including Baron Shidehara, who entered as Minister without Port-
folio—were members of the Progressive party, the largest party
of the right. Of the younger members of the Cabinet, the ablest
was undoubtedly Hiramo Wada, a radical, who took office as
Minister of Agriculture. This Ministry was the post of outstanding importance at this time owing to the policy of agrarian reform which the Japanese government had been ordered to carry
out by Allied headquarters, and owing as well to the responsibility
of the Agriculture Ministry for seeing to it that the grain produced
by the peasants was distributed to the residents of the cities and
towns.

Under the powers granted to the Allied Control Council in
Tokyo by the terms of the Moscow agreements each of the four
major powers may veto all questions which concern "fundamental
changes in the Japanese constitutional structure." It is hard to
foresee at this moment to what extent that veto right will retard
or confuse General MacArthur's efforts to help the Japanese people
construct a representative form of government and a liberal economic structure. It could obviously be employed for purposes
wholly foreign to those for which it was instituted. However, the
chief criticism to which General MacArthur has so far been subjected by left-wing elements in the United States, that he failed
to recognize the need for any fundamental reconstruction of
Japan's political and economic structure, is wholly unwarranted.
The results speak for themselves. The foundations have been
laid. What is now most urgently needed is some inter-Allied
machinery that can assist toward the desired ends but that can

under no contingencies be utilized save to further the ultimate interests of the peace-loving nations of the world. For those interests require that the Japanese people have every reasonable chance to develop their own form of democratic system. The basic question raised by the policy which the United States has so far pursued in its occupation of Japan is precisely that: Does it afford the Japanese people the opportunity to develop "their own form of democratic system"?

The American military occupation has been efficient and honest. It has been conducted along precisely the lines that would have been followed in days gone by when the War Department undertook to administer an occupied territory inhabited by "backward" peoples. It is very naturally redolent of many features of American policy in the Philippines. In view of the handicaps he has been compelled to surmount, General MacArthur's administrative achievement has been admirable. For it must be remembered that the operation of the point system has weakened the occupation forces under General MacArthur's command to such an extent that the majority of the divisions are skeletonized and by far the greater number of men engaged in the occupation are new recruits relatively untrained and entirely unprepared for the task which they have been called upon to assume. Consequently, General MacArthur has frequently been compelled to resort to measures of expediency and has often been unable to operate with the entire freedom to which he is so fully entitled.

It is, then, not the execution of the occupation policy that affords any legitimate grounds for criticism. What can be legitimately criticized is the nature of the policy itself.

The Japanese people have already been presented with a new constitution. It is notorious that that constitution is not the creature of the will of the Japanese people, but a constitution that was written for them under the auspices of the United States Army. Can any qualified student of Far Eastern affairs or any observer familiar with Japanese psychology maintain that such a constitution, however excellent it may theoretically be, will ever become a real foundation for Japanese political and social life or that it will be retained in force by the Japanese people once they are free to determine their own destiny?

Moreover, national elections have now been held in Japan. They were free and unquestionably far fairer than any national elections in which the Japanese people had previously participated. Yet here again, can it conceivably be maintained that elections held at this time, barely eight months after Japan's surrender, resulted in any real or considered expression of the will of the Japanese people?

The conduct of the Japanese occupation is probably a classic example of the manner in which the American military mind operates. It is a demonstration of the efficiency of the American Army, but it is simultaneously a demonstration of the Army's complete lack of any grasp of alien psychology. Only an astute few of the American army officers now stationed in Japan will admit that, while outwardly the Japanese people are almost excessively servile in their attitude toward the occupation, it is only too plain that privately the bulk of the Japanese are merely biding their time until the occupation ends, that their hatred for the American victors is constantly rising, and that the overwhelming national objective will in all probability be to even the score against the United States if the opportunity is later presented.

Were the American occupation of Japan to end within the near future merely on the ground that the Japanese people had now adopted a constitution and democratic form of government, that the Japanese Empire had been destroyed, and that the Japanese people would now necessarily be compelled to live quietly and peaceably within the confines of the Japanese home islands, no real change would be effected in the Japanese mentality or character.

The alternative would obviously have imposed a greater and a more protracted burden upon the United States. It would have involved a real United Nations, rather than a unilateral American, occupation of Japan, with all the attendant complications and controversies that might have arisen. It would have involved a long-continued occupation during which the Assembly of the United Nations and the agencies of that organization would have possessed real authority in Japan. It would have resulted in the gradual building up of a national democracy of the Japanese people by limiting their right to self-government to voting in local and municipal elections over a term of years, and by eventually granting them after a true period of preparation, the right to formulate their own constitution and to hold under their own auspices elections that would establish a national government prior to the termination of military occupation. That procedure would have provided the Japanese people with the means for self-education. What American policy has so far accomplished is merely to establish a simulacrum of democracy. The results are artificial. There is little likelihood that they will stand.

The basic error in our approach to the ultimate solution of the Japanese problem seems to me to lie in the assumption—an assumption altogether natural to the military mind—that Japan can be prevented from again becoming a menace to the peace and safety of the world through the enforcement of an occupation policy which is limited largely to strategic and security considerations and to the more superficial aspects of political reform.

On April 29, 1946, the Secretary of State of the United States proposed to the British, Soviet and Chinese governments a twenty-five year military alliance to provide for the continued disarmament and demilitarization of Japan through a control commission after the end of the occupation, and for joint action should there be any violation by Japan of the regulations established by the proposed treaty. The suggested provisions are comprehensive and desirable. They would constitute an essential measure of insurance.

But so long as the United States remains the *de facto* dictator of the occupation policy, and the other great powers have no real authority nor responsibility in the determination of that policy, it is inevitable that the Japanese people will later try—just as the German people so successfully tried after the First World War—to play one great power off against the others in order to secure an alleviation of the restrictions placed upon them, or to promote a conflict between the Allied nations. The four-power occupation of Germany and of Austria has given rise to endless friction and, latterly, to grave controversy between the Soviet Union and the Western powers. The chief reason for these difficulties comes from the present intention of the Soviet government to try to secure political control over the peoples of those occupied countries. Yet that difficulty would have been largely avoided had the four powers agreed in the fullest detail on every aspect of the occupation policy, and of the methods through which it was to be carried out, before the policy was inaugurated. If that lesson has been learned the same mistake can be avoided in the case of Japan. Certainly, there can be no assurance whatever that the present American occupation measures will not be tantamount to plowing the waters unless the major powers co-operate in the determination and execution of policy, and unless the United Nations, rather than the United States alone, assumes the responsibility for that transformation of the spirit of the Japanese people which is required if Japan is to become a safe member of international society.

That transformation will not be brought about by military controls nor by the enforced adoption of the forms of an alien political structure. Far more probably it will be produced by United Nations assistance to the masses of the Japanese people in the field of economic and social reform.

It is true that General MacArthur's headquarters has ordered the abolition of the large Japanese monopolies and the initiation of agrarian reform-measures. Various minor steps of the same character have been decreed on paper. Yet these adjustments, good as they are, will not by themselves create a propitious ground for the growth of native Japanese democracy. The Japanese standard of living is incredibly low. The condition of an overwhelming majority of the Japanese people offers neither hope of security nor the possibility of improving their relative status in the Japanese social system. Under such circumstances it is futile to anticipate that the occupation will be succeeded by a political structure founded upon any real comprehension of or desire for free democratic institutions on the part of the bulk of the Japanese people.

The Economic and Social Council of the United Nations is

confronted by no greater challenge than that presented in the case of Japan. It should undertake as a part of the occupation policy an immediate initial survey of the present and future needs of the Japanese people in the realm of individual freedoms, of health and social welfare, of education and of economic security. The recommendations of the council and its supervision of the enforcement of such of its recommendations as may initially be practicable should be welcomed by the United States, and by the Allied Control Council.

It may well prove to be that the achievements of the Economic and Social Council—if it is given the chance—will contribute far more to insuring the future peace and security of the world against a new Japanese aggression than the military and political measures now contemplated by the major powers.

Even the most hard-bitten British Tories were fully aware, no matter how reluctant they were to admit it publicly, that their long-promised freedom would have to be granted to the peoples of India after the end of the war. The Cripps Mission sent to India in 1942 by the Churchill Cabinet was unable to arrange a compromise that would modify the demand of some of the Indian Nationalists for immediate independence, even before the end of the war.

The propaganda of the Indian Congress (which represents primarily, of course, India's Hindu population) has been exceedingly effective in the United States in persuading a great majority of the American people that the only problem before the British government is to clear out of India, and that its failure to do so overnight is merely another symptom of the innate iniquity of British policy.

The question of India is vastly complicated. As far back as 1858 one of the truest liberals whom England has ever produced, John Bright, declared in the House of Commons that, "No man with the smallest glimmering of common sense can believe that India with its twenty different nationalities and its twenty different languages can ever be bound up and consolidated into one compact and enduring Empire confine."

The situation within India is approximately the same in its

highly complex problem of nationalities and of religions as when John Bright spoke almost one hundred years ago. For purposes of simplification, however, it should be remembered that of India's total population of some four hundred million nearly one hundred million are Moslems who will never willingly consent to a unified India if they are subjected to majority rule, since that majority rule would be dominated by the Hindus of which the Congress party is the agency. The Hindu Nationalist leaders are, on the contrary, determined upon a unified India since in no other way can they make certain that the Hindu elements will be able to secure complete control. The hostility between the Moslems and the Hindus has been traditional for many centuries. It harks back to the days of the Mogul invasion. It has been responsible for many of the riots, massacres and civil disturbances within India during the period of British domination. The Moslems are a vigorous and forceful part of the population and, should the British government give the Hindus the right to attempt to control the Moslem population, nothing is more certain than that a violent and prolonged civil war would result. The conflict between Moslems and Hindus is not due solely to religious differences. It is due also to economic causes. The Moslems have little interest in trade or in finance. They are a much poorer community than the Hindus. They are unwilling to accept any yoke that might in the future be placed upon their necks by the Hindu moneylender or the Hindu industrialist. Their attitude toward the Hindu is frequently one of individual resentment not unlike that which so many Germans felt toward the Jewish profiteer in the inflationary years after the First World War.

The situation is further complicated by the fact that approximately one-fourth of India's population lives in the so-called native states. There are actually 601 of these, of which 225 comprise large areas, some being larger than many European countries. With all these native states the British government has long-standing treaties pledging their territorial integrity and autonomy. Nor must it be overlooked that within the caste system of the Hindus, a great number are still "untouchables," with whom the majority of the Hindu population will have no social dealings, and with whom they will not be willing to develop any relations of political equality.

It is impossible for the British government to withdraw from India and turn over the government of that huge subcontinent to its inhabitants until some agreement can be found that will satisfactorily solve the problem of the native states and give practical assurance that Indian self-government will not mean subjection of the Moslems by their Hindu brethren, nor political obliteration of the individual rights of the "untouchables," or of the other communities such as the Sikhs.

The problem of India became exceedingly acute in 1942 at the time of the dispatch of the Cripps Mission. Had an insurrection flared up at that time, the possibility of a Japanese occupation of India would have been greatly increased, and had such a Japanese invasion proved successful, the war effort of the Allied powers against Japan might easily have been indefinitely prolonged. However, the Indian insurrection was forestalled, and after some critical months, the Japanese invaders were repulsed. But at that time, President Roosevelt, in personal messages to Prime Minister Churchill, strongly urged that some way be found to lay a foundation for the granting of immediate independence to India.

The general plan that the President proposed to Mr. Churchill seemed the most promising if the Indian people were to receive self-government in the light of the material difficulties above outlined. The President reminded Mr. Churchill of the difficulties that the thirteen American colonies had after the Revolution in agreeing upon a federal constitution, and of the fact that the Articles of Confederation preceded the American Constitution by many years. He suggested that something similar to the Articles of Confederation be now proposed to the Indian leaders, with the understanding that the Indian leaders would commit themselves to work together continuously, after the Articles became operative, to achieve a final form of constitutional government, which they would be more readily able to devise in the light of the actual experience that such a provisional government would give them.

It is obvious that Indian independence cannot mean the domination by the Hindu majority of the Moslem minority. Nor can Indian independence be held up, as Prime Minister Attlee has said, by the intransigence of that minority. The Moslem League headed by Mr. Jinnah has been insisting since 1933 that Indian self-government must rest upon the commitment to the Moslem people that they will be granted "Pakistan," which is equivalent to sovereign self-government and freedom from Hindu control for the Moslem populations in all those states, mainly in the northeast and northwest of India, such as Bengal, Hyderabad, Sind, Balukistan, Kashmir, and the Punjab, where the Moslem populations predominate.

Yet the solution of the problem afforded by "Pakistan" would not be as simple as it sounds. In the states listed above the Moslems possess a bare majority. In the northeastern area the Hindus constitute a minority of some forty-nine per cent, and in the northwestern states a sizable minority of thirty-eight per cent. "Pakistan" would from the outset be faced with a bitter minority problem unless many millions of people were transferred from one part of India to another.

Furthermore, India under British rule enjoyed internal free trade. Were "Pakistan" to become a sovereign state, and the Hindu portion of India to erect custom barriers, the new Moslem state could not economically survive.

In the late winter of 1946 Prime Minister Attlee announced that a special mission composed of three members of his Cabinet would go to India for the purpose of negotiating with leaders of the Congress party and of the Moslem League an agreement to provide for the immediate independence of India.

The negotiations took place in Simla under the direct auspices of Lord Wavell, the Indian Viceroy. The chief spokesmen for the two opposing factions were Jawaharlal Nehru for the Congress party and Mr. Jinnah for the Moslem League. While Mahatma Gandhi did not actually take part in the negotiations, he proceeded to Simla to remain there and direct the course of the discussions. On May 12 the British government announced that the negotiations had broken down. The chief cause for the collapse of the conference was Mr. Jinnah's refusal to accept any proposal not based upon the sovereign independence of the provinces which he claimed possessed a Moslem majority.

Shortly after the collapse of the conference the British government made public a proposal which it had addressed to the Indian peoples, and in particular to the Indian leaders, almost identical in principle with the suggestions made by President Roosevelt in 1942. While the original reactions to the proposal of the Hindu leaders of the Congress party, and notably of Mahatma Gandhi, were generally favorable, the reactions of the Moslem leaders was almost equally hostile. The British Labor government, which has patently been moved by a sincere intent finally to solve the question of Indian independence in a manner wholly fair to the Indian people, must have regretted the angry refusal of Winston Churchill four years previously to adopt the suggestions made to him by President Roosevelt. For if those suggestions had at that time been laid before the Indian leaders, it is in the highest degree likely that they would then have been accepted, and that much subsequent danger and controversy might thus have been avoided.

After much recrimination and increasing tension between the larger Indian communities the essential provisions of the British proposal for an Indian constitution were finally accepted by the Congress and the Moslem League. It represented an ingenious compromise.

The Moslems, while prevented from setting up a Pakistan, were to be given the constitutional assurance that they would not only be able to control the legislatures in those provinces where they possessed a majority, but also be able to unite two or more such provinces under a joint executive and legislature and thereby establish several regional régimes similar on a small scale to the one sovereign Pakistan which they had sought. The Hindu Congress obtained the central government it desired, to include the native states as well as the rest of India, but the powers of the central government were to be limited to a control of foreign affairs, communications and national defense, and the authority to raise the sums needed for those purposes. Otherwise the Central Government would exercise no power over the provincial governments. These would be largely autonomous.

The British proposal further provided that if the Indians, through a nationally elected constituent assembly, adopted such a constitution, that document should be open to review and reconsideration on the motion of any province after ten years, and at ten-year intervals thereafter.

The Indian peoples have now at last the grant of full independence within their reach, and the British Labor government has made the most notable, as well as the most practical, contribution so far offered toward the creation of a new world in which all peoples capable of self-government will enjoy their sovereign freedom as independent nations. The precedent has now been firmly created for the final abolition of an international system whereunder colonial peoples can be enslaved. The age of imperialism is nearing its end.

The bitter struggle of the Nationalists of Indonesia against returning to Dutch control has dragged on its tragic way during the months that have elapsed since the defeat of Japan. It is not generally known that long before the end of the war the Dutch government asked the Government of the United States for assistance in re-establishing its authority over the Netherlands East Indies, and that a tentative commitment had been made that the American forces under the command of General MacArthur should undertake that responsibility. Had that agreement been carried out, there is every likelihood that the protracted uprisings in Indonesia might have been prevented, and that a peaceful and orderly transition to local autonomy could have been arranged. Unfortunately, however, the British government insisted, upon learning of this tentative arrangement, that its prestige in the Far East would be jeopardized should American forces under General MacArthur undertake the task of liberation, since Indonesia lay within the British operational sphere allotted to the armies under the command of Lord Louis Mountbatten.

When the time came for the defeat of the Japanese forces occupying Indonesia, and for the liberation of the native inhabitants, the British troops available for the task were far inferior in number to what was required. Also they arrived six weeks too late. If a sufficient force had been immediately available on V-J Day, it is in the highest degree improbable that the Japanese armies would have had time to prepare for the armed resistance which then was carried on.

It must be remembered that two years prior to the end of the war the Queen of the Netherlands officially assured the people of Indonesia that it was the policy of the Dutch government to afford them, after the defeat of Japan, a Dominion status with rights equal to those enjoyed by the inhabitants of the Netherlands themselves. At that time, however, the Dutch government, adhering strictly to the letter of the Dutch constitution, was compelled to make the reservation that these official promises would have to be contingent upon their approval by the Dutch people themselves in the first national elections to be held after the liberation of Holland.

As soon as the government in Tokyo had capitulated the Japanese commanders in Indonesia turned over small arms and a large amount of military equipment to Nationalist youth groups in Java trained during the occupation by Japanese instructors. The invasion of Indonesia by the British forces of liberation was the signal for a Japanese-prepared resistance of these half-disciplined and largely irresponsible bands of young Javanese against any reimposition of Dutch authority. Theoretically, the chief authority within the resistance forces was vested in the self-styled "President of the Federation of Indonesia," a well-known Javanese Nationalist, Soekarno. The Dutch government had already obtained conclusive evidence that Soekarno had served the Japanese militarists as their leading collaborationist in the Netherlands East Indies, and that in recognition of his services he had been awarded the Grand Cross of the Rising Sun.

In consequence, the Dutch government was unwilling to negotiate with Soekarno, and all discussions were held with another Nationalist leader, Sjahrir, who assumed the position of Prime Minister of a Nationalist Javanese Cabinet.

Sjahrir, like Soekarno, had for many years been actively opposing a continuation of Dutch colonial rule. Both had suffered imprisonment for their activities. Like Soekarno, Sjahrir had been educated in the Netherlands, and like him he had long been in close touch with Nationalist leaders throughout the Far East. I remember that Manuel Quezon told me of the admiration he had for Sjahrir's unselfish devotion to his people, and for his unquestioned capacity.

But Sjahrir, unlike Soekarno, had been adamant in his opposition to the Japanese schemes for the subjugation of Java, and had consistently refrained from all forms of collaboration.

As a result of protracted negotiations between Sjahrir and the Dutch commissioner, Dr. van Mook, outstanding among colonial administrators of recent times because of his enlightened and liberal views, the Dutch government, once more installed in The Hague, made an official statement of policy that in some ways went still further than the official declaration previously made by the Queen. It offered the people of Indonesia Dominion status essentially equivalent to complete autonomy. Unfortunately, there was in this offer a paragraph that declared that the representative of the Crown in the future Dominion of the Netherlands East Indies in order "to be enabled to fulfill the obligations incumbent upon the Kingdom as a result of Article 73 of the United Nations . . . shall possess under his responsibility to the Government of the Kingdom certain special powers to guarantee fundamental rights, efficient administration, and sound financial management." It seemed to the Indonesian leaders that this proviso could well be employed to prevent any real exercise of independence by an elected Dominion government.

Negotiations were thereupon resumed to the accompaniment of sporadic uprisings which had now spread to Sumatra. In the meantime the Celebes, Borneo, Dutch New Guinea, and many of the smaller islands of the Netherlands East Indies had come back to Dutch rule with the assurance of autonomy or of Dominion status. The Nationalist leaders in these regions were not enamored of the project for a centralized government of a federated Indonesia since in any such government Java, because of her population of forty millions, would be able to exercise a dominating control.

The negotiations between Sjahrir and Dr. van Mook at length reached the point where the Dutch government offered a status to

Java very nearly equivalent to that enjoyed by the Irish Republic. An agreement would have been concluded except for the last-minute insistence of the Javanese that Sumatra be amalgamated with Java under the proposed régime. To that the Dutch government was unwilling to agree, since Sumatra is not inhabited by a homogeneous people, as is Java, and many of the component peoples in Sumatra were unwilling to submit to Javanese rule.

The situation in very recent months has been gravely complicated by incontrovertible evidence that agents of the Soviet Union, who have come to Java by way of Australia, have been taking an increasingly active part in the deliberations of the Javanese nationalists. At a critical moment in the negotiations with the Dutch, Sjahrir was suddenly kidnapped, and was released only after some days. The person responsible for his seizure was Tan Kanaka, a Javanese Communist recently returned from Moscow.

At this moment it seems probable that Java will secure from the Netherlands its immediate freedom, and that the remaining islands of the Netherlands East Indies will remain under the Dutch Crown as autonomous Dominions. Had the United Nations established its international trusteeship council before the defeat of Japan, and undertaken a co-operative plan for the treatment to be accorded the dependent peoples in the Far East as soon as they were liberated, much of the tragedy and ruin which has swept the Netherlands East Indies and French Indo-China could readily have been prevented.

The French government has proclaimed the establishment of an "Indo-Chinese Federation" within a French federal union, and has negotiated agreements with leaders of the small nations within Indo-China which offer hope for a more liberal and constructive policy on the part of France than has been seen during the years of France's recent colonial history.

But here, as well as in the rest of the Far East, there is no sign as yet of any realization by the present colonial powers that the United Nations can and must assume the ultimate responsibility for the great transformation of the Orient now under way if the peace of the world is to be insured.

The policy carried out by the British Labor government toward the peoples of India represents a magnificent landmark in the history of civilization. The policy of the Dutch government toward the peoples of Indonesia offers much hope for an outcome which will make for freedom and for peace.

But unless the United Nations, in the approaching meeting of the General Assembly creates its international trusteeship council so that an over-all world policy can be laid down, and so that the world organization can assume without further delay its rightful responsibility for insuring the orderly and rapid transition of all qualified colonial peoples from alien subjection to national independence, there is no certainty that peace in the Far East can long be maintained.

By her grant of full independence to the people of the Philippines the United States has given lasting proof of her willingness by her own policy to hasten the end of the age of imperialism and to recognize that the new world she seeks must be based on liberty. She has now a further opportunity to lead the forces of freedom.

The United States' greatest opportunity to eliminate the causes of war, and to further that understanding and co-operative friendship between the East and the West which alone can create a united world lies in seizing leadership now within the United Nations, in order to assure the grant of independence to all colonial peoples before it is too late.

Chapter VII

Our Foreign Policy:
Its Achievements and Its Failures

A GOVERNMENT'S foreign policy must be judged far more by its results than by its intentions. Innumerable foreign policies, like the road to hell, have been paved with good intentions. But in the atomic world in which we live, a world whose peoples have suddenly perceived that they live under the shadow of death, good intentions that are not translated into results are of no avail. It is with no feeling of vainglory but rather with a sober recognition of overpowering responsibility that the American people must today realize that the success or failure of American foreign policy may well spell life or death for the rest of humanity as well as for themselves.

We Americans consequently possess an inescapable national obligation to appraise our government's foreign policy as it was carried on during the climactic months of the Second World War, and during the year and a half which has passed since Germany's defeat, and assess objectively the results which it has achieved. At this grave moment it would be unthinkable that such an estimate should be undertaken in any carping spirit of petty or partisan criticism. It is equally unthinkable that American men and women should not speak out constructively whenever they believe the methods adopted or the ends pursued have not been in the national interest or have not been conducive to the attainment of world peace.

Let's look at the world as it appeared by midsummer of 1944. The United States was then approaching the peak of its strength. It had become more powerful than any other nation of the earth. The fate of Germany was already sealed. While we then believed that Japan would continue the struggle for a longer period than transpired, her approaching defeat was clearly foreshadowed.

It was evident that Great Britain would be utterly exhausted upon the conclusion of the war. The signs were already plain to all who cared to see them that the world order which must then be created would bring freedom to the colonial peoples, and that the liquidation of the British Empire was at hand. The British Commonwealth of Nations itself must undergo a profound transformation in the postwar period as a result of which the mother country's position would become far less dominant. The United Kingdom could survive as a major power only through a combination of favorable circumstances among which the maintenance of peace and a rapid economic reconstruction of the world would be indispensable. And even then Great Britain would need help. She would need military and political backing until she could get upon her feet again. She would need economic and financial co-operation until the British people could adjust themselves to wholly new conditions, and find the means through an increased share in world trade, whereby to meet the demands of their advanced social structure.

Such other western European powers as France, the Netherlands, Belgium and Italy, which had once played so considerable a role in the world's councils, would be prostrate as a result of the world upheaval. The smaller countries of central and eastern Europe were ravaged. Their populations were destitute. Their industries were destroyed. In the Far East, China, even if her people became united and assured of the independence and integrity of their country, obviously would require much time and far-reaching outside assistance before even the foundation for a new and progressive life could be fashioned.

The young and vigorous republics of Latin America had barely commenced the industrialization and development of their almost unlimited natural resources that would lead to the great era which should lie before them.

Asia and the Near East were seething with the suppressed forces of nationalism that would not be stilled until their peoples obtained their liberty. In many parts of Africa the same portents were to be seen.

By midsummer of 1944, it was plain that only the Soviet Union could emerge from the war in a position of supremacy comparable to that of the United States. But while her potential strength was greater than ours, she clearly would require many years before her full strength could be exerted. The German invasion of western Russia had devastated vast regions of Russian territory. A great percentage of her heavy industries had been destroyed. A larger percentage had had to be removed to other points within Russia. The Russian people, in their magnificently united effort against the German invaders, had been reduced to a standard of living far lower than that which they had enjoyed in the years immediately prior to 1941. In dead and wounded, they had lost a far higher percentage of their population than any of the other United Nations.

The resiliency of the disciplined people of Soviet Russia was greater, and her recuperative power, because of her authoritarian economy, was more rapid than in the Western democracies. But except under the threat of new aggression, the Soviet government would presumably be disposed to concentrate upon the task of reconstruction and of rehabilitation while it resumed Stalin's program of raising the Russian standard of living through increased production and through the progressive industrialization of all the Soviet Republics.

The United States had neither suffered the losses nor experienced the devastation undergone by the Soviet Union. We were already fully industrialized and our living standards were the highest in the world. We possessed by far the greatest navy and the largest and most modern air force. Some eight million of our men were under arms, and this total could be rapidly expanded if necessary. We possessed the greatest developed natural resources of any nation, and our achievements in industrial production had become a source of amazement to our allies and foes alike. Finally, although the world at large did not yet know it, the Government of the United States had within its possession the secrets of the source of atomic power, and the first weapons utilizing the force of atomic fission were already under manufacture.

The United States enjoyed an influence abroad and possessed an opportunity for leadership that no other major power had. The masses of the people, whether in Latin America, in the Far

East, or in the occupied countries of Europe, regarded President Roosevelt as their champion. The principles he had proclaimed in the Atlantic Charter were regarded by men and women in every part of the world as a source of hope and as a guarantee of a better day to come. When he spoke in the name of the American people, his words carried conviction to every far corner of the earth. More than that, the United States, because of her past history, because of the beliefs of her people and because of her democracy, was nowhere feared. She was known to possess no imperialistic ambitions; she was not suspected of desiring to extend her political or economic influence for purposes of domination, or for any other selfish ends.

As a result of the policies which President Roosevelt had carried out throughout the course of his administration, there existed in the New World a well integrated inter-American system which gave the United States, in its international relations, the potential support of an entire hemisphere.

The relations between the Chinese National Government and the United States were of the closest. So were relations between the United States and all the governments of western Europe.

The ties established by the President with the elected heads of the British government and of the governments of the British Dominions were closer than they had ever previously been between the chief executives of the English-speaking countries. And the personal understanding between President Roosevelt and Marshal Stalin, blunt as the messages which they exchanged may occasionally have been, had dissipated to some extent the old suspicions of this country which had so long controlled the thinking of the leaders of the Soviet Union. A co-operative relationship had been achieved that would have seemed altogether impossible even two years before.

Nor must it be overlooked, in taking stock of the advantages which the United States had in the middle of 1944, that in the Lend-Lease Act and in the other mechanisms authorized by the American Congress through which material or financial assistance could be rendered to foreign governments, this country possessed a great leverage which could be used to further its own legitimate objectives in its relations with other powers.

That is a summary recital of the assets that the United States possessed as the war drew to a close, and that she could use as tools of her policy to obtain the objectives sought by the American people.

It is necessary that those objectives be listed.

There can be no doubt that by the outset of 1945 an overwhelming majority of the American people had already reached a great decision. They had learned that the isolationist policies of the past were disastrous to their own interests. They had learned that in a rapidly contracting world no isolationist policy could spell safety for them. They had reached the conclusion as a result of tragic experience that the United States must, as a means of self-preservation, bear its full share of responsibility for maintaining peace in the world. They had decided that the United States must henceforth strive to create a new world order which, by gradually eradicating the political, strategic, social and economic causes of war, would ultimately bring about the rule of law rather than the rule of force. They had at length been persuaded that they could not haggle with Destiny.

They believed in the concept of the United Nations organization. They realized that the draft charter was far from perfect, but they believed that through the effective influence of the United States it could be successfully amended and perfected as the years passed. I believe it is true that the success of the United Nations was the primary objective that the American people wanted their government to secure through its conduct of their foreign policy.

Nor did they fail to envision realistically the supplementary factors which would be needed in their foreign policy if that major objective were to be reached.

The chief of these was unquestionably the establishment of a close, co-operative and friendly relationship with the Soviet Union in order that the world's two leading powers might join in making the United Nations organization work and in bringing about the conclusion of peace settlements that would be lasting. The American people realized clearly that the creation of that relationship was the key to the whole problem. Most of them undoubtedly underestimated the difficulties which would arise from the emergence in the new world of two great systems poles apart in their political and economic philosophy. But they were unhesitating in their conviction that without Soviet-American understanding, no United Nations organization could possibly fill the part for which it was designed.

A majority now also saw the need for what to some had already become axiomatic—a continuing collaboration with the British Commonwealth of Nations. They saw that the three major powers, the United States, the Soviet Union and the British Commonwealth, joined by a renascent China and a regenerated France, must use their combined strength during the adolescence of the international organization to make it succeed.

They wanted the solidarity of the Western Hemisphere to be preserved as an indispensable bulwark to the safety of every nation of the Americas.

The majority of them wanted this country to support through the United Nations the cause of human liberty and of democracy throughout the world, and in her ancient tradition to champion the cause of all peoples struggling to be free or to save themselves from persecution. They were no longer blind to the great truth that as the Four Freedoms prevail among the nations so will the masses of the people be better enabled to make their will for peace prevail.

Finally, they favored a course that would result in the joint adoption by all nations of whatever commercial and financial policies would prevent a recurrence of the economic chaos and depression of the years between the great wars, and end the autarchic restrictions and discriminations that had been increasingly imposed; thus goods might move more freely from nation to nation; might be more fairly and more efficiently distributed; and thus living standards might eventually everywhere be raised.

In setting these objectives, the American people were motivated quite as much by practical considerations as by idealism or altruism. They were guided by the conviction that a foreign policy with these aims would give them the best chance of obtaining security, of preserving their own independence and their own free institutions, and of creating a world order in which the United States could live at peace and prosper.

We must now see how the Government of the United States has utilized the immense assets it possessed two years ago to achieve these objectives.

Lytton Strachey once wrote of the temper of the British people at the conclusion of the Napoleonic wars. He speaks of them as imbued with "that sense of high exhilaration which springs from victory and self-confidence." By May, 1945, victory was already in the grasp of the people of the United States. But they showed no signs of self-confidence or of exhilaration.

As the war progressed President Roosevelt had received increasing popular support in his conduct of foreign relations. Many of his bitterest opponents in the field of domestic policy had voted for his election for a fourth term solely upon this issue. There can be no doubt that a majority of the American people still possess a lingering inferiority complex on the subject of foreign affairs. But in Franklin Roosevelt they believed that they had a leader who had already shown marked capacity to cope successfully with the leaders of the other major powers. They had confidence in his understanding and experience. They admired his demonstrated vision and courage. There is no greater fallacy than the old political maxim that the average American citizen is more apt to have faith in the occupant of the White House if he feels the President has no greater experience and no wider background than he.

When Franklin Roosevelt died an epoch ended. For the first time in a hundred years, the conduct of the nation's foreign policy had been entrusted to a man who possessed a singular flair for foreign policy, who had wide experience and great knowledge and who was capable of daring initiative as well as prudence. With his death the leadership which the White House had exercised was gone.

His unique qualifications were replaced by sincerity, a devoted patriotism and the best of intentions, but these were backed, unfortunately, by neither knowledge, experience nor strength.

Without general confidence in the capacity of the White House to guide the country through the critical complications that arose immediately after Germany's defeat, popular judgment began to flounder. Pessimism increased. The fear grew that with untried and inexperienced leaders the nation would not reach its objectives.

This growing confusion and uncertainty of the American people began to make itself apparent in two ways. An increasingly large number tended again to feel that superior military strength alone could provide security, and that a frankly imperialistic policy involving the acquisition of far-flung strategic bases throughout the world would be essential if our military might were to become predominant. Another trend was toward self-deception. Many became so concerned lest war between the Soviet Union and the United States might break out at any moment that they welcomed with jubilant acclaim any kind of agreement reached with Moscow, even when such agreements contained provisions that they would in less emotional moments have clearly seen represented concessions by the United States which could neither make for lasting peace nor prove to be in the true interest of this country.

The failure of the American people to recognize the admirable accomplishments of their government in the field of economic and financial international co-operation indicated their growing lack of understanding of the true values in American foreign policy. This was in no small part due to the inability of the White House any longer to lead, to explain and to clarify, as it had done so successfully in the days of Franklin Roosevelt, for in no other phase of its foreign policy during the past two years has the government made a greater advance toward the objectives sought by the American people.

In the attempt to obtain international agreement upon a new and liberal world economic policy, the United States had preponderant advantages. She had become the largest creditor nation in history. She had greater developed natural resources and greater assets than any other world power. During the prewar

years she had been the one major power to try by her own practices to lead the world back toward a saner trade policy and
toward the abolition of all excessive or artificial trade barriers.
With the possible exception of the Soviet Union, every nation
would look to her for help in the postwar period.

In order to enhance prosperity within the United States, as well
as to provide an indispensable bulwark to the structure of a
peaceful world order, the major aim of American economic policy
has been to establish a high and constant level of world trade
and employment. In seeking this, the United States has shown a
resolute initiative that has been altogether lacking in her pursuit
of political objectives. She has sought international agreement
that unnecessary trade barriers and inequitable discriminations
must be abolished, economic co-operation must be practiced and
multilateral trade expanded if that goal is to be reached.

She has also taken the lead in the creation of international
organizations, such as the United Nations Relief and Rehabilitation Administration, the commission on food and agriculture, and
that on civil aviation. Such organizations can help to bring order
out of chaos, provide for rapid increases in living standards, and
prevent the international cutthroat competition that would retard
rather than advance international communications.

She has procured, through the establishment of an international
bank and an international monetary fund, the method whereby
there can be created an expanding world area within which the
dollar and other currencies can be freely exchanged, and within
which, consequently, traders of the nations within that area can
function with confidence.

As a more immediate contribution to world recovery, she has
advanced long-term credits to the British and French governments
which will help to tide the peoples of those two nations through
their immediate emergency and permit the two countries to become
again active exporting and importing regions. In return for the
credit extended to Great Britain, the British government has
finally agreed to implement the fourth article in the Atlantic
Charter by breaking down the preferences created by the Ottawa

Agreements, thereby permitting the rest of the world to trade again within the British Empire.

The United States has expressed her willingness to extend, through the Export-Import Bank, similar credits to other nations desperately in need of dollar hypodermics, and has for that purpose increased the bank's capital.

She has initiated various other measures, such as a world conference on trade, to be held in the autumn of 1946, and the proposed international trade organization, which can well contribute greatly to the ends sought.

It must, however, be stated with great clarity that these ends—world trade and full employment—cannot be attained unless some means is found to enlist the co-operation of the Soviet Union, and unless the United States herself is willing to recognize the need—for her own long-range benefit as well as for the shorter range requirements of general world recovery—of becoming increasingly an importing country.

All these plans had been formulated before the death of President Roosevelt. They have been carried out with vigor and efficiency by his successor. President Truman's appointments to the key positions in the mechanisms created to carry out these projects have been altogether admirable. They have been made without regard to politics, and the men selected have been outstanding.

The President has been notably assisted by William Clayton, formerly Assistant Secretary of State and now appointed to the newly created position of Undersecretary of State for Economic Affairs. During his long years in many different public offices, Mr. Clayton has demonstrated a capacity constantly to grow in vision and in comprehension of the necessary foundations for a healthy world economy. He has shown that the qualities he employed as a keen and successful private trader can be equally useful in determining and negotiating international economic arrangements.

Nor could any better appointments have been made as head of the International Monetary Fund and as American member of the Social and Economic Council of the United Nations than Eugene Meyer and John G. Winant. The former had earlier served for some years in the Hoover administration as chairman of the Federal Reserve Board, where his grasp of international finance had been made brilliantly evident. Mr. Winant had been a progressive governor of New Hampshire, and had served with unusual distinction during the war as Ambassador in London. He had long been noted for his indefatigable interest in social and labor reform. Both appointees were known primarily, however, as ardent champions of international co-operation, and their appointment was regarded abroad as proof positive that the American government was utilizing to carry out its policies men who sincerely believed in the principles of those policies.

There can, I think, be little doubt that in the economic and financial features of her foreign policy the United States possesses a record of accomplishment which few will undertake to belittle. She has assumed practical and realistic leadership among the nations, and she has acted whenever her initiative could prove useful.

The basic difficulty she has encountered derives from the fact that until she has correctly appraised her political objectives as well, and taken whatever steps are necessary to realize them, her economic and financial objectives can be attained only superficially, if at all. For the construction of a new world economy based on liberal trade principles, on a more equitable distribution of the world's resources and production, on constantly improving living and nutritional standards, and on the full use of all those new international agencies which the United States has played so large a part in bringing into being, will depend upon a rebirth of international confidence. Confidence cannot exist until international political understanding has been reached. The economic reconstruction of the world can only be envisioned—not commenced—until such time as the nations of the earth are assured that the means of security has been found, and that peace is within their grasp. And it is in its pursuit of these political understandings that the recent foreign policy of the United States has been found wanting.

Only in the part which she has played in establishing and strengthening the United Nations has the United States shown the leadership which was expected of her in the international political field. The American people can take legitimate satisfaction from the fact that the existence today of the United Nations is due to American initiative and to American determination. The charter of the United Nations represents what was primarily an American conception. Had it not been for the unfaltering determination of President Roosevelt, during the final months of his life, the United Nations Conference at San Francisco would not have taken place before the end of the war in Europe. Late as the hour was, had the United Nations Charter not been approved before the surrender of Germany, a United Nations organization would not today be functioning. And if it were not, in the desperately troubled world which we confront there would be little if any hope for world reconstruction and for a future world order which can give mankind peace and the assurance of human progress. That is an achievement, the importance of which, in any fair appraisal of American foreign policy, can never be overestimated.

But in the long list of opportunities that the United States has had to advance world security the part played by this government has been too often bungling and prejudicial, and usually at best ineffective or sterile. In no instance has this been more evident than in its early handling of the dilemma presented by the problem of atomic energy. For the discovery of the secrets of atomic fission immediately affected every aspect of international relationships, renewed the mass fears which we had been confident the final victory over the Axis would permanently dispel, and raised at once the grave question whether the newly born United Nations could withstand the new and shattering stresses created by the antagonisms and suspicions now so rapidly engendered. The hesitant and vacillating course at first pursued by the United States was in no small part responsible for the mounting tension between the Soviet Union and the Western powers.

The Government of the United States had come into possession of the secrets of atomic fission by a strangely dramatic combination of circumstances. The basic discoveries were due in part to American and British and in part to European scientists. It was only the United States, however, that during the war possessed the immense resources required to perfect the manufacture of the implements of destruction which these discoveries made possible. Canada possessed the major part of the raw materials needed for manufacture.

The three governments pooled their resources as a part of the war effort. President Roosevelt made the decision in 1943 which placed the United States Government unreservedly behind the endeavor. Outstanding scientists of the three countries collaborated, and certain of the leading universities of the United States volunteered their services. Nor should it be forgotten that through the efficiency of the British Intelligence Service the German installations where the German government hoped to perfect the development of atomic energy were destroyed before the final secrets had been discovered.

The Soviet government was first officially informed of the discoveries of the English-speaking powers at the Potsdam meeting in 1945. The atomic bomb was first used only a few weeks thereafter. There is no doubt that the Soviet government, like the German government, knew through its agents in this country that the secrets of atomic energy were being developed in the United States, and had itself obtained through independent research knowledge of the means of atomic fission. But it had not perfected the processes of manufacture.

The impact upon the Soviet government was profound. The knowledge that the Western powers had within their possession this devastating weapon increased the suspicions and uncertainties concerning United States policy that had been mounting during the summer of 1945. Even in normal times of peace the knowledge by one major power that a group of other powers possess scientific secrets that can change the entire aspect of modern warfare, and that put to use can transform the existing balance of power, must have a disruptive effect upon international relations.

The effect upon public opinion throughout the world after the first atom bomb fell upon Hiroshima was quite as shattering as that occasioned in the Soviet Union. Mass hysteria swept through all the democracies. Fear and a panic sense of general insecurity clouded better judgment and undermined the start toward unity between the United Nations that had been achieved during the war.

There was only one way in which the United States could have prevented the rapid deterioration in international confidence. Before using the atom bomb and before officially notifying the Soviet Union that the manufacturing secrets of atomic energy were in her possession, the United States, with the agreement of Great Britain and Canada, should have presented a fully implemented proposal to all the other United Nations, providing for an effective system of control by the United Nations to safeguard against the use of atomic energy for aggression and to insure its use only for the benefit of mankind. But the United States displayed a total lack of such bold and constructive leadership. Her vacillation could only enhance the resentment and suspicion of the Soviet Union and increase the fear of all other peoples.

Without any firm and enlightened leadership from the White House, it was natural that popular opinion in the United States should manifest itself in contradictory terms. Many vehemently insisted that the secrets should be preserved solely for the use of the United States. This point of view persisted even when it became known that the United States possessed merely the manufacturing secrets, and that these secrets would be in the possession of the Soviet Union as a result of her own research within a period of one to three years. The discovery of a Soviet spy ring in Canada strengthened this demand.

Another group demanded that the secret should be immediately shared with all other countries, particularly the Soviet Union, whether or not proper control safeguards had previously been set up. This group was equally vocal in insisting that such illusory panaceas as World Government now were the only means by which humanity could be saved from imminent destruction.

It must also be frankly stated that there existed another body of public opinion, in which military and naval officials of the United States were included, which insisted that, since the Soviet Union could soon develop the manufacturing processes of atomic energy, the only safe course for the United States was to use the atomic bombs as a means of forestalling the possibility of any later aggression against herself.

The debates upon this subject in the Congress, and the hearings before the Congressional committees on atomic energy, did nothing to dispel confusion and excitement.

Only after the President summoned a conference at Washington attended by the British Prime Minister and the Canadian Prime Minister was the critical situation alleviated. The statement issued by the chiefs of government on November 15 declared that the three governments that they represented would "share on a reciprocal basis with others of the United Nations detailed information concerning the industrial application of atomic energy just as soon as effective enforceable safeguards against its use for destructive purposes can be devised."

They also proposed the establishment of a United Nations atomic commission, under the continuing authority of the United Nations, to recommend means by which atomic energy could be controlled, atomic weapons eliminated from the national armaments of all nations, safeguards set up against violations of international agreements, and pertinent scientific information exchanged between all governments.

At the first meeting of the United Nations Assembly the projected commission was agreed upon and commenced its sessions in New York in the spring of 1946. It was composed of representatives of all the powers named to the Security Council together with Canada. A representative of Canada was seated, over the vigorous objection of the Soviet Union, upon the insistence of the British and American governments that inasmuch as Canada shared the secrets with them her representative could not logically be excluded from the task before the commission. The American representative was that brilliantly qualified elder statesman and honored public servant of the United States, Bernard M. Baruch.

The Lilienthal report, previously formulated under the auspices of the State Department, had been the most constructive step taken by the United States Government prior to the appointment of the United Nations Commission. Its analysis of the fundamental issues was clear and convincing. It offered practical solutions. The McMahon Atomic Energy Control Bill, covering the control of atomic energy within the United States, in which Senator McMahon succeeded finally in inserting provisions for civilian control in place of the exclusive military control upon which the armed services had been insistent, was at length, after long debate, adopted by the Congress. The act was in harmony with the principles of the Lilienthal report. It offered assurance to other nations—if they would give satisfactory guarantees to do the same thing—that the United States had finally decided to place the determination of the problem on the high level of statesmanship rather than on that of scientific warfare.

The proposals submitted to the United Nations Commission by Mr. Baruch in the name of the United States were even more highly constructive. Their nature made it all the more regrettable that the United States had not taken such an initiative six months before, and thus forestalled much of the Russian suspicion of American intentions.

In brief, this government proposed through the Baruch formula the establishment of an international atomic development authority, empowered by all nations to hold a monopoly of all raw materials, wherever located, that may be used in the creation of atomic fission, together with a monopoly of all secrets and processes that may be used in the preparation of atomic fission. All nations would agree to refrain from research or manufacture unless licensed by the international authority, and to submit to the inspection of their territory by the authority.

The United States further agreed that once the authority had commenced to function, and "condign punishment been set up for violations of the rule of control, which are to be stigmatised as international crimes," this government would produce no more atomic bombs, would destroy its stockpile, and would transfer to the authority all the manufacturing and other secrets within its possession.

Mr. Baruch's words with regard to punishment merit quotation:

The matter of punishment lies at the very heart of our present security system. It might as well be admitted, here and now, that the subject goes straight to the veto power contained in the Charter of the United Nations so far as it relates to the field of atomic energy. The Charter permits penalization only by the concurrence of each of the five great powers. . . . I want to make it very plain that I am concerned here with the veto power only as it affects this particular problem. There must be no veto to protect those who violate their solemn agreements not to develop or use atomic energy for destructive purposes.

The attitude represented by the American proposal was wholly enlightened. It was also practical. It reflected a common-sense undertaking which could bring about an effective international control of atomic energy. But owing to the delay in its presentation as well as to the vagaries in the American position which have already been related, the proposal met, as had been anticipated, with strong opposition from the Soviet government. When the Russian views were announced to the commission by Mr. Gromyko it was made plain that the Soviet Union would not agree to renounce her veto rights in the field of atomic energy, that she would not submit to alien inspection of her territory and that all that she proposed as an alternative to the American plan was an international treaty outlawing the use of the atomic bomb, but leaving the punishment of any violation of the compact to national, rather than international, authorities. In essence the Russian proposal would possess the same sanctions as those afforded by the Kellogg-Briand pact—merely the paper upon which the provisions were recorded.

The controversy resulting from this conflict of views was fundamental. For it was clear that no plan for the control of atomic energy would work, or justify the relinquishment of the advantages presently possessed by the United States or any other power, unless it gave assurance of ironclad guaranties. And such guaranties could be offered only by an international authority which could not be hamstrung by any exercise of the veto power.

By her proposal the United States had volunteered to abandon her own veto rights in the field of atomic energy and to give up every advantage she possessed through her discovery and possession of atomic secrets. Were her proposal to be accepted, she

would be on a par with every other power, great or small. But
the United States could not afford to surrender such advantages
unless she could obtain the assurance of security thereafter.

In this issue the Government of the United States has demonstrated moral leadership and an enlightened initiative. What it
has failed to show—as has been so often the case in other crucial problems—is any adequate sense of timing. Once again this
government has been forced—after the event—to realize that
an accurate sense of timing is an essential factor in any successful foreign policy. For a proposal that is made after doubts, suspicions and even appetites have been given the chance to grow
has far less chance of being found acceptable by other governments than at the moment when the issue which requires solution first arises.

This failure to recognize the basic importance of the time
element in the implementation of American foreign policy has,
however, been only one of the defects which have gradually
become glaringly apparent as the United States Government has
charted its course in the postwar world.

Its handling in the spring of 1946 of the issues arising from
the continuation in power of the Franco dictatorship in Spain
will afford the future historian of this period an excellent example
of American official irresponsibility.

Long before I left the Department of State in 1943 it was well
known to this government that General Franco was giving Hitler
all the material assistance he dared. The unneutral activities going
on in several Spanish ports were not concealed from the secret
services of the Allies. The Gestapo was working openly throughout Spain with Franco's official blessing. The Blue Division had
been sent to fight against Russia. With the end of the war many
additional facts came to light which afforded concrete evidence
that the Franco government had gone as far as it could in support of the Axis short of risking an Allied declaration of war
and short of opening Spain to a German occupation. Of the pro-
Axis sympathies of all but a few of the members of the Franco
régime, and of the Fascist nature of the Franco government,
there could never have been any doubt.

The defeat of Germany and of Japan necessarily diminished Franco's prestige within Spain, and to a considerable extent weakened his hold on the Spanish Army which had been the chief support of his administration. Economic conditions had improved, but the Spanish people were still confronted with innumerable hardships and restrictions which continued to make for popular discontent. For some months the movement for the restoration of the monarchy, which had been encouraged by the Churchill Cabinet, seemed to make headway. Many Spanish army leaders notoriously favored the cause of Don Juan.

At the same time the republican government-in-exile, headed by President Giral, had established itself in Mexico by invitation of the Mexican government, and had been officially recognized by several Latin-American governments. It had much moral right, and some legal right, to be regarded as the legitimate government of Spain.

There was real ground for the belief that the growing support within the Spanish Army for the restoration of a constitutional monarchy, and the increasing popular· dissatisfaction with the Franco régime might result in a combination of factors which would bring about Franco's withdrawal and the creation of a provisional government under which elections might be held. Early in the winter of 1946 Franco himself was resigned to such a solution.

At that moment the Soviet government, fearing that the monarchist movement was rapidly gaining in control and that the restoration of the monarchy would establish British ascendancy in Spain for an indefinite period and thereby thwart Moscow's effort to expand Russia's influence in the Mediterranean, injected itself suddenly into the situation. It chose as its instrument the French Communist party in France.

The French provisional government, acting at the behest of its Communist members, announced that the Franco government was endangering France's security and the maintenance of world peace. The French press was filled with reports of Spanish troop movements along the Franco-Spanish frontier. To these were added stories of Nazi activities within Spain. Convincing rumors were published alleging that scientists operating in secret Spanish laboratories were engaged in manufacturing atomic bombs. The French government closed its frontiers with Spain. French mobs assaulted Spanish consulates. Diplomatic relations between the two neighboring countries were broken. France demanded that the United Nations take action to abolish the Franco dictatorship and give the Spanish people the democracy of which they had been so long deprived.

The issues which thus so suddenly arose were inherently grave. If hostilities occurred between France and Spain as a consequence of some frontier incident the fat would be in the fire. The Soviet Union would probably demand the right to assist France with military force in order to repel a "Fascist" invasion from Spain. The passage of Russian troops through France and their entrance into Spain would bring the Soviet armies for the first time into western Europe and create a situation which the Western powers could not accept. On the other hand, the overthrow of Franco, even by joint action of the major allies, would inevitably cause renewed civil war in Spain with tragic results for the Spanish people, and with the very likely probability that as an aftermath a "popular front" government would be established which would soon be found to be under the exclusive control of the Soviet Union. The Western powers had not forgotten Moscow's success in dominating the republican government in Spain during its final stages.

In such a dilemma the course which the United States should have pursued in the interest of world peace and of its own security would have seemed to be obvious. In the increasingly troubled state of the world, the elimination of the Franco dictatorship was by no means a matter of prime urgency unless it could be proved that it was actually threatening the safety of its neighbors or the peace of the world. Such charges had now been brought by France but no authoritative proof had been offered.

The United States had been losing no opportunity officially to reiterate its intention of working through the United Nations whenever international questions arose which jeopardized relations between its members. The Spanish problem was clearly such a question. Moreover the Security Council was patently the one authoritative agency capable of investigating the charges brought against Franco, and of offering world public opinion convincing evidence that the charges were true or false. The Council was likewise the sole agency empowered under the United Nations Charter to take action against Franco should the maintenance of world peace require action.

It would have seemed logical that the United States should propose that the Spanish question be at once brought before the Security Council.

However, she did nothing of the kind.

She refused to agree to the proposal of the French government that this course be adopted. She insisted that Britain and France join with her in a tripartite declaration addressed to the Spanish people assuring them that the three governments had no intention of intervening in their internal affairs, but simultaneously urging them to overthrow the Franco régime. How this was to be accomplished without foreign armed intervention, when the Spanish masses were entirely unarmed and when the Spanish Army would unquestionably support Franco in any revolutionary uprising, was not explained. At the same time the State Department published a White Book containing documentary evidence of the Axis connections of Franco and his associates.

By this strange performance, for which several of the lesser officials in the Department of State were primarily responsible, the American government achieved these results: it greatly strengthened Franco's position in Spain, since the Spaniards, like the Latin Americans, will not tolerate foreign interference in their domestic concerns, and will rally to their government at any threat to their national sovereignty; it openly sponsored action outside of the United Nations in flagrant contradiction of its professions of support for that organization; it gave the Soviet Union an added incentive to take unilateral action within Spain; it widened the growing breach between the Western powers and Moscow.

When the United States was compelled some months later to agree to permit the Spanish question to come before the Security

Council, the position which she had earlier taken made it impossible for her to assume any constructive leadership in furthering a solution which would be in the true interest of the Spanish people and prevent a further breach between the major powers. The Soviet Union and the United States continued at cross purposes.

Developments in Spain have brought out some of the gravest defects in American foreign policy. In 1937 the Roosevelt administration was guilty of its greatest error in its handling of the issues raised by the Spanish civil war. In 1946 the policy pursued by the United States toward Spain was responsible for the creation of wholly unnecessary threats to world peace. American policy also materially lessened the prestige and influence of the United States.

It is, however, in this government's approach to the problem of Germany that the inherent weaknesses in American foreign policy can perhaps most readily be seen.

There was one inescapable conclusion to be drawn from the history of the years which followed immediately after the First World War. It was this. Unless the victorious allies agreed upon a joint policy toward Germany, and unless that policy provided for the creation of a political régime within Germany that would eliminate all possibility of a resurgence of Pan-German militarism, and for the establishment of an international control over Germany's heavy industry, there could be no assurance that the German people would not, sooner or later, provoke a third world war.

A year and a half after the defeat of Germany there is no semblance of any such joint policy. There are, on the contrary, four policies. The United States and Great Britain, France and the Soviet Union are diverging more and more in their objectives. The political future of the German people has not been fixed, and bitter wrangling still continues as to their industrial future. And United States policy, so far as it exists, is intrinsically so confused, so inefficient and so hopelessly at variance with the general ends above stated that it constitutes an increasingly serious obstacle to the ultimate attainment of any effective joint policy.

The War Department has sought to place all responsibility for political decisions upon the State Department, by which, of course, they should be determined. The State Department has passed the buck back to the War Department, and has consistently refused either to accept its rightful obligation to decide all the political aspects of the occupation or to prepare for a rapid transfer of the ultimate authority within the American Occupation Zone to civilian hands.

The four-power military government of Germany has generally succeeded in disarming and demobilizing German armed forces, although it is notorious that in the British zone many German army units are still intact under British command. But the social problems that arose when the disarmed enemy forces were returned to their homes were not provided for. The re-education of the individual German during the first months after defeat would have been by no means an insoluble problem. Except in the Russian zone that opportunity has been wholly thrown away, and in the Russian zone such re-education has been in no sense in the interest of the other United Nations.

The American military authorities have pursued a policy of de-Nazification. However, many Nazis were appointed to positions of importance on the pretext that democratic substitutes were not available, particularly during the early stages of the occupation. The definition of "Nazi" laid down by the American authorities was amazingly restricted. There can be no question that both in the American and British zones many influential Nazis were protected by important interests possessing influence in the American and British governments.

An instance of the fatal harm already done by the lack of agreement between the Allies upon the political and industrial future of Germany is provided by the all-important question of the level of industry to be maintained in Germany, particularly the level of steel production. The British government originally held out for a German production of nine million tons annually. The Soviet proposal would have permitted Germany to produce three to four million tons of steel a year. The British member on the co-ordinating committee stated that the "British delegation would never agree to turn Germany into a wilderness." An agreement was later reached upon a production capacity figure of 7,500,000 tons, but with actual production not to exceed 5,800,000 tons. A week later the British government announced that it had approved the agreement only upon the understanding that the annual production should be seven and a half million tons.

In the west, Germany's industries, power installations, and research laboratories have been largely uncontrolled since V-E Day. Evidences of the influence of American and British private interests in preserving intact the holdings of the I. G. Farben Corporation and of many of the automobile production industries are innumerable. In the east, Russia has stripped every factory except those which fit into the precise plans she has formulated for making eastern Germany an economic tributary of the greater Soviet system. Without some over-all policy agreed to by all four major powers, and rigorously enforced, it is inconceivable that the industrial production of Germany will be held at a level commensurate with the security of the rest of the world.

Within the Russian zone the political structure is already Soviet controlled. Within the American zone elections were permitted long before the German people had been prepared to carry out elections. The interpretation given to this fact, not only by the German people but by the governments of the other occupying powers as well, is that the American government is forcing the Germans to accept prematurely the responsibilities of local government solely in order to hasten the day when American occupation forces can be evacuated. These assumptions have of course been confirmed by official declarations.

An exceedingly shrewd statesman from one of the smaller European countries said to me the other day, "Why is it that Secretary Byrnes finds it impossible to make a speech nowadays without harping on the theme of the termination of American occupation of enemy territory in Europe? Can't he understand that these repeated statements at such a time as this merely incite the German people, and encourage the Soviet authorities to enlarge their plans for westward expansion in Europe?"

These excerpts from a letter written to me by an American operations officer stationed in Germany present the picture with brutal clarity.

I have been in Germany over seven months and with increasing certainty of one consideration upon which American foreign policy towards Germany should be based; the German population as a whole supported the German war, does not consider itself defeated, and does not consider the acts of the Nazi régime as either hideous or brutal.

Military government in Germany today may be dealt with as a three-faceted problem.

1. The lack of a clear-cut and unswerving long-term policy has affected military government operations at all levels. There has been no decision as yet as to the dissolution of German industrial power nor has there been any clear-cut policy as to what the relations between the occupying forces and the Germans should be. The tactical troops and the local military government detachments have completely forgotten Dachau and Buchenwald and other extermination camps which were run by the Germans. They forget that the German industrial machine was the controlling factor of economic life in Central Europe. For lack of a definitive long-term policy we are steadily but consistently assuming the role of liberator and benefactor of Germany. There is, of course, a certain amount of annoyance on the part of the Germans. They are annoyed that we are here. They are annoyed conversely that we haven't done more for them. The business interests in America and in England are already fast at work both in official capacities and as private citizens in bolstering up the German economy so that Germany may again become an export market.

2. The great surge to go home which is clutching almost all Americans in Germany today is disastrous. Unless the State Department in conjunction with the War Department can recruit top notch highly paid personnel to run the American occupation of Germany, our role in Europe may well prove to be a fiasco. Most of the military government officers mean well and work hard, but they do not have the drive nor the background necessary to run an operation of this size.

3. The British occupation policy is one which aims at gaining the friendship of the Germans, in creating a Western economic unity, although not necessarily a Western political bloc. The French apparently do not desire to see any form of German government, even under Allied supervision, created. The Russians are stripping their zone as completely as they can. The Americans are attempting to run

Germany along traditional democratic lines, not realizing that the German mind as it is now constituted is incapable of democratic thought processes. The Control Council in Berlin is fast becoming a debating and consultative assembly rather than a governing body. If the United Nations Organization is to work, Germany is its first testing ground, its first chance to work. If the four occupying powers can govern Germany as a unit, then there is hope for the United Nations Organization.

The four occupying powers have not governed Germany as a unit. They have not done so because the United States failed when it had the chance—before the victory—to make certain that this would be done. The reconstruction of Europe may prove impossible for this reason. For the very key to European reconstruction lies in the ability of the four major powers, and of the United Nations, to find a policy toward Germany which will spell safety for the rest of the world. Unless it is a joint policy, no policy can spell safety.

The crisis which some of us had long feared broke in July, 1946, when Mr. Molotov, under the guise of an address to his colleagues at the Paris meeting of the Foreign Ministers of the Big Four, told the world, and particularly the German people themselves, what the Soviet government wanted in Germany.

His declaration constituted an open appeal to German nationalism and a clear pronouncement that if the German people would turn to the east, as they had in the days of Bismarck's "reinsurance treaty" with Russia, the Soviet government would bring about the resurrection of a united and potent Germany.

Mr. Molotov piously decried any "dismemberment" of Germany. But he carefully refrained from referring to the fact that Russia had already obtained the eastern half of East Prussia, and had secured for her satellite, Poland, the remaining half, together with Danzig and all of Germany's agricultural regions east of the Oder River.

He rejected France's claim for basic security by refusing to agree to the removal of the Ruhr, the Rhineland and the Saar from the control of a central German government. He placed the Soviet veto upon any plan for the establishment of a federated Germany, for a return to the healthy autonomy of the traditional

German states, or for any policy that would not serve to reconstruct a unified Germany, governed by a central government located presumably in Berlin where Russia was already in full political control.

The fatal mistake which the United States had made in thinking that the problem of Germany could be postponed for discussion upon some distant "tomorrow," and that in the meantime more than fictitious progress could be made in dealing with other European peace settlements was even now scarcely comprehended by public opinion in the United States.

If Great Britain still believed that she could hope to create a strong united Germany as a buffer against Soviet expansion in western Europe and as a profitable market for British exports she seemed destined for disillusionment, for Moscow had stolen a leaf out of the policy pursued by Britain after the First World War.

The Soviet Union had been biding its time. It had not been blind to Great Britain's ambitions. It had made effective use of every defect, every omission and every weakness in the policy of the United States and of her Western allies.

The American government has failed to carry out any positive, coherent or democratic program within its occupation zone. Its policies have not been integrated until very recently indeed with those of the other Western occupying powers. In the western zones political confusion and economic prostration are intrinsically as great as when the occupation began. I have written in an earlier chapter in great detail of the inefficiency of the American administrative machine during the occupation of Italy. The story in Germany is similar and the inefficiency has been even more marked.

The Soviet government has on the contrary succeeded admirably in achieving its objectives within the Russian zone of Germany. It has already wrought in that zone a political, economic and social transformation which has made the region an integral part—in fact if not in name—of the Soviet system.

The Soviet government has in many ways catered consistently to German nationalism. It apparently believes that it can control that nationalism to its own advantage. It is seemingly convinced that in a unified Germany the political agencies which it has successfully set up in the Russian zone would rapidly dominate any central German government that might be established, and that the masses of the people throughout Germany would soon prove submissive to the influence of Moscow. A federated Germany, in the opinion of the Kremlin, would make it more difficult to expand the Soviet system westward, and probably place Germany's major industrial resources under Western control.

Nor can it be denied, granted the failure of the United States to execute any affirmative and democratic program, from which the German people could foresee positive future benefits, that the peculiar psychology of the German masses in their present misery and confusion would probably make them as prone to accept today the tenets of a nationalistic Soviet system as they were to accept thirteen years ago the doctrines of Hitlerism.

To the United States a politically centralized Germany governed from Berlin offers no hope of future security. Yet should this come about American foreign policy will be primarily responsible.

The differences between the foreign policies of Great Britain and the United States afford a rewarding study in contrasts. The two policies differ in many of their objectives. They differ still more greatly in the manner in which they are carried on.

For many generations the basic objectives of British policy have remained the same. They have been to prevent the emergence of any one European nation as a force capable of dominating the Continent, and to maintain a European balance of power; to prevent any threat to British freedom of action on the seas; and to maintain British control of the Mediterranean and the Suez Canal as an indispensable life line between the British community of nations and the United Kingdom. British governments have been Conservative, Liberal or Labor, yet these foundations of foreign policy have remained immutable. Radical readjustments have taken place in the world, scientific developments have changed the relative value of sea power, political alignments have been transformed. But the essentials of British policy remain un-

altered, although the methods employed to secure their achievement may vary.

The power and prestige of the United Kingdom are today at
their lowest ebb in several centuries. The British government has
failed in the past decade in the first objective of its foreign policy.
Hitler's Germany very nearly conquered Europe. The Soviet
Union is at this moment an even more dominant force in Europe
than was Nazi Germany in 1939. The establishment of a bloc
of western European nations as an offset to the Soviet Union
and as a means of creating a new European balance of power is
presently impossible. The international system represented by the
United Nations has consequently become the one alternative
which can offer Great Britain hope of security in Europe and it
has become that form of collective security which she is seeking
to strengthen as the means of preventing a one-power domination of Europe.

Great Britain's third objective—the control of the Mediterranean and of the Suez Canal—is gravely endangered. The armed
force and the material resources necessary to impose her control
are no longer available. She is moving with realistic vision and
with dispatch to repair her position by new means. She has fostered the creation of the Arab federation, which is becoming not
only political but economic and strategic. In that confederation
she is prepared to join on a basis of equality. Should such a partnership be concluded her major interest—the security of the
canal and of the Near East, as well as the approaches to them
through the Mediterranean—could be protected.

The Labor government's offer of independence to India and
to other dependent areas represents a farsighted recognition of
the fact, which Mr. Churchill was unwilling to see, that Great
Britain might thus save at least a part of her world influence.
For should India or some of the British colonies break away by
force of arms, there would be little left to salvage of the vast
economic and strategic advantages which the British Empire so
recently possessed.

In the pursuit of its underlying objectives British policy has
shown itself to be realistic and adaptable. It has been influenced

very little by emotion or by questions of ideology. It has almost always had a great quality of dependability. Its more egregious blunders, such as those committed before the Second World War by the Baldwin and Chamberlain cabinets, were due rather to the blindly reactionary beliefs of England's controlling politicians, who feared Communism more than Hitlerism, than to any change in the objectives of British policy.

In contrast, the objectives of American foreign policy have changed often. Even today, when officially stated, they are expressed in very general and nebulous terms. The American people are told that their government's policy is designed to achieve for them "security," the "strengthening" of the United Nations, a "just" peace in Europe, "economic co-operation" and "friendly understanding" with all other nations. It is rare that the precise methods by which these general ends are to be attained are specifically set forth. One of the most valuable services rendered by Secretary Byrnes has been the radio broadcasts which he has recently delivered to the American people explaining clearly and in detail the problems which he has confronted in his meetings with the other Foreign Ministers of the major powers, and the precise views which this government has held with respect to each of these problems.

The objectives of our policy have tended to vary with each administration. They have not remained constant in our relations with Latin America, Europe or the Far East. Our policy was international with Wilson; narrowly isolationist with Harding, Coolidge and Hoover; once more international with Roosevelt and Truman.

The formulation of our policy has been far more subject to the influence of popular emotion and of popular prejudice than has that of British policy. The effect upon public opinion of the efforts of the Nye Committee to demonstrate that "international bankers" forced this country into the First World War, and the public stampede for the enactment of the so-called neutrality legislation in 1937, are but two recent examples.

The American people are prone to speak with much pride of the "moral leadership" of the United States. The phrase is, in fact, losing its true meaning. It has all too often been interpreted by the American people as a term which permits them to bask in the confidence of their own highmindedness, an occupation which is rendered no less agreeable by their assurance that neither effort nor sacrifice are thereby required.

To foreign peoples there are few American traits, official or private, which are more thoroughly exasperating than our tendency to deliver homilies to them on the subject of their moral deficiencies. It is unquestionably an American habit to regard the great majority of the other peoples of the world as steeped in original sin. We are apt to consider them unregenerate and as suffering from all the thousand and one defects from which, in our judgment, we ourselves are wholly free.

The geographical isolation in which the United States was permitted to develop during the greater part of its independent existence, and the political isolation in which it for so long immured itself, have prevented the American people from comprehending the continuing insecurity in which a majority of the other peoples of the earth have been forced to live, and which has given rise to many of the tendencies so scathingly denounced by the average American citizen.

But at the same time there can be no question that idealism is inherent in the American spirit. And the rest of the world has known that the United States has not in recent times jeopardized the welfare nor the safety of other peoples. These facts offer the United States a unique opportunity among the nations.

During the war years the peoples of the United Nations looked longingly to this country for positive "moral leadership." The Atlantic Charter at last furnished such moral leadership. The American initiative in bringing the United Nations into being also provided it.

Moral leadershp of a kind that will make the fullest use of this country's influence obviously implies more than the mere reiteration by the United States Government of the beatitudes in their application to international relations. Moral leadership cannot be negative. It cannot be exercised effectively unless the government which seeks to lead harmonizes its own actions with its professions.

It is unfortunate that since the death of President Roosevelt the moral leadership of the United States has been for the most part limited to the proclamation of righteous principles, while at the same time many of her acts have raised grave doubt in the minds of other peoples whether the policy of the United States was any less selfish or any less shortsighted than their own.

The question of strategic bases furnishes an apt example of official action by the United States which is construed by public opinion in other countries as running counter to her moral professions.

The defeat of Japan left the United States in military occupation of a number of strategic bases in the Pacific formerly under the jurisdiction of Japan, or under the sovereignty of other powers. In July, 1945, President Truman, in a speech to American troops in Potsdam, declared emphatically that the United States would not take one inch of additional territory as a result of the part she had played in winning the victory. An uproar arose in the Congress, and from American army and navy leaders. They protested that the United States must retain as her exclusive property all the strategic bases in the Pacific which American forces had captured. The President thereupon let it be known that he had not meant precisely what he had said.

A powerful element in the American press took up the issue. Voices were soon heard declaring that the United States not only must retain such of the former Japanese islands as she required for strategic purposes, but that she must likewise retain any other islands in the Pacific which she might need, even though these were the property of Great Britain and France.

The effect of these incidents was much more far-reaching than has generally been recognized. Many of these Pacific bases lay within a short distance of the Soviet Union's Siberian provinces. The United States' claim for permanent possession could only create deep-rooted suspicion on the part of the Soviet government. A few officials in the State Department expressed their view that an effort would be made to place all the strategic islands captured from Japan under the International Trusteeship of the United Nations, provided the United States were designated as the administrator of those bases. But no public commitment was made to that effect. Nor could any categorical announcement then be made that the United States had no designs on the property of its allies, because of a continuing conflict of views within the executive and legislative branches.

Had the United States at the end of the war possessed a definite policy on strategic bases throughout the world, she could have demonstrated "moral leadership" by informing the United Nations of her intention of transferring to it, once she was satisfied that adequate trusteeship and policing machinery had been established, and that other powers would take similar actions, all the Japanese islands which she had seized during the war. By so doing she would have strengthened immeasurably the trusteeship machinery of the United Nations, and would have forestalled the suspicions of other colonial governments. She would also have lessened the probability that the Soviet government might later, as it now has, present claims for the exclusive possession of strategic bases which have passed under its control.

Another specific instance where the United States has failed to live up to its professions of moral righteousness is represented by its approach to the problem of the tortured peoples of the Jewish faith in Europe.

President Roosevelt took the initiative in 1938 in bringing about the establishment of the Inter-Governmental Committee on Refugees. The basic purpose in creating the committee was to provide havens or new homes for the refugees who might be able to escape from Europe. Later, after the outbreak of the war, it was intended that the committee should secure the resettlement of those refugees who might still survive after the defeat of Germany.

It cannot be said that the committee has been worthless, since the fact that it existed at all provided a demonstration of the truth that this problem can be solved successfully only if its solution is accepted by all nations as a common responsibility. But had the leadership of the United States been truly effective, the committee during the early stages of the war could have drawn up a resettlement program, and by negotiation with individual governments willing to receive immigrants after the war could have perfected preparations for the transfer of refugees to their new homes as soon as hostilities in Europe had ended. This could have saved the lives of many hundreds of thousands of unfortunates. The concentration camps for displaced persons would not still be filled fifteen months after Germany's defeat.

The only voice of real moral leadership on this subject which has been recently heard from the United States was that of Mrs. Franklin D. Roosevelt when she served as a delegate from the United States at the first session of the United Nations Assembly. It was she who was largely responsible for the rejection by the Assembly of the Soviet government's contention that all refugees in central Europe who had previously been residents of areas now under Soviet control should be restored to Soviet jurisdiction whether or not they wanted to be. It was her insistence upon the right of the individual to freedom and security, whether or not he supported the political régime in control of his homeland, that prevented the perpetration of a crime which would have set an evil precedent for the future.

In its handling of the question of Palestine the United States has been guilty of the same dereliction. This government has been guided by humanitarian motives, but its objectives have been halfheartedly carried out. Its attitude has been flabby and timorous. It has rarely shown less ability in making the nation's influence effectively felt. Through its agreement to take part in the Anglo-American Palestine Commission and in the later Anglo-American Cabinet Committee, it was persuaded by the British government—bent unfortunately upon strengthening its influence over the Arab world at the expense of the Jews—to assume responsibility without securing in return any commensurate authority.

Had the United States been determined to promote a final and equitable solution of the question, it would have refused to acquiesce in the British government's assertion of its alleged right to impose its own decisions in Palestine. For the imposition of such decisions would result in a repudiation of the pledges given the Jewish people, permanently shut out from Palestine all but a handful of European refugees, and by an illusory partition create accomplished facts which would later have disastrous consequences for the world.

The solution of the Palestine question concerns all countries. The United States should have insisted that only the United Nations, through its Trusteeship Council, could legitimately assume the responsibility for finding a solution.

A further instance where the United States refrained from exercising moral leadership is to be found in the question of the dependent peoples. Those who originally drafted the United Nations Charter intended that the charter should establish the principle that the United Nations would guarantee to dependent peoples freedom from exploitation, and would assure them of eventual self-government or independence.

Long before the end of the war it was apparent that unless such international guarantees were made, victory would bring with it, particularly in the Far East, a tidal wave of revolt among many hundreds of millions of people who were demanding the severance of their ties with the colonial powers. The United States had the chance to secure the adoption within the charter of concrete provisions which could have averted chaos and paved the way for the orderly liberation of the colonial peoples. It is true that the colonial powers, such as Great Britain, the Netherlands and France, strenuously objected to the inclusion within the charter of any such specific provisions. But had the United States insisted, the colonial powers would have acceded. The violent upheaval which has now taken place in the Far East, and which may increase in intensity in the immediate future, might have been prevented.

It was the Soviet government that at San Francisco seized the moral leadership from the faltering hands of the American delegates. It is the Soviet government that today, because of its insistence at San Francisco upon the recognition of these essential principles, is regarded as their champion by the colonial peoples. The nationalists of the Far East, notwithstanding the liberation of the Philippines by the United States, look to the Soviet Union rather than America to procure their freedom for them.

The foreign policy of the United States during the past two years has far too often failed to show the dependability which has generally marked British policy in the past. In the Atlantic Charter, in the Declaration of Moscow of October, 1943, and in the Yalta agreements, the United States pledged herself to support certain general as well as certain specific principles of international conduct.

She declared in the Atlantic Charter that she desired to see no territorial changes that did not accord with the freely expressed wishes of the peoples concerned, and that she respected the right of all peoples to choose the form of government under which they will live.

In the Moscow declaration the United States reaffirmed her support for the principle of the sovereign equality of all nations, great or small.

In the Yalta agreements the United States pledged herself to bring about the establishment of democratic and representative governments in all the occupied or former Axis satellite countries of central and eastern Europe through the holding of free elections.

None of these pledges have been respected. Yet their fulfillment involved the creation of the very basis for that kind of free world order which the United Nations fought to establish and which would have provided the greatest measure of security that the American people could obtain.

The peace treaties with Italy, Finland, Hungary, Rumania and Bulgaria, drafted by the Foreign Ministers of the Big Four, which the American government has officially committed itself to "advocate" before the Peace Conference of the twenty-one United Nations at Paris, are a flagrant repudiation of the pledges of the Atlantic Charter. By agreeing to them the United States Government has chosen to stand for the compromises suggested by power politics and weak-kneed expediency. She has violated the principles which she so solemnly proclaimed.

By refusing to insist that the smaller members of the United

Nations should have a real share in the final conclusion of the peace treaties, and by permitting them to be relegated to the role of "advisers" whose "recommendations" need have no determining weight in the final decisions, the United States violated the essential principles of the Moscow Declaration of 1943 proclaiming "the sovereign equality of all nations, great or small."

By his agreement at Moscow in December, 1945, to the Soviet proposal for a merely nominal participation of two opposition representatives in the Communist-dominated governments of the countries of eastern Europe occupied by Russia, Secretary Byrnes abandoned the fundamental principles of the Yalta agreements. Free elections cannot now be held in those countries, and their peoples will be deprived of democratic and representative government. The Moscow agreement represented official acquiescence by the United States in the Soviet Union's extension of its sphere of influence over eastern Europe and the Balkans.

If the United States is to exercise any effective influence in promoting world peace and a better international order, other nations must be confident that she will abide by her pledges. American foreign policy must possess the all-important quality of dependability.

The United States continues to possess the influence in world affairs which is derived from her potential military might and from her material resources. But the moral influence which she possessed during the war years, derived from the belief of other peoples that she was determined to support those principles which are indispensable if a peaceful world is to be established, is rapidly vanishing. It would be far better for the United States to refrain from giving assurances, however noble they may be, than to fail to carry out her solemn pledges. For she cannot exercise any effective moral leadership until all peoples know that she means what she says.

The United States has squandered many of the assets she possessed when she entered the Second World War. She has wasted invaluable resources derived from what Wendell Willkie well termed this nation's international "reservoir of good will." And she could ill afford to lose any asset, or to suffer any decrease in her authority and prestige among the nations of the world, as she confronted the gravest problem with which American foreign policy had to deal within a century—the problem of her relationship with the Soviet Union.

The future safety of the United States depends upon the rapid consolidation of the United Nations and the creation of that One World which it symbolizes. The charter of the United Nations was drafted with a realistic recognition of the fact that during an indeterminate period of transition no international organization could function successfully unless the major powers were able to co-operate. The success of the United Nations is predicated upon the ability of the United States and the Soviet Union to resolve their differences and to work together at least during the initial period of the new world organization. Later, if a régime of law regulated by a more democratic and a more effective United Nations replaces the present régime of force which is necessarily controlled by the great powers that possess armed forces, the differences which may arise between the two major countries can be settled by resort to the law of nations. But now, any insoluble differences must be prevented through their joint willingness to harmonize their policies and their actions.

The alternative is only too apparent. If agreement becomes impossible all hope of a peaceful and stable world order breaks down. The result will be two worlds rather than one. The United States, to guard its own security, will be compelled to engage in an armament race, especially in the fields of aviation, of atomic weapons, and of scientific and biological warfare. The manner of living of the American people will have to be radically transformed. An American trend toward imperialism will be inevitable. The United States will head a bloc of Western powers, endeavoring to draw within their orbit additional allies in other parts of the world. She will be opposed by an ever more powerfully armed Soviet Union surrounded by her satellites. Ultimately the clash between two hemispheres would destroy the remnants of our present civilization.

At this moment the fatal drift toward the two-world order is becoming ever stronger. In the United States it is being accelerated by some of our official policies, but even more by an increasingly passionate popular prejudice incited by many potent American influences determined to block any possible understanding between Communism and the Western world. It has been rendered far more rapid by the recent policies of the Kremlin in Europe, the Far East and the Near East, and by the fears and hatred of the "capitalistic nations" which Soviet authorities are deliberately inculcating in the Russian people.

One of Europe's ablest officials said to me not long ago, "Why do you here in the United States always talk so much about your obligation to try and understand Russia? It seems to me that you are developing an inferiority complex on the subject. What is needed is for the Russians to try and understand you. The trouble is that the Russians don't want to try and understand anybody except themselves."

His estimate of the present Russian tendency is, I believe, entirely accurate. But in my judgment that does not mean that in their own interest, and as the surest way of deciding what their own policies toward the Soviet Union may most wisely be, the American people should not continue to try to understand the Russian point of view and to grasp what lies behind much that has seemed both dangerous and sinister in the course which Russia has been following. For the present generation of Russians is a race apart.

I happen to come from a stock that for three hundred years was rooted in New England. I have always believed that the highest form of democratic freedom that civilization has yet given to society was to be found in New England before the Industrial Revolution transformed her earlier economy. By inheritance and by personal convictions it would be impossible for me to support a system in which the individual is subordinated to the state. Communism is the denial of individualism, and is consequently the antithesis of the democratic system upon which our American policy has been developed. Communism could never be acceptable to more than a handful of Americans.

Yet I also believe that Soviet Russia represents one of the greatest attempts to attain human betterment that the world has ever known, and that society in every part of the earth will eventually be profoundly affected by it. It was forged out of such suffering as the Western peoples have never dreamed of. In a quarter of a century it has given health, education, economic security and the hope of happiness to one hundred and eighty millions of human beings who had previously known only misery. It has not only created a new social structure out of the ruins of a barbaric feudalism, it has, within a short generation, changed the medieval agricultural economy of an entire continent into an economy of advanced industrialism.

The founders of Soviet Communism attempted to deny not only the Divinity, but also the soul of man. Yet the greatest of them all, Lenin, wrote these words:

Man's dearest possession is life, and since it is given to him to live but once, he must so live as not to be seared with the shame of a cowardly and trivial past, so live as not to be tortured for years without purpose, so live that dying he can say; "All my life and my strength were given to the first cause in the world—the liberation of mankind."

The democracies of the West are too prone to underestimate the religious force of the fanaticism which such ideals of Soviet Communism can inspire, and the political strength engendered by the individual Russian's recognition of the concrete benefits he has received from Communism.

The Russian people for thirty years have been living in mental as well as physical isolation from the rest of the world. An isolation that may earlier have been a source of strength in the Soviet experiment has now become a source of weakness. For the Russian people have been taught actually to believe that the amazing progress which they have made has already placed them far ahead of all other peoples. The artisan or the farmer in Soviet Russia cannot be made to think it possible that other peoples may be enjoying a higher standard of living, may possess a greater degree of individual liberty, or may have developed a more rounded or more advanced culture. Political freedom, freedom of expression or of information, are not missed because except to a few score of Russians these are phrases devoid of meaning. Such mental isolation has become a weakness because once the rudimentary foundations of a social structure have been laid, the structure cannot be fully perfected unless its human builders are given the chance to learn from the errors and the successes of other builders.

Added to the unshakable conviction of the Russian people of the superiority of their own political and economic system is a factor that is even more significant in Russia's relations with the outside world. That is the fanatical fervor of the Communist party leaders. To them Communism is a religion as proclaimed by Lenin. They are willing to go to any limits to serve their ideals, and with the mysticism of the Slav their own lives are of little value to them if by dying they can advance those ideals. We cannot afford to forget that the Soviet government is run by Marxists who sincerely believe that war and poverty will never be conquered until an international socialist world is created, and until that world is directed by the Communist party in Moscow. Under the commandments of Lenin, to do right is to do that which is in the interests of Communism. Anything which obstructs the realization of the policies of the Communist party in Moscow is criminal. Those beliefs are the driving forces back of the Soviet government today, and they present some explanation for the undoubted fact that all the horrors of the concentration camps in Siberia, all the purgings and liquidations undertaken by the N.K.V.D., all the restrictions upon individual freedom, all the continuing official emphasis upon the need for sacrifice, are gladly accepted by the Russian masses as necessary means to the attainment of a great ideal. This popular conviction could not be better interpreted than in the words that Rosita Forbes quotes as having been said to her by a Soviet professor in Samarkand: "We are making something bigger than mere history."

It is because of their own success in forming and in controlling public opinion within Russia that the Communist leaders find it hard to understand that a free public opinion in the Western democracies can frequently determine official policies. The greatest statesman who has guided Russia's foreign relations once said to me that his greatest difficulty in interpreting the West to his

Communist colleagues in Moscow lay in their inability to comprehend how public opinion can really shape the course that the Western democracies pursue. It is equally difficult for the members of the Communist oligarchy, for Stalin and the members of the *Politburo* and the Council of Ministers, to believe that it is not solely the three or four persons who hold the top executive offices in the Western powers who dictate the policies of their governments, or that the legislative and judicial branches have any say in the matter.

It was for that reason inevitable that the death of Franklin Roosevelt should have inaugurated a new period of doubt and suspicion among the Soviet leaders in their appraisal of the United States. They knew Roosevelt. In 1933 he had made the resumption of relations with Russia a cardinal principle of his foreign policy. He had personally tried to solve fairly each of the difficulties that subsequently arose between the two nations, and had been personally responsible for the scope of the military and economic assistance rendered to the Soviet Union after Germany's aggression of 1941. He had invariably insisted that the only way to create confidence between the two greatest powers in the world was to start by having confidence. He had put to one side all questions of his Presidential prestige in his insistent desire to meet Stalin face to face and to find with him an understanding covering every controversial question that had arisen or might arise. The Soviet government and Stalin in particular recognized that there were strength and sincerity behind this insistence. The fruits of the Roosevelt policy became apparent at Teheran and at Yalta. Then, suddenly, the direction of American policy passed to other hands. The dire change this brought in Soviet-American relations was apparent to every objective observer present at the meeting at Potsdam.

Naturally, the Soviet government knew that President Truman was beset by conflicting advice as to the methods he should adopt in his dealings with it. It was fully aware that one group of advisers, who decried what they termed the "appeasement of Russia" policy of Franklin Roosevelt, was asserting that strong-arm tactics constituted the only means of achieving success. It also

knew that another group was urging that concessions on Near
Eastern and eastern European questions could be advantageously
used as a bargaining point in order to secure Russian assent to
American objectives in the Far East and in western Europe.

It became speedily apparent to the Soviet government that the
United States was following no consistent policy, and it doubted
that she had any fixed objectives. The Russians were increasingly
convinced that the United States was following a line of momen-
tary expediency, rather than a policy founded on immutable principle and legitimate self-interest. It looked to them as if the
executors of American foreign policy did not even know precisely
what they themselves really sought. It likewise, and most unfortunately, began to be suspected in Moscow that American policies, especially in Germany, in the Mediterranean and in the Near
East, were being deliberately or unwittingly subordinated to
decisions laid down in London.

The Soviet government never doubted, so long as President
Roosevelt was in charge of American policy, that the relationship
between Great Britain and the United States was inviolable. But
it likewise never doubted that the President desired to find some
way of creating precisely the same kind of relationship with the
Soviet Union. The United States had not agreed to back British
aims against the Soviet Union except when she was convinced that
they were desirable from the standpoint of world relations and
wholly compatible with a healthy collaboration between Moscow
and Washington. President Roosevelt had made it clear that the
United States would at all times be prepared to mediate between
Great Britain and the Soviet Union when critical controversies
arose between those powers, but that the United States was not
prepared to back the British Commonwealth, right or wrong.

By his traducers, by those who misrepresent or distort every one
of his official acts, as well as by those critics who have opposed his
policies because of an honest difference of views, Franklin Roosevelt has been charged with the commission of a fatal diplomatic
blunder when he sought to find the means of reaching a friendly
understanding with the Soviet Union. It is said that he knowingly
undertook a "great gamble" although he had been warned it could

not succeed. It is said that he should from the outset have adopted a policy of open coercion, which it is alleged would have been made feasible by our superior military power, designed to cow the Soviet leaders into acquiescence in every American objective at the war's end.

Leaving aside the questions whether such a policy would have made for effective military co-operation against the common Axis enemy, whether it would have averted all possibility of a separate peace between Moscow and Berlin renewing the German-Soviet pact of August, 1939, and whether the American people would have stood for a policy which risked involving them in a new war before their victory over Germany and Japan had even been won, the policy should be considered objectively from the standpoint of the long-range interests of the United States.

I have set forth, in a previous chapter, the basic considerations that President Roosevelt believed should guide our relations with Russia. He was not blind to the fanaticism nor to the ulterior motives of the Communist party leaders in Moscow. But he was equally aware—with that capacity for seeing the forest rather than the trees, which always distinguished him—that the present régime in the Kremlin was not immortal. Stalin would some day have a successor just as Stalin himself had succeeded Lenin. The proponents of policies inimical to the United States or to the cause of collective security might be eliminated from the Communist party hierarchy just as Trotsky had been. The tendency toward imperialistic expansion and militaristic domination, already apparent before the end of the war, might some day be replaced by a trend back to Lenin's policies of anti-imperialism, nonannexation and respect for the sovereignty of every nation, however weak.

President Roosevelt was confident that if at first any head-on clash of interests could be prevented, if peace in the world could be maintained and if the United Nations could be given a chance to work, living standards in the Soviet Union would rapidly rise, trade with the outside world would become steadily greater, the walls of isolation around Russia would gradually be razed, cultural and intellectual ties with the West would increase and the Russian people themselves would eventually obtain freedom of information as to what was really going on in the rest of the world. If time could be made available, the President had confidence that time would be on the side of world peace.

Which was the policy of statesmanship, and the policy that was in the true interest of the American people and of humanity? The policy of the "fight-now" school, the policy of that group which declared that conflict some day was inevitable and that consequently it was "realistic" to force the issue while the United States was the stronger, and to pursue an overbearing course which might well lead to war unless Russia backed down on every issue on which the United States demanded her own way? Or was it the Roosevelt policy of standing resolutely upon questions of principle but of trying steadfastly to find a way to co-operate, of securing the participation of the Soviet Union in the United Nations, and of proposing then to deal patiently with each issue which arose until time had given the new world order a chance to weld all peoples more firmly together?

The Soviet government has recently undergone a significant reconstruction. We are so accustomed to think of Stalin as the one effective power in Russia that we are apt to forget that the day cannot be far distant when the controls must pass to other hands. Stalin's supremacy was never greater than it has been since the end of the war. He has become the symbol of security, regeneration and success. Yet he is now approaching the proverbial age of three score years and ten, and his life, tough as he is, has been spent under the stress of a never-ending tension.

The Supreme Soviet of the Union, nominally the agency of the people, although in reality of course merely the mouthpiece for the directorship of the membership of the Communist party (which numbers only a very small percentage of the Russian population) lately changed the title of the Council of People's Commissars to the Western title of Council of Ministers. The number of ministries was at the same time greatly increased. The former large economic ministries have been split up into a number of portfolios. The key figures in the Council of fifty-odd ministers are simultaneously members of the *Politburo*—the highest policy-making agency in the Communist system—in order to insure co-ordination and unity of policy.

There are ten members of the *Politburo*—Stalin, Zhdanov, Molotov, Voroshiloff, Andreyev, Malenkov, Mikoyan, Beriya, Krushchev and Kaganovich.

The secretariat of the party, and the *Orgburo*, the executive agency of the Party Central Committee, nominally have equal authority with the *Politburo* in their control within the party. Only three men are members of all three organs. They are Stalin, Zhdanov and Malenkov.

Stalin has shrewdly divorced the political and the military hierarchies. No military hero has been permitted to hold any political office, or to receive appointment to the chief political organs. Stalin himself remains Supreme Commander-in-Chief. Outstanding marshals, like Zhukov, have recently been relegated to subsidiary posts outside of the sphere of potential influence. Yet while Stalin can continue to exercise supreme control because he led the military hosts to victory, were he to vanish, no one can foretell whether or not the Russian Army would name his successor. What is unquestionable is that the military influence is greater today than at any time since 1917. That is one reason why the foreign policy of the Soviet Union has grown consistently more nationalist and more expansionist, in the old tradition of imperial Russia, since the Potsdam meeting.

A further reason for this development is found in the policy pursued by the United States since that time. At the time of Franklin Roosevelt's death, he had taken only the first steps in seeking a co-operative relationship between the system of American democracy and the system of Russian Communism. He had been fully aware that it would require years to perfect this relationship. The history of the years between the great wars was too recent; the ultimate purposes of the Soviet Union were still too little known; the inherent differences between the two political and economic systems were too great for any assurance to exist that a perfect collaboration was possible. But an actual start in the right direction had been made. Foundations had been laid. Within twelve months after his death those foundations had vanished and the friction, misunderstandings and suspicions between the peoples of both countries were even greater than they had been prior to 1941.

Since the death of President Roosevelt, American policy toward Russia has continually vacillated between two extremes. Washington has blown now hot, now cold. At the Council of Foreign Ministers of London, in September, 1945, Secretary Byrnes adopted a position of intransigence. At the Moscow Conference the following December the Secretary of State reversed himself. He abandoned the fundamental principles established by the Yalta agreements in order to appease the Soviet government. In a further effort at appeasement, we have recognized the Communist minority dictatorships in Yugoslavia and in Rumania, counter to our solemn professions to the peoples of eastern Europe. At almost the same time we sent the battleship *Missouri* to Turkey as a gesture of the big stick. We sat by while Russia consolidated her political influence among the German people, and while she obtained over three billions of dollars of reparations in kind from the territories that she has occupied, and then after the horse was stolen we closed the barn door by refusing to permit any further reparation transfers to Russia from Germany's western zone, and by suggesting an economic union between the American, French and British occupation zones of Germany.

But most prejudicial to American interests and to the prevention of a clash with Russia has been the inability of the American government to recognize in any practical way the fundamental truth of what Winston Churchill said in his Fulton speech. The Soviet government respects strength above all else. The headlong demobilization of the United States after the war, the constant cries in the Congress that all the boys should at once come home, the skeletonization of our air force, the evident war-weariness of the American people—these provided the Soviet Union with a greater incentive for expansion than any other one factor. The Communist hierarchy not only realized that the United States did not want to fight, they began to think that she could not even if she wanted to.

That is, however, no indication that the Kremlin desires war.

There is every reason to believe the contrary. Even though Stalin calls for the increase and perfection of the Soviet fighting forces, the Soviet government knows that Russia needs peace, the chance to repair the ravages of war and to build up a program of internal development.

Yet the party-state in Russia will seize every advantage afforded it by the vacillation and weakness of the United States, as it maneuvers for what it claims is security and for increased influence in the world.

The Soviet government has made its own mistakes in its foreign policy, and these have greatly weakened the ideological prestige which Russia possessed among the masses in many countries at the end of the war. The Soviet government, during the years between the two great wars, had gained a deserved reputation for complying with the international commitments which she contracted. By her flagrant violation of her agreement to evacuate Iran on March 2, 1946, Soviet Russia lost that great asset overnight. Her recent policies of expediency, and of utter ruthlessness in the countries she has occupied, have diminished the support she possessed among the intelligentsia and the laboring classes in many parts of the world.

The Soviet leaders are demonstrating their failure to understand alien psychological factors. They are still obsessed with the doctrinaire conviction that Communist ends invariably justify any means employed to achieve those ends. They are impervious to the arguments by which most Western statesmen are moved.

No Westerner who has conferred with Mr. Molotov could fail to realize that he speaks not as an individual empowered to negotiate in the reasonable exercise of his own discretion, but as the bureaucrat automatically pursuing the lines laid down for him by the party. Mr. Gromyko's "No's" in the Security Council are not the expression of his own cantankerous disposition; they are purely the orders coming down to him from the *Politburo* and the Council of Ministers.

And as the months pass and the recurrent crises in the relations between the United States and the Soviet Union increase both in gravity and in number, the growing fears and suspicions in one country are sharpened by the fears and suspicions in the other.

Both countries are rapidly becoming involved in a vicious circle which—unless it is promptly and cleanly cut—may well presage an atomic war. Both countries must modify their recent course if there is to be any hope of avoiding the division of the world into two opposing armed garrisons with all the calamities which that portends.

Stalin and his colleagues have often before modified their course from one day to another. At Yalta Stalin recognized the need for compromise. It is more than ever needed today if Stalin is to lead the Russian people to ultimate success in their great national experiment.

But American policy must also change before it is too late. It must be consistent. It must be firm upon great issues, conciliatory on minor issues. It must be predicated upon the demonstrated strength of the United States—internal, diplomatic and military —until the United Nations has become strong. It must be predicated as well upon a fact which has been almost wholly disregarded —that both the Soviet Union and the United States are equally pledged to the principles set forth in the Atlantic Charter and in the Yalta agreements. Unless both governments enforce those principles, there can be laid no solid foundation for world reconstruction. The United States must persistently strive for economic co-operation, freedom of information, and the advance of human liberties. She must persistently follow a policy toward Russia based upon the realization that if a clash can be avoided, if each incident as it arises can be patiently resolved, the chances are in our favor for avoiding war and for advancing the cause of liberal democracy in the world.

The analysis of American foreign policy undertaken in this book is necessarily critical. It has been written with no intention of minimizing the unique difficulties which the present directors of our policy have encountered, and with no failure to recognize the untiring devotion to the interests of this nation which they have brought to their task. But if the American people are to see clearly where they are heading they must analyze objectively and dispassionately every aspect of their national policy. Nothing could be more dangerous to the security of this country than their complacent acquiescence in official assurances that lasting peace is at hand, merely because they so greatly desire to believe those assurances. "Wishful thinking has slain its millions." Popular understanding, popular discussion and constructive criticism of the government's course in its search for peace and in its dealings with other governments are needed today more than ever before.

I do not believe that public opinion attributes sufficient importance to the need for perfecting the administrative mechanism through which our foreign policy is carried out. That machinery should today be functioning with the highest possible efficiency, but it is notorious that it is not.

There are three improvements which could very rapidly be made.

The first has to do with the organization of the Department of State, and with the instruments by which this country's foreign policy is carried out. The second involves the information concerning foreign relations which should be given to the American people by the White House and by the Department of State. The third would be aimed at securing more effective co-operation between the executive and legislative branches of the government in matters of foreign policy.

Lord Curzon once said that "epochs arise in the history of every country when the administrative machinery requires to be taken to pieces and overhauled, and readjusted to the altered necessities or the growing demands of the hour."

In the case of the machinery established for the conduct of American foreign policy that epoch is long overdue.

The public has in recent years been led to believe that the State Department has undergone a miraculous "streamlining." To those who know the Department, it has been shocking to see how the public has been misled. A recent Secretary of State who suffered from the delusion that to be successful a Foreign Office need only be run like a business corporation proudly announced that the reorganization which he was undertaking would be such as to end the need for all further reorganizations. When the job was done the walls of the building had been repainted, the lavatories had been moved, the messenger service had been adjusted and the names of many bureaus and divisions had been changed. That any observer could see. What most observers did not realize, however, was that the permanent service of the Department had been nearly disrupted, that the morale of the key men and women in the Department's personnel had been impaired, and that this government's most vital agency at an exceptionally critical moment had been rendered fifty per cent less efficient than it had been before.

To place the Department of State upon a truly efficient basis is not a task that can be accomplished by a new Secretary of State in a couple of months, even if the services of publicity agents are utilized. It is a task which requires the personal attention of the President and of the Congressional leaders who are familiar with the practical aspects of the government's foreign relations. It requires also the participation of men who have devoted themselves to the foreign service of the United States throughout their lives, and who have proved their fitness to formulate expert recommendations as to the technical reorganization needed.

The Department of State in its present form is an inefficient machine. The Department is not a business corporation and it cannot function effectively if it is set up as a business corporation. It requires the kind of readjustment that will make it possible for the permanent officials under the State Department, that much maligned and unappreciated branch of the government, to put their technical knowledge and experience to the best use.

Under President Roosevelt, permanent members of the foreign service and of the State Department's administrative staff were for the first time given full recognition by receiving appointment to positions of the highest responsibility. The value of the services they could render when they were given the chance was proved during the war years.

In recent months the Administration has selected for almost all key diplomatic missions either political appointees, or military or naval officers. The average general or admiral possesses neither the resiliency nor the knowledge of foreign psychology needed for successful negotiation with other governments. He has been taught primarily to take orders or to issue orders. He too often lacks imagination and the capacity to understand the other fellow's point of view. Certainly there are exceptions to the rule, as there have also frequently been outstandingly useful ambassadors who were appointed for political considerations. But the able and patriotic Americans who have spent their lives in their country's foreign service are usually more likely to understand how her foreign policy can best be made effective, as they are more apt to possess the special qualities needed to represent this government, than those who have had no previous reason to train themselves for the critical responsibility of negotiating with foreign governments, and of knowing how the interests of the United States may best be served abroad.

The people of the United States are not taking full advantage of the great asset they possess in the permanent foreign service. It is a body of men drawn from all ranks of life, and from every section of the United States, who have shown themselves to be fully as competent, if not more competent, than the diplomatic and consular officials of any other government. They have been as tragically underpaid as the members of Congress or the members of the Presidential Cabinet. Legislation just enacted has in some degree remedied this situation. But the appropriations granted by the Congress to the State Department for salaries and for the duties with which it is charged are still far less than is needed to obtain a proper standard of efficiency in the conduct of this nation's foreign relations. A few million dollars more in appropriations each year would represent a vast saving to the nation in the way of permanent security.

The public press has made much of the recently announced intention of the Department of State to enlarge its public relations services, and to make available in foreign countries through official agencies a greater volume of news from the United States. The interests of the United States will be advanced by a more accurate knowledge among foreign peoples of American policies and of American life. The press associations of the United States have been of the highest value in this regard. They perhaps could have done more, but it would be ironical if the transmission of official information abroad reduced or eliminated the service which the American press associations can render in that field. It would be still more harmful if news from the United States were officially doctored, as is the news from official Soviet sources.

More necessary than official propaganda is fuller and more accurate information to the American people covering their country's foreign relations and their government's conduct of their foreign policy.

The London and Moscow conferences of the autumn of 1945 demonstrated the harm that results from every failure of this government to recognize the right of the people to know what decisions it makes in their name. The agenda of these conferences were not published. The American people were given no opportunity of knowing beforehand the questions that were to be dealt with. They consequently had no chance to make their wishes known as to the course which the United States should take.

At London the American delegation shunned the press. At Moscow the press was excluded. Neither the American press nor the American radio was given any authoritative guidance as to what was going on, or any accurate knowledge of what the American delegates were trying to accomplish. The inevitable result was erroneous interpretation and dangerous confusion.

If the foreign policy of the United States is to become a democratic foreign policy, American public opinion must be helped, not hindered, in its attempt to appraise correctly the significance of events in the field of foreign relations, so that it may decide the policy to be adopted.

During the first months after the end of the war public opinion was given no chance to demonstrate its approval or disapproval of this country's foreign policy. It was kept largely in the dark. Yet the government could have possessed no more valuable asset than the knowledge on the part of the other powers that it was fully supported in every step it took by a majority of the American people.

Secretary Byrnes in recent months has done much to remedy this grave defect in the conduct of our foreign policy. His recent broadcasts have given the American people the detailed information they had a right to. At the Paris Peace Conference he has stood for open negotiations. Yet the harm resulting from his earlier course has not yet been dispelled.

Finally, the executive branch of the government has failed to establish the full measure of co-operation with the legislative branch that is indispensable if the conduct of our foreign policy is to be successfully carried on. The need is not fully met by the admirable steps taken by President Truman in associating the ranking members of the Democratic and Republican parties on the Foreign Relations Committee of the Senate with the Secretary of State in his peacemaking negotiations.

In practice, the opportunities for official co-operation between the executive and the legislative branches of the government are at present limited. The Secretary of State and other officials of the Department of State appear before Congressional committees, most of which meet in executive session, but the information thus obtained is confined largely to the members of these committees.

It is also true that both the President and the Secretary of State often confer with the leaders of the Congress in both Houses on the more important questions of foreign policy. Here again, the information obtained rests with the Congressional leaders who attend the conferences.

There is no continuing means of making available to the whole Congress the information regarding foreign policy which all its members should legitimately have. Any inside knowledge of the conduct of our foreign policy is withheld from a majority of the members of the House of Representatives, and, to a lesser degree, of the Senate. They have no more detailed information than what they read in the daily press.

The collaboration between the executive and legislative branches of the government must be far closer in the field of foreign affairs if the Government of the United States is to be able to act with full assurance of popular support in the determination of foreign policy, and if the people are to be given an opportunity of making their wishes heard through their representatives in the Congress. The rules of the Senate and of the House of Representatives should be modified so as to permit either the Secretary of State or the Undersecretaries of State to appear at reasonable intervals on the floor of either House in order to answer questions which may be put to them by the members of Congress concerning the conduct of the country's foreign relations. Such an arrangement should naturally not preclude the right of the executive branch of the government to refrain at any time from divulging information when in the judgment of the Executive to do so would be incompatible with the public interest.

From the analysis of the character and conduct of our foreign policy made in the preceding chapters a balance can be struck.

Because of the vision and resolution of President Roosevelt in the final months of his life, the United Nations came into being. The United States has shown initiative and determination in strengthening the authority of the new world organization.

The United States has taken the lead in establishing the financial and economic agencies which are indispensable if international co-operation in world reconstruction is to succeed. The American government has buttressed these agencies through the credits it has made available to foreign governments.

President Truman has made it possible for the foreign policy of the United States to become a national policy which is now far above the sphere of party politics. In that endeavor he has had the unswerving co-operation of such leaders of the Republican party as Senator Vandenberg, Senator Austin and Governor Stassen.

These are great achievements to be recorded on the credit side. Their full significance can already be appreciated.

But unfortunately the failures that make up the debit side must represent a cause for increasing anxiety to every American citizen.

Solely because of the failure of the United States to abide by the true principles of the Good Neighbor Policy the solidarity of the American Republics has in three short years been disastrously undermined. The United States has thereby lost her greatest assurance that the security of the Western Hemisphere can be preserved.

The United States has failed in her attempt to promote unity within China and thus to avert the possibility of a protracted civil war, with all of its attendant threats to international co-operation in the Far East. In her policy toward Japan the United States has pursued a course which may not insure any real regeneration of the spirit of the Japanese people and which, because of its unilateral nature, offers no certainty that the major powers will adopt identic policies in their future relations with Japan.

By her failure before the end of the war to secure a common agreement between the Big Four upon a long-range policy to be pursued jointly toward Germany, the United States has made possible the conflicts resulting from four divergent policies. There is no greater threat to world peace and to European reconstruction today than the increasing differences between the major allies with regard to the future of Germany.

The United States has ceased to be regarded by the smaller powers as the champion of their legitimate rights in the community of nations. By her failure to support in practice, as she has supported in her official declarations, the principle of the "sovereign equality of all nations, great or small," she has forfeited much of the added influence which the backing of the lesser powers would have afforded her in the pursuit of her objectives.

The United States has failed to exercise any vigorous or effective moral leadership in such issues as that of Palestine and the future of the colonial peoples.

Assurance after assurance has been given by the highest authorities of the American government that this country's policy was based upon "the principles of the Atlantic Charter." Yet the European peace treaties which the United States has helped to draft, and which she is pledged to "advocate," contain provisions in flagrant violation of those principles.

The United States has failed to find any basis for agreement with the Soviet Union upon the essentials of a peaceful and stable world order. The responsibility for such failure must be shared by both governments. Yet the American people are compelled to recognize the dangerous fact that suspicion and antagonism between the two greatest powers in the world are steadily mounting.

The hour is already very late. Remedial action, in the sense of any radical transformation of American foreign policy, is infinitely more difficult today than it would have been two years ago. Every failure to take action bravely and wisely and at the right moment has brought into being a chain of events which have each in turn increasingly darkened the international horizon.

Yet even now it is not too late for the American people to secure such changes in their foreign policy as seem to them necessary in the interest of world peace and for their own welfare.

I am fully persuaded of the present truth of Stalin's statement at the last Red Army Day exercises: "Neither the nations nor the armies want any new war." The danger is that without continued agreement between the major powers, and without a constructive and enlightened policy on the part of the United States, the nations will drift into two increasingly hostile blocs. There would then be two worlds, and if two worlds come into being, war will sooner or later become inevitable.

The peoples of the earth are shaken today, more than ever before, by the passion for liberty and by the impelling force of nationalism. Some day, the anarchy of unrestrained nationalism will give place to an international federalism; some day the spiritual and political liberty of the individual will be consecrated by universal law, and his economic liberty will be assured by the discovery of the means of ending poverty in the very midst of potential plenty.

It may be that great social convulsions and new wars will come to pass before these ends are attained. But these ends can be achieved—and achieved by peaceful means and by friendly co-operation—through the United Nations. That is the challenge which the American people confront.

They failed to meet that challenge in 1919. They cannot risk not meeting it today.

"No wave on the great ocean of Time, when once it has floated past us, can be recalled. All we can do is to watch the new form and motion of the next, and launch upon it to try in the manner our best judgment may suggest our strength and skill."

INDEX

Afifi, Dr., 54
Ala, Hussein, 255
Alem, Leandro, 188
Alvear, Dr. Marcelo, 190
American Foreign Ministers,
  Panama meeting, 34
  Rio de Janeiro meeting, 20
"American Relief for Italy," 137
American Zionist Emergency Council,
  272
The Anatomy of Peace, 46
Anglo-American Cabinet Committee,
  367
Anglo-American Palestine Commission, 367
Anglo-Iranian Oil Company, 258, 262
Arab League, 246-247, 259, 263, 281
Arabian-American Oil Combine, 261,
  262
Aranha, Dr. Oswaldo, 221
Argentina, 185-219, 228-237
  admission to United Nations, 41,
    208, 209, 213
  United States policy toward, 186,
    198-201, 203, 205
Armaments, reduction of, 8
Armour, Norman, 195
Armstrong, Hamilton Fish, 21
Asia, nationalist surge in, 284
Atlantic Charter, 2-3, 6-18, 65, 233,
  337, 342, 364, 369, 382, 389
  Churchill draft, 7
  Welles draft, 8-16
Atlantic community of nations, 26-27
Atomic energy, 2, 67, 106, 313, 314,
  345-348
  control of, 70, 72, 347-350
  Washington Conference on, 70, 348
Attlee, Clement, 63, 243, 327
Augusta, 11
Austin, Senator, 22, 207, 225, 233, 388
  representative to United Nations, 54
Australia, 55

Austria, 81, 167-170
Aviation conference, 33
Azerbaijan, 57, 58, 252, 253, 257, 258
Azores, as United Nations headquarters, 32, 49-50

Badoglio, Marshal, 131, 132, 149
Balfour Declaration, 277
Balkans, 116, 150
  peace settlements, 60, 62, 72
  standing army in the, 4
Baruch, Bernard M., 348-349
Belgium, 111
Beneš, Dr. Eduard, 165-166, 275
Berle, Dr. Adolph, 223
Bevin, Ernest, 63-64, 71, 107, 243
  Palestine problem and, 266
Bidault, Georges, 175, 177
Bloom, Congressman, 22
Blue Book, 229-230, 232
Blum, Léon, 178
Bolivia, 196
Bonnet, M. Henri, 54
Bonomi, Ivanoe, 133
Borneo, 331
Bowman, Dr. Isaiah, 21, 22
Braden, Spruille, 215-219, 223-225,
  233, 235
Brazil, 220-224
Brett, General, 235
Bretton Woods Conference, 32
Briand, Aristide, 115
Briga, Italy, 145
Bright, John, 324
British Foreign Office, 26
Bulgaria, 72, 153
  peace terms for, 64, 74
Burma, nationalism in, 287
Byrnes, James F.
  abandonment of Yalta agreements
    by, 72, 152, 370
  appointed Secretary of State, 214

Byrnes, James F.—*Continued*
  Council of Foreign Ministers, 66-67, 380
  German policy and, 88
  Japanese policy and, 316
  Moscow Conference, 71, 72, 380
  Paris Conference, 111
  Potsdam Conference, 63
  radio broadcasts, 363, 386
  Security Council and, 254-255

Cadogan, Sir Alexander, 6, 11-16
  representative to United Nations, 53
Cairo Declaration, 29, 308, 310, 313
Callender, Harold, 88
Castillo, Dr. Ramon S., 192, 194, 197, 203
Celebes, 331
Chamberlain, Joseph, 13
Chamberlain, Neville, 267
Chapultepec, Act of, 207, 224
Chiang Kai-shek, 28, 71, 291-296, 302, 305-307, 310
Chicago Aviation Conference, 33
Chile, 193
China, 104, 286, 290-308, 388
  support of National Government, 71, 302
Chou En-lai, 293, 295
Chu Teh, General, 293
Churchill, Prime Minister Winston,
  Atlantic Charter and, 2, 6-18
  Fulton speech, 380
  on peace settlements, 61
  Palestine White Paper and, 267
  Potsdam Conference, 63
  replaced by Attlee, 63
  Teheran Conference, 28
  Yalta Conference, 38
Ciano, Count, 167
Cirenaica, 146, 147
Civil Aviation Conference, 33
Clayton, William, 343
Cobden, Richard, 8
Colombia, 231
Combined Chiefs of Staff, 62
Communism, 1, 37, 102, 154, 240, 372-375
  growth of, in France, 176
Connally, Senator Tom, 21, 207, 214, 225, 233
Cooke, Dr. Juan, 206
Council of Foreign Ministers, see Foreign Ministers Council

Council of Foreign Relations, 22
Cripps Mission, 324, 326
Cromer, Lord, 246
Curzon, Lord, 383
Czechoslovakia, 128, 161, 164-167

Dairen, 299
Daladier, Edouard, 177
Damaskinos, Archbishop, 161
Danzig, 120, 121, 126
Dardanelles, 69, 160, 244
Davis, Norman, 21
Democracy, 1, 37, 117
Dimitroff, George, 154
Dodecanese Islands, 244
Doenitz, Grand Admiral von, 81
Dulles, John Foster, 66
Dumbarton Oaks, 26, 34, 35, 210
  proposals, 33, 34, 42
Dutch New Guinea, 331
Dutra, General Enrico, 222, 224

East Prussia, 120
Eaton, Congressman, 22
Economic Warfare, Board of, 21
Eden, Anthony, 63, 245
Egypt, 289
Eichelberger, Dr. Clark, 21
Eisenhower, General Dwight, 82, 86
Epirus, 126
Eritrea, 69, 146, 147, 148, 244
Europe,
  federated, 115-118
  frontiers in, 119
  living standards in, 116-118
  reconstruction of, 60, 114-181
Evatt, Dr. Herbert, 40, 41, 69
Export-Import Bank, 184, 343

Far Eastern Advisory Commission, 315
Farouk, King, 246
Farrell, General, 196-198, 201, 203, 208
Feisal, King, 259
Finland, 119
  peace terms for, 64, 74
Fiume, 123
Foch, Marshal, 75
Food and Agriculture Conference, 32
Food and Agriculture Organization, 117
Forbes, Rosita, 374

Foreign Affairs Committee, 21, 22, 208, 225, 233, 387
Foreign Ministers Council,
  established, 64
  London meeting, 64-69, 179, 380
  Moscow Conference, 71-73
  Paris Conference, 74, 100, 110, 125, 147
Foreign policy,
  Roosevelt and, 3, 18, 19, 102, 105, 340, 375
  Soviet Union's, 6, 64, 102
  time element and, 36, 111
  United States', 18, 68, 73, 88, 173-174, 334-390
Foreign Policy Association,
  Welles address to, 287
France, 173-180
  American policy toward, 173-174 177-180
  Balkan peace treaties and, 69, 72
  German policy, 92-93
  Italian peace settlement and, 64, 74, 179
  relations with Spain, 352-353
Franco regime, 56, 351-354
Frazer, Prime Minister, 41
Free enterprise, 108

Gandhi, Mahatma, 327, 328
Gasperi, Alcide de, 135
Gaulle, General de, 41, 83, 174, 175
  resignation of, 176
George, Mr. Lloyd, 277-278
George, Senator, 21, 233
Germany, 116-117
  after World War I, 75-77
  after World War II, 77
  Allied Control Commission, 82, 83
  decentralization, 88, 92, 122-123
  educational program for, 96
  frontiers of, 92, 120-123, 179
  occupation zones in, 81-93, 96
  policies toward, 74-101, 110, 355, 389
  reparations, 78, 83, 88, 97-100
Ghavam, Ahmed, 255, 257, 259
Giral, President, 352
Gomes, General Eduardo, 222-224
Good Neighbor Policy, 118, 240
  jeopardized, 118 (fn.), 183-184, 199, 201, 210, 224, 233, 388
Gouin, Felix, 175, 177

Great Britain,
  foreign policy, 63-64, 107, 361-363
  occupation of Greece, 159-161
  policy toward Germany, 88
  preparatory postwar plans, 26
  supremacy in Near East, 243
Greece, 244
  British occupation of, 159-161
  Northern frontier of, 126
Gromyko, Andrei, 53, 57, 350, 381
Grotewohl, Herr, 84
Guani, Dr. Alberto, 196 (fn.)

Hassan, Mahmoud, 54
Hatoyama, 319
Higashi-Kuni, Prince, 318
Hodgson, Colonel, 55, 255, 256
Hopkins, Harry, 11, 13, 15
Hot Springs Conference, 32
House, Colonel, 20
Hudson, Judge Manley O., 51
Humber, Mr., 46
Hungary, 161-164
  peace terms for, 64, 74
Hurley, General Patrick J., 295, 301-302

Ibn Saud, King, 259-261, 263
  Conference with President Roosevelt, 264-265
Ickes, Secretary, 258, 261
India, 324-329
  independence for, 326-329, 362
  nationalism in, 287, 289
Indo-China, 332
  nationalism in, 287
Indonesia, 262, 329-331
  nationalism in, 287
Inflation, in American Republics, 239
Information, need for, 386
Inonü, President, 248
Inter-American Committee on Political Defense, 196
Inter-American Conference (Mexico City), 41
Inter-American Conference (Rio de Janeiro), 193
Inter-American Consultative Meeting of Foreign Ministers, 34
Inter-American Financial and Economic Advisory Board, 241
Inter-American Juridical Committee, 34, 208

Inter-Governmental Committee on Refugees, 280, 366
International Bank for Reconstruction and Development, 32-33, 117
International Court of Justice, 51
International Labor Organization, 31, 33
International Military Tribunal, 94
International Monetary Fund, 32, 33, 343
International organization, see also United Nations
  policing powers and, 4-5, 24
  Roosevelt and, 3-6, 19, 26
  Russia and, 28, 29-30
  State Department plans for, 19-26, 27, 34
International Stabilization Fund, 117
International Trusteeship Council, 42, 50, 51, 68, 147, 278, 289-290, 366, 368
Iran, 57-58, 104, 251-259
Iraq, 259, 262
Irigoyen, Dr. Hipolito, 188-190, 202
Isolationism, 3, 17, 18, 338, 364
  Russian, 373-374
Istrian Peninsula, 123, 143
Italian Red Cross, 137
Italian Somaliland, 146, 147, 148
Italy,
  Allied Control Council, 138-142
  Allied Military Government, 138-141
  frontiers, 123, 124, 143
  peace treaty with, 64, 68, 73, 74, 142
  policies toward, 130-150
  reparations, 111, 143
  territorial possessions, 143, 146-147

Jackson, Justice Robert, 94, 95
Japan,
  occupation policies in, 71, 313-324, 388-389
Java, 330-332
Jinnah, Mr., 327
Joyce, Major General, 138
Justo, General Augustín P., 190, 197

Kanaka, Tan, 332
Killearn, Lord, 246
King, Prime Minister Mackenzie, 40
Korea, 104, 310-313
  agreement on, 71
Koudenhove-Kalergi, Count, 115

Lange, Dr. Oscar, 54
Larreta, Dr. Rodriquez, 225
Laski, Professor Harold, 107
Latin-America, 102-241
  Dumbarton Oaks Conference and, 34-35
Latvia, 120
Lawrence, Colonel, 245
League of Nations, 3, 24, 42, 61
  comparison with United Nations, 42, 43, 44
  defects of the, 24, 43
  Latin-American governments and, 35
  Roosevelt and the, 3, 5, 15
  United States refusal to enter, 76
Lend-Lease Act, 11, 251, 252, 337
  Argentina and the, 193-194
  termination, 107
Lenin, 373-374
Leopold III, King, 171
Libya, 69, 146-147, 148, 244
Lie, Trygve, 50-51
Lilienthal report, 348-349
Lippmann, Walter, 26
Lithuania, 120
Litvinoff, Maxim, 53
Living standards, 116-118
London Conference, 48, 74, 386
  Foreign Ministers, 64-69, 179, 380
Lowdermilk, Dr., 276
Lush, Brigadier Morris Stanley, 139-140
Luxembourg, 171

McCormick, Anne O'Hare, 21
McMahon Atomic Energy Control Bill, 349
MacArthur, General Douglas, 316-317, 320, 329
MacFarlane, Lieutenant General Sir Mason, 138-140
Machek, 155
Manchuria, 303-304
Maniu, 154
Mao Tse-tung, 293-294, 306
Marshall, General George C., 302, 303, 305-307
Masaryk, Dr. Thomas, 165
Messersmith, George, 233
Mexico City Conference, 41, 207, 208-209, 238
Meyer, Eugene, 343
Michanowsky, George, 219

Mihailovitch, General, 155
Military establishments,
  in small European countries, 4
Missouri (battleship), 380
Molotov, V. M., 65, 71, 212, 240
  attitude toward Latin-America, 211
  Council of Foreign Ministers, 69, 100
  German policy, 359
  San Francisco Conference, 40-41
Monfalcone, Italy, 145
Monroe Doctrine, 184
Montreaux Convention of 1936, 250
Mook, Dr. van, 331
Moral leadership, 74, 363-368, 389
Morgenthau, Henry, Jr., 97
Moscow Conference, 30, 369-370, 386
  Foreign Ministers, 71-73
Moslem League, 327, 328
Mountbatten, Lord Louis, 329
Mussolini, Benito, 123, 127

Najera, Dr. Castillo, 55
Near East, 242-283
Nehru, Jawaharlal, 327
Netherlands, 93, 171-173
  postwar suggestions of the, 26
Netherlands East Indies, 329, 331-332
Nicola, Enrico de, 133, 148
Norway, 171
  postwar suggestions, 26
Nürnberg trial, 95

Oder frontier, 120-121
Orgburo, 379
Ortiz, Dr. Roberto, 190-191, 192, 197
Ottawa Agreement, 8, 12, 13, 15, 342-343

Padilla, Dr. Ezequiel, 211
Pahlevi, Mohamed Reza, 252
Pahlevi, Reza Shah, 251
Palestine, 260, 263-281, 367-368, 389
Palestine White Paper, 266-267
Pan-American Union, 204-205, 208, 227 (fn.)
Pan-Americanism, 185
Panama Canal, 185
Paris Conference of 1919, 43, 60, 61
Paris Peace Conference, 1946, 74, 111, 112, 386-387
Parodi, M. Alexandre, 54

Parri, Professor Ferrucio, 135
Pasha, Nahas, 246
Pashitch, Mr., 144
Pauley, Edwin, 99
Peace,
  desire for, 1
  settlements, 60-113, 369-370
Pearl Harbor investigation, 18
Peron, Colonel Juan D., 194-196, 203, 206, 216, 228-237
  letter to President Truman, 235
Philippines, independence of, 284, 285, 333
Pieck, Herr, 83, 84
Pola, Italy, 126, 145
Poland, 41, 56, 120, 121, 212
Politburo, 378-379, 381
Port Arthur, 299
Postwar planning,
  Great Britain, 26
  U. S. State Department, 19-26, 27
Potofsky, Jacob, 219
Potsdam Conference, 63-65, 106
Prestes, Carlos Luis, 222
Public opinion, 9, 18, 67, 68, 109, 386

Quezon, Manuel, 285, 331
Quo, Tai Chi, 54

Ramirez, General, 195-198
Rawson, General, 194, 195
Reconstruction, European, 60, 114-181
Regional systems, 23, 25, 117-118
Rennell, Major General Lord, 138
Renner, Dr. Karl, 82, 168
Reves, Emery, 46
Reynaud, Paul, 177
Rio de Janeiro Conference, 238
Roberts, Justice Owen J., 46-48
Rockefeller, Nelson, 205, 207, 215, 219
Roosevelt, Franklin D.,
  Atlantic Charter and, 2, 6-19
  conference with King Ibn Saud, 264-265
  death of, 2, 39, 106, 107, 375
  foreign policy and, 3, 18, 19, 36, 102, 105, 340, 375
  illness, 28
  international organization and, 3-6, 19, 26-32
  League of Nations and, 3, 5, 15
  Moscow Conference, 30

Roosevelt, Franklin D.—*Continued*
  Palestine policy, 264-265
  postwar planning and, 22, 27
  Teheran Conference, 28, 30, 103
  Yalta Conference, 38, 103, 104, 152
Roosevelt, Mrs. Franklin D., 367
Rumania, 72, 153
  peace terms for, 64, 74

Saenz Peña, Dr. Roque, 188
San Francisco Conference, 38-42
Saracoglu, Turkish Prime Minister, 249
Saudi Arabia, 260
Savannah, Georgia, 33
Schacht, Hjalmar, 8
Selective Service Act, 3
Senate Foreign Relations Committee, 21, 22, 208, 225, 233, 387
Sforza, Count, 134
Shidehara, Baron, 318, 319
Shotwell, Professor James, 21
Siam, 308-310
Sino-Russian Treaty, 298, 304
Sjahrir, 330-332
Smuts, Marshal, 40
Soekarno, 330
Soong, Dr. T. V., 292, 297
Soviet Union, 372
  Dumbarton Oaks Conference and, 35
  foreign policy, 6, 64, 102
  frontiers, 119-120
  German policy, 101
  international organization and, 25, 28-30, 38, 40
  isolationism, 373-374
  Nazi invasion of, 5, 103
  Near East policy, 243
  war against Japan, 65
  world government and, 46-47
Spaak, Mr., 40
Spain, 56, 64, 351-354
Spears, General, 246
Stalin, Joseph, 37, 65, 377-379, 382
  Potsdam Conference, 64
  Red Army Day statement, 390
  Teheran Conference, 28, 29
  Yalta Conference, 38
Standard Oil Company of California, 261
Stark, Admiral H. R., 17
Stassen, Commander, 41, 388

State Department, U. S.,
  postwar policy plans of the, 19-26, 27, 34
  reorganization, 383-384
Stettinius, Edward, 53-54, 205, 207, 211, 212
Stone, Admiral Ellery, 140
Strachey, Lytton, 340
Sumatra, 331, 332
Sun Yat-sen, 291, 293, 297
Syria, 262, 281

Tabriz, 253
Tamborini, Dr., 228, 233
Taylor, Myron C., 21, 22, 137, 280
Teheran Conference, 28, 30, 57, 103, 113
Tenda, Italy, 145
Texas Company, 261
Thomas, Senator, 21
The Time for Decision, 2, 281
Tito, Marshal, 124, 144, 151, 154, 157-158
Trade Agreement program, U. S., 7
Trade policies, 8
Transjordania, 246, 259
Transylvania, minority problem in, 128-129
Treaty of Versailles, 3, 19, 40, 60, 61, 75, 114
Trieste, 111, 123-126, 143-146
Tripolitania, 146
Truman, President Harry,
  appointments of, 343
  Army Day address, 233
  atomic energy control and, 70
  lend-lease termination by, 107
  letter from Juan Peron, 235
  Palestine problem and, 266, 272
  Potsdam Conference, 63
  Soviet government and, 375
  statement on Chinese policy, 302
Trumbitch, Mr., 144
Turkey, 247-251
Tuscaloosa, 10, 15

United Nations, 2, 38, 114
  Atomic Commission, 70, 348-349
  Charter, 26, 38, 40, 42, 43, 214, 288-289, 344, 368, 371
    amending, 42
    defects in the, 42
    proposed amendment, 25-26

United Nations—*Continued*
comparison with League of Nations, 42, 43, 44
criticism of the, 44
Declaration, 2
Economic and Social Council, 42, 44, 51, 323-324, 343
foundation of the, 2
General Assembly, 32, 40, 42, 52
first meeting, 48, 51, 74, 243, 348
International Court of Justice, 51
International Trusteeship Council, 42, 50, 51, 68, 147, 278, 289-290, 366, 368
police power, 43
Preamble, 42
Preparatory Commission, 49
purpose of the, 2, 43, 60
regional systems and, 214
San Francisco Conference, 38-42
Secretary General, 50-51
Security Council, 24, 26, 29, 31, 35, 40, 42, 43, 44, 50, 51-59, 110, 254-255
New York City meeting of the, 51
problems of the, 56
site for the, 48-50
veto issue, 24, 25, 35, 40, 44-45
United Nations Relief and Rehabilitation Administration, 32, 158, 342
United States,
Argentine policy, 186, 198-201, 203, 205
co-operation between executive and legislative branches, 20, 387-388
foreign policy, 18, 68, 73, 173-174, 334-390
French policy, 173-174, 177-180
German policy, 86-90, 99
isolationism and, 3, 17
Latin-American policy, 182-241
League of Nations and, 76
military government of Germany, 86-92
moral leadership, 74, 363-368, 389
postwar policy, 20
relations with Soviet Union, 6, 28,

United States—*Continued*
29-30, 36-37, 46, 72-73, 100, 103, 104-106, 109, 110, 112, 282
Trade Agreement program, 7
United States of Europe, 115
Uriburu, General, 190, 194, 201
Uruguayan proposal, 225-227

Van Kleffens, Dr. Eelco, 40, 55
Vandenberg, Senator, 41, 214, 225, 233, 388
Vargas, Getulio, 220-224
Vatican, influence of the, 149
Velloso, Dr. Pedro, 54
Venezia Giulia, 111, 123, 143, 145
Versailles, Treaty of, 3, 19, 40, 60, 61, 75, 114
Victor Emmanuel III, 148, 149
Vienna, Congress of, 114

Wada, Hiramo, 319
War criminal trials, 94-95, 317
Warren, Ambassador, 235
Wavell, Lord, 327
Weizmann, Dr. Chaim, 264, 274-275
Western Hemisphere, unity of the, 182
Wherry, Senator, 219 (fn.)
White, Senator Wallace H., Jr., 22, 233
Willkie, Wendell, 370
Wilson, General Sir Henry Maitland, 138-139
Wilson, Woodrow, 19, 20, 22, 105, 119, 123, 124
Winant, John G., 343, 344
World Court, 51
World government, 46-48
World Order, progress toward, 1-59

Yalta Conference, 38, 103-104, 152, 369, 382
Yemen, 260
Yoshida, Shigeru, 318
Yugoslavia, 123-125, 143-144, 154-159

Zhukov, Marshal, 379

Date Due